READING BETWEEN THE WINES

With a New Preface

Terry Theise

University of California Press   Berkeley   Los Angeles   London

University of California Press, one of the most distinguished
university presses in the United States, enriches lives around
the world by advancing scholarship in the humanities, social
sciences, and natural sciences. Its activities are supported by
the UC Press Foundation and by philanthropic contributions
from individuals and institutions. For more information,
visit www.ucpress.edu.

University of California Press
Berkeley and Los Angeles, California

University of California Press, Ltd.
London, England

First paperback printing 2011
© 2010, 2011 by Terry Theise

ISBN 978-0-520-27149-4 (pbk. : alk. paper)

The Library of Congress has cataloged an earlier edition
as follows:

Library of Congress Cataloging-in-Publication Data

Theise, Terry.
    Reading between the wines / Terry Theise.
       p.   cm.
    ISBN 978-0-520-26533-2 (cloth : alk. paper)
    1. Wine and wine making—Miscellanea.   I. Title.
    TP548.T48   2010
    641.2′2—dc22   2009050516

Manufactured in the United States of America

20 19 18 17 16 15 14 13 12 11
10 9 8 7 6 5 4 3 2 1

CONTENTS

To Karen Odessa and Max

PREFACE TO THE PAPERBACK EDITION

This book was completed a little over two years ago. It has its share of unfinished business, and that is partly by design, as one of its theses is that unfinished business is fun.

I have an abiding and evanescent concern about wines that show a strange force of gentleness that makes us grope for a language by which it may be described. Or so I have supposed. I've just finished a helpful book by Stanley Fish called *How to Write a Sentence*, and in the course of ruminating over transparency in language, Fish writes, "A lapidary style is polished and cut to the point of transparency. It doesn't seem to be doing much. It does not demand that attention be paid to it. It aspires to a self-effacement that allows the object to shine through."

I have always admired this effect in writing, as in Bernhard Schlink's exquisitely careful, judicious prose in *The Reader*, or the recent poems of Robert Hass, which seem so plainly written as to cause us to question just what we think poetry is, or should be. And I've found—or imagine myself to have found—the same effect in certain wines, such as Helmut Dönnhoff's, or those of the Saahs family at Nikolaihof. I didn't have a word for it, and so I shot a pile of arrows toward it. Now there is this fine word *lapidary* that will shove all the other adjectives out of my quiver.

Still, even after I've gained a helpful new word, the old questions persist. How can these ostensibly demure wines convey such numinousness? And when I am caught in the web of this mystery, what is the nature of this place? Who, what lives here? Is it as still as it seems? Why do these wines affect me so keenly? How can they exist at all?

This book seeks to explore not how such questions may be answered but how they might best be framed. What is happening to us in the moment when we have formed the question but don't know the way to the answer? It's like the holding of a very small breath, a pause among the beats of living. There are worse things to preoccupy a fella.

I was on the Mosel, and it had rained for days. Good weather for working, people said. Dreary, though, and each morning I'd peer out at the still-sodden sky and wish there were a treadmill somewhere nearby.

But then it dried out one day, and there were even furtive bolts of sun, so I announced I was going to walk the seven kilometers through the vineyards from Zeltingen to Graach, and would try to be on time for my visit with Willi and Christoph Schaefer.

In the last few years a path system has been completed that carries the happy walker straight through the vineyards from village to village. You used to have to scramble in the Wehlener Sonnenuhr vineyard, but now you can tromp like the civilized gentleman you assuredly are. (That would be you, not me: I was schvitzing like a donkey and loving it.) It's a mid-slope path, well above the river, and you can look down into the lunatic steepness and up to the twittery woods. I got the lovely lostness you get when you walk awhile—no more thoughts, just a slow dissolve. Now and again there'd be a wan shaft of sunlight. The air smelled like wet slate.

So I walked and dreamed, and I dreamed about this book, which was finished but for the final proofs, and would be published later in the year. You dream all your life about such a thing, and then once it's done you do nothing but angst over it. I laid bare my heart, and feared looking foolish. Still, looking at this miraculous valley, washed in its pearly light, I hoped my little testament to a heart's love of wine would take its place, find a corner to curl up in.

Thus dreaming, I missed the path down. That's what I get for being blissed out. When I finally did descend into Graach, there was the little *gasthaus* on the corner where I once burned the roof of my mouth on a Schnitzel, and there was the house of the Kunsmanns, who had a B&B where I once slept in the attic under the eaves, and awoke one morning to the deliberate creeping of a huge spider and five smaller ones behind her, moving single file along a huge wooden beam toward the center of the ceiling.

That was thirty years ago. It was lovely how little had changed. I turned the corner and the Schaefer house appeared.

It was a momentous year for the family. The parents—now grandparents—were handing over the house to the next generation. "It's more space than we need," Willi said, "and if Christoph's going to keep producing grandchildren"—here Christoph blushed becomingly—"they need room to play." Schaefers *senior* would move to a little house on top of the hill—

"But I'll be down here at the winery every day"—and I enjoyed the thought of them having their breakfast and looking at the view over the valley. All of this was discussed as if it were merely pragmatic. But of course it isn't. Something the French might call a *patrimoine* was being handed down. *You have arrived; it's yours now.*

An hour later I was looking at a map I'd asked to see, a satellite view of the hillside, on which the Schaefers showed me each of their various parcels. They own roughly sixteen in the Domprobst vineyard, and several dozen in the Himmelreich, where the EU-wide land consolidation hasn't yet occurred. I wondered whether the organic purists would be brought up short at the logistical nightmare of trying to farm that way when your land consisted of thirty or forty postage-stamp-sized parcels scattered hither and yon over the hillside. But even more I wondered at the many wines the Schaefers bottle that are parcel-specific, and how these multiple bottlings of wines with the same name seem to annoy people; it's just those Germans being insufferably exact.

What they really are is a thing we should preserve as an endangered species. Look: a few people still exist who are willing to show you the *intimacy* of their accord with the land, and the beautiful detailing of nuance that results.

So we tasted, and then had some supper. We drank some old wine from Willi's cellar, but nothing extravagant. We laughed and were silly, as we often are together. Yet there's a happiness in this house that doesn't express as jollity. It has very little affect at all. You know, you try to be open-eyed, to convince yourself there are dark veils of shadow and *thanatos* even around these happy-looking lives. You don't want to sentimentalize them.

But you sit in the house with parents and children and look at pictures of the new babies, and you see everyone glowing just because—I mean, why wouldn't you glow? And you find yourself, your miserable skeptical self, thinking, "Life is supposed to be like this, and sometimes is." And a sort of dopey desire visits you. *Pare it down. It isn't that hard to be happy.*

Families like this one are why I believe in *terroir*. It's neither a dogma nor a faith. It's just a simple fact. The wines themselves lead me to this belief. It's not only a rational empirical matter; it's also a question of Goodness. And this leads me to consider the schism between two groups of vintners and drinkers: those who feel wine is "made," and those who feel it is *grown*. It is a fundamental split between two mutually exclusive approaches to both wine and life. If a grower believes from his everyday experience that flavors are *inherent* in his land, he will labor to preserve them. This means he does nothing to inhibit, obscure, or change them. He does not write his adorable agenda over his raw material. He respects the material. He is there to release it, to take this nascent being, slap it on the ass, and make it wail.

If, on the other hand, your work as a "winemaker" is all about the vision you have *a priori*, the wine you wish to "sculpt," then your raw material is a challenge to surmount, almost an inconvenience. You learn to be expert at systems and procedures. You make wine as if you were piloting a plane, and there's nothing wrong with being a good pilot. But terroir-driven vintners make wine as if they were riding on the back of a bird.

This implies a modesty that we rarely understand, we worshippers at the altar of self-esteem. One effaces oneself without diminishing oneself—rather the opposite. And sometimes one's wines assume similar virtues, which we also misinterpret.

It is because of our thirst for wines that put on a show for us. But some wines are content to be the straight man and let the food get all the funny lines. One night I had a jar of some black truffle goop or other, and I wanted to use it. I thought of Daniel Boulud's notorious black truffle and foie gras hamburger, and I thought *I too can be decadent*, so my wife and I got some ground veal and made us some slutty patties with the truffle stuff, and just to totally gild the lily we stuffed a pat of D'artagnan black truffle butter in the middle of each patty to melt as the burgers cooked. Oh yeah, baby, it tasted as good as it sounds—but what do you drink with it?

We alighted upon a "basic" St. Laurent from Austria, from Erich Sattler. We might have also been happy with something like a modest Chorey-les-Beaune (assuming we wanted to pay triple the price), and though we had the option of upgrading to the "Reserve" quality wine, it would have had *too* much fruit, and maybe oak would show, and these wicked little burgers don't need all that mojo. They have their own. Our wine was so seamlessly perfect it was as if it too could taste those truffley burgers.

We're all insanely busy stretching toward the stellar; we've really got to *RAWK* the carafe. But if I stand for anything in this little wine-life of mine, it is to insist we learn to cherish wines of modesty and quiet. It will help us understand the beauty of the humble. *Pssst!* It'll also save us money.

I have a fantasy that somewhere up on a stage, some international wine megastar—Guigal comes to mind—is getting a big, ostentatious trophy for attaining an average "score" of 98.3 points for his over-$300 wines. Back in the big general tasting, they're cleaning up, and a guy approaches a Rhône grower whose $12 Côtes-du-Rhône gave him pleasure, and he says to the grower, "Thank you for this wine. It makes me happy."

No question in my mind where I'd rather be, and who I'd rather be.

Things of noise lead us inexorably into greater and greater coarseness and sensual incoherence. Noisy wines are fun from time to time, but like most of the coarser pleasures, they are easy to abuse and very bad for us. I publish a wee manifesto in my sales catalogues, and I recently updated it with a deliberately ambiguous statement: *Many wines, even good wines, let you taste the noise. But only the very best wines let you taste the silence.* Few have commented to me about that thought. I suspect they're being polite because they find it silly. Who knows, perhaps it is. But I know what I mean by it.

First we need to understand this: silence isn't merely the absence of noise. It is the presence of eternity.

A wine that can offer such a thing to you is a wine that breaks bread with the angels. And yet I am aware that I've taken one ethereal statement and elaborated upon it with another. Let's try to get concrete. What do I want you to understand when I write about "tasting silence"? Is it just me indulging a taste for poetry, or is it palpable?

Think of the way a wine comes to greet you. Some tasters refer to it as "the attack," the very first instant when the wine presents itself. It may be assertive, brash, massive, or it may be demure, flowing, bashful. But there is always that very moment with every new bottle, and I am aware that I anticipate it, as if I'm asking, "Who will this be?" It's like meeting a new person, before you know anything about him; you respond instinctually, chemically. There is something remarkably *alive* about us in that moment. Our receptors are buzzing, and we are alight with interest.

Some wines announce themselves. They really push at you. They work the handshake, they're riffing right away, full of schtick, one-liners, they want you to like them, and they work to amuse you. But sometimes you feel a melancholy suspicion it isn't at all about you; they do it with everyone—they need to be liked and approved of. It's their act. And often it's fun to encounter such people. And sometimes there's even a genuine and substantive person, underneath the bluster.

In wine terms that's "tasting the noise."

Other times you meet someone who seems oddly composed and at peace. She doesn't seem to care what impression she makes on you, because she has nothing she's driven to demonstrate. Yet often she directs a lovely beam of attention on you, as if you are a surprising delight, and you spend minutes talking with this compelling new person, and you come away feeling roused, glad, as if you'd been seen in some keenly approving way. Yet *she* is still a blank. She didn't talk about herself. She seemed to be demure.

You become extremely curious about such a person. What is the source of her composure? How does she seem so sure and so stable? How graceful she is, and how effortless she makes it appear! While the high-affect fellow seems to spring into action when he feels the spotlight hit him, this lady seems to be lit from within.

In wine terms, that's "tasting the silence." These introverted wines seem to draw some sheer curtain, and suddenly the world falls away. They banish preoccupation. They deliver repose.

They embody a calmness, they channel the daydreams. And they do it with no perceptible effort. They combine a serene diffidence with a strangely numinous beauty in a poignant and haunting way. And such wines are *full* of flavor, often the most searching and complex wines we'll ever know. But they hold you in their theta-dance, and some crust starts to dissolve in you, and you liquefy to your core, a place hardly anyone ever sees, and the wine seems to know you, like some strange angel.

Such wines are never noisy. They don't know how to be. They won't reward superficial attention. But the deeper you go, the greater the prize, for these aren't merely great wines, they are great moments of life. They show that a certain thing is possible, something you never saw and doubted existed—a mysterious miracle you didn't know you carried with you. You realize that hedonism washes away—it won't adhere; it's why we chase it so desperately. This, though, this stays. This actually changes your life. It might not be a huge change. It's not like getting your first degree or losing thirty pounds or having your first child. It's just a small glimpse of a possibility you can't fathom, tiny, delicate, impossible to forget.

If it moves you, and if you try to talk about it, you feel like a fool. You don't have the language you need, and so you fumble, and people think you've been hitting the bong pipe. For you it is entirely definite as feeling and spiritual sense, but in language it's nebulous. How do we delineate between wines that *enact* and wines that reveal?

Enacting wines can be brilliant and scintillating, but I sometimes feel them straining to ravish me, busy being amazing. Revealing wines just sit there being themselves, as if they were born knowing repose. Think of the way a person's face is most revealing when it isn't busy with gestures and expressions; while reading perhaps, or even sleeping. You look at the face and see the person behind the personality. That is what revealing wines reveal.

You can call it spiritual, but that poor word's been debased. It's easy to distrust spirituality or the life of the soul, because the words are wielded with what sounds like a rebuke, that we should live in spirit or that our souls should live our lives for us. Well, phooey. Yet very often we make the opposite mistake; we insist on banishing soul from our lives. Quite an effort, that is, to push away soul, to reassure ourselves and others that we're matter-of-fact, as if soul were a kind of spiritual elitism. Personally I think it's useless to pull soul in or to shove it away. Better to ignore it and go about your life, as long as you *are* alive, by which I mean attentive and available. Soul is pretty smart and will show up when it's warranted. And these aren't always the moments we think are exalted. Baseball season just started, and I can't wait for that first night game. I'll buy my soul some chicken fingers. My soul likes the fried stuff.

When you taste silence in a wine, you sense a peace that lives on the far shores of all the urging and pushing. It's like making up after a fight: I love her; why are we fighting? It's a strange and stirring peace that seems to come only this way, to take us to this place where everything belongs and everything's all right. These wines that seem so quiet only whisper to you *so that you will quiet down and listen,* and listening, be finally able to hear not only their own psalms of flavor but the tenderness and serenity around us always.

I happily confess I was touched and amazed at the way people responded when this book came out in September 2010. I knew that the people who'd like it would like it a lot. I figured there'd be a few of them, and what the hell, I stuck my neck out and risked seeming mawkish. But I started to get the impression that the book talked to some forbidden place in some of us, somewhere we felt ashamed, as if wine were too ephemeral to cause such emotion, or as though there were no greater values in play.

But as this paperback edition of *Reading between the Wines* appears, I want to reassure you that none of what follows is a command. It is merely a proposal. It's all right to think of wine like this, and it's all right not to. A range of possible experiences exist, and we take the ones we like. Wine is a tactful invitation, not a summons. But let us be available, when it asks, to go quietly soaring, because the earthbound life is finally too small.

INTRODUCTION

Some people will never learn anything, for this reason, because they understand everything too soon. —*Alexander Pope*

I owe my life in wine to two people: Hugh Johnson and Rod Stewart.

Rod came first. It was a Faces concert at the late, lamented Fillmore East on Second Avenue in New York City. Somehow I'd scored a front-row seat. Faces concerts in those days were like big drunken ramshackle rehearsals, with lots of boozy bonhomie. Rod would swig from a bottle of Mateus Rosé, and on one occasion he passed it down to some twitching rocker in the front row, who took a greasy hit and passed it along. Then it got to me. First sip of wine. I *hated* it. Passed the bottle to the next guy. Finally the last hippie handed the bottle back to Rod, who pantomimed being seriously pissed off to find it empty.

Metamessage for me: wine is cool, rock stars drink it. I want to *be* a rock star. This was crucial information. I had to at least pretend to like wine.

Looking back all these years later, I see that this was the very moment wine, or the *idea* of wine, came to reside in my life. Not because I liked the stuff, but because I'd absorbed the idea that wine was crucial as a social-sexual marker.

As I grew older, I (and my girlfriend du jour) would often score a bottle of wine—most of which I hated—for a Saturday night. The first wine I ever drank and actually wanted to drink again was . . . (here go my credentials) *Blue Nun*. It was a novel feeling to enjoy drinking wine. It was a relief to drink something with low alcohol and fruitiness.

I'd lived in Munich, Germany, as a middle schooler; my father was head of the Voice of America's European division from 1965 through 1968. Those middle-school years are when you form your persona and self-image; the bands and clothes you like, what pack you prefer to run with (or which pack will have you). For me, this seminal time was forever connected to being in Germany, and I was eager to return someday. I took what purported to be a hiatus from college and went with my girlfriend to Europe, where we drove around in a severely beat-up old Opel we bought on the street.

After many months of wandering, we ended up back in Munich, since old family friends had told me the army usually had jobs available for civilian "components" of the Department of Defense, and of course we'd run out of money in a fraction of the time we'd imagined. This, improbably, is where Hugh Johnson comes in.

Our Saturday evening bottle soon morphed into our Friday *and* Saturday evening bottles, which in turn became Friday-Saturday-Sunday. We liked drinking wine more often—fledgling sybarites, you see. I shopped for wine each week, and all of it was supermarket plonk. Then three things happened.

I'd bought a random bottle we happened to like a whole lot, and when I went to buy more it was all gone, *ausverkauft*, never to return. The moral: when the wine's good, buy more fast. Thus was born a wine cellar, a terribly important way of describing our few dozen bottles on plastic store-bought racks. But any bunch of wine in excess of what you're drinking right now is a de facto cellar, and now I had one.

Second, I bought a bottle of something called "Riesling" for the first time. This was different! I had never tasted a wine with so *much* flavor that wasn't "fruity." It tasted like mineral water with wine instead of water. I needed to know what this odd new thing was.

One of our benefits was access to the army library, and one of the books in the army library was, yes, Hugh Johnson's *World Atlas of Wine and Spirits*. "The pictures are pretty, in case I can't deal with all these words," I reassured myself. But what words they were! Open to any page and there was something, an urbane turn of phrase, a stray bit of poetry, and, most striking to me, an unabashed emotionality. The Saar (which I could reach in a few hours' drive) "makes sweet wine you can never tire of: the balance and depth make you sniff and sip and sniff again . . . every mouthful a cause for rejoicing and wonder."

Rejoicing and wonder? All right, I can see rejoicing; I mean, after all, there's a moment of rejoicing in the first bite of a perfect cheeseburger if you're alert to it. But wonder? Was there more to this whole wine thing than I'd imagined? Was wine an object of beauty?

So I set about locating the wines Johnson wrote about, as best I could, and as best I could afford. I tried to taste them more attentively, to see whether they spoke to me. Sometimes they did, and sometimes I was groping. But the pictures in the book sure made wine country look pretty. Maybe it was time to see for myself.

And since we lived in Germany, and since these were the days before German wine became uncool, German wine country was the shortest distance from us. Armed and provisioned with maps and lists of recommended vineyards and producers, off we went. We parked at the edges of many wine villages, and went knocking on winegrowers' doors.

I don't suppose many of the growers we visited had ever been dropped in on by some hirsute freak with a list of geeky questions and a minuscule budget. But to my immoderate good fortune, then and many times since, I found German wine-growers to be *the* most generous and hospitable people I'd ever encountered. If you were interested and curious, there were few limits to the time they'd take or the samples they'd pour. If I asked about vineyards, they'd grab my arm and walk me up into the hills, explaining minutiae of geology and microclimate; if I asked about vintages, out came the bottles and the corkscrew. I protested lustily, but for naught. I said I needed to buy small amounts of a lot of *different* wines so that I could learn by survey-ing, to which they answered, Buy what you buy, it's no problem.

My entire world changed. It was May 1978, and I had found the thing I didn't know I was seeking. Or it had found me.

Wine, I discovered, could indeed be a thing of beauty. It could make you feel. It was endlessly changeable, and it played ever-wonderful variations on its themes; it wasn't just lovely, it was *interesting*. It was made in beautiful countryside, by sweet-natured people. And in many wines there were flavors I couldn't begin to account for. Music was similarly evanescent, but music's effects could usually be described; happy, sad, eerie, morose, pastoral, ecstatic, tender . . . but wine? What was going on here?

I lived five more years in Europe and visited most of its important wine regions, spent far too much money on wine and far too much time obsessing over it, not to mention boring the eyelashes off anyone around me if, God forbid, the subject of wine came up. We are all a little insane when we're infatuated. But my run of good luck continued; I experienced each new wine region by actually being there, absorbing its vistas, smells, horizons, whether the dogs were on leashes or roaming free, if it seemed welcoming (like Burgundy) or austere and taciturn (like Bordeaux), and I did this with Johnson's (and others') prose playing background music in my mind. There is no better way not merely to learn but also to *know* about wine. I belonged to no tasting groups, attended no wine classes. There was no Internet with its bulletin boards and exchanges of geekery. I did it alone and feverishly. My girlfriend became my first wife, Tina, and she was a very patient woman. Wine, for me, became something most vitally *intimate;* only later did it become something I connected to social life and conviviality.

I was driven to write about it long before I had anything of value to say. I liked to write; it seemed to complete my experiences, both of individual wines and of wine in the abstract. Somewhere in a dusty old shoebox is a primitive manuscript of a wine book I had no business producing. I could find it, but I doubt I could bear to read it. Yet even that early need to catalog information and describe experience was helpful, not least when

I cannibalized sections of the book into magazine pieces for an American journal called *Friends of Wine.* They paid me! Spent the first check on wine, of course; 1970 Montrose and Las Cases, as I recall. Finally opened the Montrose after staring at it nostalgically for twenty-six years.

In early 1983, when I returned to the United States after ten years in Germany, I wanted a job in the wine business. Suffice it to say I made my way. My progress was hardly picaresque; it was tedious. But it was progress. I put together a little portfolio of German wines from most of my old friends. Years later I helped introduce the splendid new wines of Austria to the States, and, undeterred by the indifference and derision that had become my daily lot, I assembled a slew of small Champagne growers to sell to the wary trade, effectively strapping a safe to my back to add to the grand piano already there as I pushed my rock up an endless hill. I seem to have had a fiendish gift for selecting uncool wine categories. For reasons still obscure, German wine was dead in the water in the mid-eighties. Nine years later, no one had heard of Austrian wine except that they put antifreeze in it some time ago. And *no one* believed they could sell "no-name" Champagne.

It's not that I relished a challenge; I just wouldn't shrink from one. But I didn't go looking for weird or difficult wine categories, I just followed my odd little bliss. Years later, when interviewed for a magazine profile, I was asked, "So how does it feel to have perennially unpopular taste?"

"Just lucky, I guess," was my reply then, and it still would be today.

In June 2008 I received the James Beard Award for outstanding wine and spirits professional, our industry's equivalent to an Oscar. As I accepted the award I flashed back on those first formative years, overwhelmed with all I'd been given. This book will tell you how I got from those early quiet walks through remote, hilly vineyards to the longer-seeming walk onto the stage at Avery Fisher Hall after my name was called. It's time to give back. It's time to tell what wine can mean in a person's life.

But to do this I have to ask you to accept the ethereal as an ordinary and valid part of everyday experience—because the theme of this book is that wine can be a portal into the mystic. And we hate the very thought of the mystic, which seems so esoteric and inaccessible. But it isn't; it happens all the time.

A batter in a slump says (as one of my hometown Orioles did, just this morning), "It's like the ball is invisible." Another batter on a tear says, "I'm seein' the ball real good." Well, just what is happening here? It isn't mechanics; hitters and their coaches are seasoned professionals who know the basics. How does one describe these states of being in or out of "the zone"? I think we start by trying to describe what "the zone" itself is. And you can't do that without recourse to the mystic.

Musicians will sometimes reach zones of their own, often saying something like "I felt like a vessel through which the music was playing, as if I weren't generating it at all." And since that state exists but we don't know how to access it, what is its nature, and how do we find our ways to it?

My central argument is that wine can be a bringer of mystical experience—but not all wine. There are prerequisites, and I'll discuss them. In addition, there are collateral benefits to allowing oneself to be prepared for wine's mystical capacity. We also become sensitized to wine's *fun* capacity. But what is the process of cultivating this preparedness? That has been the subject of millions of words on Eastern thought, but when has it ever been applied to wine?

It begins with understanding what a "palate" actually is, and how to truly know one's own. It continues with cultivating a particular approach to wine, whereby one prefers the finer over the coarser virtues, the quiet over the noisy.

The ethereal can be forbidding when it isn't grounded in counterpoint to the ordinary. I wish this book to be ethereal, since it is defending the mystic, but I don't want it to be slack or nebulous. Neither do I want it to be too linear, though, because I don't hold that all experience is reducible to logic. I understand the difficulty of using language to describe evanescent or ineffable states. But instead of surrendering vaporously ("such things are beyond words . . ."), I'll confront the very limitations of language itself by asking what purpose it serves.

If you want to experience wine with your whole self—not only your mind and senses—the wine has to be authentic. And what confers authenticity is a rootedness in family, soil, and culture as well as the connections among them. These are aided by intimacy of scale. And they form the core of a value system by which *real* wine can be appreciated and understood.

Part of advancing this point of view is to identify what opposes it. It cannot suffice only to find the good and praise it, because the good is under ceaseless threat from the bogus and ostentatious. This tension forms the basis for a large quarrel between two sorts of wine drinkers, and they don't always play nice. I'll try to help us steer a decent person's way through.

I was fortunate to learn about wine in the best possible way, in the Old World among the vines and in the company of the families who grew them. One could call this a "classical" education, to learn the benchmarks of the subject firsthand, to place in the center what belonged in the center, and to appreciate the borders between the central and the peripheral.

In the end I'll share a few wine experiences with you, which will put these principles inside an actual life with wine.

If the text seems to meander or to sometimes repeat itself, I don't mind; in fact, I hope it does. It is less a strict cerebral argument and more a piece of a lifelong incantation. At times I might frustrate you by defining terms you already know, or failing to define terms you don't know. The actual you won't always be congruent with the many hypothetical yous I've had looking over my shoulder. I beg your pardon in advance.

Although this is not a wine primer, if I were an educator, the first thing I'd tell you is this: anyone learning about wines should begin in the Old World, where wine itself began. It's more grounded there. All things being equal, it is more artisanal, more intimately scaled, humbler, and less likely to be blown about by the ephemeral breezes of fashion. Its wines are made by vintners who descend from other vintners, often for a dozen or more generations. They are not parvenus, arrivistes, or refugees from careers in architecture, dermatology, software design, or municipal garbage disposal systems. They don't know about the wine "lifestyle," and if you tried to tell them, you'd likely draw a blank stare. You won't see a huge white stretch limo pulling out of their courtyards like the one I saw emerging ostentatiously from Opus One in the Napa Valley last year (I doubt it would *fit* in Ürzig or Séguret or Riquewihr or Vetroz). You'll never find *Bon Appétit* taking pictures in these growers' kitchens or at garden parties on the grounds.

Starting with Old World wines is also useful because they

don't do all the work for you. Non–wine people will wonder what I mean. Climate change notwithstanding, Old World wines (especially north of the Alps) have about them a certain reserve. They're not aloof, but neither are they extravagant, gregarious, life-of-the-party wines. They don't play at top volume, and they can seem inscrutable to people with short attention spans. They are, however, kinetic; they draw you in, they make you a participant in the dance. They *engage* you. They won't let you be passive, unless you choose to ignore them—in which case, why buy them? Yes, of course, I'm painting in broad strokes, but I won't clutter the prose with qualifiers; this is what I believe. Old World wines ask you to dance *with* them; New World wines push you prone onto a chair and give you a lap dance, no touching.

Other writers have clarified the disparate paradigms of Old and New World wines, and the rule of generalities applies; they are never more than generally true. Yet they exist for a reason. Notwithstanding the various honorable exceptions, New World wines are marked by a kind of effusiveness that turns the drinker from a participant into an onlooker. These big, emphatic wines put on quite a show: explosions and car chases in every glass. If you're new to wine, this can be reassuring. You get it. You needn't worry there are subtleties you don't grasp. But eventually such wines begin to pall.

Most New World wines cue off an Old World benchmark. The original is the great novel; the newbie is the made-for-TV movie based on the great novel. Not only is the complexity of the story squandered, but the entire experience of receiving it shrinks to a passive "entertainment" and obliterates the vital, breathing, imaginative life we bring to the act of reading.

Go on, call me opinionated! I accept it. But also call me a

man who stands for something. The alternative seems to be to stand for nothing, and that won't do.

I'm sitting at my dining room table with a glass of wine. On the walls around me are all the pieces of art I've collected. Laughably, these are mostly prints from calendars, but in my own defense they're Old World calendars with superior print quality! The scenes are all *peaceful;* they show cows, ponds, cows grazing near ponds, ponds reflecting the faces of cows, all these theta-wave-inducing scenes for which a city boy hungers. I have a stray thought: what will my son make of these? How will he remember them? Will they grow nostalgic for him; will he love them in retrospect? (I'm sure he finds them seriously boring right now.) My folks had a reproduction of a van Gogh that showed sailboats on a shoreline. It's probably famous. I saw it constantly when I was a kid. If I see it now, some kind of membrane grows permeable inside me. I don't even *like* the painting. But I'm plunged back into old, familiar waters. It's not associated with any discrete memory: I don't link it to my father burning the lamb chops or my mother cracking us all up. It is the sum of all the ethereal memory of being little, all the mystery of what I didn't know then and will never know, all the mystery of what becomes of the time, all the longing for what might have been said, said better, done better, how we might all have been better, starting with me. Sad, wondering, uneasy, oddly sweet.

Wine can talk to this thing in us. Some call it soul. Wine is not apart from this being within us. It doesn't have to be. It fits in tidily, and takes its place. All it needs is a soul of its own. It can't be manufactured; it can't have been formed by marketers seeking to identify its target audience. It needs to be connected to families who are connected to their land and to working their land and who are content to let the land speak in its own voice. Wines like this are valid because they don't insist you leave 90 percent of yourself at the rim of the glass. This trait stands apart from how good they are; that comes after. Plenty of wine can be contrived to bring you to a kind of peepshow of flavor, if that's your idea of a good time. *True* wine takes its legitimate place as part of your entire, true being. You are complete and human. You have not been reduced to a consumer unit whose behavior can be anticipated.

I didn't know any of this in 1978 when I started. No one explained it. I was shocked later on when I saw that wine could be otherwise, could merely entertain with its noise and phony seductiveness. Wine, it seemed, could be just another thing, *product*, disconnected from any reason a human being should care about it. My spirit felt starved when the caring wasn't there. I found the any-old-soil, technical nirvana New World ideal to be vacuous and lamentable. And yes—*of course*—there's no end of schlock from the Old World, but the Old World is hospitable to meaningful wine in a way the New World hasn't yet attained. A couple hundred years from now, it'll be a different story. Or so I hope.

In the pages to come I will challenge many common fallacies about wine, and I will show how wine can enrich your life by describing how it enriched mine. This isn't any sort of challenge to you, innocent reader. I've always cringed at the self-help "wisdom"-dispensing swamis for the rebuke underlying their message: *You live these pathetic, suffocating lives because you're not as smart as I am, but I'll consent to get you smart for $18.95 and a donation to my ashram in Boca Raton, Florida.* One of the great things about wine is that it will meet you wherever you manage to be.

I want to give you choices, and you can swallow what works for you and spit out the rest. I will make the case that wine belongs in a life of the soul, in an *erotic* life (in the Greek sense of *eros* as the force of life), but to encounter it there you have to be unsentimental and willing to demand authenticity from the wine and from yourself.

This doesn't guarantee exalted experience. It guarantees *real* experience. It guarantees that you won't have to curtail any aspect of your humanity to have a relationship with wine.

When my son was old enough to wonder what Daddy did, I had a hard time feeling satisfied with the answer that Daddy sold wine. I tried expanding it by explaining that Daddy sold wine he himself tasted and chose, but even then it seemed pretty mingy. Daddy sells stuff. Doesn't matter how adorable it is: Pop's a salesman.

How then does one define the larger questions? Is it even possible? It seems as if it must be, since I feel so stratified all the time. One layer is the garden-variety mercantile wine guy dealing with all the "issues" surrounding the zany categories with which I work. Everyone in the wine biz knows those issues: education, marketing, perseverance, dog-and-pony shows, "working the press." I try to be good at those things, or as good as my fallibilities allow. The other (perhaps deeper) layer is less concerned with the job and more concerned with the *work*. I have a voice in my head that always says, "Yes, *and?*" So if I ask myself what is the net effect of what I do, this voice propels me through ever more big-picture considerations.

I sell wine. *Yes, and?* I help ensure the prosperity of good artisanal winegrowers. *Yes, and?* I contribute to the continuing existence of cultures *containing* small artisanal winegrowers. *Yes, and?* To remain sustainable, I need to tell people why this is a good thing. *Yes, and?* In telling people why this is a good thing, I have to detail the reasons, which compels thoughts of soil, of family (the two are often combined into the word *terroir*), of a person's proper relationship with nature and to his human history. In short, I have to assert *values. Yes, and?* In delineating these values, I find I can't escape matters of soul. *Yes, and?* If soul enters the equation, you can't select what it inhabits, because soul inhabits either all of it or none of it. So what I finally end up doing is placing wine in the context of a life of the soul. *Yes, and?* So now I am defending and delineating the idea of living with conscience, gratitude, eros, humor, all the things soul imbues us with. And further, I'm placing wine squarely within this matrix and insisting that we don't have enough time to settle for less. *Yes, and?* And we seem to need certain things: to know where we are. To be connected to something outside ourselves. To be connected to something *inside* ourselves. And the only wines that actually speak to our whole lives are *authentic* wines, which are themselves both located and connected. Confected wines are not designed for human beings; they are designed for "consumers." Which do you want to be?

one

BEFRIENDING YOUR PALATE

First you master your instrument. Then you forget all that shit and just play.
—Charlie Parker, when asked how one becomes a great jazz musician

You're at home watching TV in the evening. Let's say you're watching a DVD of something you really like. Unless you have some monstrous home-theater system, you're looking at a relatively small screen across the room. You can't help but see all your stuff strewn about. Usually you have a light or two on. You hear ambient noises.

Now pretend you're at the movies. The lights go down, and you're sitting in a dark room with a bright screen encompassing your whole field of vision. Even with others around you, there is a strange, almost trance-like intimacy between these huge, bright images and your emotions. All great directors are acquainted with this spell; it's the essence of cinema. And it arouses a deep, almost precognitive attention from us.

We often think of palate as our physical taste receptor, the mouth itself, and, more saliently, the sense of smell. But a palate is more than what you taste; it is your *relationship with* what you taste. Palate isn't passive; it is kinetic.

Palate is really two things. First, it is the quality of attention you pay to the signals your taste receptors are sending. Second, it is memory, which arises from experience. A "good palate" is able to summon the cinema type of attention. An ordinary palate—more properly called an *indifferent* palate—is watching TV with the lights on.

Most of us are born with roughly the same discrete physical sensitivities to taste. (But there are said to be so-called supertasters who may have a larger number of taste buds than the rest of us do, in which case, lucky them; they're getting bombarded with signals.) What varies is our sensitivity to this . . . sensitivity. It seems to be an irreducible aspect of temperament, how the gods arranged the goodies in the box called you.

I remember when I was a wine fledgling being complimented on my palate by people more experienced than I was. It wasn't as gratifying as it may seem. I had no idea what a good palate was supposed to entail. I guess it was good that I had one. Then what?

Later, when I taught wine classes for beginners, I did a little exercise at the beginning, putting four different brands of tortilla chips on numbered plates, and asking the eager wine students (who must have been wondering when their refund checks would be mailed) to taste all four and write down which one they liked best and why. A lively discussion never failed to ensue: "Number three has the deepest corn flavor" or "Number one wasn't salty enough" or "The taste of number four lasts the longest time." When it was all over I'd say, "Okay, guys, now you know everything you need in order to become good wine tasters." *Ah, excuse me?* But these students tasted variations on a narrow theme; they paid attention because they had to, and they put their impressions into words. They were *tasters*, and the medium didn't matter.

Yet the approach path to wine seems so fraught (compared to tortilla chips!); there are so damnably *many* of them, they change all the time, and just when you think you're getting a handle on the whole unruly mess you read about yet another obscure place entering the world wine market with labels that look like anagrams without enough vowels. It's dispiriting; I feel your pain. But you're completely wrong.

When I started my wine life I made the same mistake. I imagined some theoretical point of mastery that lay on the horizon, and I would reach it eventually if I just kept walking. But horizons are funny: they keep moving just as we do. The more urgently you walk, the more they recede. Bastards, mocking me like that; don't they know I'm *tryin'* here? Sure they know! They're just going to keep frustrating me until I finally get the message: enjoy the journey, and notice your surroundings.

But aside from this corner-store Zen wisdom, here's a practical suggestion: If the sheer cacaphony of wine cows you, just ignore it. For at least three months—ideally even longer—choose two grape varieties, a white and a red, and drink *nothing but those*. Let's say you chose Sauvignon Blanc and Syrah. First you drink all the Sauv Blanc you can lay your hands on, California, New Zealand, Austria, all the various Loires, Alto Adige, and Friuli; you steep yourself in Sauvignon, seeing how the wines differ and what core qualities they all seem to have. Write each impression down. Do the same with Syrah: Australia, Rhône valley, Languedoc-Roussillon, California. When you start getting antsy for change, that's when you're ready for the next duo. You're getting bored with Sauvignon and Syrah because they aren't surprising you anymore. But boy, do you ever know them. You know them in your bones and dreams. Your very breath smells like old saddles and gooseberries.

Let's say you opt for Pinot Blanc and Cabernet Franc for your next duo. Right away you'll notice the newness of these wines, not only *that* they are different, but *how* they are different. You've immersed yourself in those first varieties, and every subsequent variety will automatically be contrasted with them. To know wine, learn its elements deeply and deliberately. Then your knowledge will be durable and your palate's vision will inexorably widen. Trying to skim over hundreds of different wines all at once will only make you cross-eyed.

This is hard for most of us because of all the many wines coming at us. Trust me, though: it's mostly static, and if you really want to learn you'd best find a system, or use mine. It builds your knowledge slowly, but what you build stays built.

The palate is an instrument played by the taster, and you're practicing and doing your exercises until you become facile. When that finally happens you think you've attained your goal, but you're still in a primitive zone of merely demonstrating the mastery you have obtained by practice and repetition. Eventually, if the gods consent, you stop worrying about *how* and start worrying about *what*. You forget about playing your horn (or your ax in my own mangy case) and just start to play the *music*.

You go to a party in a house you've never been to, and they have a really cool dog. You like dogs. But this particular dog is introverted or bashful, and the more you approach, the more he backs away. All you want to do is scritch him! But looks like it isn't happening, so you merge back into the throng and forget about Towser. Later you're sitting talking with some fetching young thing and suddenly you feel something cold and wet on the back of your hand. Well, look who's there: it's old Towser, sniffing you, checking you out. *Now* you can scritch his handsome head all you want. Scritch away—what a good boy! You go back to complaining to your friend about how no matter how much you study wine, it doesn't seem to get any easier. . . .

Wine is like a shy dog. Lunge for it and it backs away. Just sit still and it draws nearer. Wine is less about what you can grasp than about how you can *receive*. You grasp it more firmly if you grab it less tightly. It will resist you if you insist on subduing it. You can accumulate only so much knowledge in quantifiable bits, but you accumulate *understanding* if you learn to relax. Wine doesn't like being dominated. It prefers being loved and wondered about. It will do anything for you if you're curious and grateful.

I learned this the hard way, and so will you, if you don't already know it. I made quite an ass of myself strutting with my sexy-pants wine knowledge, and I wasted far too much time arguing with other wine geeks to prove my alpha cred. Learn from my sad past! The first hint I can offer is to try to distinguish between true complexity and mere complicatedness. The latter is usually frustrating, but the former is usually wonderful. You have to direct a beam of mind to pick a way through complicatedness. You set your jaw and grind your teeth until you've prevailed. You've nailed the flavors, quantified and named every nuance, and decided precisely how much you liked the wine on whatever scale they told you to use. But complexity asks the opposite. It is an immediate sense of something you *can't know*, something you won't be able to isolate or explain. Complexity is quiet; complicatedness is noisy. With complexity you have to relax your mind and see what happens. I can't promise this mental state is available to most of us, unless you are the Dalai Lama, until you reach a certain . . . ahem . . . age. It has been years since I worked *at* wine. I work *with* it, of course, and it's fun work, but I'm sure that after a certain point, the more we work at our pleasures (we say we "pursue" our pleasures, tellingly), the more they'll back away from us. Show me someone who "plays hard" and I'll show you someone who has forgotten how to play at all.

Of course, it *is* play, for many of us, to deconstruct and describe all of a wine's elements. But to the extent that they can be detected, what we're describing is intricacy, not (necessarily) complexity. A wine is complex when it suggests something that can't be seen or even known, but it is definitely, and hauntingly, there. A complex wine seems to channel the very complexity of living. A complicated wine is just a mosaic we piece together with our senses.

Here's what I think you're after: a point of utter receptivity in which you're seeing only the wine instead of seeing *yourself* seeing the wine. Oh, it does sound very Zen. But I'm persuaded it's the way to pleasure and sanity. If you don't see past your own discrete palate, you can't get past *What am I getting from the wine?* It starts and stops with "I." What am *I* getting, what do *I* think, how many points will *I* give it—all I can say is, if you drink wine this way, I sure hope you don't make love this way, because your partner's bored.

I know how it is; you're trying to get a handle on wine, and so you grasp for a handhold. If you're drinking a wine you like and someone tells you it was fermented with cultured yeast, the lightbulb goes on over your head: *Aha!* Cultured yeast = wine I like, thus I must posit the theorem that better wines are made from cultured yeast. Innocent enough. The problem arises when you cling to your belief despite any new evidence. It's tempting to add knowledge nuggets to your basket, and discouraging to chuck them away. But you have to; wine will force you to. It will lie in wait the minute you get certain about something, and trip you up in front of your friends, your sommelier, and the date you hoped to score with. Not that this has ever happened to me personally. . . .

It's actually best when you make a mistake. And the easiest mistake is thinking you've got it aced, because now you're not asking questions anymore, you're waiting for each wine to confirm your conclusions. Yet wine will contrive to confuse your assumptions in order to force you to still your ego and listen. If you hold wine too tightly, it can't dance with you. Hold it just right and it will glide over the floor with you as if you were a single body.

Remember, your palate isn't a thing you possess; it is part of you. You don't taste with this thing; you taste with your whole self. Some years ago there was a story about a so-called Robotongue the Japanese had developed, a machine that could be programmed to identify wines based on predictable markers (acidity, sweetness, and tannin, among others) and that was able to "perform" with uncanny accuracy. So the actual physiochemical reception of flavor can be bettered by a machine, which can register and catalog what it "tastes." But does it actually *taste?* We are entire human beings tasting wine; we bring our memories and longings and anticipations to every glass.

Each of us relates to our palates based on our temperament: a geek will have a geeky relationship with his palate, a right-brainer will have an elliptical and inferential relationship with his palate, and a linear, cataloguing person will organize his palate like a well-oiled machine. No single system is "best"; it's important to have the relationship that comes naturally. If you try to force it, you'll be doomed to frustration.

These relationships change over time. In a wine lover's early days, he's usually (and usefully) an obsessive note-taker. Notes help hone his powers of concentration and help him remember what he has tasted. My closets are laden with dusty old notebooks so full of entirely tedious tasting notes that my wife's running out of space for her shoes. She's right, I probably ought to chuck 'em. I hardly write notes anymore unless the wine is seriously moving. And I'm confident I can deconstruct a wine's flavor if I have to. In the early days I wasn't, none of us is, but like every muscle, this one got stronger the more I used it.

The greatest wines are the ones you can't write notes about because you're weeping, overcome with their loveliness. This happened to me in a restaurant in Paris one evening; the waiter must have thought my wife had just told me she didn't love me anymore and was absconding with the plumber. Nah, it was just the damned Jurançon. This, like all wine experiences, will jump out of the darkness at you, but it's okay, it's part of the spell. Don't fear the weeper.

There's no need to posture with your palate. Unless you publish tasting notes for a living, no one knows what you think or feel about the wines you drink except you. So don't play games. Don't grope for extravagant language, don't confuse what you admire or find interesting with what you spontaneously *like*, and please, if the wine smells like roses, it doesn't make you a better taster if you find some esoteric flower like buddleia to compare it to. Trust any impulse that emerges spontaneously, as these are most authentically *you*. Some wines intrigue with their mosaiclike arrangement of nuances, and it's fun to root around and glean the intricacy of the design. Other wines seem to be pure image. If you're at all in the synesthesia continuum you'll find color images come to you immediately. I definitely receive some wines as "green" or "orange" or "purple," and while some of this is reassuringly literal—purple as aromas of irises, wisteria, lavender, violets, for example—other times I have no idea why a wine seems "silvery" or why it might play in a "major" key. I just know the image makes sense even if I can't make sense of it. Your notes should help you remember not only how the wine tasted, but what it was like to drink it.

And what of the notorious practice of blind tasting? What, indeed.

For some people it is the sine qua non of wine knowledge. Many of the exams for various wine titles (Master of Wine, famously) require proficiency at blind tasting. Why, I don't know. Once a guy can bench-press three hundred pounds, he needs a way to employ that strength; otherwise, he can show off his irrelevant prowess only on the bench. Blind tasting as such is hardly a skill that will be put to use in a wine career, unless you plan to make a living playing parlor games with wine. Importer and author Kermit Lynch said it best: "Blind tastings are to wine what strip poker is to love."

Let's come back to the musical instrument metaphor. The palate is an instrument played by the taster. As you learn your instrument, you practice exercises and repetitions until you are skilled. Then it comes naturally. You don't get on a stage and play your exercises in front of an audience, and blind tasting is the equivalent of playing scales: valuable, necessary, but not to be confused with playing *music* or tasting wine.

When Keith Jarrett recorded *The Melody at Night, with You*, he was recovering from chronic fatigue syndrome. He couldn't play concerts; sometimes he could barely even sit at the piano for more than a few minutes. The CD is a recital of standards and folk melodies, played very straight, with little embellishment or technical bravura. The result is nearly sublime, tender, deliberate, caressing, essential, and pure. One time I answered the phone while the disc was playing, and as I walked back into the room I realized that if I'd been listening casually, I might have thought it was merely cocktail-lounge piano. Knowing the artist, his history, and the conditions under which the recording had been made gave it resonance and meaning.

What, then, is the value of reducing wine to a thing without context? What game is this we're insisting wine play along with? What's the *good* of tasting blind? Where's the silver lining of experiencing wine in a vacuum? Yes, it can train us to focus our palates and hone our powers of concentration. Then we can discard it! It has served its purpose. If we persist in tasting blind we run a grave risk—because it is homicidal to a wine's *context*, and wine without context is bereft of meaning, and the experience of meaning is too rare to be squandered.

But, you protest, blind tasting makes you objective! Oh, nonsense. Can anyone who has ever tasted blind really assert any pure motivation toward truth and objectivity, or does that person simply need to win the game by making the right guess? Besides, blind tasting will guarantee your "objectivity" only if this objectivity is so fragile it needs such a primitive crutch. If you're too immature (or inexperienced) to be objective when you have to be, blind tasting won't help you. It will, however, confuse you as to the purpose of drinking wine. And I'm not talking about only recreational drinking (remember *fun?*); the only genuinely professional approach to wine is to know as much about it as possible. Who made it, under what conditions, what are the track records of the site and the vintner—then and only then can a genuinely thoughtful evaluation of a wine take place in the fullness of its being.

I wish I could tell you how to hasten the process of relaxing into wine. But it takes the time it takes. It can't be forced. Here's how it was for me.

One morning I woke up thinking about a high school teacher I hadn't remembered in years. Jane Stepanski taught honors English, which I took as a junior. I had no great love of reading, but I had all the love I could stand for Mrs. Stepanski. Looking back on it now, we were an awfully fatuous bunch, and it's touching how she forgave us.

I needed the pack. I wasn't a nerd; I was what used to be called a "freak" exactly two years early. So I needed shelter, and honors English provided it, 'cause all the misfits were there. Oh, I read a little, but mostly I was earnest and clueless. I recall when my classmates were especially derisive of what they called truth-and-beauty poems. I went along with the prevailing contempt: truth-and-beauty poems—*ptui!* Only ignorant clods liked those. What kinds of poems did I like? Um, er, ah . . . well—*ahem*—um, y'know, all *kinds* of poems as long as they were *not* truth-and-beauty poems.

Looking back, what can you do but laugh? I don't disdain how we were, how I was. I was pitiable, I was so needy, we all were; we hungered for any scrap of certainty, any solid bit of floor to stand on, and so we struck our attitudes and Jane somehow didn't spit at us. She let us be, and was respectful, and steered us gently away from our silliness.

When I first got into wine in my mid-twenties, I was like every fledgling wine geek. It consumed my every hour, and sadly, it also consumed anyone in my proximity for a couple years. But I was greedy for knowledge, or rather for *information*, and I did what every young person does: I sought to subdue the subject by acquiring mastery over it. Ignorance was frustrating and uncertainty was actively painful.

Wine was behaving like the mechanical rabbit that keeps the greyhounds running the track. No matter how much knowledge I hoarded, the ultimate target remained the same distance away. The "truth" of wine, it seemed, was a sliding floor . . . and even then you had to gain access to the room. It frustrated my craving for certainty, for command and mastery. And for a time I was angry at wine.

Now I think it was wine that was angry at me. But as patiently as my old honors English teacher, wine set about teaching me what it really wanted me to know.

First I needed to accept that in wine, uncertainty was an immutable fact of life. "The farther one travels, the less one knows." There was no sense struggling against it; all that did was retard my progress toward contentment. But it is a human desire to ask why, to seek to *know*. Would wine always frustrate that desire as a condition of our relationship?

Far from it. But I was asking the wrong *why*. I clamored to understand "Why can't I know everything about wine?" But I needed to ask why I *couldn't*, why none of us ever can. Wine's essential uncertainty existed ineluctably, it seemed, and the most productive questions finally became clear: *What purpose does this uncertainty serve? What does it want of me?*

The first answer was quite clear: there wouldn't be one. There would, however, be an endless stream of ever more compelling questions. I often think you know you've asked the right question when the answer is an even deeper question. The "answer" is the end of the line. For me, answers were actually frustrating because they quashed the curiosity on which I'd learned to feed. It seemed, after all, to be questioning and wondering that kept my *élan vital* humming.

The less I insisted on subduing wine, the more of a friend it wanted to be. It let me understand that it was more responsive to love than to "knowledge." It showed me which came first, that knowledge derived from love and not from will. Wine is an introvert who likes his private life, I learned, and so I no longer had to seduce away its secrets with my desire to penetrate. The very uncertainty kept it interesting, and wine grew to be very fine company. These days I'm inclined to guess that wine's uncertainty wants to remind us always to be curious and alert to the world, grateful that things are so fascinating. And to be thankful for the hunger. Because the hunger is *life*. Accepting the irreducible mystery of wine has enabled me to immerse myself more deeply than I ever could when I sought to tame it.

Immersion is the key. I am immersed in the world, the world is immersed in me. There are filaments and connections, always buzzing and always alive. The world is not a commodity designed for my use; its cells are my cells, its secrets are my secrets. And every once in a while, usually when I least expect it, wine draws its mouth to my ear and says things to me. *Time is not what you think. A universe can live inside a speck of flavor. There are doors everywhere to millions of interlocking worlds. Beauty is always closer than it seems. Passion is all around us always. The brightest secrets play on the darkest threads. When you peer though the doorway, all you see is desire.*

You hear these words and maybe it all sounds like gibberish, a stream of sound that doesn't amount to anything and only confuses things more. But if you've ever held a restive infant, there's a little trick you can do. Babies like to be whispered to; it fascinates them. They get a wondering, faraway look on their little faces, as if angels have entered the room. And so I don't need to explicate what wine may be saying to me. It is enough that it speaks at all, enough that it leaves me aware of meanings even if these don't fall neatly into a schema; enough how sweet it feels, the warm breath of beauty and secrets, so soft and so close to my ear.

two

WHAT MATTERS
(AND WHAT DOESN'T)
IN WINE

Have you ever tried to field the question, What kind of wine do you like? Hard to answer, isn't it? At least it's hard to answer briefly, because often the kind of wines you like need a lot of words to describe them. I recently answered, "I like moderate wine," and I knew what I meant by it, though I'm sure my questioner found me a tough interview.

Part of the business of deepening both your palate and your acquaintance with your palate is to pay heed to what it responds to. Eventually you organize that information as patterns manifest themselves. These patterns are almost never random. They tell you not only what you like and dislike, but also what you believe in, what you cherish, and what you disdain.

I want to suggest a kind of charter of values by which we enjoy wine, understand it, appreciate it, and place it in a matrix of principle and judgment. I'm hardly qualified to do this for "humanity," but I need to do it for myself, to locate where I am at this point in my wine-drinking life. Test these ideas against your own experience. Use what works, discard what doesn't, create your own charter; in short, think about wine as something *ineluctably attached to your life*, not merely a diversion or entertainment.

Let's begin with how wines actually taste. It's the only reason to drink the stuff. It only *seems* imperative to our lives, but we can live without it. When we begin we drink wine because its taste is pleasurable, and indeed it remains so; it is only later (if at all) that we begin to realize we've formed a set of principles by which we've organized our wine experiences and learned to appreciate the many *forms* of pleasure.

Consider the following an attempt to codify a set of First Principles of Wine, starting with the way it tastes.

Aspects of Flavor: The Ones That Matter Most

Clarity
Distinctiveness
Grace
Balance
Deliciousness
Complexity
Modesty
Persistence
Paradox

These aren't the only aspects of flavor that matter, but when I delineate the relative importance of the things that make up Flavor, these matter most.

Clarity: Without clear flavors, none of wine's other aspects can be easily discerned. Clarity can connote brilliance, but it doesn't always; I think of the soft-lighted gleam of a Loire Chenin or dry Furmint, or the smoky evening-light depths of Barolo. But we should be able to see into a wine's flavor, even when it shows that which we *cannot* see. Clarity also suggests the work of an attentive vintner with a desire for candor and nothing to hide. For me it is the first of first principles. Flavor should be clear. The question of what the flavor is comes after. This is so obvious that no one considers it, but it is not self-evident. There are, distressingly, loads of blurry, fuzzy wines. I'm driven half-crazy if I'm riding in someone's car and he hasn't cleaned his windshield. Clarity!

Distinctiveness: Call it what you will—taste-of-place, terroir, "somewhereness" (author Matt Kramer's telling word)—but whatever you call it, it's the thing that says your glass contains *this* wine and no other, from *this* place and no other. Distinctiveness can include idiosyncrasies and quirks as long as they are spontaneous and not mere affectations. But it needn't imply quirkiness if it is a wine's innate nature to be classical and symmetrical. Some individuals are angular and others are rounded; what's crucial is that the *particular* is what shows. Distinctiveness makes a wine valid. The *Wine Advocate*'s David Schildknecht wrote, "Wines of distinction are wines of distinctiveness." The reason some of us are cool toward the "international consultant" school of winemaking—expert enologists-for-hire who fly around the world working their magic (and their formulas)—is that we feel these wines, no matter where they're grown, are stamped with a certain recipe, irrespective of what's at the market or in the pantry, so that we encounter big oak-aged ripe-fruited wine from this grape here and that place there, all melding into a big, bland glom. It's often an attractive glom, but how important is attractiveness, really? Should we pursue it at all cost? I don't believe we can even consider the question of "greatness" in wine until its uniqueness is established. I'll examine this question in more detail in a later chapter about globalization in winemaking. But suffice it to say, it's not enough for wine to have a passport; it needs a birth certificate. I'd rather drink something that tastes like *something* and not like everything. Anything can taste like everything, and too often does, and bores the crap out of me.

It's only a small digression to wonder at the whole international wine personage phenomenon, as it seems inimical to the rootedness that is inherent in authentic wines. I'm not sure why it's chic for someone to fly thousands of miles to make wine. I appreciate wanderlust, but I'm happier when people choose a place and make wine there, ideally the place they were born and raised. They then become linked to that place, and their wine expresses the connection. Otherwise wine becomes little more than a plaything. Don't misconstrue me; there's nothing morally wrong with making wine anywhere you please. I just don't think it's inherently fascinating or desirable. It rather adds to the incoherence of the world. And whatever it is, it ain't glamorous.

Grace: This quality can apply to wines of various degrees of strength, body, or ripeness, and it can be found in both polished and "rustic" wines. It allies to modesty, but not every modest wine is graceful. Grace is rather a form of tact, a kindness; it rejects coarseness and is even more dismissive of power merely for its own sake.

Balance (and its siblings, Harmony and Proportion): Balance is not to be confused with symmetry, as there are asymmetrical yet balanced wines. Balance is simply the palpable sense that no single component appears garish or inappropriate. It is a quality of flavor that draws you away from the parts and toward the whole. It is a chord of flavor in which no single note is out of tune. If you hear any one of its component notes, it's probably for the wrong reason.

In a balanced wine the flavors seem preordained to exist in precisely that configuration. You sit by the stream. The water is clean and cold. The mountain peaks are clear. There are no beer cans or cigarette butts in sight. You've been hiking for a few hours and you feel loose and warm and hungry. You unpack your lunch and take the first bite, and then you see your sweetheart coming up the path, smiling. The air is soft and cool under a gentle sun. Things are absolutely good. Happens, what, once in a lifetime? In a balanced wine it happens with every sip.

Deliciousness: It is strange to have to mention this, but deliciousness is hardly ever spoken of or written about. A wine can meet every other criterion for success and yet not *taste good*. Then what? Do we outgrow appreciating deliciousness? Do we cultivate more auspicious tastes? Well, poo on us. Deliciousness ignites something in us that delights at the scent of pleasure. Is it wise to quash this thing? What else dies with it?

Complexity (and its siblings, Ambiguity and Evanescence): There is *explicit* complexity, wherein each component of a wine can be discerned and we are delighted by how many there are and how they interact. There is also *implicit* complexity, in which we sense there is *something* present but oblique to our view. Finally, in the few best wines there is a haunting sense of *something being shown to us* that has nothing to do with discrete "flavor." This is the noblest of wine's attributes, but the hardest to contrive by design. It seems to be a by-product of certain vintners' philosophies and practices, but neither formula nor recipe exists; this aspect is found when it is found, often unexpectedly. Some wines are complex in themselves, and it stops there. Other wines seem to embody *life's* complexity, and this is when we see the view from the sky.

Modesty: This denotes a wine that seeks to be a companion to your food, your state of mind, or the social occasion, as opposed to a wine that needs to dominate your entire field of attention. Some wines deserve your entire field of attention, but they don't need to shout for it. Modest wines are endangered in these times, when power is overvalued. Just because your text is written in boldface doesn't mean you have anything to say. Modest wines are tasty, tactful, and confident, and they don't show off.

Persistence (and its siblings, Depth and Intensity): This attribute properly comes *after* the ones cited above, since a persistent unpleasant wine is no one's idea of fun. A good wine is elevated by persistence, a bad wine diminished. Nor does persistence have to do with volume; the best wines are the ones that *whisper* persistently. We misunderstand the idea of intensity because we conflate it with volume. Bellowing flavor isn't intense; it's adolescent and irritating. Intensity arises not from a will to express, but from the thing that is being expressed.

Paradox: I can scarcely recall a great wine that didn't in some sense amaze me, that didn't make my palate feel as if it were whipsawed between things that hardly ever travel together. My shorthand term for that experience is *paradox;* again, this component is in the hands of the angels and doesn't appear susceptible to human contrivance, but when it is found it conveys a lovely sense of wonder: How can these things coexist in a single wine? And not only coexist, but spur each other on; power *with* grace, depth *with* brilliance. . . .

Aspects of Flavor: The Ones That Matter Least

Power

Sweetness

Ripeness

Concentration

It's not that these aspects don't matter at all, but too many think they matter too much. They appear near the bottom of my scale of values, but they do appear.

Power: Power matters only when you're planning a menu and selecting the wines. You want to align the power of the dish with that of the wine, so one doesn't subdue the other. But power inherently is a quality neither desirable nor undesirable; it needs to justify its existence by combining with grace, distinctiveness, and deliciousness. Too often it stops at mere incoherent assertiveness: I'm putting my fist through this wall *because I can!*

Sweetness: In the wine world there's no single component of flavor subjected to more obsessive dogma and doctrine. The prevailing (and I'd say *pathological*) aversion to sweetness has diminished many wines. Sweetness figures in menu planning and in forecasting the way a wine might age. It is sometimes helpful. Like acidity, tannin, or any other single facet of flavor, sweetness matters only when there is too much or too little of it. Yet we focus on it in isolation, insisting that it be reduced or removed at all cost, unaware that we are misguided and have taken balance, length, and charm away from our wines. Sweetness should be present when it is called for and absent when it is not, as determined by the flavors of individual wines and not by any theory we have promulgated a priori.

And a lot of us are confused about sweetness. I'm here to help. There's the sweetness of an apple, and there's the sweetness of a Twinkie. They're not the same!

Ripeness: I refer especially to *physiological* ripeness, sometimes called phenolic ripeness, which is seen when a grape's skins and seeds are ripe. It would seem to be desirable, but the singular pursuit of physiological ripeness as an absolute has wrecked many wines by condemning them to a power they can't support, and it has removed the nuance possible when wines are made from grapes of different degrees of ripeness. When ripeness is sufficient, how do we assume overripeness will be preferable? It only brings more alcohol and an infantile swaddle of fruit.

Concentration: Concentration matters only after this question is answered: What are we concentrating? Tannin, viscosity, alcohol? Are these things we want even more of? In itself, concentration is merely an adjective, not a virtue.

Taking a Stand: What Is Not Important

Why begin by discussing the unimportant? you might ask. Because these ephemera take up far too much of wine discourse, deflecting us from more important matters. I remember Gore Vidal's famous answer to the question of why academic quarrels were so fierce: because the stakes were so low.

You might expect the wine world to be a gentle and civilized place, but you'd be wrong. You'd think habitual wine drinkers would be less querulous than other folks. Wrong again. Then you'd get tired of always being wrong, and realize that wine can be a lightning rod for many other debates—or arguments—that are conducted with humanity's usual standards of skill, intellect, civility, and tolerance. In other words, it's Mailer versus Vidal, minus the erudition.

Important matters become obscured by opinionated posturing from people who've succumbed to the modern inability to distinguish conviction from pugnacity—not to mention the temptation to make simplistic intellectual fast food out of complex issues. I call them "thought Twinkies"; they masquerade as substance while offering only spuriously seductive assertion. I expect such things from beginners intimidated by the intricacies of wine, but some of the worst offenders are some very powerful elders of the wine world, who ought to know better, or *be* better.

Wine people get combative when they fear a threat to the existence of the kinds of wines they like. But combativeness becomes a habit, a default position for people unwilling to make the effort entailed by reasonableness. And suddenly every little nonissue is absurdly exacerbated by people staking claims on categorical positions. If we don't, we look, what—weak? We are often wrong, but never uncertain!

Don't mistake my meaning; there are many places where values belong, and when you're in such a place you're a coward if you don't assert yours. But when you're asserting value judgments over work you yourself don't actually *do*, you risk sounding fatuous. And the need to see wine merely as a warren of opportunities to decide rights and wrongs is a blind alley, and it hinders both knowledge and appreciation. I thus assert the value of knowing when asserting values is called for.

Here are a few of the prominent issues around which opinions orbit, beginning with the silly ones.

Yields: This issue is rife with truisms. The prevailing assumption is that you must have low yields in order to have any claim to quality. Ostensibly, it makes sense; the less fruit per acre, the more flavor in each bunch of grapes. But more flavor doesn't always equal *better* flavor. Our obtuse insistence that low yields will always give better wines has given rise to a community of clumsy, opaque, and joyless wines, overconcentrated, overendowed, just plain *overdone*. The simplistic equation—low yields = superior wine—is true only if *concentration* is the sole criterion of quality. But any good restaurant line cook knows how to reduce a sauce to just the right point, and he also knows what happens when you go too far. You get an opaque substance that's like a black hole from which no flavor can emerge. The entire matter of yields needs to be seen as a mosaic winemakers evaluate according to the kind of wine they wish to make. Sadly, when you dare to suggest this you'll get mocked by the lovers of forceful wine, as if their own bellicosity were validated by the wines they prefer.

They will accuse you of mounting an elegant rationalization for thin, anemic wines. And sometimes they are right. Other times they can seem obtuse to the value of transparency. Certain kinds of wine aren't meant to be "intense" and musclebound. Nor does each wine drinker enjoy the same things in wine. Some people like to be overwhelmed. I like my whelm the way it is. I don't like Hummer wines.

And when we earnestly measure yields in terms of hectoliters per hectare (or tons per acre), we're laughed at by most serious vintners, who know how those numbers can be fungible and manipulated. You can say you made your wine from fifty hectos per hectare, but maybe you actually grew seventy-five and sold off the excess twenty-five. Maybe your yields were low because your husbandry was lousy. Maybe your vineyard was sick with rots and mildews and when you finished picking out the healthy fruit your "yield" looked tiny. Yield per vine and vines per hectare get us closer to the truth. Seeing the question as an interface of economic sustainability for a vintner along with an appropriate—an *appropriate*—degree of concentration in his wines is more flexible and realistic. For proof that "high" yields can give lovely wines, consider the entire Mosel valley! Its yields seem high on paper, but the wines have the concentration they need, and no more. In fact, the entire region is in retreat from the era of ever-lower yields, as they learned they had too much overripe fruit, which led to shortages of the scintillating light Rieslings for which the Mosel is beloved.

Yeasts: I've witnessed fairly new wine lovers eager to make value judgments on this subject. They don't see the vintner snickering behind their backs. Mind you, the question of what yeast a grower uses to ferment his juice is interesting and worth discussing, but it is almost never decisive. Even so, it is perhaps a useful illustration of wine people's need to take categorical positions. Wine gets uncomfortably near to theology at such times, and it seems a pity to reduce this sensuous, civilizing being to a mere object over whose nonsalient details we squabble desperately. Still, in the context of a list of tangential matters that wine folk spend far too much time obsessing over, the last thing I need to do is indulge in obsessive detail to prove my point that detail isn't warranted! Still, maybe a little footnote-type diversion might prevent opacity. In that spirit, and do skip ahead the moment your eyes start glazing over . . . I present the Apostasy of the Yeasts!

Vintners have two options for fermenting their grape juice. Either they let nature do it for them—spontaneous or "ambient" yeast fermentation—or they inoculate their juice with cultured yeast. Within the latter choice lies a range of options. All yeasts form flavor, but some are more aggressive than others, and a case can be made that the most aggressive ones cross the line into confecting flavor not inherent in the grape itself. That is as far as I will go in suggesting a value judgment, and I'm not entirely sure of even this much.

Growers who use cultured yeasts usually do so in order to have a predictable fermentation, especially if their cellars are naturally cold and they want their wines to be dry. In some instances growers desire a very cold fermentation because they like the aromas that naturally result. Some tasters dislike those very aromas, which can recall pear drop or banana, but that is solely a question of taste.

The range of possible yeasts is greater than one might suppose. There are mass-produced industrial yeasts, and there are specific yeasts for certain grape varieties and also for highly concentrated dessert-wine musts. I know of several instances in which growers had cultures made from their own wild vineyard yeasts, and one of these growers went further and had variety-specific ones made, that is to say, a special yeast cultured from a vineyard in which only a particular variety was planted. And even among the commercial cultured yeasts are types that purport to be entirely neutral.

But there's a lot we don't know about the process, including what yeast actually starts a fermentation, because even if you inoculate, can you ever be certain it was *that* and not an ambient yeast that got the party started? It sounds laudable to culture one's own vineyard yeasts, but it has yet to be proved that it's anything more than a seductive romance to assume yeasts are a crucial, inherent aspect of terroir.

Assuming a grower has a conscience, he'll choose cultured yeast to create a certain texture and transparency in his wine and to avoid bacteriological or sulfide problems that would require technological interventions to solve. He chooses what seems to him a benign fermentation method up front so as to avoid a more serious agitation of the wine later. I know a great many growers whose methods are as rigorous as the most devout wine purist could require, yet they ferment with cultured yeasts.

What of the ones who go wild, as it were? In some cases it is part of an overall hands-off approach, which one can certainly appreciate as long as the wine tastes good. But in some cases it's an affectation; it gives growers a fashionable thing to say while at the same time they may be doing all kinds of things we might find unsavory. But let's posit a wild-yeast-fermented wine as part of a general tolerance of "naturalness" (if you approve), "funkiness" (if you disapprove), or "animalness" (if you approve of funkiness!). If you are an experienced taster, and I emphasize *experienced*, you might sense that the wine is unpolished, undeodorized, hewn a little more toward "country" rather than "city." Maybe you prefer the style. Fine! I like it, too. But I don't conflate it with All That Is Honest and Moral in viticulture. Surely we understand that persons of conscience do not make identical choices.

Each option for starting fermentation has advantages and disadvantages, and almost without exception none is "morally" preferable to another. I'm inclined to sympathize with growers who insist on letting their wine ferment spontaneously, but what am I to make of the many growers equally passionate about terroir who use cultured yeast? Are they disingenuous, misguided, ignorant, poseurs? Or am I just being a pill?

One grower told me, "There's entirely too much conversation about this really minor issue. I doubt if even experts could tell you which wine was fermented which way more than 5 percent of the time." And he's right. Yeast is almost never more than an *inflection*. But it has become a coat-hook upon which we hang all kinds of categorical value judgments. I suspect that ten years from now we'll look back and ask, "Why were they obsessing about yeasts in those days?"

Winemaking methods: Of course, these are significant in descriptive terms, but rarely in forming absolute judgments. Oxidative (vinification with oxygen encouraged) or reductive (vinification with oxygen discouraged); which is "better"? Steel or cask; which is "better"? Whole-cluster pressing or conventional crush-and-press; which is "better"? The answer—*always*—is *It depends.* The common risk we run is that we fall in love with an estate and learn how the vintner makes the wine, whereupon we conclude, *This must be the way to make great wine.* And we memorize the formula (if there is one) and think we've learned something. But I guarantee you that soon, very soon, you're going to fall in love with another wine estate that makes wine completely differently than the first one. Each vintner can defend his or her preferences with great conviction, yet the two methods are mutually exclusive. And you, poor you, are trying to suss out who's right. Sorry, but they're both right; it's you who's wrong. You don't have to choose! You just have to *pay attention*, consider, and understand what prods different vintners to make wines in different ways. It says something about them; what they like to drink, perhaps, or what they learned from their fathers. The value lies there, in human terms.

Taking a Stand: What Is *Important*

I'll outline my position here, and elaborate at length in subsequent chapters.

Artisanality: By this I mean a connection between the worker and the work made possible by intimacy of scale. I think this is a first principle, if only to establish a beachhead against the seductions of industrial, "product"-driven winemaking. This leads to . . .

Connections: Various connections are important: first, the connection of the vintner to his land (and the inseparable connection of flavor to that land); then the connection of the worker to the work; then the connection of the family to the culture of family estates; and finally, our own connection as drinkers to something we know is true, important, and worth defending and preserving. When we insist on these things as preconditions for attending to wine, we will know when they are absent, and the wine will lose its savor and its claim on our attention.

How the soil is treated: This one's a sticky wicket for people with an environmental conscience. How vineyards are treated is manifestly important. But it doesn't invariably follow that a continuum of "purity" exists upon which each vintner can be measured. And how could we presume to do the measuring? I take a dubious view of people who never had to support a family growing grapes and making wine preaching to those who do about living up to their precious purity standards. Between the total hack working with any and all chemicals at one extreme and the organic or biodynamic grower at the other, there lies a complex spectrum of values and possibilities. We need to attend as concerned and reasonable beings, but we do not need to assign points on some green-o-meter. What we should do is look and listen—to each grower's ambient conditions (dry versus humid, flat versus steep, among others) and to the values by which the grower works. Absolute judgments on our part are liable to be fatuous. We'll know a grower's conscience when we see it, and persons of conscience may make decisions different from those we *think* we'd make from our remove.

True flavor: This comes from the land, not from the cellar or from any of its bazillion possible treatments. Mosel grower Karl-Josef Loewen says, "In the modern world there are hitherto unimagined possibilities to form the tastes of wines. In my region there are people using *barriques*, using the most current techniques to concentrate natural musts, special cultured yeasts to form the characters of wine, and special enzymes to form bouquets. Is this the brave new wine world? I have a different philosophy." Bearing in mind that all viniculture is manipulation, it follows that we'd be better served attending to agitation, to anything that diminishes a wine's inherent vitality, and to any and all practices that add flavor not inherently there. Oak is the most blatant example, of course.

To the extent that a wine culture exists where it should and as it should, these things tend to apportion themselves properly. A simple example is Mosel Riesling: the vine clearly thrives in that land, the wines are holistically appropriate; a normal year, the grapes are *just* ripe enough while still laden with crisp, refreshing acidity. The wines convey an energy that corresponds to the effort needed to grow grapes on the killing-steep mountainsides.

If, in order to make potable wine, it must be subjected to manipulations bordering on (or becoming) falsification, then something is askew. Suppose I like golden retrievers, and say I live in a very hot climate, and say this breed of dog is extremely uncomfortable in very hot climates. Obviously I should get a different breed of dog. What I shouldn't do is to shave the poor bastard bald or give him some drugs to make his coat fall out. If you have to diddle your wine to remove the undesirable facets with which it was born (or that you brought about by insisting, among other things, on "physiological ripeness"), then you're not hearing what nature is saying: *You're growing the wrong grapes in the wrong place.* You're picking overripe grapes because you're scared they won't be "physiologically" ripe. Your wine has far too much potential alcohol, so you add water to the grape must. That takes color away, so you add it back with a compound called Mega Purple, an extract of grape skins. You also "adjust" alcohol by using spinning cones or reverse osmosis. For the drinker, to take a stand against such manipulated wines is to assert the value of the right thing grown where it belongs, and the distinctiveness and honesty of the results in the glass. Little enough to ask, it would seem; yet it is everything.

It's time to elaborate on one of this book's most crucial themes, which breaks down into three ideas: connectedness (the most important), attentions, and the thing to which the first two lead, artisanality.

Connectedness

I woke up this morning thinking about Germany's Mosel valley, and about a vintner family I know well, the Selbachs of Zeltingen. I first met them in 1985; it was Hans and his wife, Sigrid, in those days, with eldest son Johannes waiting in the wings. Hans died recently, and suddenly, and when I visit the Mosel each March to taste the new vintage, I pay a visit to his grave, which has a view of the silvery river and the village of Zeltingen, where he and Sigrid raised their family. Indeed, if the steep hill behind the St. Stephanus church weren't a cemetery, it would certainly be planted with vines, and Hans and his vines alike rest deep within the slate.

He died at home, surrounded by family. His body was carried through the house, through the bottle cellar (one of his sons told me, "Terry, it was as if you could see and hear the bottles stand and applaud Papa"), before it was placed at last in the ground, perhaps three hundred meters from the house. It is not only his spirit that lingers genially among his survivors; his body itself is near at hand.

My own father died abruptly. I was about to be a senior in high school. I came home one afternoon from my summer job and he was slumped over the kitchen table. He died six hours later in a hospital room while I waited at home with my small sister. He is buried in an enormous cemetery in Queens, New York; I doubt if I could even find the gravesite.

My story may not be typical, but neither is it all that unusual. We were suburban folk, and a certain existential disconnect was a defining parameter of our experience. Nor do I claim this is necessarily tragic. Disconnection has its silver linings if you're a lone wolf.

But when I contemplate the connectedness the Selbachs nurture and presume upon, it becomes clear that their wines are also connected, that *they* are a defining parameter in a complex of connections. This is as invisible and vital as oxygen to the Selbachs and people like them.

Johannes speaks nearly perfect English. In fact, he gets along in French and for all I know can mumble articulately in Chinese. What I didn't know, or had forgotten, is that along with his native German he also speaks *Platt*, or regional dialect. I heard him speak it when we visited another grower together. It was the Merkelbachs, two bachelor brothers now about seventy, who have barely ever left their village and who make a living from a scant five acres producing some thirty different casks of Riesling, each of which they bottle separately. As I heard Johannes lapse into dialect it struck me what a piece of social glue this was; it was Johannes's way of reassuring Rolf and Alfred, *We are brethren*, another marker of connection and identity. One might almost claim that Mosel Riesling is what it uniquely is because of the dialect *it* speaks.

I find I am *satisfied* in some essential way by connected wines. It doesn't even matter whether I like them. I happen never to have met a Priorat I enjoyed, but I respect Priorat for its authenticity—it is manifestly the wine of a place, speaking the dialect of the sere, barren terraces in northeastern Spain. I may not like it—I have issues with high-alcohol wines—but I'm glad it exists.

I can't summon up anything but weariness for the so-called "international" style of wine (ripe, "sweet" fruit, loads of toasty oak, a spurious seductiveness), since it's either connected to things I don't care about or connected to nothing at all. I've had more than enough disconnect in my life. Many of us have. When I consider a Mosel family like the Selbachs—like any of the people with whom I work—everything I see expresses an identity rooted in connection; they themselves, their wines. You could not disconnect these things even if you tried.

And it salves a kind of loneliness. Though it isn't my home, it is at least *a* home, and the people are particular people, and the wines are particular wines. I spend too much of my life driving among strip malls and their numbing detritus, and so when I descend the final hill over the Eifel and the village of Zeltingen comes into view, sitting peacefully along the Mosel, I have a momentary thrill of *arriving*. Here is *somewhere*. I see it, I know it, I will soon embrace people who embody it—and I also get to *taste* it.

I will not settle for less from any wine. Nor need you.

When I'm there I stay at home with the Selbachs, and since the family likes to eat and knows how to cook it is an ongoing challenge to maintain my trim, boyish profile. I need to tramp, ideally every day, and the surrounding vineyards are ideal for tramping, steep and beautiful. One morning I set off into the misty, moist freshness, with a high fog riding about five hundred feet above the valley. I stamped up to a trio of wild cherry trees blooming halfway up the Himmelreich vineyard. I pushed at top speed to get warm. Kept climbing. Got up into the woods too high for vines and listened to the birds fluting away, new birds with unfamiliar voices.

The Himmelreich hill leads back into a small combe that gives way to the next hill, corresponding to the Schlossberg vineyard, and this in turn leads southeast to the great Sonnenuhr. I was on a high path with the Mosel vertically beneath me through the vines, and only the woods above. Some workers were pruning and binding here and there, and it seemed lovely to be out on such a sweet, cool morning working with the vines in such pretty surroundings. I know very well it isn't always like this—these vineyards get hot in the summer, or grapes wouldn't ripen—but I seemed to have passed through a membrane, and everything was suddenly and clearly *divine.* The small teams of people working, the birds noisily peeping, the languorous Mosel below, the smells of slate and wet trees. These fugue states are so sudden; you just take a small step through what you thought was yourself, and you're in some silent, airy space that's strangely durable while you're there. I passed a group of workers replanting in the Sonnenuhr and bade them *Guten Morgen,* glowing and goofy with joy and certain we all were as giddy as I was.

But of course to them I was probably just another crazy tourist blown away by the view.

I turned to head back down and walked past Hans Selbach's grave, and I wanted to stop and talk to him, to tell him, *It's still like it always was, old friend; it's a beautiful foggy morning and the workers are working and the birds are birding and it's all as it should be, and you were right, it is divine and full of love and patience, this little bit of the world.* I got back late and my colleagues were waiting impatiently, but I didn't feel too bad; I'd burned a bunch of cals *and* had a mystical reverie—all before 10:00 A.M.

Visiting Hans isn't a duty; I need to do it. I love that he lies in the slate, the soil where his Riesling grew. I love that he views the village and the river. I love thinking of harvesttime, when the air will be full of the voices of the pickers and the thrum of the tractors, all nearby. Later the first snow will sift and settle over the graves where Hans and his neighbors lie in the slate above the river.

I think that we who love Mosel wine do so with a special tenderness. That is partly because of the wines' particular sparrowy charm, but if you have ever been there you find in these wines a taproot from which you can drink from your soul's purest waters. These wines do not merely hail from a culture; they're so deeply embedded in that culture you can't tell anymore where one ends and the other begins. The cohesion is both stirring and unnerving. Looking at the mourners at Hans Selbach's funeral, many of their faces could have been carved on Roman coins. They were the people of *this* place in the world. It's no accident that there are almost no international consultants, the "flying winemakers," from here. The Mosel gives its vintners all the stimulus they need.

Yet as much as I love this culture, I recognize its shadow side. It is not exclusively lyrical. If its air is rarefied, that's partly because it isn't always as fresh as it might be. There are all the petty jealousies and Hatfield-McCoy chicaneries that afflict small-village life around the world. But there is more.

I represent two Mosel producers who are neighbors on the same site; their parcels are contiguous. One producer hadn't quite finished picking grapes when his Polish harvest workers' work visas expired, meaning the crew had to return to Poland. No problem, said the neighbor; we'll pick for you. *We'll pick for you!* It really is another world. People may know one another for twenty years and still address each other as *Herr*-this and *Frau*-that. They have all the ratty bullshit that can possibly exist among people, but—"We'll pick for you."

Sigrid Selbach (Hans's widow and the matriarch of the family) told me a story once. "We picked our Eiswein last year on Christmas Day," she began. "The day before, when we saw it might be cold enough on Christmas morning, we hesitated to call and ask for help with the picking. But you know, we called twelve people, and they all agreed to help, and they were all *cheerful* to do it. We went out into the vineyard before dawn to check the temperature, then phoned them at 6:00 on Christmas morning, and they all came and all in a good mood. Afterward they gathered here at the house for soup and Christmas cookies. And when they left they were all singing out *Merry Christmas* as they went home to their families. Isn't that wonderful?"

I ask you! I too am amazed that people would cheerfully agree to get out of their warm beds before dawn on Christmas morning while their loved ones slept, to go out into the frigid vineyards and gather enough fruit for a few hundred bottles of wine that nobody makes any money on. This is more than mere neighborliness. It is simply assumed that certain traditions are ennobled by observing them with a hale kindness. When nature gives you a chance at an Eiswein, you *celebrate* the opportunity. Your grapes might have rotted or been eaten by wild boars. But this time the gods smiled.

Being a Mosel vintner signifies membership in a human culture much deeper than mere occupation. This is true of every vintner, whether his wines are great, good, or poor. This may seem abstruse to the "consumer," but there are many ways to consume and many things to *be* consumed in a glass of wine. You can see it merely as an object and assess it against its competitors using some arbitrary scale. Or you can drink something that tells you it was made by human beings who want to show you the beauty and meaning they have found in their lives. *You* decide.

A few years ago I saw a newspaper piece about a wine salesman who was realizing his "dream" by making wine—or "making wine"—in California. He owned no vines. The fruit he bought was crushed for him (they call it custom-crushing out there) by I don't remember whom. His winemaker was a hired gun out of U.C. Davis. All of this was unremarkable; it is the common and vapid story of much New World wine. Their first vintage was offered to the market for $125 per bottle (a small fortune in those days), and then I knew the world had gone mad.

Let's call such a wine Hubris Hill. The "producer" doesn't tend a vine or make the wine, doesn't even own a vine, but he's sure willing to claim your $125 because he knows how many suckers are born per minute, and how easily they'll pony up if the reviewers gush about the wine's *oodles of jammy hedonistic fruit erupting from the glass in subatomic orgasms of delirium: 95 points.*

This, we are led to believe, is wine. *Wine* (n)—anything anyone can contrive to make, detached from nature, detached from culture, connected to nothing but our infantile need to be entertained and our adolescent need to be fashionably correct, to be sold at the highest price that some desperate hipster can be horsewhipped into paying.

If this were the summit of wine's aspirations, I wouldn't shed a tear if it disappeared from the world. It feels as if we move through life in a fog sometimes. And when we alight on something real, someplace real, it's like putting on eyeglasses that suddenly show what's blemished and bogus around us. To me it is urgent that we recognize those things and avoid them. The bogus isn't good for us. It's like a sugar high that leaves us crashed and wretched later. We get confused, and lose our bearings.

But Mosel wine hails from someplace true in the world, and from the people connected to it and the culture they created, which honors the connection. Can we ever have too many reminders that such places persist? If you're sinking into ennui as yet another corporate type presses his marketing strategies on you, as yet another former dermatologist or veterinarian lords his milk-and-honey lifestyle over you and you wonder what any of it has to do with wine, with why you first fell in love with wine—I have places to show you. If you're weary of reading about grape-skin concentrates and oak chips and spinning cones and must concentrators and debt service and consultants who guarantee a certain critic's score—if you're weary of even thinking about scores—I have places to show you.

If you read a passage of poetry and feel that sudden silence as the world expands and deepens, and you hear yourself wonder, *I used to have this thing in my life; where did it go?* I have places to show you. They are what I wish to capture here, because the world keeps grinding us down to the nub until we forget we are even hungry or alive. But *these places are still here*. You can go to them whenever you want. You can live the life they offer. You can remove the thorn from your paw.

Attentions and Artisanality

Let's put aside for a moment the question of spirit of place. It is so important that it will return in a later chapter. Right now I want to tell you what I've found in common among the people who make connected wines.

First, they all detest the term *winemaker*. A Pfalz grower named Lingenfelder once told me, "We are not wine*makers*; we do not *make wine*. We simply prepare the environment for wine to come into being." The German-speaking vintner prefers the term *cellarmaster*. I like it too; it's humbler, more craftsmanlike.

My term *attentions* is ambiguous, I know. But it is always useful to consider a vintner in terms of this question: to what is he attending? To his skill at manipulating machines and systems? To his ability to "sculpt" a wine? To getting a couple more points for his wine than his neighbor does? To beaming with pride when you say you like his wine? To letting you see what a total hot-shot he is?

Or is he attending to the flavors that come from his land, and his sensitivity in nurturing them and letting them be? The greatest German cellarmaster of the late twentieth century, Hans-Günter Schwarz, put it as perfectly as can be said: "Every time you handle a wine you remove something that cannot be put back. The smartest thing a cellarmaster can know is the right time . . . to do nothing." The worldview of such people can be summed up as: Grow the best possible grapes and then get out of the way. And growing grapes, when you do it yourself, is of course a form of tending, of working with *life*, of subsuming yourself so as to hear what these other lives need and desire, to give of their best. For such vintners, machines are a necessary evil; their real work is done with nature. It is the difference between "Hey, check *me* out, look at *my* adorable talent," and "Come with me and I'll show you this place that I love."

You see it in the elders when (if they're lucky) their children grow up to take over the estates. I've been doing this work for most of my adult life, and in nearly every instance of generational transfer, the parents *go back into the vineyard*. It is the work that most fulfills them. They are away from sales, tanks, pumps, presses; they are back with living things. I'll never forget the Austrian vintner Engelbert Prieler, deflecting my compliments toward his daughter Silvia, who had taken control of the cellar. He wouldn't even field a question: "Oh, don't ask me, I'm just a simple farmer now. . . ." He did, however, claim all the credit for the *quality* of the wines, much to our mutual amusement—Silvia knows her dad much too well to be offended. Whatever compliment I gave, even the most innocuous, Engelbert grinned and twinkled and said, "Yes, the quality here was the result of scrupulous viticulture," or "Indeed, it goes to show what is possible when you have a genius working the vines," until finally I got it. And when I liked the next wine I turned to Dad and said, "Wow, there really was some bloody fabulous vineyard work here," and he replied, "Yes, wasn't there?"

But it's all quite sweet, you know. The older man likes being outside among the vines he has known his whole life, by himself in the fresh air. It isn't so fast out there. He can pay the kind of attention he has learned how to pay, without which one doesn't hear the earth twitter and hum. I am happy to think of these happy men.

I've seen my share of great vintages over the years, but I don't recall when I've ever seen a grower strut or preen. Most recently a fellow named Hexamer had such a remarkable vintage that he said, "I'd be lucky to have two or three more vintages like this one in my whole life." At such times I love what I see on the grower's entire visage, a thing I've seen many times when great vintages were on the table, the same thing you see on a ballplayer's face when he crosses the plate having hit the game-winning home run. He knows he has worked hard, spent his life preparing, hoping for a moment like this one. But when it comes, all he does is wonder. He's too amazed even to feel proud. He is almost embarrassed to be showered with such good fortune, as if it had nothing to do with him. *Look what happened*, he seems to say.

The pride these people feel is a craftsman's pride in work well done. When we think of "humble," we call up images of pathological self-debasement or else some mumbly "Aw, shucks," but there's another way it shows. The ego's need to insist on alpha status is calmed when one is fundamentally content, and what makes you content is to be gratefully aware that *you get to do this work*. I have never seen good wine come from an unhappy vintner. I doubt if it can. Being grateful doesn't banish the ego; it matures it. And the mature ego is reinforced when it is grounded in the natural world.

You can try to impose yourself over nature, but it leads into a blind alley and you do collateral damage to your soul. Every vintner I know is content to exist in nature as a listener who wants to hear what it asks. Few of them are mystical at all that I can see. But all of them are partners in a world where nature is as alive as they are. "The vineyard teaches me to wait, absorb nature, and understand my own boundaries," says Heidi Schröck, a vintner in Austria. There's a fellow feeling in such sentiments, a kind of friendliness. I don't think that beautiful wine can be made without it. You can make good wine, and you can damn sure make *impressive* wine, when you work from ego. Those wines always "show" well, but there's a coldness at their core. One symptom of this is the reduction of wine to a specimen to which a score is given. And this in turn is based on the idea that "perfection" is attainable—or even desirable. When someone says, "This is as good as it gets," I always want to reply, "Really? *How do you know?*" We'll revisit this topic, believe me.

Fundamental to the idea of artisanality is the appreciation of imperfection. Imperfection squares with what we observe in ourselves, our fellow humans, and all throughout nature. The natural world may be sublime, but it isn't perfect. When you make love to another person, you bring your fallibilities and flaws to hers or his. Maybe you feel fat or achy or preoccupied, or maybe you feel wonderful, but the point is that *you can't predict how you'll feel*, and you damn sure can't predict how your partner will feel, but in this collision of imperfections something valid occurs. Alternatively, you could watch porn; it's always perfect there, and you can rewind and watch your favorite parts again and again. But you are ineluctably *separate* from the images on the screen. No, it isn't perfection we need to seek; it is imperfection, because the assumption of imperfection is the thing that allows the miracle, and the swoon.

The tender attentions of the artisan are the most important prerequisite for authentic, meaningful wines, to be enjoyed by each of us imperfect beings, in our imperfect lovely world.

three

REMYSTIFYING WINE

First of all, everything is unified, everything is linked together, everything is explained by something else and in turn explains another thing. There is nothing separate, that is, nothing that can be named or described separately. In order to describe the first impressions, the first sensations, it is necessary to describe all at once. The new world with which one comes into contact has no sides, so that it is impossible to describe first one side and then the other. All of it is visible at every point. —P. D. Ouspensky

Either nature has a kind of consciousness, and therefore a purpose, or it does not. In our present state of development, there's no way to know. It's my experience that nature—whether metallic (like my car) or organic (like a plant) or neither (like the wind)—behaves differently if one relates to it as though it is conscious; many have experienced consciousness in rocks, flora, fauna and objects, but our subjective experiences are difficult to demonstrate and impossible to prove. If nature has no consciousness or purpose, I don't see how humanity can, so I choose to believe we all do. That's my sense of things. Again, impossible to prove, especially when the evidence appears to point the other way. —Michael Ventura

James Hillman and Michael Ventura published a provocative book called *We've Had 100 Years of Psychotherapy and the World's Getting Worse*. Well, we've had what seems like a hundred books purporting to "demystify" wine, and wine is more mysterious than ever. Not that the technocrat-enologist complex hasn't been furiously laboring to remove every pesky variable from wine—damn that nature!—and Lord knows we're ever more inundated with all manner of mass-produced industrial swill, but true wine is *supposed* to be complex, and if you think you know it all, well, pal, you don't know nuthin'.

Ah, but the poor hapless consumer, faced with the groaning shelves of wine bottles with gobbledygook on the labels, or the Talmudic opacity of some eight-pound document called the restaurant wine list—what can we do to help this innocent waif, terrified he'll pick the "wrong" wine? The first thing is to remind him of the nature of the risk. Let's remember, he probably has little to no idea how an automobile actually functions, and if you stuck his head under the hood, he'd think, *Hmm, why yes, that's an engine, all right*, while remaining clueless about how it makes his car move. He's getting ready to spend serious money on a machine whose operation he doesn't understand, yet we're writing books fussing over how difficult wine is? What are you out if you make a "mistake" and buy the "wrong" wine, twenty bucks in a store? This is not a major disappointment.

Underlying the wine-simplification industry is an inferiority complex. Actually, two inferiority complexes. The first belongs to the reader, who thinks he should know more about wine since apparently he can't escape it, and he hates to feel incompetent. The second belongs to wine writers, who feel themselves part of a collective failure to get Americans to drink more wine. Anything we can do, they reason, to make wine *safe* for the novice will cause him to snuggle up to wine, and this is good because we who sell wine for a living want more wine drinkers.

But what if we were talking about literature? Not enough people read, that's for sure. But they like looking at images, this we know, so let's simplify this whole literature business by making graphic books out of all those annoying *wordy* things. Once that's done, let's see if we can eliminate even *more* words, and tell the whole story with drawings. Oh, hell, let's forget about even having an object you have to hold in your hands; let's make a video of it and shove it onto a screen. I mean, it's the same story, right? Anna still throws herself in front of the train. Holden's still fussing about the stupid ducks. What's the difference?

What often underlies the desire to simplify wine, to make it more "accessible" to everyman, is perilously close to pandering: "If I kill its essence and make it incredibly simple, then will you start drinking it?" Why should we enable everyone's childish desire for things to be predictable? You want predictable, stay clear of wine. Oh, there's plenty of predictable wine made, and if you find one you like, then by all means keep drinking and enjoying it. But if you find yourself curious about wine, you have to accept that uncertainty is inextricable from the experience. Vintages vary, at least in many of the Old World's uncertain climates, and the crisp wine you liked this year could be a voluptuous wine next year. Different growers with adjacent parcels in the same vineyard will make different-tasting wine. It isn't total chaos—there are threads of consistency running through artisanal wines—but to appreciate these wines you need a tolerance for surprise.

Put it this way: Would you rather watch a ballgame as it's played, not knowing the outcome? Or would you rather cue up the DVD player and watch a tape of a game already played, maybe a great game, but one with no element of surprise?

There's very little that's inherently mystifying about wine; there's just a huge number of them, from different grapes and different places, and most of them change their taste a little each year. It's a lot of data, but it isn't integral calculus. There is, though, something that summons the *mystical* in fine wines, and this experience is available to anyone who's willing to prepare for it. It begins with being available—in other words, allowing both your attention and your emotions to respond to sensation, and to feelings of joy in the face of beauty. This is not a big deal. Say you go for a walk but you're preoccupied (that damned Blauman contract still isn't signed, and little Johnny needs braces). You see nothing of your surroundings. But then your cell phone rings, and it's Jenkins with good news: "Blauman signed!" And now your mind is liberated, and you don't just notice things, you notice *everything*. You pick up a leaf and turn it over, and the pattern on the underside is astonishing, my God, look at this, was this always here, do other people know about how amazing this is?

There is nothing esoteric or inaccessible about this state of mind. If you are aware of the world, things will come to your attention. One of them is beauty, and one of the beautiful things is wine. But wine's abilities do not stop at mere sensual beauty. Wine is able to channel multiple currents of beauty, from the pretty to the charming, from the fleeting to the logical, from the passionate to the pensive. And great wine will take you to a question and, wonderfully, deposit you there, without an answer or a map—just looking at the question.

Ambiguous? If you're sitting on a hilltop enjoying a view, you may be able to say, "This is beautiful because I can see a great distance, and the hills fold into one another in an especially comely way, and the river is perfectly situated to give depth to the scene," and that is certainly part of the truth. But beauty has a face that's turned away from the light. Think of music. Can you say *why* a certain piece of music makes you feel so intensely? Probably not. But it has happened to most of us, and we don't think ourselves weird or "new agey" when it does, because this experience, though mystical, is commonplace. It happens with wine too, but it seems outré because wine drinking itself seems the purview of the arugula munchers.

Wine may have a particular hold on this mystical faculty based on the proximity of the parts of the brain that process smells and memories. I've never had my own Proustian moment, but for me wine does something even more astounding than that. I may not suddenly recover my own memories, but a few great wines have seemed to dilate the world so that I seem to experience a *collective* memory. I might smell an old Loire valley Chenin Blanc, and it makes me think of an armoire. That's not too fanciful. But it makes me think of an armoire in a room in a French country house, and I can see the other furniture too, and the view of gardens and fields out the window, and I can almost hear the voices of the people who live in the house, and smell the body scents on the clothes hanging in my make-believe armoire.

So here is silly old me, in my imaginary room with the armoire; I hear the voices and see the fields and smell the smells, but then I sense a kind of rising; I am in the sky somehow, I see the roads linking "my" house to the other houses and then to the market village, I see the forests and the horses in the fields, and the kids playing or stealing apples, and the orchard owner running behind them swearing, and then I think, *They're not here anymore, where did they go?* And I sense an endless succession of brief lives, of people trying to work, and love, and be safe, and understand what it all means, and I am further away than ever from what it all means but there is within it all a tremendous gravity, tenderness, and sadness for our strange species so heed-less and so angelic.

Now, who knows; maybe I'm recovering an embedded mem-ory of some inconsequential scene in Turgenev I read thirty years ago. Or maybe it's a manifestation of wine's strange ability to arouse the imagination. This is the "mystical" facet of wine, and I don't think we should apologize for it or be embarrassed about it or seek to quash it. I think we need not to demystify wine, but to *remystify* it!

I return to the wine in my glass. What I just described took place in a second or two. I haven't figured out how to summon it, but I try to be there when it summons me. It means well by me.

I work with a grower named Martin Nigl, who makes espe-cially ethereal wines, the kinds of wines that pose questions we never thought to ask: How far can refinement be taken? What do we find there? Clarity reveals flavor, as we know, but what is on the far side of clear flavor? I also wonder how wines like Nigl's make me feel, because they don't generate a volume of emotional affect. They are too searching. Perhaps what they generate most is curiosity. If I haven't imagined that wine can offer such pure refinement, what else haven't I imagined?

I think that wines like Nigl's can inculcate an appreciation of detail and design. They're like dew-covered webs you see in the morning, when you pause to appreciate the craft of the weaver, all curled into a tiny nugget, waiting for the sun to strike her. Or hoarfrost on your windows some winter morning, as you study the intricacy of the crystals. When I was a little guy I had a microscope, just a little one but more than a toy, and I loved to look at my slides. And now flavors are under a microscope, showing all the worlds within worlds, all below our vision.

This is not to say that Nigl's wines leave all sensual life

behind; far from it. They are feasts for the senses, but theirs is an esoteric cuisine that will feed the hungers you know, and the ones you're unaware of. But you have to be available for this experience, and to listen in a different way. It won't leave you happier, but it does leave you wondering, because there is *more* of you on the other side. And you don't need to contrive some great vast rapture in order to know this moment. It can live, and lives quite easily, in a single sip of wine.

So why not just relax with wine? Don't worry about what you know or don't know. Don't even worry about what you're "supposed" (according to the likes of me) to feel. Just daydream and release your imagination. Believe me, it's more fun than trying to grab a wine, to nail the poor bastard, to dissect it in order to show how cool your palate is. What a pitiable waste! It's like ignoring a rainbow so you can balance your checkbook.

Bear in mind, the cultivation of the mystic isn't only a pursuit of refined experience—in fact, it isn't any sort of *pursuit* at all. The mystic also reveals itself by presenting and encouraging intuition and metaphor. Each of these can come to you if you're relaxed. I recall sitting in a tasting room at the estate of Carl Loewen (from whom we heard in chapter 2) and noticing that I always heard blackbirds when I tasted there. I found a charming connection between the companionship of the songbird and the unassuming but lovely wine. This is probably because Carl's tasting room is just inside his garden, and there's always a blackbird trilling away in the background. Nature does enjoy showcasing her metaphors! But I delight in the juxtaposition of the wine in my glass with the whistling and warbling outside. Here's this little blackbird singing its tiny lungs out, all that energy and melody coming from such a tiny, delicate body, and in the glass there's a wine with 8 percent alcohol, all that energy and melody coming from such a tiny, delicate body. I wonder what the metaphor would be if you were tasting, hmm, in Australia. Some huge malevolent beast bellowing outside in the dust.

If you see the world sacramentally—apart from whatever religious affiliation you may have, or even if you have none at all—you find you have learned to assume that things are connected. Austrian grower Michael Moosbrugger has leased a venerable monastic estate called Schloss Gobelsburg. The land was superb, but the current generation of monks wanted help in modernizing the property and aligning the wines with prevailing standards of quality.

Michael went about upgrading the wines squarely within the context of modern quality-oriented winemaking, and his wines quickly became excellent, even great, as these things are currently understood and evaluated by the critical establishment. Within a few years he had accomplished his goal, only to learn that his true goal lay elsewhere, somewhere both further on and deeper inside.

It started when he tasted through the estate's cellar of old vintages. The wines were different, less modern; the current wines seemed almost sterile in contrast to these mossy old things. And Michael wondered, What guided the old wines? Did those old monks simply lack the know-how of modern cellarmasters? Or was something else at work? The monks kept detailed records. It was easy to see what they did with their wines. But all this did was to ignite a deeper curiosity. What if he went *very* far back, to the period between the end of the Franco-Prussian War and the start of World War I? What did those monks know that we have forgotten?

It is so easy to make this sentimental and trivial. "Return to the wisdom of the monks" is guaranteed to make my eyes glaze over. It is not what I mean. Michael set about to produce a wine—eventually, two wines—as they would have been made almost one hundred years ago. He didn't intend them as an "homage," and certainly not as a pastiche. He couldn't be sure how the wines would be. He only sought to *know*.

"If you consider the span of time between the Romans and the nineteenth century, a Roman who would have been catapulted forward in time would not have been surprised by what he saw," Michael says. "But in the last hundred years, everything has changed, and our own mentalities have changed also. These days we seek to preserve primary fruit as much as possible, and the ways we do it are to ferment at lower temperatures and not to agitate the wine. But until very recently none of this was technologically possible. In those days the guiding idea was that a wine was *schooled*, like a child is schooled—the French call it *élevage*—until it reached a stage in its development when it was ready to drink. And then it was bottled."

How did they know? I asked. "They knew by taste, and also by the extent to which the wine attained the Ideal they had for it." It sounds like a kind of *ripening*, I said. "Yes, exactly; the wine said when it was ready, when it reached the development they'd guided it toward."

Therefore Michael had gone back to a time when oxygen wasn't feared in winemaking. Indeed, it couldn't be avoided, so you adapted to it. You understood wine as a beverage *dependent* on oxygen to create the nongrape flavors by which it was *wine* and not just fermented grape juice. In place of the modern trend for whole-cluster pressing (and the crystalline texture it creates), Michael crushed and pressed his grapes on their skins; he fermented the juice without clarifying it (the old ones used to say he "fermented with all the *schmutz* and bacon"); he eschewed temperature control; he put the wine in old casks and racked it often to *encourage* secondary flavors, the nongrape flavors we call "vinosity," all to replicate this old vinous dialect, which was almost extinct.

What moves me most, apart from the quality of these wines, is what I interpret as Michael's search for *soul*. I imagine we all suspect that soul is, or can be, crowded out by technology, if only because it is so tempting to surrender to the machine's ease, its sterile exactitude, that which we once knew in our fingertips. Each time you flick a switch on a machine you erect a membrane between yourself and your wine. Sometimes this is a necessary evil. I don't want to endorse any kind of feel-good nostalgia. But I like to make meatballs, and while I could easily do the mixture in a food processor, I prefer doing it with my hands because I like that my hands know when it's ready. So I can see how a vintner could be prone to ennui if he merely flicked the switch and the machine did the rest.

I'm not making any sort of Luddite case for pretechnological wines, nor do I suppose they have a nostalgic value. I only share Michael's fascination with how it must have been for the people who made wines as best they could in those times, and created a set of values predicated on what was, and was not, possible. I share Michael's intuition that something of soul, something we may have misplaced, is there to be found. I share that hunger, and I know the rare thing that feeds it. When intuition is all you have, you nurture intuition! And intuition isn't quantifiable, and whatever we can't quantify slips between the threads of what we call understanding. And what we don't understand we call mystic, with mistrust and derision.

There's a lot we can understand about wine, and among those things there's nothing more salient than understanding the *limits* to understanding. Wine is bigger than us, and this is perfect, it is why we spend our lives in love with it; and if this is mystifying, then please, *bring it on*.

four

THE THREE HUMORS

O ver the course of three decades of drinking wine, I began to realize which among its enticements were most important. This has to happen empirically; you can't go in with assumptions already formed. You have to learn to recognize the difference between what you think you value and what you actually do. For me the things that matter become apparent when I see which topics I get into arguments about. I am not by nature a quarrelsome fella; I believe in sweet reason. But that doesn't preclude passion, so here are the facets of wine with which I'm most absorbed, and which I'm most convinced are central to understanding and appreciating wine, and its place in a rich and juicy life.

I call them the three humors, but they can just as easily be called the three cruxes. They imbue my every thought and feeling about wine. Yet I barely ever actually *do* think about them discretely (I spend most of my time thinking about baseball, sex, and guitar solos . . . ever the rock-star wanna-be) because I'd be paralyzed with self-consciousness. Nonetheless I find myself asserting and defending precisely these three values when I talk or write about wine.

- One, wine should express an emergence from its particular origin.
- Two, in considering this and other abstract values, we should never forget to respond spontaneously to wine's sensual value. Laugh when you're tickled, please!
- Three, we should be aware that wine takes us to the edge of language, and sometimes to the edge of what we can know. I'm instinctively sure that this is centrally important—not only to our lives as wine drinkers, but to our entire lives.

These three "humors" could be called the spatial, the sensual, and the spiritual. Their borders are porous: each inheres in the others, and all of them permeate everything we experience in wine.

The First Humor: Specificity

Why should wines taste of their origin? The question is not rhetorical. Wines should indicate their specific origins in flavorsome ways because, in part, many of us *want* them to. But we are a great mess of different temperaments, and some people claim that only sensual pleasure is important, no matter how it might be contrived. Sensual pleasure is crucially important, and sometimes it's the right place to stop, but not always. Some people seem uneasy with the notion that wine could *signify* something. I'm not here to throw psychobabble at their motives—tempting though that is—but rather to try to answer the question inherent in their challenge. I am claiming that the flavor of origin *matters*, and it's reasonable to be asked why.

In the not-very-distant past there were lots of people who said that terroir—which for my current purpose I'm defining as the particular flavor from a particular place, based first on soil— is a lot of meretricious mumbo-jumbo. Doesn't exist, except as a romantic notion cherished by those who drink with extended pinkies. Well, that idea didn't seem to gain much traction. Many New World vintners who were among the most vocal opponents of terroir as a core factor in flavor have since signed on, or would like you to think they have. Perhaps they are evolving, perhaps it's a matter of can't-lick-'em-join-'em, or perhaps it's a wee bit cynical. . . .

There are wine drinkers whose vector is hedonistic, and in many cases they're proudly pragmatic. Wine, in their view, is a thing that can be engineered to press certain pleasure buttons. These pragmatic hedonists eventually (and grudgingly) yielded the point of terroir when they could no longer reasonably deny it. But even as they mumbled, *Well, yes, it does seem to exist, I guess*, they claimed (in very loud voices now) that *it didn't matter.* Terroir might well be real, they said, but if it isn't blatant enough to nail reliably in a blind tasting, then how important could it really be? I'll tell you.

That an effect is subtle doesn't make it unimportant. Significance is not established or validated by obviousness. If for argument's sake I grant the point that terroir shows only in delicate ways, how does that make it any less significant? Yet this is not the crucial issue at hand. To identify that issue I'm going to proceed elliptically. My argument is more holistic than linear, though *holistic* does not connote *illogical*, but only asks for a tolerance for fluid logic—a hard proposition for the pragmatic hedonist. Remember, I'm asking, Why does this all matter? And here's what I'd say.

Some years ago I was a panelist at a sustainable-agriculture conference. Our topic was spirit of place, and toward the end of the discussion a Native American woman to my left said something I have never forgotten. "The salmon do not only return to the stream to spawn," she said. "They also return to respond to the prayers and hopes of the people who love them."

I think that's a lovely thing to say—to believe—and quoted it in one of my sales catalogs. I also thought the statement was innocuous enough to be accepted at least as a bit of poetry. So I was taken aback when a reader called it "pretentious new-age bullshit." I had to ask why anyone could be so enraged by what struck me as a commonplace enough statement from someone who sees the world sacramentally. I recognize there are sensibilities other than mine, more logical and prosaic. Yet with all respect, most thoughts along the "mystical" continuum can be rephrased in linear equations—if one insists.

No, the salmon aren't actually thinking, *Let's hurry back to the river, guys, 'cause the Indians are waiting for us.* No one means to say that. There is, though, among certain people (and peoples) an assumption of immersion in nature that is essentially different from the subject-object relationship most of us presume. I am not *apart* from nature, I am *a part* of it, as it is of me, and everything I see tells me that all living things are unified. The idea of the salmon "responding" may be poetic, but the notion of life's basic interconnectedness is entirely reasonable. That doesn't mean I don't swat as many flies as the next guy, but it's hardly mystical to recognize that each of our discrete lives is part of a general life force. If someone wants to believe the spirits or gods inhabit the salmon too, I find it less objectionable than to assume that we humans have perfect knowledge of where the gods do and do not live!

Life takes many forms, as of course we know. But how often do we actually pause to consider how lucky we are that people look different from one another? I wonder how it would be if we could be engineered to look like some standardized ideal of beauty. Everyone would be attractive, or "attractive," and we'd all look the same. I wonder if someone would yearn for the good old days when people were idiosyncratic and asymmetrical and sometimes not all that gorgeous—but always unique and recognizable, *because of where they came from.* I think it's better—not relatively better, but truly inherently better—when wine shows us its origin. Because if *it* has an origin, then *so do we;* so does every true thing. Wine that expresses its identity reinforces the value of identity. That's part of why it matters, but not all.

Although I assume there is unity among all living things, I don't imagine that this is pretty, and sometimes it's damned inconvenient. But I can't find reason to believe otherwise. Thus it isn't much of a stretch to infer spirit into places, based on the varieties of lives to be found there. Qualities of light, of vegetation, of fauna and people, and of the things people do—what they grow, how they celebrate, how much their ears stick out: all of it. Wine is one of the ways a place conveys its spirit to us. And this matters because we *are* in fact connected—even if we deny it, and even if we aren't aware—and if we claim that wine is important in our lives, then wine must also be bound into and among the filaments that connect us to all things. Wines that are made for commercial purposes and exist merely as products have to take their place alongside all such commodities: soda, breakfast cereal, vacuum-cleaner bags. They can be enjoyable and useful, but they don't matter. They don't matter because they don't *live*. They don't live because they don't come from a recognizable place.

Spirit of place is a concept that's like really good soap; it's lovely, it feels good when it touches you, and it's slippery as hell. It isn't announced with billboards, you know. SPIRIT OF PLACE, FIVE MILES AHEAD; BEAR RIGHT TO ACCESS. Not like that. Nor is it necessarily beautiful. The northern section of the New Jersey Turnpike is *full* of spirit of place, repugnant though it may be. I think spirit of place comes at the moment of ignition between your soul and that place, and a condition of that union is that you don't notice it happening. It is an inference, as all soul things are.

I'll give an example. In Champagne there is a road I like, down an alley of fine old elms leading to the Marne at Damery: France at its most sylvan and tranquil. At first I thought it odd that such a serene landscape should yield such a vivacious wine. But then I realized that the vivacity of Champagne is not only the voice of the landscape, but of the crisp nights in early September and the cool days in June and the wan northern sun that seldom seems to roast. And the still wines of Champagne are rarely vivid in the way young Riesling or Muscat can be. They are pastel, aquarelle, restrained, gauzy. Add bubbles and they get frisky, but they aren't born that way.

Champagne grower Didier Gimonnet told me that a wine writer had been pestering him to bottle a separate cuvée of superrich wine from an eighty-plus-year-old vineyard he owns.

"I'll never do it," he insists, "because the wine would be too powerful." *But isn't that the point?* I thought. Isn't that what wine's supposed to do in our skewered age? Density, opacity, power, flavor that can break bricks with its head! No, said Gimonnet: "I think Champagne needs a certain transparency in order to be elegant." And then it came to me.

Here was the aesthetic to correspond to the gentle Champenois landscape. A *pays* of low hills, forested summits, and plain, sleepy villages isn't destined to produce powerful wines. We might demand them, but we've become so besotted by our demand for impact that we're forgetting how to discern *beauty*. And who among us ever tilts a listening ear to hear the hum of the land?

Is that, too, insignificant? One reason the Old World calls to us is that these lands *do* hum, in a subterranean vibration you feel in your bones, especially if you are an American unaccustomed to the experience. The hum existed for centuries before you got here. It isn't meant for you to fathom. It is mysterious, and you are temporary, but it connects you to vast currents of generations and time. And you are tickled by a sense of meaning you can't quite touch.

It is rarely the same for Americans. Each of us is the crown of creation. We invented humanity. Nothing happened before us, or in any case nothing worth remembering. Memory is nothing but a burden anyway. We turn to the world like a playground bully looking to pick a fight. "Whaddaya got *today* to amuse me, pal? How ya gonna impress me? How many *points* will this day be worth?" Oh, maybe our little slice of earth rumbles with its own hum, but if so then few Americans want to know how to hear it, and most are suspicious of the value of listening at all. For me and my countrymen the taste of place is an anchoring we don't know how badly we need.

Does spirit of place reside integrally within a place, or do we read it in? The answer is *yes*. We are a part of all we experience, and if we glean the presence of spirit of place, then it's there in part *because* we glean it—we bring it to consciousness, one might say. I want to emphasize that point. The soul records, but does not transcribe. Because we are part of nature, what happens to us also happens *in nature*. This is self-evident. From this point one ventures forth according to one's curiosity and temperament. I prefer to believe that spirit of place registers with us because *nature wants it to*, because everything that happens in nature is part of a—dangerous word coming up—design. Not the "design" co-opted by the religious right seeking to challenge Darwin, but an ordering of existence and experience that we humans discern, which is also part of the self-same design.

Whether this design has purpose can be reduced to our sense of faith or just to intellectual entertainment. If I choose to believe there is no purpose, then there's nothing left to think about, it's all random and senseless, and let's see what's on TV. Assuming that things aren't mere chance is, at the very least, an invitation to *keep thinking*.

How do we know when wine is expressing spirit of place? This is actually easier than it might appear. Tangibly, a wine expresses its origin when it *flourishes* and tells us it is happy. It says, "Here is where I'm at home," and I believe we taste flourishing when a grape variety speaks with remarkable articulation, complexity, and harmony in its wines. Generations of winegrowers had centuries of trial and error to learn which grapes made the best wine on their land, but one taste and *we* know immediately. And the noblest grapes are persnickety about which places they call home. Grapes grow mute when planted in foreign soil. Riesling planted in warmer climates than it likes, or on over-rich soils, gives a blatantly fruit-salady wine that most people correctly reject as dull or cloying. Has Chenin Blanc ever made great wine outside of Anjou and Touraine? Nebbiolo seems not to flourish outside Piemonte. I'd even argue that Chardonnay is strictly at home in Chablis (and possibly also in Champagne), since this seems the only terroir where it is inherently interesting and can manage without the pancake makeup of oak or other manipulations.

When a vine is at home, it settles in and starts to transmit. We "hear" those transmissions as flavors. A naturally articulate grape like Riesling sends clear messages of the soil, a panoply of nuances of fruits, flowers, and stones, flavors that are consistent, specific, and repeated year after year, varied only by the weather in which that year's grapes ripened. Vintners know those flavors in their bones. They don't have to wait for the wine in order to detect them; they can taste them in the must. They can taste them in the *grapes*. You wouldn't have to sermonize to these people about spirit of place. They are steeped in that spirit as a condition of life. Indeed, their inchoate assumption that a place contains spirit is *part* of that spirit.

An invitation is implied in spirit of place. When someone like Mosel grower Willi Schaefer goes about his work, he does so with certainty that the Domprobst vineyard will taste one way and the Himmelreich another. He doesn't think about it abstractly—he's too close in—but if you asked him, he'd say he likes that the earth expresses itself in *various* ways. He is also aware of his place in a continuum of generations who have worked the land, land that existed before him and will exist when he's gone, and which has always given the same flavors in the same ways. Willi takes his place within nature and cares for his vines and soils; he would never dream he had *dominion* over nature, or that a vineyard was merely a production-unit to be bent to his will. Unique flavors come into his wine because they are *already there* and he gets out of the way. Why would he do otherwise?

When he tastes his wines, he is fascinated with each unique nuance of identity, and we can likewise be fascinated when we drink his wines, linked together in mutual fascination, he to his land and we to him. And so we are also linked to his land. None of this is "mystical"! Wines of distinctiveness will ground us in a nexus of meaning. Humility before nature is meaningful. Connection to our fellow folks is meaningful. Connection to places we don't otherwise know is meaningful because it stimulates dreams and longing, of faraway places and of the lovely multiplicity of things.

But spirit of place doesn't dwell only in the details. The Mosel, that limpid little river, flows through a gorge it has created amid almost impossibly steep mountainsides. Its people are conservative, and they approach the sweaty work on the steep slopes with humility and good cheer. They are—global warming notwithstanding—northerly people, accustomed to a bracing and taut way of life. Is it an accident that their wines are also bracing and taut? Insist that it's pure coincidence, and I'll wager you were never there. If you were there and you still don't see it, Customs must have confiscated your imagination.

We need wines that tell us in no uncertain terms, "I hail from *this* place and this alone, not from any other, for only here am I at home." Such wines transport us to those places. If we are already there, they cement the reality of our being there. We need to know where we are. If we do not, we are *lost*.

I don't have time to waste on processed wines that taste as if they could have come from anywhere, because in fact they come from nowhere and have no place to take me. We crave spirit of place because of our own need to be located, which reassures us that we belong in the universe. We want our bearings. We want to know where home is. We can deny or ignore this longing, but it will scrape away at us relentlessly while we wonder why we feel so homesick, why we never feel whole.

Or we can claim this world of places. We can claim the love that lives in hills and vines, in trees and birds and smells, in buildings and ovens and human eyes, of everything in our world that makes itself at home and calls on us to do the same. The value of wine, beyond the sensual joy it gives us, lies in what it shows us—not only its own hills and rivers, but the road home.

The Second Humor: Fun, and Why It Runs from Us

I had two unsettling anniversaries in 2008: thirty years of drinking wine seriously, and twenty-five years in the wine business. And as these dates approached, I began to wonder whether the longer we all drink wine, the less fun we have with it.

I don't think this is necessarily because we grow jaded, but rather because of the kinds of wines we select for ourselves: *earnest* wines, emblems of a "serious" or "passionate" approach, wines that compel our full attention. A metaphor for this phenomenon is the creature called the restaurant wine list, which, if you're ordering for the table, means that for minutes on end—often many, many minutes on end—you are ignoring your guests. These tomes insist that we pay heed: *it's all about the wine*, you see.

Many wine professionals were wine hobbyists to start out, and we head-butted our way into the business because it seemed like fun to make money doing what we were doing anyway: obsessing about wine. In my early days there was no difference between the "work" I did and the place of wine in my private life. For me it was kind of sweet, but for those around me it must have seemed that the business was open 24/7.

A few years ago I started to see the roads diverge. When I drank wine at home—drank, not tasted or "appraised" or evaluated from any professional standpoint—I wanted something *recreational*, ideally something different from "work" wines. At least, I wished for a wine that would be wholly satisfying but not necessarily demanding. What kinds of wines would these be? Did my portfolio already contain them, my work encompass them? If not, *why not?* And what did this all say about the kinds of wines I actually, spontaneously, sensually found *yummy?*

I know full well that wine can be important, that it can be an embodiment of culture, that it can be a messenger of meaning, a portal into the mystery. But if wine must always be solemnly Important, then life gets pretty dour. Here are some other things wine can be.

It was a pretty midday in early May when I visited Jamek in Austria's Wachau. Along with the winery there is a venerable restaurant that should have a high place as a culinary

UNESCO heritage site, and I was asked if I wanted to sit and taste outdoors—"It's the first day we've set up the tables in the garden." And so I did. I was alone, with the superattentiveness one has at table alone. At Jamek you always taste somewhere in the restaurant, as if to emphasize the connections among wine, food, regionality. The garden slowly filled with people pausing to enjoy their lives on a soft spring day among the flowers and the blackbirds and the trees. Some brought their dogs, who lay cooperatively under the table as well-behaved Eurodogs do. I watched food and wine being served and wondered, *What role does wine play here? To what does it pertain?* Do wine professionals ever think about how wine fits into other aspects of our lives, or is it just wine qua wine for us?

It is something to see wine drunk without fuss in a spring garden as the world twitters and blossoms and people eat their salads and schnitzels and pike perch. However much *we* may obsess, wine itself goes about its genial business of washing down people's meals and gracing their lives for an hour.

At the end of one year's tasting tour of Austria, entailing much concentration and many days of writing tasting notes, I took myself off to the Alps for a couple of days to clear my head. At times the need to write tasting notes is intrusive, like pausing to describe the giddy ecstatic running of a dog for whom you've just thrown a stick. The grinning beast lopes back to you with a big ol' drool-covered stick in his slobbery maw, and he's looking at you as if every scintilla of his happiness depends on your throwing that stick again, and what are you doing? You're writing! Put down the pen and throw the damn stick, man!

My friends at Jamek had given me a bottle of a Muskateller they saw I enjoyed. Once in the mountains, I spent the afternoon hiking, enjoying my solitude and blissful not to have to think. I ate a simple dinner and washed it down with a carafe of pretty dubious Blaufränkisch. Up in my room again, the sun was setting and the peaks were napped in that late-day amber, and I had my bottle of Muscat. So I went down and asked for a wineglass. I took it upstairs, sat on my little balcony, and glugged a wine that seemed to encapsulate the keen mountain air. Eventually I jettisoned the glass and just drank from the bottle. Those moments were perfect: the wine was content not to occupy my whole attention, but rather just to keep me company.

It can grow tedious, you know, to encounter a "great" wine that spends the whole evening talking about itself. Obviously the truly great wine both compels and warrants all the attention one is willing to give it, but for every sublime and articulate wine there are a few dozen chatterboxes and bores.

We risk squandering the capacity to enjoy that which is simple because we seemingly need to insist that it be *merely* simple, or that simple isn't good enough for us. Great, complex wines are wonderful, enthralling, life-affirming, soul-stirring, but it's worth asking whether they are *relaxing*. Good, simple wines are. Good, simple wines speak to our spirit of play and ease and repose, exactly because they don't demand our exclusive attention.

One summer I met a friend in San Francisco and we played hooky and took a picnic up to the cliffs of the Marin headlands, where we sat watching pelicans dive into the Pacific. We had a bottle of Bardolino rosé, but no glasses. No matter! That bottle emptied pronto. My companion was a "wine friend," but we spoke not a word about that Bardolino. Yet we were limbically united in the almost animal pleasure each of us took in it.

What has to happen in such moments? The wine has to be good enough that you can trust it without having to think about it. There's a tiny second of ignition—yup, it's good—and then you return to your life. Great wine would be too intrusive, but a wholly *good* wine is ideal.

I've taken customers with me to Austria from time to time. One has to be careful how to stage these trips. You can't front-load too many serious estates when people are still tired and jet-lagged. So on the second day of one such trip I took the group to Hans Setzer and Erich Berger, and taught myself a lesson in the process. Both of these estates make wines of charm. That doesn't preclude significance as we might measure it, but it refers to a different aesthetic. I suddenly found myself inside a kind of spell: "These wines, whatever else they might be, are *delicious*," it said.

Delicious. Who uses that word to talk about wine anymore? A hamburger might be delicious, but a Gigondas? And what makes a wine delicious? Can we isolate its elements? Should we even try?

I believe we should try—not to kill it by dissection, but rather to contemplate the value that such deliciousness deserves, and seldom receives. And I would argue that the first element of deliciousness is *charm*.

Of all the aesthetic virtues, charm is perhaps the most imperiled. We have a little carousel at our county's regional park, and I like to pause there during a long walk and watch the little kids whirl around on the painted horses. One week I noticed they'd given up the usual calliope music in favor of—god help me—disco. And it was just so damn *wrong*, all these three- and four-year-olds riding along to "I Will Survive." Is calliope music supposed to be too goofy or unhip or some stupid thing?

Charm is among the highest virtues. In people it denotes an effort of behavior whereby you feel appreciated and cared for. In wine or music it creates a response of palpable delight. I find this feeling more pleasant than many other feelings that have greater *prestige*. Of course, there's a place in me for being knocked out, blown away, stunned, impressed, but none of these is as exquisitely joyful as feeling charmed. Also, charm is a flexible virtue, able to exist in big wines, medium wines, or little wines. I prize this quality of charm because it seems less reducible to recipe. Any grower of unexceptional talent can make intense wine, but to craft charming wines is less a matter of formula than of intuition and attending to myriad tiny details, knowing all the while that your wine won't be the biggest, boldest, or loudest wine on the table. Instead it will insinuate, will crawl inside a certain temperament and sing its lyric song, and this is the pleasure for which we live.

Do I perhaps overstate the case? Charm isn't all that impossible; just ferment with aroma yeasts at cold temperatures to get those sweet banana aromas and leave a little residual sugar behind, maybe throw a little Muscat into the Veltliner and *presto*, there's your charm. Not so. Lovers of true charm are not seduced by the specious or formulaic. Charm asks the grower to pay heed to *texture* and, even harder, to attend to flavor in a different way: not how much of it there is, but how *pleasing* it is.

The mere affectation of charm is indeed abhorrent, and such phonies are all too easy to spot. The awareness of being seduced usually precludes the seduction! The truly seductive wine ignites a spontaneous and irresistible delight, a flush of animal pleasure at its sheer deliciousness.

At this point I'll pause to consider how I've come to worry at this possibly self-evident point. As a wine pro, I spend a great deal of time assessing wine. Does it make the cut? Is it worthy? Further, I spend a great deal of time describing wine, which often involves a kind of vivisection of its components. None of this is exceptional; professionals *work with* wine, after all. But I fear we all, pros and amateurs alike, are in danger of working *at* wine. The blatant example of this melancholy activity is the point score. I'll reserve my dudgeon at that all-too-easy target for a later chapter, except to point out an inherent limitation in all scoring systems: they cannot speak to how wine is used, but only to how it is "judged."

And at the end of a day working with wine, by evening I want a wine with which I can relax, a delicious, companionable wine. All of us in the trade know—or ought to know—that the most successful wine isn't always the one with the highest score, it is the one the tasters reach for to drink after the tasting. "The best bottle is the first one emptied," is a wise proverb.

My friend Erich Berger's wines are wines of *humor* in the classical sense, graceful and pleasurable, gregarious and celebratory. Please consider: often, when we drink a wine for "celebration," we forget what we're actually celebrating and end up celebrating the wine. Be honest, now, you know it's true! But whatever it is—your novel got published, you have an anniversary, your biopsy came back negative, your computer is fixed, you finally got laid—don't you actually need a wine that won't draw attention away from the reason you popped it in the first place? If you want to drink a great wine, or Great Wine, then celebrate *that*. Otherwise, drink a wine in which the spirit of celebration lives.

If we reorient the way we think of wine to favor wines of usefulness and companionability, interesting things happen. Wine draws closer to us. It becomes our partner in a dynamic relationship. And as we consider which wines we want in our cellars or in our lives, we find our thinking becomes more ecumenical. We appreciate wines in broader echelons of "stature." We stop insisting, and start accepting. We no longer see from the top down, grasping for the "best" without reference to the rest of our lives. We start to think about what we eat, *how we live*; which wines we drink at what times of year, whom we drink with: in short, we think of wine as we actually use it. And we let it take its natural place as a helpful being who keeps us company and eases our ways.

To know what you *really* like, look at what you're always buying more of. Speaking again of Austria, I am certain her best wines are her great Rieslings. But I'm just as certain her Grüner Veltliners are more useful to me, since I'm always reaching for them and constantly running out. Strict evaluation of wine certainly has its place, and great wine has a very noble place in our souls; but I suspect we are all too greedy for exalted experience. I like Anaïs Nin's quote "Beware of the esoteric pleasures; they will blunt your appreciation of the ordinary ones." Our craving to have our worlds rocked is a filter that excludes the very experience we so urgently clamor for. Great wine will come to you if you're calm enough to let it. And in that calm you will find a renewed (and renewable) joy in wines of loveliness, goodness, and charm.

So we've considered the value of located wines as a marker

of authenticity and meaning, and we've considered wine as an agent of fun and delight. What is left is to look at wine's strangest ability: to channel the inexplicable. And so we arrive at the frontiers of what can be said, and it's time to go exploring. Who, what lives here, and what oxygen is here to breathe?

The Third Humor: Ease with the Unknowable

We begin with a strange and unsettling thing that happened in Washington, D.C., in January 2007. The story (by the wonderful Gene Weingarten) was published in early April in the *Washington Post*, on a day when we awoke to a tracing of snow on the newly unfurled leaves.

It seems the great violinist Joshua Bell agreed to play as a busker during morning rush hour in a D.C. Metro station, just to see whether passersby would notice the presence of the extraordinary. It won't surprise you to learn that almost no one stopped to hear Bell's performance, and that many who did were actually annoyed by what they perceived as an intrusion. Yes, of course, the deck was stacked. Obviously the lives we live are all stupefying to some degree, especially when we're shooting robotically through space on our way to work, latte in hand, iPod bud in ear. We cannot reasonably accuse those heedless commuters of being (in Anne Lamott's lovely phrase) worthless philistine scum. They're merely busy drones who've accepted that much of their lives—*our* lives—will be lived on autopilot. But why am I telling you this?

This book considers a commodity that none of us needs. We can live without wine. We might not want to, but we can. Yet we care about wine in many and varied ways. At the very least it gives us sensual pleasure. Others become cerebrally intrigued by its multiplicity. Still others are more serious about wine's role in culture and history. And some of us, when we experience a wine of great beauty, are compelled to speculate on the meanings of the aesthetic experience. And we feel the curiously powerful emotion that beauty evokes. Wine is singular in this respect. Beautiful flavor can be found and appreciated in food, of course, but there is appetite involved. We seldom drink wine because we are thirsty.

I am concerned with the ways we form our relationships with beauty. Some of us don't form them. I'm also curious to know how we live when there is, by circumstance or design, a paucity of beauty in our lives.

I suspect we are all more thirsty for beauty than some of us know, or would admit. What differs is our *awareness* of the need. Temperament plays its usual role, and I suspect I am especially sensitive, not because I'm a superior person, but just because I am made that way. If you are made differently, I'll be the last guy to try to force you to fake beauty orgasms to demonstrate your sensitivity. But I believe in a universal thirst for beauty, which gets ground out of us by the sedative effect of the everyday.

I am also convinced of this: no matter how much we have or have not cherished beauty in our lives, at some point we'll regret that it wasn't more.

Wine, for me, has always been an unusually pure bringer of beauty. It is something akin to music in that respect, that is, it moves us without recourse to narrative and without stirring our empathies. In that sense it is perhaps even more pure than music, which is often contrived to produce certain emotions.

Wine is music in the form of water. Since it is such an unspoiled conveyor of beauty, I respect it in a very particular way, and I feel it needs protecting. It's way too easy to stamp wine into the ground by manipulating it in the cellar and obsessing over it in the parlor. Not too many things convey beauty to us in a form as pure as wine's.

However, a life in pursuit of beauty is vulnerable to a certain neurosis, and it can quickly grow merely precious. Groping for beauty is a good way to send it packing. Insisting that all wines must be measured by how skillfully they wiggle your beauty knob or how quickly they open your tear ducts is more than tiresome. Some wine is exceptionally vivid, and demands attention, and most of the time I am gratefully and respectfully willing to give it. Other times I want to be left in peace. There are stunningly compelling wines and there are "let me keep you company" wines, and we need them both.

And once in a great while, there are wines like those of the great Nahe vintner Helmut Dönnhoff, which simply play for you like Joshua Bell busking in the subway; they open a door but do not tap you on the shoulder—they just open the door. If you are *awake* to possibility, you'll notice the portal, and if you're curious, you will wonder where it leads.

But here, a small digression. These ways are serpentine and mossy. . . .

Like most lovers of German wine, I love Auslese, the not-quite-dessert wine that begins to show a grape's ripe essence. I buy more of it than I drink. It piles up in the cellar, and at such times it is useful to have thirsty friends and a lot of cheese—both of which I gathered together a little before Christmas one year, to drink a whole slew of mature Auslese and chow down with suitable nibbles.

The wines were very fine, all of them kinetic and articulate, some of them exciting and gripping. Then I opened a Dönnhoff, the 1990 Niederhäuser Hermannshöhle Auslese. The game was, we (or rather, *they*) tasted the first sip blind, not to guess the wine but simply to receive its signal without the noise of identity. As this wine was poured, I watched a kind of spell settle over my friends. I hadn't planned it, and I didn't suppose the wine was any better than the wines around it. But the chatter died down, and people went from witty and sociable to pensive and meditative.

What in a wine can bring about this rare and strangely truthful quality of evanescence? This strikes me as a vital question. When a wine is this searching, probing, it seems to offer something that is found no other way.

One gropes to find words. There is a saying that we should be suspicious of things for which no words exist, and although I imagine this to be true, it can't be the whole truth. Words may not exist, but *something* does. There's a drawing among the many aching works of Käthe Kollwitz called *Prisoners Listening to Music*. In it we see the wretched trying to endure the divine. We suppose that beauty has been banished from their lives. And here it is, restored; their faces are afraid and hesitant and wondering, as they see perhaps for the first time the tiny cloisters that live inside each of them, and each of us.

There are wines that convey these moments. There are wines that express without asserting, wines that show the little penumbra between joy and serenity, between brilliance and luminosity. I have tasted them, as I hope you have. Such wines are sometimes a little unnerving because they resist being grasped and they don't make statements. It also seems impossible to contrive them. And this quality confounds a certain kind of drinker who likes to vivisect how a "well-made" wine is constructed.

Recently I had an absolutely marvelous wine from the Nahe's Schlossgut Diel; it was the 2006 Goldloch "Grosses Gewächs," and it is admirable in every way. There's a lusty vein of minerality and all the baroque fruit of great Goldloch; the wine is superbly balanced, delicious, and sophisticated. It demonstrates care and intelligence, and gives a tasty joy. Yet it is entirely *tangible*, and all of its delightful facets are readily discernible.

A few evenings later I had a 2005 Steiner Hund Riesling from Austria's Nikolaihof and was once again thrust into something irreducible. Sure, I could have written a tasting note and broken it down, but there was something elusive here. Where the Diel was expressive, this wine was serene. Where the Diel was complex and delicious, this wine was exquisite and mysterious. Where the Diel was a glorious fanfare of flavor, the Nikolaihof was a lullaby. May I go further and risk looking silly? Where the Diel was giddy with its own beauty, the Nikolaihof was content with its own calm, cheer, and tranquillity. It asserted nothing and conveyed everything. And it is precisely this almost eerie self-possession that creates such an oddly compelling itch. What flora and fauna live in this place? What does it want us to see? Why, when I am so hyper, is this damned wine so calm?

This is by no means to cast aspersions on those wines that are deliberately and explicitly great. Far from it. But such wines *come at you*. They are not ambiguous, nor do they hint or imply; they come straight to the point. They are great. And that is, of course, a very good thing.

But to return to Dönnhoff, with few exceptions I don't think this can be said of his wines. They are difficult to study because they don't hold still; they are too busy melting. They don't thrust at you from any particular angle; rather, they invite you to enter a larger nexus that includes them but doesn't stop at them. Diel's Goldloch is the tower of a great gothic cathedral, mighty and filigree, rising to a definite point that the eye follows up into the sky. But when I think of Dönnhoff I think of the peaceful little cloisters nearby, and the deliberate birds who live in their shady air.

This has to do with texture, but not only with texture. I have no idea whether Helmut Dönnhoff would endorse any of this—I suspect he thinks I have a screw loose—but neither do I think there is any formula that can explain his wines. One can try, certainly; is it harvest selection, method of pressing, choice of yeast, temperature of fermentation, choice of aging container, cellar temperature, all of the above, none of the above—all *and* none of the above? Or shall we simply admit the mystery of how a wine with such unearthly glassy smoothness can also contain so much information?

However, it isn't information that will answer my questions or yours. It will instead pose even more inscrutable ones, because the wine is seldom what we'd call "intense"; it doesn't land with huge impact, but instead envelops you in a sort of tenderness you cannot identify, isolate, or explain.

There is something sapid and companionable about such wines. They don't talk only to your senses; they talk to your *life*. They seem almost entirely without affect. They are serene in themselves, numinous in their very lack of thrusting and pushing. They are all of the reasons we should love wine, but few of the reasons we actually do. We are busily determined to place our pleasure on a scale, locked in our solitary confinements. It's all about us.

I have never tasted a Dönnhoff wine and felt that it was out to thrill me or to "entertain" my senses. It simply expresses the pure honesty of itself. It hasn't a thing to prove. You almost can't believe it exists, because there's no GPS to get you there, no recipe you can follow to create *that* result. It isn't like arriving, it isn't like winning or prevailing or mastering; it is in some strange way like breathing, or daydreaming. At the end of H. G. Wells's lovely novel *The History of Mr. Polly*, the hero, who has spent his life urging and asserting, has finally learned to admit contentment into his life. We find him "not so much thinking as lost in a smooth still quiet of the mind." I think that when we look back on our lives we will know those were the times we were happiest.

Here's another way to view it. The idea of "forest" is different from the notion of "a lot of trees." The notion of "a lot of individual tones and pitches arranged in organized and pleasing ways" is existentially different from the idea of "music." "Landscape" is different from the hills and rivers it might contain. There are wines that live in the Whole, which is not only greater but also *other* than the sum of its parts. Yet it often seems that wine trains us to examine and live inside the parts. And when certain wines come along shining with their Whole-ness, we've never been taught how to respond. That's because this "Whole-ness" is very real and almost impossible to explain.

One year at Dönnhoff we had something to negotiate, and

I made a second visit in order to do so. A colleague was with me, and Helmut brought the wines out for us to taste. I passed through them unthinkingly, busy with our conversation, rather like the commuters who didn't hear Joshua Bell in the subway station that morning. Yet luckily for me, a wine found a seam and soaked through it, and suddenly I was invaded by silence. It was a tiny, lovely moment, nothing dramatic at all. But it asked a question I like to remember: *And what of this?*

My wife likes to remember her dreams, and I find this quite endearing but don't at all share it. It seems ordinary enough that our subconscious hums and buzzes all the time and we see it only when our waking consciousness is out of the way, just as we see stars only in a dark sky. But the stars are always there even when we don't see them, just as the dreams are always there even when we don't dream them. And there are wines that speak to the dreams and the stars and the beauty that is always there.

I love the phrase *vini di meditazione.* There are take-a-brisk-walk wines and there are sit-still-and-be-quiet wines. When you're out on a hike and you've walked a while and you stop to take a drink of water, the world rearranges itself. Suddenly you see leaves fluttering and grasses dancing and critters crittering, all the things you don't notice when you're making tracks. It's funny how glad you can be, as William Stafford wrote, when all you have is the world.

The truth is that I don't know how certain wines are like this, I don't know why, and I am very sure if I did know I still wouldn't know how they get that way. What I do know, or think I know, is that while brilliance, explicitness, and assertiveness are wonderful things for wines to have, there's a point at which they *stop;* they're only an amusement, even if sometimes a very fine and even noble one. The wines that go deepest seem to steal over you. You're prepared to admire them or to deconstruct them appreciatively, but these oddly haunting wines don't care what you think or feel. Something materializes out of the ether, something you knew but forgot was there.

My friend the wine writer David Schildknecht is fond of quoting F.H. Bradley's saying that metaphysics is the finding of bad reasons for what we believe on instinct. I like the quote too, especially when we're trying to clarify the inexplicable. My point here is not to explain these slippery ambiguities, but rather to pause before them and ask why they visit us and what they want.

There is a kind of beauty that is unconcerned with whatever pleasure it gives us. If and when we are aware of this beauty, it can lead to a rare kind of gratefulness, a compassion that isn't sentimental. It says that the world finds you when you are prepared to admit it, but will assault you if you are not. It says that we are not merely life-support systems attached to a taste motor. We are humans who can bring our entire selves to a glass of wine. In the quiet of these calm, exquisite wines we hear a kind of divinity. And we see that the world is charged with it—it is, we are, the current that passes between us is. And it is *always* there.

And loveliest of all, you don't have to attain this by dint of some tremendous effort or "spiritual practice"; you don't have to meditate or hold séances or even do yoga. You just have to be willing to relax and step out of your damned life for a few minutes. Nor will this make you a beatific and benign person. It's not about "self-improvement." I'm as cranky as the next guy. All it will do is stop you from wasting too much of your little brief life.

There is a saying that the last notes of a piece of music are the silence that follows the final note. Robert Frost said that if a book of poems has twenty-four poems in it, the book itself is the twenty-fifth. There are wines that let us hear the beat of time between the tick and the tock. It hardly matters how they got that way; it matters that the world includes them, and we respond. For we are all prisoners, listening to music.

five

PRESSING HOT BUTTONS

Is All Taste Equally Valid? A Defense of Elitism

The question of "validity" arises in matters of taste only when one struts one's democratic cred by claiming that one man's taste is as good as another's. The idea for this chapter came from a magazine article by a wine journalist who had a moment of awakening in which his idea of taste dilated to include *tout le monde* in its sentimental embrace. Anyone with intellectual aspirations knows this feeling, the groping toward the common touch, as if dropping your *g*'s and drinking beer from the can will transform you into someone socially and sexually desirable. Show me someone who insists that all taste is equally valid and I'll show you someone who doesn't know he isn't discussing taste—he's discussing himself.

How, after all, can taste even touch on validity? Taste is either fine or coarse, cultivated or heedless, even *good* or *bad* (and often good and bad within the same person), but "valid"?

Two things are valid. First, hierarchies exist throughout

nature, and when hierarchies exist, then so do elites. The lion is the "elite" among carnivores. Second, we're all expert at something, and we manage very often to contemplate expertise without screaming about snobbery or elitism. If we approve of the field in question, we respect the elite in that field. "Albert Pujols is one of the game's elite hitters." No one quakes at the word *elite* in this context; Albert's a hitting machine, and he's one of a tiny, select group at the top of his field. If instead we fundamentally disapprove of a subject, then expertise seems egregious: *I feel inferior before this subject, so I'll accuse you of being an elitist snob for caring about it at all.* "The intellectual elite in the foreign policy field suggest that negotiations are more productive than may at first be apparent." Oh, right, ivory-tower snobs who never had to change a tire; who cares what *they* think?

One evening at a ball game, I had the good fortune to sit next to one of the advance scouts who attend every game, gathering intel on the players for the next team they'll face. It was a slow night, and I asked if he could think out loud for me, tell me what he saw. Turns out he watched a whole different ball game from the one I did. I sat in admiration of his trained eye. I'd thought the game was exciting, and said so. "It was actually a poorly played and managed game," he responded. "Not one of baseball's finer examples." When I pressed him to elaborate, he opened a new world for me. I didn't feel inferior or rebuked; I felt educated. And I realized again the value of training and discernment.

Did I see all subsequent baseball games through these newly expanded eyes? In fact, no. Sometimes I *liked* watching the game like a simple fan. But now I'd been given a choice, to see the game analytically or as simple entertainment.

Similarly, when I take my car to a mechanic, he hears different things in the engine's hum than I do. A piano tuner hears minute tonal variances to which I am effectively deaf. A massage therapist discerns muscle tensions of which I'm not consciously aware. All of these are examples of expertise we take for granted. And yet if someone asserts expertise in wine, we are promptly suspicious; we sniff for snobbery, we get defensive. Why?

As I've discussed, wine writers often feel a degree of responsibility to "demystify" wine in order to make it accessible to everyman. That way, they reason, more people will drink it and the world will be improved. If some people like trashy wine, be gentle with them; they may grow into appreciation for the kinds of wines *we* like. Maybe, maybe not. I rather think that innate taste will show itself apart from experience. Would we argue that today's Burger King diner is tomorrow's Thomas Keller aficionado? "Let's applaud them for just being in a restaurant at all!" It seems improbable, this logic.

Other wine writers want to reassure you that there are no "rules" and that you should always just drink what you like: reasonable advice on the face of it. If you like drinking young Barolo with a dozen raw oysters, I won't stop you (though I'll shudder to think what's going on inside your mouth). If you like a cognac with a fistful of sardines steeped in it for twenty minutes, go on and drink it that way. No one wants to keep you from the consequences of your perverse taste. No one denies your right to it.

Some of us, however, like to call things by their proper names. Not from snobbism, sadism, or any other ism, but because it helps to order the world of experience. It fends off the chaos. And whatever expertise we may have attained in the things we love, there are plenty of other things to humble us. We're all on both sides of this divide all the time. I have a fascination with fragrance and am a fledgling amateur of perfumes and colognes. I thought I had good taste, because it was mine! Then I read some of Chandler Burr's writing about perfumes and colognes and was nonplussed to learn that he found many of my favorites quite despicable, and a few that he lauded to the skies were scents I found repugnant. It's self-evident that we perceive things through subjective membranes, and even if tannic red wine and shrimp conspire to produce a strong metallic flavor in the mouth, I'm sure someone somewhere *likes* that flavor and resents being hectored about its undesirability.

If you like Twinkies, eat them. Don't apologize. Have all the fun a Twinkie delivers. But don't claim it's just as good as a home-baked brownie from natural fresh ingredients, or that anyone who believes otherwise is a food snob. *It's only sugar and chemicals, but I like it.* I'm sort of a cultured guy, and yet I can't abide opera, whereas I have a perverse tolerance for professional wrestling. Again, we're all admixtures of high and low tastes, and this is fine, as long as we don't confuse them.

I had a conversation on an airplane recently with a cellist in her twenties. We talked about music, naturally, and it became clear to me that her tastes were wider than my own. (I'm an ossified old geez in his mid-fifties.) I remarked upon her ecumenical listening habits. "Well," she said, "don't you think one should search for the virtues in everything?" Much as I yearned to say yes, to do so would have been false. Instead I said: "No, I think *you* should seek the good in everything; that's where you are in your life. But what I need to do is identify that which annoys or wounds me, and avoid it."

Wine writer Stuart Pigott once wrote, "We should . . . start making wines with balance, elegance and originality sound so astonishing that our readers feel they've just got to try them," and this of course is true. Critics must stand for something; otherwise we are merely pusillanimous. The first task is to find the good and praise it. But anytime we take a stand *for* something, we imply the thing's shadow; that is to say, the thing we love suggests—it can't be helped—the thing we don't. And we must not shrink from naming both things, especially not for fear of wounding the delicate sensibilities of the philistines (who, by the way, are robustly insensitive and also have no scruples about insulting *us* with labels such as "snob" or "elitist"). God knows we'd prefer to be everyone's best friend, and we feel humane and generous telling those with unformed (or simply atrocious) taste that their taste is as good as anyone else's. But it's a lie we tell so that *we* can feel noble, and furthermore it is unfair to the recipient, who, if he's being patronized, is entitled at least to know it.

But this does not confer any sort of carte blanche to offer gratuitous insults. Good-taste bullies may have better taste than bad-taste bullies, but they're still abhorrent. Making clear distinctions in matters of taste does not grant license to be arrogant or inhumane.

Pigott went on to claim that any wine anyone likes is ipso facto "good" wine, and this is just the slippery slope we can't help sliding down when we try to be "democratic." It is manifestly impossible to support a definition of *good* as "wine that someone, regardless of who it is, finds to taste good." This is irresponsible and it ducks the question. Once at a presentation I was terribly busy and opened bottles without a chance to screen them. A punter remarked that a particular wine was "fantastic;

I never had anything that tasted like this, wow, how was this made?" His enthusiasm infected me, and I poured myself a taste. Corked! What should I have done, based on Pigott's definition of *good?* The gentleman liked a wine that was patently flawed. He has every right to like it; no one disputes this. But I felt honor-bound to (discreetly and tactfully!) correct him.

Thus I can't endorse a definition of *good* that is as inclusive and democratic as Pigott and others desire. I do not believe nature has any use for our democracies. Some things *are* better than others, and one of our functions is to guide our readers toward appreciation of these distinctions as gracefully as we're able.

If we take these democratic principles and apply them to any other thing about which aesthetic or cultural criticism is warranted, do they stand up? Shall we endorse a statement such as "All art is good art as long as someone likes it"? Does this sentiment apply equally to architecture, poetry, cuisine? Or is wine somehow "special" because too few people drink it? And should we pander to every sort of unformed or misguided taste because we're trying to get more people to drink wine?

Let me be clear: no one has to like wine the way I like it, or the way any "expert" likes it. If wine is a casual beverage for you, then the discussion ends. Wine is complicated and therefore intimidating, but I'll make you a deal: you promise not to lash out at me for what I know because you feel intimidated, and I'll promise not to guilt-trip you into acquiring expertise in a subject you don't care that much about.

Writers are well advised to write humanely, because it is good to be humane. Any professional who uses words does well to shade them so as not to deliver gratuitous insults to people with dubious or uneducated taste. But that doesn't mean he abrogates responsibility to exercise the entire range of his judgmental faculties—which by the way are *why he was hired*—in search of some romance about inclusion or democracy.

There are no "invalid" moments of pleasure in wine. But there are higher and lower pleasures. Once you have graduated from the low you can always return. It's fun to return! You *should* return, frequently, because it's good to stay in touch with your inner redneck, or you risk your taste becoming precious. But if you're in the process of honing your wine taste, and you want to continue, no one helps you who fails to delineate the distinctions among inadequate, ordinary, good, fine, and great—or between mass-produced "industrial" wines and small-scale "agricultural" wines.

Maybe there *is* a thin line between this and Pigott's concern that we will insist on our notion of high quality as an imperative. But the way through asks us to remember to be kind (or at least, not unkind) and to hone our craft with words. I feel it is indeed unkind to flatten all taste to a specious equality, made even more pernicious by encouraging the philistines to set the level.

I have a powerful aversion to prefab wines and to wines that gush and scream; they annoy me, I tell you why, and you make up your own mind. My imperative isn't everyone's, but I strive to send clear signals, to advocate what I think is worthy and to identify and explain what I think is unworthy. If my tone is (in Pigott's terms) "superior, even dictatorial," then the fault lies with me. I have failed to communicate my point.

But the point remains. Taste moves along a continuum of discernment and refinement. Each of us moves as he can, and as he wishes. It is helpful to delineate all the places along the way, and it's helpful to recall that when we cherish the best—the "elite"—in a given field it is a gesture not of snobbery, but of love.

"What's All the Fuss? Wine Is Only Fermented Grape Juice"

Aaahhh . . . right. That's all it is. And Mount Everest is just a really big pile of rock. And *Crime and Punishment* is just a long story about a student who whomps some old lady upside the head with an ax. You know, I agree with you; life is just too damn good. I'll be right there to help you suck all the blood out of every possible transcendent moment just so we can make our lives even more diminished and paltry. But let's work fast, 'cuz I've got tickets to the ball game.

But look: the batter swings and the ball rises in a soaring arc (its whiteness looks so lovely against the black sky . . . but no, it's just a hard-hit ball, keep calm, damn it) and jeez, all forty-something thousand people sitting here are suddenly on their feet watching the little ball fly, and when it lands in the seats in deep left field they all start cheering and high-fiving their neighbors and, I mean, come *on:* what possible joy can derive from this? The twenty-five overpaid athletes who happen to play in my town are now likelier to defeat the twenty-five overpaid athletes who play in *your* town, and for this I am ecstatic?

We care because we want to. We care because human beings are *made* to care. Caring feeds a hunger. Caring affirms our lives. It doesn't matter what we care about, whether bridge or crossword puzzles or lacrosse or twelve-tone music or sitcoms or sustainable agriculture or gardening or wine. Wine at least rewards our caring by giving so much back: family, culture, hospitality, beauty. And wine is entirely tolerant. You don't have to care if you don't feel it naturally. Care a little or care a lot, your wine will meet you wherever you are. But don't let anyone—let me emphasize this: *anyone*—tell you not to care, or that caring makes you some kind of geek. Everyone's a geek about something, so don't be meek, embrace the geek.

Pointless Scores

It won't hurt to repeat this: point systems, any of them, may or may not be useful in strict consumerist terms. They are probably useful or they wouldn't have metastasized as they have, though the system of thought they enforce is a feedback loop in which the reader is infantilized and thus comes to depend on the score. But we'll leave that aside for the moment. I agree for argument's sake that scoring systems are attractive to the wine consumer who wants a shorthand buyer's guide. But no scoring system can possibly work in holistic terms, because there's an inherent problem with the notion of "perfection" and because wine is not only judged, it is also *used*, and enjoyed, in many and varied ways.

To use one example, are riper wines inherently better than less-ripe wines *because* of their additional concentration? What possible answer can there be except *It depends?* Maybe the answer is yes if one is obliged to score on an absolute scale, but certainly not if one permits relativity and equivalence to enter the equation; for instance, a zippy, light Sancerre can be a "perfect" wine with oysters for which the higher-scoring wine is too concentrated.

The question of perfection is more difficult because when we feel intense pleasure, it is so awfully tempting to think, *This is as good as it gets.* But the quest for perfection is useless; it takes us down myriad blind alleys, it sticks us in a maze and then lies to us about where we are. There's little question that a *very* thin line can exist between the perfect and the bland when it comes to wine. It's not that the flaw needs to be forgiven; it's the opposite. We like the flaw (or so-called flaw) because it makes the thing interesting, animate, approachable. I mean, my Christmas tree is a little droopy on one side, and it's definitely not as picturesque as a fake tree would be, but it smells so good, and it's alive. If perfection is attainable, then it can't be miraculous, only improbable. The assumption of imperfection is the precondition for the miracle.

But buyer's guides aren't concerned with miracles; they just want to throw a lifeline to busy consumers who don't know what to buy or whether they can trust their local retailer to tell them. Fair enough. But must the scales be (or appear to be) so exact? Back when Pierre Rovani worked with Robert Parker, I asked him why it wouldn't suffice to simply have groups—fair/good/very good/excellent/superb—and rank the wines in order of preference within those groups. "Good question," answered Pierre, "so what you're proposing is a five-point scale." Touché! Hoist on my own Bâtard. My mistake was to debate the issue on the terms of the point defenders, whose logic is self-enforcing and circular. Critics have a responsibility to take a definite stand, and scoring forces them to do so. They can't hide behind vague or nebulous language. The wine is an 88, and that's all there is to it. Please read my prose too, they say, because that's where I get to use all my flavor associations and groovy locutions, but the score's the mojo.

The role of the critic in this Weltanschauung is to handicap the entrants and tell you who won the race and by how many lengths. It's all very clear, and its intentions are benign. And its logic isn't false, only incomplete.

First, any point system misleads in direct proportion to its affect of precision. The more exact, the more misleading. We all know that wine is a moving target. Even industrial wine, made to be predictable, is a moving target. Why? Because *we* are a moving target. We feel differently on different days, at different times of day. Our bodies are changeable, our palates are changeable. The overly tart salad dressing we ate at lunch will affect every wine we taste all afternoon. It doesn't matter how responsible we try to be; the moment we assign an absolute value to a wine, we have misled. And the more specific we purport to be, the more we mislead.

Yes, experienced professional tasters will allow for the variables I cited (and others I didn't cite), but even if they wanted to give themselves a little wiggle room, their hands are tied if they're selling *omniscience*. Every time someone asks Robert Parker if he has ever made a mistake or changed or regretted a score, I have to laugh. Ask the oracle all you like whether his advice or predictions are ever false, but he won't remain the oracle if he answers, "Oh, well . . . yes, my advice has sometimes proved unwise." Oh, really? Then why should I listen to it? To remain credible you have to affect (or feign) omniscience, and wine does not welcome omniscience. So we have some cognitive dissonance.

Let's also remember we're setting an example for readers, whom we are training to consider wine in terms of how many points to "give" it, and this is mischievous at best. Even if I yield the point that scores are a necessary evil—which, by the way,

I don't—how many innocent consumers of wine journals are savvy enough to know that the writer may have to use points but the *reader* doesn't? Sadly, the metamessage of point obsession is that "scoring" wines is the sine qua non of wine appreciation.

Oh, lighten up, I hear you say. What's the harm? The harm is subtle because its symptoms appear mild, but the long-term effects are pernicious.

Here's a quote I like, from John Berger's essay "The White Bird": "The aesthetic moment offers hope that we are less alone, we are more deeply inserted into existence than the course of a single life would lead us to believe." Wine is just such an aesthetic moment. It doesn't have to be great wine, it only has to be *true* wine, connected not to the factory but to the family, not to the lab but to the earth. We're invited to respond with our souls, for wines like these will open doors by which we enter a larger world than we normally inhabit. All we need is to be available for the experience.

But we will squander this opportunity if, in that very moment, we are scrolling through our egos to see how many points we're going to "award" the wine. Has no one noticed how suspiciously pompous even the language is? "We *awarded* Château Bluebols *xx* points on our 100-point scale." How nice for you. How many points did the wine give *you*, Ace? Is the whole thing really about *you?* Does the cosmos really care at all how many points you bestowed upon some mere wine? That wine was a *gift* to you, and all you can do is "evaluate" it as if it were a DVD player or a Dustbuster.

Among the various online wine bulletin boards this is a hot topic, as you might suppose. I remember one gentleman writing (and I'm paraphrasing now) that he grew *into* using the 100-

point scale when he felt his palate was mature enough. This poor lamb is running blindly toward the cliffs.

Ah, but maybe he's right. After all, I've been using the 100-point scale to assess literature ever since I turned fifty. I'd finally read enough to know exactly how good stuff was. I give Molly Bloom's soliloquy at least a 94. That ranks it among the great literary scenes of all time, along with Stavrogin's confession (95), Levin's day with the threshers (97), Gerald's walk to his death in the mountains (94+), and the death of Ben Gant (99). I didn't used to give scores to great scenes in literature. But eventually I came to realize that all pleasure was in effect a commodity, and I *owed* it to myself to quantify the little suckers. So now, when I read novels, I'm constantly thinking, *How many points is this scene worth?* I judge on imagery, diction, overall rhetoric, whether it advances the plotline and/or develops the characters, and finally on how close it brings me to tears. Eyes barely moist gets 90. Eyes barely moist plus a catch in the throat gets 91–92. Eyes full of tears but no drippage gets 93–94. Between one and three tears slipping down my face earns a 95–96, and full-bore blubbering earns the highest scores. Since I started doing this I have just gotten so much more from all these great books!

Why stop at books? Let's declare all of our pleasures subject to a precise analysis of their *extent* on an absolute scale. Then we can see what 100-point *joy* is about. "I can't possibly be happier than this"—are you *sure?*

Perhaps we're at cross-purposes. I'd rather that wine writers tried to deepen people's love of wine, but they do what they can and what they've trained their readers to expect. Robert Parker may be a convenient target for my frustration, but the truth is more complicated because he has done the wine world enormous good over his storied career, more good than whatever harm he may have caused. But I also believe, as St. Peter opens the gates to admit Mr. Parker, he'll peer through Bob's valise, pull out the folder marked "The 100-Point Scale," and say, "I'll just hold on to this. You won't be needing it here."

"Globalization" in Wine: Menace or Straw Man?

Fifty years from now it may seem quaint that a single critic wielded so much power, let alone that he became the crux of a contention that wines around the world, fashioned to appeal to his taste, were all beginning to taste the same. The shorthand for this complicated question is "globalization." A lot of people fear it's a threat to the very existence of fine wine. Other people dismiss it as a slogan for a polemic. Reason abides on both sides of this issue—to a point.

If you still doubt that civil discourse is in mortal peril, just take a peek at how this discussion is carried on, especially on the Internet. I shall try, in my uniquely unctuous fashion, to state the case for both sides and see if there's any common ground.

In my wilder fantasies I allow myself to believe this book might be read many years from now, and in the unlikely event that I am right, I wonder how readers in the future will see this issue ramify, if it does at all. Will wines have become stultifyingly homogeneous? Will the very name Robert Parker be anything beyond a historical blip? For it is Mr. Parker who, fairly or unfairly, has become the lightning rod for this tussle, and because I do admire (and like) him, I wish I could say he has risen to the occasion and comported himself with the civility incumbent upon a grand elder of the wine world. Alas, he hasn't. Each time he has written about this issue, whether in magazines (his own or others') or on his Web board, his many reasonable points are frequently diminished by a tone of defensiveness, invective, and name-calling. Persons taking views contrary to his are accused of membership in the "pleasure police" (since evidently they, unlike Parker, have a taste for wines that don't give pleasure?), peering over our collective shoulders to ensure we're all drinking lots of tight-lipped Calvinist wines. He has also trotted out that hoariest of labels, "pseudo-intellectual," to characterize his opponents. Curious. Granting the point that pseudo-intellectuals actually do exist, so do bona fide intellectuals, and I wonder how Mr. Parker tells them apart.

Wherever there is power there's also resentment of power, and a lot of power has accrued to Robert Parker. Most of the criticisms lobbed his way are unwarranted, and many of them are the incoherent irritations of people without a fraction of Parker's experience and essential seriousness. Yet some of the challenges have merit.

A few years ago, a very fine book was published, Lawrence Osborne's *The Accidental Connoisseur*, in which, under the guise of a search for "taste," the author raised the issue of whether wines the world over were endangered by a kind of uniformity of type. He did it obliquely and with exquisite slyness, and raised only the faintest of ripples. Who, after all, reads books?

Shortly thereafter a friend of his (and mine) named Jonathan Nossiter made a film called *Mondovino* that tackled the same question, this time with direct and polemical passion. Now the fur was flying. People see movies. Nossiter was accorded all the horror and loathing invited by anyone who challenges the basic orthodoxy of his time. Much of the criticism was petulant and insulting, as it often is when one strikes a nerve.

But *why* would this issue strike a nerve? My usual theory is that we overreact when we feel something we value is threatened. But the style of wine that makes Osborne, Nossiter, and myself uneasy is so prevalent that no reasonable person could claim it's under any kind of siege. No, there's some shadow here. There is reason on both sides of this dialectic, but the argumentative tone from one side tends toward hectoring and bullying, and their argument is strong enough that such tactics are unwarranted. Unless some people simply are bullies and never learned how to disagree respectfully. Interesting, then, their taste for bellicose wines. . . .

I'll try to summarize each camp's position. My biases are clear, but I have empathy for the other side, and I think they deserve better than the voice they themselves have often used. First, to define the term: *globalization* denotes a phenomenon in which wines from around the world are striving toward a similar formula, in order to appeal to Mr. Parker's taste. (This is perhaps a misuse of the broader term *globalization*—though there are concerns over multinationals in the wine world—but it has been appropriated as a shorthand term for the basic debate.) The formula, as I understand it, favors a lot of ripeness (and the high alcohol it brings) and overtly expressive flavor, *gushing* flavor in many cases, along with a certain sheen, a lashing of oak, a sense of "sweetness" based not on residual sugar but on what's called phenolic or "physiological" ripeness, achieved when the grape's skins and stems are ripe. These wines tend to be straightforward, symmetrical, and generous—and pleasurable in basic sensual terms. *Hedonistic* is an adjective much beloved among proponents of this wine style. Who doesn't like hedonism?

Globalization's critics are suspicious that wine is becoming too uniform, and they worry about the rote application of formulas or recipes to bring about the prevailing styles. They wonder whether the quirky or idiosyncratic wines they like are in danger of being crowded out by the new buxom starlets from hither and yon. For the sake of brevity, I'll call these folks "romantics."

Proponents of globalization—let's call them "pragmatists"—argue that wine in the aggregate has never been better, and that good wines are now hailing from a greater variety of places than ever before. They do not perceive a problem, and think a bunch of fussbudgets are trying to rain on their picnic.

I don't believe it's reasonable to deny their argument. There are certainly many more competent and tasty wines (and concomitantly fewer rustic, dirty, or yucky wines) than there were twenty years ago. The romantics' argument would be stronger if it conceded this point. The floor has been raised, and wine overall is the best it has ever been.

But even if the floor *has* been raised, has the ceiling been lowered? The romantics fear it has. They also fear that the pragmatists are too concerned with results and less concerned with how the game is played, as long as they are entertained. During the height of this argument the steroids scandal hit baseball, threatening the integrity of the sport. But too little attention is paid to the role we ourselves play in bringing such things about. We'd rather wish it all away. Honestly, a lot of us *enjoy* the spectacle of Herculean demigods bulked up on chemicals hitting baseballs five hundred feet. This becomes our ideal, and players who embody the ideal command the highest salaries and put the most butts in the seats. They're also the envy of other, less "enhanced" players, some of whom seek to climb aboard the gravy train.

The metaphor is temptingly apt. There is no doubt that the prevailing recipe for modern wines with commercial aspirations is easy to apply and effective at churning out ripe, sweet wines with softly embedded tannin, large-scale and concentrated, regardless of where they came from or what grapes made them. I believe the pragmatists care less about how such wines get that way than they do about being titillated and thrilled by juiced-up slugger wines hitting flavor out of the park.

Should we conduct this discussion in grayer shades? Quite possibly. Parker has often expressed his admiration for moderate, elegant, temperate wines. He typically scores them in the high eighties, and he has told me he wishes more people prized and drank such wines. Yet he must be aware that the commodity called a "Parker score" effectively damns such wines with faint praise. And although Parker himself might admire them well enough, he reserves his love and his most emotional prose for their bigger, more "hedonistic" cousins.

Thus a particular idiom becomes the prevailing idiom, because everyone wants the scores and the financial juju they engender. And superficially, this flavor idiom is persuasive, though it is at best singular and at worst predatory of other flavor idioms. The romantics struggle against the monofaceted and bland. They (we) are innately wary of uniformity, as it is contrary to nature. We're also alert to an insidious effect uniformity can create. We risk becoming passive, infantilized, dulled;

when all things are a single way, there's less reason to pay attention, as they can't surprise us anymore.

The pragmatists will claim I'm overstating the case; none of them argues that all wines should taste the same. (Few of them see that many wines *are* starting to taste distressingly similar.) Fair enough. Yet they often accuse romantics of wishing to return us to some imagined Eden of dirty, weird, and rustic wines—which, they sneer, we excuse by citing terroir. It's the classic war of straw men. Is there a sane way through?

I ask the pragmatists to consider this question: How, in a world of wines made by an indisputably prevailing set of practices in pursuit of a predictable result, will there still be room for the quirky, the angular, the evocative—the heirloom varieties of the wine world? Or are we content to let such wines disappear? Is this the wine world—is it the *world*—we wish to live in? If not, how do we prevent it?

I place no value judgments on "modern" methods per se, many of which are benign. But some amount to outright falsification. Yet this isn't the time to inveigh against even those— some people think it's fine for ballplayers to use steroids. I'm asking the pragmatists to consider the consequences inherent in their belief system. It's certainly true that good wine's coming from many regions that were unknown and unavailable twenty years ago. Yet to my palate this signifies very little, for many of these wines join an international glom of hot-climate wines whose effect calls to mind the old British phrase "much of a muchness." So there's yet another source for the same kind of wines we already have plenty of. I'm not sure why I should care.

And much of what we see from these new sources is little

more than plausibly attractive in a style we already know. It took the Old World many hundreds of years of trial and error to learn which varieties and what kind of winemaking would best capture terroir. The New World displays its customary derring-do, and presumes it can learn these lessons in the first thirty years. It can't. There are no short cuts.

In cuisine there comes a point of ennui when all you see are the same luxury ingredients in nearly interchangeable preparations. Monday it's squab stuffed with foie gras in a truffle *nage;* Tuesday it's squab stuffed with truffles in a foie gras emulsion; Wednesday it's truffle-crusted foie gras in a squab jus, and eventually it becomes a meaningless farandole of dishes constituting the "luxury dining experience," which you could have in Hong Kong or Los Angeles or Las Vegas or New York or Kuala Lumpur. It becomes a membrane separating you from the world, swaddling you in a specious bliss, seducing your senses, starving your soul. I think of this when I taste yet another big wine indistinguishable from myriad other big wines, and yes, it might well be superior to the odd little wine that grew there before—*might* be—but what does it signify? That people in lots of different places can suss the formula and apply it? I'm not sure why I should care.

Thus it doesn't really matter that good wines are coming from a greater number of places than ever, if most of those wines are cut from the same pattern. A mere grape or place-name we haven't seen before is immaterial unless the wine offers a *taste* we haven't tasted before. That's the crux of the romantics' argument.

Sometimes in our righteous passion, we romantics can also forget to be reasonable. We *must* yield the point that the floor has indeed risen for wine quality, and this is a good thing. Our struggle is to applaud this while also protecting the ceiling. And that "ceiling" isn't merely new stratospheres of hedonism (even *more* ripe fruit, even *more* intensity, always *more*), but instead it is those wines that are uniquely great, and significantly unique. There are very good Syrahs and Cabernet Francs coming from Switzerland's Valais, but these offer less to cherish than the singular and remarkable Humagne Blancs and Amignes—which don't grow anywhere else, and which taste lovely.

What other great wine is great as the best Loire Chenins are great? As the best Barolos? As the best Jurançons, the best Nahe Rieslings, the best grand cru Chablis, the best Grüner Veltliners? Ultimately it isn't greatness we must protect, it is uniqueness. Preserve the unique, and greatness takes care of itself.

Here's how it happens. To the extent that drinkers value distinctiveness in our wines, the people who make them will learn there's a market for their *particular* wines, and we'll have fostered a community of vintners who cherish what is uniquely theirs. This doesn't mean all of their wines will be great. But it is the basis, the prerequisite for greatness.

The pragmatists would do well to remember the risks inherent in their aesthetics. And we romantics need also to realize we *have* misapplied the concept of terroir to excuse feeble or flawed wines. This concept is precious, and we need to respect it and use it with care. And we romantics have sometimes been guilty of a form of Puritanism; if it tastes unpleasant, it must be virtuous.

But the pragmatists ought to acknowledge that theirs isn't the only form of pleasure. There are worlds alongside the sensual. Wine can be intellectually and even spiritually nourishing. People can desire those things, and the true hedonist isn't threatened by them.

I wonder if we cannot all unite behind the value of diversity. I'd like to think so, though sometimes I despair. From my high-rise window I often see raptors soaring on the thermals, especially in fall and winter, and I love watching them swoop in elegant arcs across the sky. But I could never imagine myself feeling, *I sure love these hawks, and all the other big birds, eagles, buzzards, falcons, and it would be great if all birds were like these because they give me so much pleasure.* What about the assertive, gaudy cardinal? The pensive heron? The silly woodpecker? The delicate little finch? I want to live in a world of thousands of *different* wines, wines whose differences are deeper than zip code, each of them revealing fragments of the unending variety and fascination of this lovely green world on which we walk.

six

OF PLACES AND GRAPES

When you look at bottles of Mosel wine from the 1960s and before, even from the best vineyards, you will hardly ever see the word *Riesling*.

Burgundy labels do not contain the words *Pinot Noir* or *Chardonnay*. Vouvray and Savennières do not proclaim *Chenin Blanc*, and neither Barolo nor Barbaresco says *Nebbiolo*. The classic Old World model was always based on the *place* from which a wine hailed. We needed to learn the name of the grape.

When wine was marketed in the New World, it was first labeled with place-names to which it wasn't entitled. Thus *Chablis* was stripped of its meaning as a particular place in northern France, and diminished to a spurious synonym for white wine, just as *Sauterne [sic]* was used to denote a sweet wine. It is still being done with *Champagne*. I dream that someday a vigneron in the Languedoc will bottle something he calls Napa Valley Cabernet Sauvignon, and when the Californians react in righteous outrage, our canny hero will mildly say, "Well, you know, here in France we understand *Napa Valley* to be a generic term for any Cabernet that grows under a hot sun"—and then the fur will fly.

Later the more ambitious and conscientious New World vintners sought to distinguish themselves from the rabble who used "borrowed" place-names, and thus was born the era of varietal labeling. And consumers who began their wine education with New World items got the message that Grape Is All. Alas, in doing so they missed something crucial about wine. Burgundy is a reality apart from the grapes that happen to grow there. You'll know when you visit. It's *Burgundy*, not merely "Pinot Noir from eastern France." To focus on the grape detached from the context of place is to lose the forest for the trees.

Wine historians more erudite than I have detailed the often centuries-long, painstaking trial and error by which it was eventually understood that a particular grape seemed to make the best wines in a given spot. But we need to remember what guided the search. It wasn't only the desire for the "best" possible wine; it was also the desire to hear the voice of the land in the form of flavor. You might protest that this is just poetry, but when the land was worked by hand, the worker was closer to it, more aware of its life and of his own role in keeping it vital and healthy. Arriving at the best choice of grape is like tuning the dial on an old-fashioned radio; you tweak and shift in tiny increments, and suddenly there's a clear signal. When a grape feels at home, its voice is clear as it narrates the text the land has written.

Once the choice of grape is established and codified, one starts to look at the different ways it expresses itself in various plots of land within a region. This expression involves more than ripening alone, because the grape would not have been chosen at all if it wouldn't ripen. Vintners couldn't survive. There has to be an accord among grape, land, and person whereby all three of them know that things are in their proper places. (I realize such statements raise the hackles of some of the linear technocrats populating much of the New World, but I am at the very least *intrigued* by Michael Pollan's audacious notion in *The Botany of Desire* that we didn't choose the plants we cultivate, the plants chose us. I wouldn't insist that this is true—or True—but I'm willing to believe in a symbiosis between cultivar and cultivated whereby it's hard to recall who asked whom to the party.)

We always return to the place—because the place isn't the same as other places, and sometimes a place is different from any other place. If you are growing the same grape throughout a region, place becomes the crucial variable. Yes, I know about clonal variations in grape varieties—there are lots of small rogue variables, and more in some regions than in others. But taking, say, the Nahe region of Germany, you have basically two clones of Riesling at play, which no one could tell apart by flavor alone. But beneath the vines is a Valhalla for the amateur of locale, a geological miasma, with soil changing every few meters. Spend a day tasting Nahe Rieslings, and then try to defend the notion that grape is supremely important. Place seems to matter just as much.

All Nahe Rieslings taste like Riesling, and no one would dispute that Riesling is the best variety for the region's prevailing conditions. But the taste of Riesling per se is of little import here; it is the astonishing variation in flavors arising from one vineyard and its neighbor that fascinate us. One site may be flowery and its neighbor fruitier, and *their* neighbor more minerally, or there may be variations among fruits, flowers, and minerals, and these variations can occur in sites just a few meters apart. It seems miraculous. But it's also fun, because we humans enjoy contrasting, comparing, and cataloguing when the theme is so replete with telling distinctions. And one of the things we discover is how easily we recognize the consequences of extraordinary land. A great vineyard's wines are not merely riper; they are in every way more expressive, more complex, more beautiful. They may not be riper at all. But there is something singular about them, a libretto to accompany the varietal music.

I sometimes call this the grand cru effect, something profound that isn't derived from fruit, and where such fruit as may be present is absorbed into a deeper whole. Grand cru lands are the earth's erogenous zones, some confluence of nerve endings that tingle at the touch of sunlight. It's why the old ones didn't include the grape name on the label—the place mattered more.

If I'm asked to choose among grape varieties, or to identify the ones I think are ordinary, good, or great, I don't stop at the tastes of the wines. There are some grapes whose wines taste distressingly similar wherever they're planted, and some that taste wonderful in certain places and yucky in others. I like the temperamental ones. To cite a common example, Cabernet Sauvignon; there's no question that great wines are made from this variety (though the greatest employ other varieties as blending partners), but there's also no question that they are all great *in the same way*, regardless of where they're grown. And their innate style is so seductive that they are grown all over the place, and most of the time the place is trampled underfoot by Cabernet's overwhelming "varietality." If a decent taster can't tell a Napa Cabernet from a St. Julien, then the world has something to grieve, not celebrate.

Chardonnay is the other variety most conducive to ennui—maybe we should refer to it as *Chard-ennui*. It has certainly flooded the world with oceans of stupefyingly mundane, "spoofulated" wines. (I adore that coinage, which so perfectly evokes wines that are amped up or "pimped" with extraneous flavor designed to get high scores.) Chardonnay seems to lend itself to palate pandering, and this is a shame because there's at least one place where it speaks with profound, articulate force—Chablis. But consider: Chablis is considered an "undervalued" wine, and it's because it's too expressive and idiosyncratic for a wide market to appreciate. I sometimes wonder if a talented but inexperienced taster, given Chablis for the first time, would even know it was made from Chardonnay. I also wonder whether Chardonnay is ineluctable to the identity of Chablis. Imagine if Sauvignon Blanc and Aligoté were "promoted" from the second-class land they grow in now, and were introduced to the premier or grand crus. What if Riesling were planted in Chablis? But if we assume Chablis is what it is *because of* Chardonnay, then we have to conclude that Chardonnay is at least *capable* of greatness if it's grown where it belongs. Champagne also comes to mind, and some of the most resplendently beautiful and complex wines you can taste are old Blanc de Blancs.

But what of this silly notion of Chablis planted with Riesling? It can sometimes be difficult to separate grape variety from terroir, because terroir speaks, of course, *through* the grape, and because it is quite rare to see more than one grape planted in great terroirs. Rare, but not impossible.

Consider Austria's Wachau. This region and Alsace are the only places I can call to mind where grand cru vineyards are often planted with more than one variety, in this case Grüner

Veltliner along with Riesling. Yes, there are certain sites (most often flat vineyards on alluvial soil) where Riesling doesn't belong but where Grüner Veltliner makes at least middling-good entry-level wine. But many of the top vineyards, such as Kellerberg, Steinertal, Loibenberg, and Achleiten, are planted with both, offering the drinker a rare chance to see terroir *abstracted* from grape. And what do we see?

We see that these grand crus have identities so powerful as to supersede grape flavors—not to quash them, but to put them in their proper place. It happens that I taste Steinertal and Loibenberg each year from both varieties as rendered by the angelic Leo Alzinger. And believe me, Steinertal is *always* itself, "green," wildly herbal, piercingly limey, narrated by Riesling in this glass and Veltliner in that one. Same for the smoky, tropical-flavored Loibenberg. It compels a few of those lovely unanswerable questions that make wine such fun. If Riesling didn't exist, would we taste those Veltliners and think, *This is the perfect grape for these soils; how could anything be better?* What do the two varieties have in common that lets them transmit terroir so precisely? Is it their deep root systems and late ripening? Can we know at all? Even more curiously, Riesling was rather scarce in the Wachau until the advent of drip irrigation; the sere terraces were formerly planted with Neuburger. But when irrigation enabled Riesling to grow, grow it did, and the land found its noblest voice of all.

My favorite grapes are those so woven into where they grow that grape and place are no longer extricable, like when you pull one thread and the whole sweater unravels. But when pressed to consider grape alone, there's no question in my mind at all which is the greatest grape, of either color: Riesling.

If there's any problem with Riesling, it's that it will spoil you for anything else. Hans Altmann of the Jamek estate in the Wachau once said, "There are times when I think that any sip of wine that isn't Riesling is wasted." Riesling is so digitally precise, so finely articulate, so pixilated and pointillist in detail that other wines seem almost mute by comparison.

And if you grow Riesling where it belongs, its wines come out of the ground already perfect. They are inimical to the diddlings of hotshot "winemakers" eager to strut their cellar chops. Riesling resists the face-lift depilation tummy-tuck breast implant school of vinification. Riesling does more than just imply terroir: it subsumes its own identity as fruit into the greater meaning of soil, land, and place. Riesling knows soil more intimately than any other grape, perhaps because it ripens so late in the fall and is thus on the vine longer than other varieties, and because it thrives in poor soils with deep bedrock strata into which it can sink its probing roots. Riesling is beloved of all who grow it for being so cooperative—the furthest thing from a diva. It survives all but the most brutal frost, is hearty in its resistance to disease, and yields well without sacrificing flavor—perhaps because it ripens late in the fall when everything is taut and crisp and golden. Riesling wines are the afterglow of the contented world.

Riesling will thrive in any idiom. Its dry wines can be superbly focused and expressive, its almost-dry wines can be even longer and more elegant in flavor, its going-on-sweet wines are the apotheosis of fruit and mineral flavor, and its truly sweet wines are uniquely piquant.

It is also food's best friend. If, from this day forward, you swore to drink nothing but Riesling and eat only the things that went with it, your diet would hardly change, unless it consists of rare unsauced red meat and eggplant Parmesan. You would also discover the wine you'd been seeking for any number of dishes you'd thought were too "difficult" for wine. Riesling wine may be the most complex in the world, but it's never boastful; it is a team player, there to make food taste better. Riesling isn't shy or demure, it is modest and tactful, but if you pay attention to it—which it never *insists* you do—you'll discover how deep these still waters run. Ironic, isn't it? The grape with the most to say is the very one that speaks in a moderate voice.

Riesling often provides two things wine drinkers need: acidity and low alcohol. Acidity is innate to the berry, and it's acidity that creates the greatest magic at the table. Low alcohol is a gift to the drinker who'd rather not to be semicomatose by the time the main course arrives. Riesling needs a certain ripeness, but once this is reached it needs no more, and its value is not demonstrated by ripeness per se. Nor do we sacrifice flavor as we appreciate Riesling's sheer drinkability. There is no wine on earth with more flavor than a tingly little Mosel Kabinett with its 8 percent alcohol.

Riesling's aging capacity is legendary; no other grape undergoes a similar metamorphosis over time. When you taste a great old Riesling you can barely infer the taste of the young wine. If you saw a butterfly without knowing whence it came, would you assume it derived from a caterpillar?

Riesling is also particular about where it's planted. It is at home in the Rheinland (Germany and Alsace) and in Austria, and there are stirring signs it may be at home in certain parts of Australia—time will tell. It doesn't pout when it's planted in "foreign" places; it just goes mute, giving a simple wine that can cloy if it's too ripe or too sweet. Riesling is aristocratic, yet it's also down-to-earth because it knows it is translating a text that was written in the ground. Its fundamental humility is reflected in the people who grow it, love it, and delight in it.

Similar claims are often made for Pinot Noir, and people who love Riesling almost always love Pinot Noir too. As do I. But the argument for Pinot Noir is clouded by the complexity of its winemaking parameters. Riesling on the other hand is simple. It begs for (and receives) a less-is-more approach in the cellar because all of its flavor is already there. You can clean the juice in different ways, though the best growers just let gravity do it instead of agitating with centrifuges, filters, or separators. You can crush and press it if you want a chewier, more tactile wine, or you can press the whole clusters if you want a gossamer, crystalline wine. You can ferment *au naturel* with ambient yeasts or else use cultured yeasts, and only the very best tasters could tell the two apart. You can make it in steel if you want to preserve the utmost primary fruit and mineral, or you can make it in *neutral* wood if you want more vinous, tertiary flavors. But these are all issues not of text, but of font.

The question of minerality is inherent to Riesling, because the variety is, in its essence, more mineral than fruit. The Riesling genre is one of a mineral-tasting wine into which are woven various strands of fruit, depending on site and vintage. But there's a lot of (sometimes willful) distortion of the M-word. It's a lightning rod for an often contentious debate that's usually conducted dishonestly.

We don't know whether the flavor we call mineral results from an actual trace of dissolved literal mineral in the wine. I personally think it doesn't. More accurately, I'm agnostic on the question, because it hasn't (yet?) been demonstrated to be true. But *something* is creating that definite, tangible flavor, and we don't know what or how. Tasters of varying types and temperaments use all kinds of phrases to describe it—"crushed rocks," "wet stones," among others. I once heard a beginner describe the taste of Champagne as like "licking the shell of an oyster," which is almost literally true: chalk is nothing more than an agglomeration of the shells and skeletons of sea creatures, and Champagne grows on chalk.

I think minerality is perhaps the noblest of flavors *because* it is metaphorical, and metaphors work on the imagination. Fruitiness, on the other hand, is a simple matter of identification—it tastes like this apple or that pear, this peach or that melon—and once you've identified it, you don't think anymore. Minerality in contrast is suggestive, even mysterious. We don't know what it is or how it got there. We grow alert to the loveliness of the unknowable.

I don't drink Riesling all the time, though I'd hardly mind doing so. Still, there are occasions when something more pagan is called for, and that's when I summon my guiltiest of wine pleasures: Scheurebe.

Scheurebe *(shoy-ray-beh)*, often shortened to "Scheu," is Riesling just after it read the Kama Sutra. Put another way, Scheu is what Riesling would be if Riesling were a transvestite. If Riesling expresses all that is Noble and Good, Scheu offers all that is Dirty and Fun. It is Riesling's evil, horny twin.

The variety arose from a crossing done in 1916 by a botanist,

Georg Scheu. It is certainly emphatic next to Riesling, but it takes what is essentially a Riesling *type* and ladles a wicked blast of sauce over it. Scheu's usual associations are pink grapefruit, sage, cassis, and elderflower, and when it isn't ripe enough you'll probably think of cat pee. But Scheu has magic tricks it won't explain. However blatant it may be, it can also show remarkable class and elegance, and it will work with food for which Riesling may be too delicate. Every Asian-fusion place in the world should have fifteen Scheurebes on its list. It makes an excellent dry wine (it needs to be ripe enough or it can seem bitter), a wonderful barely sweet wine, and an amazingly exciting sweet-ish wine in which its earthy-spicy-floral thing seems to twirl the palate away from the sweetness.

Tastes differ, of course, and what's sizzling and emphatic to me might be blatant and vulgar to you, but if you love Scheu you're really in a kind of thrall to it. It has little of Riesling's spiritual depths, but neither does Riesling have Scheu's erotic power. We need both for a balanced diet. Yet however writhing and sweaty our Scheu may be, it doesn't preclude a certain poise, a certain stature, a certain . . . dare one say, aristocracy? Scheu may be blatantly flirtatious, but it's far from ignoble, and I doubt there's an equivalent in the world of wine.

Scheu will keep, but it doesn't change with age as Riesling does. It's more partial to some soils than to others, but not as sensitive as Riesling. Indeed, it enjoys conditions similar to Riesling, which is probably why we don't see more Scheu; given the choice, most vintners would plant Riesling, which has a wider audience and fetches a higher price. Scheu is almost never minerally, yet planted in a grand cru it can restrain its extravagance and offer a complexity of its own. It's fun enough to be a wine geek's guilty secret, but fine enough not to insult one's intelligence. Still, it must be said that Scheu expresses *itself* more than its place, and that's why, though it can be very good, it is almost never great.

The greatest grapes are those that carry you away, and among these is the singular and searching Chenin Blanc. An extremely finicky fellow, Chenin Blanc seems to give its best only in a small fillet of France along the Loire River and its tributaries.

If Riesling is a brilliant wine, Chenin is more *luminous;* its light softer, more dispersed. If Riesling is vigorous and energetic, Chenin is more stately. It reflects the sweet light of the place it is grown, where the most classical and perfect French is spoken, and there is a corresponding perfection in the voice of fine Chenin. It has yet to make great wine anyplace else, and there isn't all that much truly great Chenin even along the Loire. But when you find one it can be soul-expanding as few other wines—few other *things*—can be.

It's usually described in terms of quince, rosewater, and lanolin, and I often find the smell of a blown-out candle. (I remember an '82 Coulée de Serrant that smelled like a whole church's worth of blown-out candles, and I half-expected a procession of monks to parade through the dining room.) Chenin is also more yielding than Riesling, but it can't be called soft. Everything about it is allusive.

As I write I find I am also thinking about Piemonte's Nebbiolo, which offers something of the same experience. If Chenin sings of the light of the Loire with its gauzy, breathy voice, Nebbiolo sings of the fogs after which it is named, and of the earth and the animals and the dark flowers scattered over it. Truffles, violets, leather, but none of it blatant, and all of it in a murmuring thrall of beauty. Great Barolo and Barbaresco, Nebbiolo's utmost expression, are perfectly inscrutable and wonderfully mysterious. To be sure, a lot of the wines are made in modern idioms specifically to be *more* visibly and tangibly flavorsome, but the old-school wines hold a séance on your palate.

Indeed, thinking of Chenin and Nebbiolo in the same breath, I find them kin, or perhaps they are the king and queen of a rare hidden kingdom of ghosts whose dreams they allow you to hear. An old Barolo or an old Vouvray or Savennières offers an invitation with no equivalent in the world of flavor; they will take you to the wellspring, to your own wellspring. I have often felt them melt away the membrane by which I'm separated from the world. This can be unsettling.

Such wines are not easy to find. We drink them just a few times in our lives. But we never forget them, or the places they lead us to. A few weeks before writing this, I dined with my wife in the Austrian Alps, in a restaurant whose chef worked with wild local herbs. We drank two stunningly brilliant dry Rieslings that buzzed and crackled like neon, and then we drank a '93 Barolo from Bruno Giacosa, a so-so vintage but fully mature. To go from the giddy, giggling clarity of those Rieslings into the warm murmuring depths of that Barolo was moving in a way I grope to describe. It was as if the Riesling prepared us somehow, it reassured us that everything was *visible*, and then that smoky twilight red wine . . . like the moment it gets too dark to read, and you get up to turn on the light and see a tiny scythe of moon low on the horizon and you open the window and smell the burning leaves, night is coming on, and there will be dinner and the sweet smells of cooking, and then at last the utter dark, and the heart beating darkly beside you.

I did something I seldom do—got just a bit plastered that evening, for which I blamed the altitude, though I knew better. But I wasn't letting a drop of that Barolo go to waste. It stirred the deepest tenderness because it possessed the deepest tenderness. Tenderness is different from affection. Tenderness has a penumbra of sadness, or so I have always felt. Tenderness says there is an irreducible difference separating us, although we might wish to dissolve it. But we can't quite, however close together we draw; it is there as a condition of being. And then we see the sadness that surrounds us, wanting to merge into one another and finding it impossible; and then there comes a compassion, it is this way for all of us sad hopeful beings; and *then* the membrane melts away, even without touching it melts away.

I don't know how it is for other people, but I myself know a wine is great when it makes me sad. Not a bitter, grieving sadness, but the thing the Germans call *Weltschmerz*, "the pain of the world," a fine kind of melancholy.

I pause before writing about Pinot Noir, and I don't think I have much to say about it. Some have called it the "red Riesling," which makes sense. Burgundy, which is more than merely Pinot Noir, is a heartrendingly beautiful and frustratingly irregular being. Pinot Noir is difficult in the vineyard, and persnickety overall. And what sensible wine drinker doesn't love it? Burgundy is satisfying and life-affirming; I couldn't live without it, I adore it young and I love it old and when I'm a hugely successful author I'll be able to afford it more often.

Forgive my brevity regarding Pinot Noir. It is wonderful. It is suave yet rustic, polished yet earthy, intricate yet forthright, and somehow it is both sensual and, at its best, mystic. Great Burgundy seems to claw right into your viscera, yet its call is angelic. We talk about Cabernet as we talk about sports, but we talk about Pinot Noir as we talk about religion. If I could drink all the great Burgundy I ever wanted, at a price of having to forgo Cabernet for the rest of my life, I'd miss Cabernet, but I'd do it. I would not do the reverse.

And then there's my beloved Muscat. Of all the wines I know, good dry (or just off-dry) Muscat is the most lovable. I realize that love is subjective and irreducible, and that you might not love it as I do, or maybe not at all. I won't understand you, but there it is. But even knowing my drooling crush on Muscat is just me being me, I think there's a claim to stake for this variety.

Muscat can restore us to an almost primordial innocence of the senses. I was watching a young father wheeling his little boy in a stroller. He picked a dandelion and handed it to his child, who was just transfixed, grinning and beaming at the common little flower, his entire being numinous with delight. It doesn't take a great thinker to observe that we lose this quality as we grow up, just as it doesn't require a remarkable soul to miss it. But we don't have to meekly surrender. Muscat can bring it back.

When I drink good Muscat it is always one of those almost precognitive moments of recovering an embedded and inaccessible memory of how *wonderful* a thing can taste. It's as if you entered the butterfly house and suddenly all those colorful little guys were flittering around and you were dumbstruck by how comically gorgeous nature can be.

You do have to watch out, as all Muscat isn't the same. In Alsace it can be a blend of the so-called Yellow Muscat (a.k.a. the small-berried Muscat) and an inferior variety called Muscat-Ottonel, inferior by dint of its more specious perfume and softer structure. Yellow Muscat is the very bitch to grow, which tends to imply a degree of utopian fanaticism among those who brave its challenges of late ripening and uncertain yields. You can find wines made with 100 percent Gelber Muskateller (as it is called) in Germany and Austria, and they can make you weightless with happiness.

The last among my favorite varieties is, of course, Austria's Grüner Veltliner, henceforth abbreviated GrüVe. Why "of course"? Because it is a hugely important variety both for its flavor and also for its *usefulness*.

You may recall my effusions on behalf of Austria's magnificent dry Rieslings. They are her finest wines. I rejoice in each one of them I have in my cellar. And yet I drink three bottles of GrüVe for every one Austrian Riesling. Grüner Veltliner is by far the most flexible dry white wine in the world at the table. Someday a really headstrong, visionary sommelier will have only GrüVe as a dry white selection, and where food is concerned, few would miss the absence of other options (unless the menu was fusiony-eclectic and needed whites with residual sugar). GrüVe shines in so many idioms, from light wines you

gulp like springwater to medium-weight wines that just insinuate themselves to your food to big, resonant wines that offer a
profundity to partner your "important" dishes.

But can't the same be said about a dry Riesling? Said, yes, but
not defended. Dry Riesling is among the world's *more* flexible
white wines, but GrüVe overtakes it with a larger body, a more
capacious structure, and a particular set of flavors that harmo-
nize with Riesling killers. If it were Italian instead of Austrian
it would be called Valtellina Verde and the wine world would be
abuzz; finally, a truly *great* Italian white wine! Its carafe wines
would be slurped outdoors *(alfresco)* while its serious wines
would be offered for grand *(grande)* occasions. We'd also rejoice
at how well it partnered peppery, difficult salads using mizuna
or arugula *(arugula)*, not to mention going perfectly with every
veggie that's usually homicidal to wine—artichokes, asparagus,
avocado, and all the ones that stink up your house when you
cook 'em, like broccoli or cauliflower or brussels sprouts.

GrüVe seems entirely particular to Austria. It has the Vien-
nese wit and insouciance and it has the robustness and sinew
of the countryside. It is baroque in the ways the churches are.
But its wines are more corporeal than German wines, which
are more mystical. Even mature GrüVe (and the variety ages
deliberately and for a great many years), while it is thrillingly
complex, is still more *food* than ether.

GrüVe has two sets of flavor according to the soil it grows
in, though there's a degree of overlap among them. In loess (a
glacial sediment extremely rich in minerals) it goes in a "soft,"
lentilly direction. One hears talk of legume, sorrel, meadow
flowers, mimosa and oleander, rhubarb, green beans, and, if one
is fanciful, moss and heather and vetiver. On the volcanic and

metamorphic soils called primary rock, it's another story; pepper is the archetypal descriptor, along with peppery greens such as bok choy and cress. There are scents of boxwood, tobacco leaf, strawberries if it's very ripe, and a minerality so dense and compacted one thinks of ferrous ore.

GrüVe is like some hypothetical spawn from a union of Sauvignon Blanc and Viognier, with Daddy's green, flinty, herbal flavors and Mommy's flowery flavors. Yet it isn't quite literally like either. It is in fact its own ornery self, and once you encounter it, you may not be able to imagine life without it.

seven

WINE FROM OUTSIDE

M ine is not the first book by a professional wine importer, and I hope I'm not contributing to any sort of genre— "The beautiful things I've done, and the colorful people I've known. . . ." That I-focus seems to distort the experience somehow, as if it were seen in a fun-house mirror that made some of it smaller and some of it larger than it really was. But how can I be sure what it really was or, in my case, still is?

I have developed a portfolio of estates whose wines I select and advocate and sell. Every choice I've made has been for my own pleasure only, never with a market in mind. The portfolio reflects my preferences, partly from self-indulgence but also plain pragmatism, because I know I'm not a good enough salesman to push what I don't believe in. As the years passed, patterns emerged, and I began to glean an anchoring pattern from which a system of values began to arise. This book is concerned with those values. But if I consider the prosaic tasks in the work I do, selling wine and being loyal to my growers and customers, I find I feel a certain shame. It feels as if whatever I have done, it should have been more.

I am mindful of the people my work has aided. There are growers who had worked in obscurity and for whom I helped earn a worldwide reputation. There is at least one grower to whom I brought prosperity who would not otherwise have had it, a small domain that had sold nearly all its wine in bulk until I arrived, after which a great many wines were bottled for me to sell, wines that would not have existed had I not wanted them.

Time is always too short. I know a grower in Germany who is a practicing Buddhist and whose entire conversation about his land, his vines, and his wines is concerned with their "energy fields," and how his choices either block or encourage these forces. I'm agnostic about the Buddhism but enormously intrigued by the practice of mindful viticulture, and I agree the work is more authentic when the vintner feels that his land and vines are every bit as real as himself. I yearn to spend a day with this man, walking the rows of vines, naming the bugs and birds, putting our hands in the dirt, prompting him with the occasional question and hearing how it is for him. I want this, and he deserves my full attention for as much time as it takes or as much time as he's willing to give me. But when? I have sixty-nine more growers to visit, and I can't spend six months in Europe; there's wine to be sold.

I wonder about this Buddhist grower and about nearly all of his colleagues whom I represent. Do they get enough of me? Do they know I believe in them and the work they do? How do they feel when I dash away for the next appointment? What can I really say about their experience?

Individual winegrowers, of course, are as diverse as people in any profession. But over the years I've noticed a few common facets. One of them is this: however beautiful the results may be, the actual work is sweaty. I think growers everywhere enjoy a slim edge of derision regarding us aesthetes. For each of us who cherishes a bucolic fantasy of the harvest there's a winegrower whose hands are stung by bees. And so there's a fraternity of growers united by knowing things the rest of us don't know. You hear it when they talk with one another. They rarely linger over the aesthetics; they talk about *the stuff they did*, the myriad mundane details of the job.

The profession doesn't tend to attract the mystic temperament. Nor does it necessarily coddle the introvert who likes to express himself in writing. Most growers I know are more farmers than *artistes*. I've sometimes sent them questions of a searching nature, which they could ponder and answer at their leisure. It seemed reasonable, but it flirts with arrogance. I eventually learned that many growers found the questionnaire "too much like school" (which many of them hated) and, even more salient, what little free time they had was for family, amusement, recreation; answering the importer's earnest queries was a priority roughly between obtaining a root canal and scrubbing lime deposits off their shower stalls.

But I feel a city boy's guilt about my remove from the plain hard work of viticulture. If I were a grower, I'd despise me. So I seek to understand the grower's experience at the ground level—not when we're in his tasting room or making sales calls, but what his work is like when none of us is there to observe it.

Here's Mud on Your Shoes

Yesterday it was late April, and where I live we have catbirds passing through. I was walking across a numbing strip-mall parking lot when I heard the gorgeous, unearthly sound. I followed it to a tree and found the crazy bird on a low branch, indifferent to me even as I drew closer. I stood there at least ten minutes before I heard him make any single sound twice. I even called my wife and held out the phone for a few minutes. If you've never heard a catbird, you can't imagine their creativity and insouciance.

I thought of it because I've had many winegrowers tell me they like to hear the birds when they're out in the vineyards. One very rugged guy astonished me when he said he was counting the days till the nightingales would come. He seemed the kind who'd rather talk about tractors, but people will surprise you.

It is very easy to make puerile romance out of these lives. "People of the vine" is typical of the fulsome language used by dewy-eyed writers. People of the antiperspirant or the bee sting would be closer to the truth. I've spent the past quarter-century of my life doing business with winegrowers, but unlike some of my colleagues I have no ambition to make wine. I'm effete and I'll just handle the aesthetics, thanks. But I wonder whether there is a common temperament among the people who choose this work. And I wonder what rewards them.

Bear in mind, I deal in the Old World, and only with family-owned estates. Children born into winegrowing families experience a very powerful cohesion, similar to that of small-farm families. It chafes some of them. Others are indifferent, and some are attracted. Parents pay lip service to the children's right to make their own choices, and to be fair it's often more than lip service. It is by no means inevitable that the youth will follow their parents, and if they do it is a great relief. For Americans this may seem rather quaint, because part of our national mythos is the perfect right to make our own way. That current has traveled to Europe as well, and it has trickled down to the rural life. Yet they have their own mythos, having to do with the dignity of successive generations engaged in a family enterprise, and if you're a young'un who stands as the umpteenth generation in a family wine estate stretching back centuries, you need a pretty compelling reason to break the chain. Americans might feel yoked to a life they didn't choose. Europeans might discern a beauty in the passage of generations carrying the thing on. And they're both right.

Many of the growers I've worked with are now retiring and handing the estate off to a daughter or son. I'm fascinated with what informs that young person's choice. It seems improbable to me, because I don't romanticize viticulture; most of it is a pretty brusque affair. And so I ask myself, What does this life entail? Who chooses it, and why? Once chosen, what aspect brings the most satisfaction, even the most joy?

The answers are many, and some of them are obscure. I know people who seem not to have thought about it. It was "assumed" they'd carry on the winery. Yet they don't seem at all unhappy. They show no signs of yearning for the choice they didn't get to make. Perhaps they are relieved because they didn't face the crucible of self-invention. Or maybe they saw the vintner's life and liked it. In Germany, the custom is to shove fledglings out of the nest and encourage them to travel widely. Young Sebastian Strub of Nierstein's is a typical story; he spent a semester in New Zealand, went to Japan to see Strub's importer at work, did *stages* in Austria and Germany, and so when he returns to the estate to accept the reins he'll have gotten the wander-bug out of his system, and learned a few things besides. Modern young German vintners may be rural, but they aren't provincial.

Caroline Diel went another way. Her family's estate is blue-chip, and her father casts a giant shadow. Armin Diel is one of Europe's most important wine journalists, a formidable lord of the manor and of all he surveys. Caroline is smart, charismatic, very beautiful, and connected. She could have done almost anything.

She apprenticed in Burgundy and at a couple of estates in Austria, and wandered in a picaresque drift with no particular end in view. She proceeded to New Zealand, and got work with a family winery. And there she had her awakening. "It wasn't the work per se," she says, "though of course I was always interested in grape growing and winemaking. It was that I saw this young couple working at something *that belonged to them*, where they could enact their visions and build something of their own."

"What was that like?" I asked.

"I couldn't wait to get home," she said. "I mean, there it was, all waiting for me; it was mine if I wanted it." And so she returned to the tiny village of Burg Layen and began to establish herself as proprietress, no mean feat with Power Dad looming in the background. She also needed to forge her own accord with the estate's established cellarmaster and vineyard manager, whom Dad had hired. Fast-forward two years: I've arrived early for my annual visit, and Armin and I are kibitzing and fussing over all the polemical disputes of the day—the tasting can't begin until Caroline's there, you see. And in a moment there she is, clomping into the tasting room ruddy and schvitzing from the vineyards, resplendent in her heavy boots. And so we taste the new vintage between stories of how it was grown, and at some point I ask Caroline what she likes best about the work. She answers promptly, "For me, the best part is getting to know the vineyards, because you can't rush it. You really have to spend time in them to see what makes them tick."

I remembered Helmut Dönnhoff saying something similar. He'd obtained a parcel in a great site called Dellchen, and after about four years the quality of the wine took a big stride forward. I noticed it and remarked upon it, and he agreed; the new vintage had jumped ahead of all its predecessors. I asked, "Is it because the vines are older?"

"No—although they are," he replied. "I'm not sure there is a *reason*, except that I'm getting to know the vineyard better. We're more at home with each other." I can just see my concrete-minded, linear-intellect friends groaning and rolling their eyes. What's all this *mysticism?* What, indeed. Dönnhoff is about the most matter-of-fact guy I know, but he talks about this aspect of a vintner's life quite explicitly: "I hope my wines convey a *story*," he says. "Otherwise they're just things, bottles of wine, good wine certainly, but I want them to tell the story of a man in his landscape."

Is this really so nebulous? I wonder. Anyone who has ever tended a garden experiences the same thing. You get to know your garden, and it responds to you. How can it do otherwise? It might respond with vigorous growth if you're a skillful grower, or it might respond with weeds and blight if you're careless or inattentive—but respond it must. Is it such a stretch to imagine that it responds in some way to the *love* you show it? If you like being in your garden, if you observe it with interest, curiosity, appreciation, should we really insist that it *cannot* respond? Why would we rather believe that?

Of course, there are shades of temperament among growers, but the overwhelming majority of vintners I know would agree that they are happiest among the vines.

Still, with the Diels and Dönnhoffs of the world we receive something extraordinary at the end of their labors. It isn't always easy to know why or how a wine becomes extraordinary, let alone a group of wines, year after year. The notion of the vintners dazed with love among their vines is a telling image, but by no means an explanation. We want to have great wine explained. But what about ordinary *good* wine? If there's anything to this notion that a vineyard responds to being known and appreciated, is that response always in the form of the marvelous?

I'm thinking again of Erich Berger, whom we met in chapter 4. An importer like me is always aware of his competitors, both in his own areas of focus and across the entire world of wine. My Rieslings compete against the other guy's, and Riesling itself competes against other grape varieties for a claim on the drinker's attention. Competition makes us insecure. We hate to admit it because we have to exude confidence to make the sale, but we're always scared the other guy's wine will kick sand in our faces. So we fuss and strain to have *stellar* wines.

But there are types of wines that confound this assumption. Berger doesn't set out to make the "best" or highest-scoring wine; he wants to make *tasty* wine. "It was always drummed into me by the family, to be above all honest, straightforward, and willing to develop," he says. "It's why I want to make consistently good wines. I want my children to inherit values as I did as a child. My own philosophy is to always be in accord with nature and to understand the environmental signals it gives." Well, sure, you say; that's the usual boilerplate. But what I see is a thoughtful life of hard work in the service of wines that won't make him famous. He could force them to be more ostentatious. Every grower knows how, and Erich's land can give "impressive" wine. But he seems content to make self-effacing, enjoyable, and delightful wine, almost as if doing so were inextricable from his duties as citizen, father, and husband.

Willi Bründlmayer, one of the great Austrian vintners, said, "I try to get each vintage into a spirit close to *This is my first vintage* or *This is my last vintage*, in order to draw as much joy and affection for the grapes as possible. Chase away all routine and find the singularity of each vintage and of each grape."

Austria's Heidi Schröck puts it like this: "My inspiration is the vine itself. With its powerful roots it collects the life force which comes from deep below the surface. As the root system grows deeper and more complex, the wine becomes more interesting and multifaceted. Being in the vineyard helps me to understand nature and to know my own boundaries." Interesting, isn't it: a crux of viticultural experience is *something that you can't see*, something welling up from inside the world.

Sometimes a grower's inspiration is elusive. He probably couldn't put it into words. Sometimes it is so intimate he prefers to keep it to himself. At times he may not even know. I do not suppose this matter of inspiration is always linear—"I sing when I'm spraying because my dad always sang when he sprayed," or "I use yeast number 817-B because that's the one my dad used." When I first got to know Laurent Champs of the Champagne estate Vilmart & Cie., I saw a number of stained glass panels throughout the winery and cellars. Was it merely a leitmotif?

"No, actually," said Laurent. "My father is a worker in stained glass. You'll meet him when we go there for lunch."

Laurent's parents live in a timbered house in a woodsy dell. My knowledge of French is that of a moderately gifted kindergartner whose hobby is wine, but I managed to convey how much I'd enjoyed the stained glass. I was offered a peek into the workroom. It was as chaotic as most workrooms, a jumbly refuge with a boom box. What sort of music does a worker in stained glass listen to? I stole a glance at a pile of CDs, expecting to see Arvo Pärt or Hildegarde of Bingen, but all I could see was Miles Davis's *Kind of Blue*.

That first visit was twelve years ago. This year I asked Laurent how his father was doing. "He's working on a book," he replied. "The subject is the three Oriental religions, as seen through the symbolism of light, and what light means to them."

"Your dad's quite the mystic, isn't he?" I said.

"Oh, yes, very much so."

Laurent himself is capable and dashing. He's the kind of guy you imagine striding purposefully to catch his plane, wheeling very sleek luggage behind him. I've only seen a couple photos of him in jeans in the vineyards. But sometimes a veil will part, and he'll say something remarkable and searching. He once mused that 1996 "isn't a vintage of pleasure; it's a vintage of desire." I loved the deliberate ambiguity of that statement. It's wise in some way, to understand that desire is deeper than pleasure.

I sat with him in the cellar and thought about his father's book, a study in the mysticism of light written by a lifelong worker in stained glass, stories told in light, a narrative of the divine itself rendered by the divine. And Laurent is his father's son; his wines also express light, as if their flavors were swinging from a Jacob's ladder of luminosity. I had always seen Vilmart's Champagnes as infinitely yet tenderly bright—he uses a majority of Chardonnay in a commune where Pinot Noir typically rules—and now I wondered at the connection. Vilmart's best Champagnes are serene and *beautiful.* They are objectively wonderful and superb, like many wines I drink, but the others don't all move me as Vilmart's do. I scribbled in my notebook, and this is what I wrote: "Flavors as shafts of brightness, the eerie sweet feeling of being visited by whoever or whatever your god is, gods are; just that reassurance that we aren't forgotten, and that every tiny floating speck of dust is also deserving of the light."

I thought of asking Laurent, "Can you tell me exactly how your father's work influences your wines?" But it seemed rude and intrusive, and I wondered whether it was even necessary. I can *taste* the answer. And even if this is all a conceit of my imagination, the wines of this father's son compel such imaginings. I prefer to believe in these connections because the belief aligns with my intuitive life. In any case, it's harmless. It would be illuminating to hear why those who adamantly *disbelieve* in such connections—and for some reason it is always "adamantly"— feel the way they do.

Sometimes when I talk with growers they like to remind me that they're *farmers* first, before anything else. That's easy to forget if you're dealing with the New World, but in the Old— or the parts of it with which I'm involved—you never forget. Yet their world is not only farming; it's also selling, marketing, publicizing, engineering, and craftsmanship. If you plant carrots, you eventually harvest carrots. There are things you can do to ensure you have wonderful carrots, but once you put them in the customer's basket, your work is done. Imagine if picking the carrots were followed by processing them into a soup or a beverage that was then evaluated alongside everyone else's carrot product, deconstructed, given scores, and all of this so you can be ranked as a producer of carrot drinks. I don't know about you, but this would make me bonkers. Small wonder the vintner likes to be out in the vineyard where he can escape the noise for a while.

Knowing vintners helps you understand about palate, because you see how they steer their wines toward their own palate's preferences. I doubt if vintners ever construct an a priori *idea* of their wines—"I want to make a rugged, rustic wine with high alcohol"—rather, they make the kind of wine they themselves like. Later on they may describe their principles, but any overriding philosophy has arisen from their spontaneous preferences. As these develop, their wines change. Heidi Schröck started out making somewhat rural, antique-style wines, gentle, evocative, influenced by the acacia casks she had in the cellar. Later she began to favor more compact and focused wines, steering toward the brilliance she was learning to treasure.

She is not alone, but Heidi is one of the better tasters and more thoughtful folks out there. A common mistake among wine lovers is to assume that all growers have what we'd call good palates. Many do, but not all. The Germans have a tidy word, *Betriebsblind*, which describes the blindness (or lack of perspective) caused by overimmersion in one's own business. And yet even this isn't always bad. To be so imbued with the place and grape you work with that it is *inside you*, you are not separate from it, expresses such a powerful locating of identity in your wine that we drinkers experience it as soul. Such a pure unity of worker and place conveys a startling power. I remember hearing Ürzig's Alfred Merkelbach being asked if he ever took a vacation. Sigrid Selbach had been showing him pictures from a recent trip to South Africa, and he was clearly quite amazed. So where did he like to go?

He hemmed a little (as he often does when asked a direct question), and finally said, "Vacations? I don't really take vacations." Really? we asked him. With all the marvelous places in the world to see? "Oh, I don't know . . . where would I go? When I'm in the vineyards on a nice summer day, with the Mosel behind me, I have everything I need to be happy."

It is one thing to try to "understand" wine in terms of causes and effects by using the work of vintners grand and wonderful. Because the wines are superb we assume the story of their making to be significant. Sometimes it is, but that can never be the whole truth. The lives of Rolf and Alfred Merkelbach offer another angle for viewing an equally valuable *tranche* of truth.

No one knew who they were, except for a few merchants who bought wine in bulk from them and a handful of Mosel insiders. Luckily, one of those insiders was a friend of mine, the endearing Willi Schaefer, of Graach, with whom I'd made friends during my ten years living in Germany. I reached out to him immediately when I looked for estates to include in my first portfolio. We were happy to be back in touch, and Willi asked me whom I was considering working with. "Well, I was kind of hoping you could help me with that," I replied. "Who do you know who makes excellent wine that no one knows about?" He'd have to think that one over. And a day later he called, saying,

"Terry, I think you'll be happy at Alfred Merkelbach in Ürzig. Especially as you like my wines."

Off I went. I didn't make an appointment, and I went alone. I met two middle-aged Moselaners who looked as if they'd been sent by Central Casting to answer a request for colorful Old World German winegrowers. I think they'd never met an American. They were very shy, and answered many questions with a giggle. And they were very much a *they*, Rolf-and-Alfred. Their current vintage was almost sold out, but I'd be back next year to taste the new one from cask, before it was bottled or otherwise claimed.

In the early '80s there was nothing so remarkable about the Merkelbachs. They were small-scale (barely five acres of vineyards), hands-on, and obscure, in common with thousands of other Mosel growers in small villages. But two things were remarkable: first, it was just the two of them, for neither had married; and second, their wines were remarkable. And so we began doing business.

Over the years many things changed along the Mosel. Many of the small growers couldn't survive; they had no children who wanted to carry on, or they were part of the herd-thinning that occurred as wine scaled up from being an everyday part of life to being the purview of connoisseurs and "experts." An activist wine press came into being, and you had to make the cut if you were going to be successful. All the articles described the change in wine consumption, and the shorthand was, "We're drinking less wine but *better* wine." The old generation, who drank wine as a daily beverage without our fanatical concern for how "good" it might be, was dying out. And so the ordinary grower sold his vineyards, if he could, and folded up shop. If he had a child who wanted to continue, the young person knew the only way to prosper was to go all out for top quality and get on the journalists' radar. This meant lower yields (or so it was believed) and other investments, which in turn meant higher prices. Thus advanced the world, except for a small corner of it on the Brunnenstrasse in Ürzig, where Rolf and Alfred Merkelbach just carried on.

I arrived there one year to see a shiny white Volkswagen Jetta parked in front of the house. When Rolf and Alfred answered the door, I said something like, "Hey, some wheels, eh!" To which they answered, giggling, "Well, you bought it for us!" And I realized that the effect of my patronage was to keep this estate alive in its original form. It hasn't grown larger, and the prices barely seem to have budged, and these days people talk of Merkelbachs as if they were some open-air anthropological exhibit.

The brothers are adorable. They're older and more rumpled now, but everyone who meets them adores them. I have known them a quarter-century, and they remain as shy as the day we first met. That's probably why they remained bachelors, although the scowling-with-disapproval portrait of Mama in the parlor-cum-tasting room offers perhaps another clue. And I myself made hay from their cuteness in my writings for customers. But I got older, and something happened.

I say I've "known" Rolf and Alfred for all these years, but "known" isn't really apt. When I'm there we taste the wine and I enthuse and they giggle, and unless a Selbach is present (they act as brokers for me and often join my visits) there's hardly any schmoozing—sometimes even then. I'm sure the Merkelbachs are glad of me, but I have no idea what they make of me—nor I of them, if I'm entirely candid. Of course, I adore them, because they're adorable. But when I think of them now, I find myself immersed in a kind of mystery. Who are they? *What are their lives?*

They're closing in on age seventy now, yet they still do all the work themselves (with a little help at harvest), and the steep slopes are not for parvenus. They live simply and give every appearance of perfect contentment, and I believe they are contented. I *hope* they are; it's part of a faith I hold. Theirs are lives reduced to a degree of simplicity and integration we wouldn't tolerate. Now when I look at their adorable faces I hear an inner voice that both stirs and challenges me. *Look at those faces, and now tell me how valuable all your hip, arch postmodern affects are.* But not only that. *Feel the divinity in these simple lives.* I think of Zen, and how arcane and mysterious it all seems. Monks, retreats, silence, monasteries, all that jazz, and that strange calm no one seems to be able to explain. And here are Rolf and Alfred, effortlessly embodying the Buddhist ideal of contentment. They are at home in their lives. They have what they need to be happy. And they *are* happy. I don't know what they say to each other over breakfast, or in the vineyards, or how they decide what to watch on TV in the evening, and I have no idea what each man thinks as he's falling asleep at night. But I know they're happy.

And the mystery haunts the wines, precisely because the wines are anything but mysterious. Instead they're so *essential*, so euphorically pure and expressive they display a categorical identity you might be tempted to call honesty, except that "honesty" implies the option of being dishonest. Everyone who knows Mosel Riesling agrees; Merkelbach's wines are *ur*-Mosel, stripped of all affect or the artifices of ego. It's as if some kindly old Mosel-god speaks through these two shy men. And no one would claim the wines are "great," but to paraphrase Andrew Jefford, they are infinitely *good*. That this species of wine exists at all is great enough.

This hadn't occurred to Germany's Channel Two television when a producer sent out a reporter to film a brief "lifestyle" piece on the Merkelbachs. Alfred asked, with exquisite shy pride, if I'd like to see the DVD, and of course I would. The interviewer milked the human-interest angle, of course. Poor thing; it was rainy the day they shot, and she looked pretty forlorn in her slicker. Rolf and Alfred couldn't help being "colorful." If they were bemused at being described as the last of a dying breed, they didn't let it show.

The reporter got some footage of the housekeeper. She'd worked for the Merkelbachs for twenty-five years but would soon leave; her husband was ill and needed her full-time care. She was a stern-looking lady, the kind who weeps easily. Had she liked working for Rolf and Alfred? "Yes, it was good here," she said, as they quick-cut to the brothers at their little dinner table eating the meal she'd cooked. It was a ceiling shot that made them look very lonely. Who will cook for them now? Or maybe it was I who was lonely. I sat with my back to the room and cried, and hoped nobody could see me.

We left and walked to the other side of the village to our next appointment. My old friend Sigrid Selbach walked with me. I was still weepy. Sigrid put her arm through mine. I told her, "I haven't always been as good as I wanted to be, and there are things in my life I am ashamed of . . . *(pause)* . . . and at times I feel the weight of those regrets . . . *(pause)* . . . but something with which I can console myself is that I brought appreciation and prosperity to Rolf and Alfred during these years of their lives. . . . *(pause)* . . . I sometimes think of that." Sigrid, perfect friend that she is, looked into my face and said nothing.

eight

WINES THAT MATTERED

Or, "The Dog Ate My Point Scores"

This thing we tell of can never be found by seeking, yet only seekers find it.
—Abu Yazid al-Bistami

When you're new to wines, they all matter. You write notes to focus your palate, hone your concentration, and remember what you tasted. You read other people's notes, too, so as to taste vicariously (especially if you can't afford the glam wines you read about) and try to suss what tasting notes are "supposed" to be, and whether yours measure up.

But eventually you reach a dead end with the whole tasting-note thing. It becomes a form of absurdity. Most tasting notes are associative (describing wine flavors in terms of other flavors), and this is of course tautological: saying a wine smells like peaches is to say that peaches smell like peaches. Nor is it any help if your reader has never smelled a peach.

There are basically two ways to taste wine. You don't have to pick just one, but eventually most of us settle on the one that comes naturally. You can taste "aggressively," that is, aim a beam of concentrated attention directly at the wine, using your palate to take a sort of snapshot. This is entirely desirable, but taken to extremes it has the effect of seeming to torture a confession from the poor wine.

Or you can taste "passively," or peripherally; you look away from the flavors and see what the wine says when you're not trying to nail the sucker down. You quietly let the wine come to you. This approach brings you closer to the gestalt—I might even say the *truth*—of the wine. But the liability is that it's very hard to verbalize, unless your tasting note takes the form of a Zen koan.

On the other hand, for most of us, no one is going to read our tasting notes, so we can write whatever we want. I say this notwithstanding the distressing phenomenon of Internet wine bulletin boards wherein people share their tasting notes with other lonely wine geeks. I'm sure this is fun for them, but I find it a little sad. I have a melancholy feeling that lots of people spend their weekends drinking wine *in order* to post their notes on Monday. "Look what I drank!" The cork is pulled, and suddenly there are all these hypothetical eyes upon you. Your life becomes a kind of performance. But don't mind me. I'm just a private, introverted guy, and my relationship with wine has always been intimate.

As a merchant I have made myself write tasting notes because I want to help my customers determine what to buy, and because I seem to have lost the omniscient recall I had in my thirties, when I could remember every wine I tasted. These days I have to consult notes for a wine I tasted ten days ago. The job requires me to write notes on a thousand to fifteen hundred wines per year, which may be why I almost never write tasting notes at home.

But some wines embody a story—not merely a narrative, but a kind of curiosity, as if they cast out tentacles into the ether. Other wines stimulate the imagination, and you're off and running. I am very sure these things are worth getting down, but if you seek to share them you will sometimes run afoul of a certain kind of person who actually *does* want to know that your 2004 Domaine de la Crachoir tasted like "beer-battered kiwi fritters, boysenberries, and pork snouts." When Hugh Johnson's charming memoir *A Life Uncorked* was published, someone on the Internet was bemused. The book was useless to this person because "He never says how the wine tastes; he only says what it was like to drink it." Well, my good man, that there's the very *point* of the thing. I'd far rather read the genial musings of a humane spirit mulling over the little nimbus between his soul and the wine in the glass than to see how many arcane adjectives some anal geek can string together.

You've read such notes, I'm sure. *This dramatic wine has the burnish of torched sienna, that hint of Tuscan chickens, perhaps even pullets, that gamey, feathery aroma; a dishy first impression of guppies spawning and bracken roasting in the Castilian sun, and the high wind blowing from offshore when a garbage scow has recently run aground, not exactly fresh passion fruit, but passion fruit after it has been chewed by a horse that's just run through a heathery dale, you know, sort of sopping wet fetlocks and old dogs; and the finish, oh, just a portrait of nasturtium, or shuttlecocks dipped in quince jelly, or the stench on a fox's muzzle after he's eaten a number of small rodents or the ice caked in a refrigerator in a Paris apartment, or like new sandals, especially if the feet in them have been soaked in a bromide solution—and revisiting the nose is all rotty mulch sluicing out of a bilge pipe in a fetid stream of sweetly blooming hawthorn in a flighty perfume of freshly starched uniforms of a flight attendant in the first-class cabin in a manly swill of gassy medicinal opaline mordant porcine gratuitous acetate begonia-laden air freshener or like the fannings from a fire of souchong tea or like . . .* Somebody make him stop! *Just one more thing: Am I the only one who finds this wine a bit* hirsute?

One of the early wine books I read was the (tragically out-of-print) *Fireside Book of Wine*, a compilation done by the late Alexis Bespaloff. Among the works were many old tasting essays (it's mingy to call them mere "notes") by a few of the old-school British writers such as Maurice Healy and the great André Simon. If you read some of the travel literature of the nineteenth century, you'll discover that the ostensibly staid and prosaic British were wont to spout extravagantly emotional and flowery prose. As a fledgling reader of wine lit, I was getting the message that intense emotion was a normal response to intense beauty. I was in effect given permission to respond in this way myself. I was also reading Hugh Johnson, of course, and Gerald Asher's elegant columns in *Gourmet* magazine, and so all of the writers whose work shaped mine were either excellent writers or wore their hearts on their sleeves. People new to wine these days are just as apt to be corrupted as to be inspired; there's a lot of lousy prose and shallow thinking out there.

I want any tasting notes I care to read—my own or others'—to be *visceral*. Most of the time the telling image is more valuable than the literal description. You risk incoherence and self-indulgence if you write intuitively, and I'm sure I resemble that remark now and again, but it's a risk worth taking.

For laughs, I'll deconstruct a tasting note I wrote for a young wine while on the job. I was tasting at Müller-Catoir, a supernal estate in the Pfalz in Germany, and we were partway through the Rieslings. The wines were incandescent, as usual, and I noticed the way that beauty consolidates when you taste one superb wine after another. Each wine falls like a small snowflake, but they settle into a blanket of snow. We tasted a Spätlese from the Bürgergarten vineyard, and I wrote, "Well well well . . . so this is the view from the summit [I was still trying hard to be matter-of-fact] . . . Inconceivably exquisite. Plum essence in a perfect duck consommé. Spice spice spice. Mineral sings, 'Honey, I'm home!'" The wine was great, but I was essentially in control, lambent and receptive.

There was another Bürgergarten Spätlese, a sister cask to be bottled separately (reason alone to cherish German wines, this lovely determination not to sacrifice individuality). I thought we were through with the Spätleses. I wrote, "I didn't know this was coming. How do you get higher than the summit? Stand on tiptoes? Now comes the saltiness to shimmy into the sweetness and glide in an itchy, urgent gorgeousness over the palate [here it is, the precise moment I lost it and let myself be carried away] . . . profound and magnificent yet without opacity, rather delineated to the last molecule of detail." I tasted it again and again as if to break the spell, but the wine was bigger than I was, and I vanished through the membrane. "It tastes this way for the same reason blossoms open—for the bees to be useful, for the plant to live and make new plants, for a few human passersby to pause, sniff, delight, and feel a strange longing, not quite sad, wanting to touch another warm skin, oddly happy and alone in the odd lonely world."

On the surface the passage makes no sense. Yet it describes as accurately as my talents allow just how it was to taste that wine by saying where it took me. But first you have to surrender control, and then you have to be willing to risk looking silly. And it never works to force it. You let yourself dance to the particular music of that wine—which recalls a quote I like, from George Carlin: "Those who dance are considered insane by those who can't hear the music."

On the occasion when I wrote that note, I had a young colleague with me at Catoir. She didn't speak any German and couldn't follow the chatter, and I was loath to break the flow by pausing to translate. So she attended to the wines. At one point near the end, she rose and walked over to the oriel window, looking out into the gray March light. I knew why. She came back with glassy eyes and an out-of-body expression. Later in the car, as we headed to dinner, I said, "It's surprising how *wrenching* it is, don't you think?"

"Yes. Yes!" she said. "I mean, two or three of them you can withstand. But one after another, it just overtakes you."

For me, part of the fascination in how we respond to beauty is the very curiosity beauty engenders. *What is the nature of this experience?* I'll try to say how it is for me.

Beauty dilates the senses. That's the first thing that happens. Any beauty, whether of language, flavor, or sound. It penetrates us, and we absorb it with such a charged vividness that we suddenly grow aware of this quality's absence from ordinary experience. If the beauty is complex, we feel our minds scrambling to take it all in before it's gone, to make sense of it. This often happened for me at Müller-Catoir, and I was always constrained from examining it by the ambient conversation. They should have sat me in a quiet chapel and had a young novice monk bring me another wine every twenty minutes.

As the senses dilate to admit this strangely stunning beauty, a silence enters, too. For now, there is only *this*. You'd forgotten the mere world could include *this*, and something dormant in you awakens. The ordinary you will not suffice for *this*. Such beauty is a pledge to which you must attend.

As the senses focus and deepen and probe, the emotions also begin to dilate, unless you are inured or cold to beauty. The first things felt are gratitude and wonder. But there's more. Beauty is a fierce thing. It doesn't let up, it invades you, even *violates* you; it will have its way, and that way is ecstasy. And of the many notes in the ecstatic chord, one of them is rage. I don't know why, but it's there. Maybe it's because we can never seem to rise high enough to meet beauty at *its* level. Maybe it's because we spend so much time subduing rage and frustration, that when pure emotion is finally unleashed we get the whole sloppy mess, not just the pretty parts. Maybe the charge isn't selective—it electrifies all of you. The effect is strangely violent, even as it overwhelms you with pleasure.

And on the far side of this incandescence, we start to think of the people whose work brought this about. Suddenly their dedication seems astonishing. What does it entail, to offer this beauty? Sitting there receiving it, we suddenly grow somber. We're not thankful enough. Not just in this moment—*ever*. Yet we were invited.

And so we walk to the window with our back to the room, and weep.

In many cases the quietest beauty and the deepest stories live in older wines. That is in part because they grow less brash and frisky, less explicit—but more searching and, at best, more sublime. I have young colleagues who sometimes travel with me on my rounds in Europe, and I always thrill to see them respond to very old wines—in some cases older than they themselves are—for the first time. If you've never visited German growers you have no idea how these wines truly age, when they've never been moved from the perfect cellars where they've rested since the beginning. That first taste is nearly unbelievable, even if the wine is an unremarkable citizen of an ordinary vintage. There is a kind of *tenderness* in such wines, and many a grower, witnessing our wondering responses, has disappeared into his cellar to unearth another bottle, or bottles.

For many of these mature Rieslings it isn't just how well they've preserved, and it isn't even how many facets they've integrated or what complexities they've attained. It's more. It is, first, the extent to which they have stayed *alive.* They are neither relics nor objects of curiosity nor even of astonishment; they are still with us to serve their original purpose, to keep our food company and to make us happy. And it's also the way they've made peace among their factions of flavor. The French call this process *fondue*, a melting together of elements into a seamless whole. The tenderness I speak of arises here.

But it is also a quality of deliberateness. "A twenty-five-year-old Kabinett, and yet it tastes so *young!*" is not where it ends, but where it begins. The wine is going nowhere fast. It has much life before it, it has all the time in the world. Such wines do not only exist in time; they appear to *embody* it. We think of time as a thing there's always too little of, against whose relentless limitations we constantly bang our heads. But wine can show us another kind of time, a more meandering and forgiving time. There's an old saying: "The oxen are slow, but the earth is patient." Wine can bring us to the patient earth, of whose existence we are often not aware, though we live here. We do well to consider not only how wines age, but *why* they age. It is because they have something to show us, stories to tell us.

You could well be thinking, *Something to show us? What, exactly?* And if that were your thought, I would sympathize. I'd like to be more concrete, but the experience itself is too fluid. Still, I can offer an example. This evening I happen to be drinking a 1985 Riesling Grand Cru Kirchberg, from Louis Sipp (great name for a winery!) in Ribeauvillé, Alsace. The wine is almost a quarter-century old, and the bottle—luckily—is in excellent shape. It has the sort of *strict* character of Ribeauvillé Rieslings. It isn't hedonistic. But it begins with an up-close miasma of quince and ginger and a subtle stoniness. After an hour or so it gets a little crazy, like some potion of wild mountain herbs, Chartreuse almost, and tart berries like juniper. It's as if the wine were releasing something, its id, maybe. And after two hours, with the final bit in my glass, it's all burning leaf and kiln, but the oddest thing is how the flavor both compounds and retreats, on one hand growing ever more complex, and on the other drawing ever farther away. That sense of something wafting to you from across the hills and fields is awfully haunting. Maybe you've tasted it, and walked away, but my own weird temperament compels me to consider the spell. How many things bring it? How often? Why does it come, and what does it want? I find myself swimming in a liquid ether of leaves, trees, winds, burning. The leaves are burning because soon it will be winter. The trees will hunker down. They'll be bare and thready. We will see nature when it isn't putting on a show for us. Winter is like a dress rehearsal for death, but it isn't really death. It's just how we dip our toes in the dark water, and then go back to life. A long way to travel from a bottle of wine, isn't it? Yet really not very long at all.

Here's a wine with a story. During the decade I lived in Europe, from 1973 to 1983, I became solely and passionately devoted to wine. I promptly became a wine tourist, and one of the first places I visited right away was Burgundy. I lived in Munich, and Burgundy was closer than, say, Bordeaux, plus it was far more interesting and hospitable.

While there, knocking around earnestly (albeit cluelessly), I stumbled across a domaine off the main routes, in a corner of Beaune. I'll take a small degree of credit; even as a beginner I knew the wines were special. I bought what I could afford.

I returned a few years later. No appointment. Arrived just as a busload of Belgians was pulling away. The proprietor was doddering through the room consolidating the remains of tasting glasses into a large plastic bucket. "Ah, he'll top up his casks with that," I assumed. When all the glasses were emptied, our vigneron placed the bucket on the floor and issued a shrill whistle, whereupon his *dog* trotted in and proceeded to lap up what must have been several hundred dollars' worth of premier cru Burgundy. (Somehow I can't quite imagine a similar thing taking place in Pauillac. . . .) This time I had more money and I'd learned to allocate a lot of my Burgundy budget to this domaine, and so I bought and bought and bought.

And finally the very last of those bottles was being drunk, on New Year's Eve 2006. I had shipped it back from Europe along with its companions.

The bottle didn't look promising. There were at least three inches of ullage and, let's face it, I hadn't stored it perfectly. But these wines appeared indestructible, and a couple of months previously another old bottle from the domaine had been wonderful. So once more into the breach. Wine lovers all know the feeling—the final bottle! You can't stand to part with it, and in a strange way you almost want to wait till it's past its best; perversely, it's less heartbreaking that way.

The color was fine; mature, of course, but not decayed. It needed decanting to separate it from its heavy, gritty sediment, and even after the bottle had been vertical for forty-eight hours, the best I could do was leave an inch in the base. The bouquet of this wine was a force of spirit. If truffles had orgasms, they might emit this fragrance. Soy, sandalwood, shiitake, you know: Burgundy. Like the fat cap on a roast after you've studded it with cloves, sweet and caramelized and bloody. You know: Burgundy!

On the palate the tannin was durable and unpolished, in the old-fashioned way. Honest, nothing to be ashamed of. The fruit, or its echo, was something that reminded us how we blow silly things out of proportion. I could try to say what it tasted like, groping for literalisms, but I'd rather say it made me want to forgive. It melted away the trivial grudges I've clung to. It even said, Next year will be better, next year you'll let it go and let the kindness come.

We carved our roast, and my sweetheart and I sat down to dinner. The wine smelled like all the sweetness of the country, like the redeeming kindness of people. Thank you, old Albert Morot, for this Beaune Bressandes, 1969.

I love the varieties of beauty wine can display. Old Burgundy with its murmuring sensual depths, all the way to my cherished Riesling and its lyric, sprightly music. I am sometimes asked why I spend my career selling German wines. Did I see a marketing opportunity because the wines were so "underrated," or do I simply have freaky taste? I have, as you've noticed, a special fondness for German Rieslings along with a huge, unseemly crush on the entirely kinky Scheurebe, and drinking these wines, with their extraordinary vividness and complexity and delicacy, spoils one for wines of coarser virtues—which basically means everything that isn't German.

But for me it has become something other than the tastes of the wines *as such*. I glean a sort of meta-identity, a *species* of wine toward which I've become very fond.

One night while on my Germany rounds, I returned to my hotel, turned off the car, and climbed out into the early spring cold. And I heard a thing I hadn't heard in years: three nightingales were singing their dark and eerily beautiful song. Suddenly the world went silent and it was the beginning of time. I walked in the hotel's garden and listened to the three tiny birds until it was too cold to stay out any longer. Inside, I opened my windows—they were still singing there in the middle of the night—and snuggled under the comforter and let them sing me to sleep.

Each day as I'm making the case for German wines, I remember that night, and I realize that I am unnecessary; *nature* makes the case for German wines constantly, with every lark, thrush, or nightingale, every snap and crunch of apple, every swooningly fragrant linden tree in blossom, everything that makes us pause when we are visited by the electric hum of the world. German Riesling is a small bird that sings in the darkness, a seemingly minute thing that can tingle your pores, and haunt you your entire life.

To complete this tale, I should mention telling Helmut

Dönnhoff of my night reverie. Dönnhoffs are often considered among the world's most sublime Rieslings, and people feel an almost religious awe when drinking them. But the man himself is down-to-earth. "You wouldn't think those birds were so pretty on a hot July night when you're sleeping with the windows open," he rebuked me. "I want to take a rifle to the little bastards." Way to bust up my moment, dude!

Last summer my wife put a hummingbird feeder on our balcony, and lo and behold, they came—three of them, to be exact. I named them Nate, Alice, and Zippy. Nate is gray and handsome, with a long neck and a comely head, and if Alyosha Karamazov were a hummingbird, he'd be Nate. Alice is smaller, and she has emerald tail feathers. More skittish than Nate, Alice hovers when she feeds, while Nate will perch there as if no one could hurt him. The littlest one, Zippy, comes and goes. She never stays long. She seems a little hyper.

Nate is my favorite, because he will pause between gulps of sugar water and just look around. Hummingbirds beat their wings more than fifty times per second; they are extraordinarily kinetic. But in repose Nate looks like a miniature dove, a small happy saint, peering around with the pleasure of the world and a full belly. I was moved to see this little life pause and muse so calmly, just a few feet away.

It is precisely this equipoise of energy and delicacy that I love most about German Riesling. No other wine is quite the same. As I've gotten older I seem to have excavated some kind of compassion for little beings. I feel it when I think of Mosel Rieslings, especially a Kabinett or Spätlese with 7 or 8 percent alcohol, so slight you think it might not really be there, beating its wings faster than your eye can absorb, singing and singing.

It's curious how often Riesling and birds are connected. On one suddenly warm March day we arrived at the Karlsmühle estate in the little Ruwer valley near Trier. It would have been cruel to sit indoors. So we tasted alfresco, the way young Ruwer Riesling *should* be tasted, it so embodies the spirit of springtime. It was just the second time in seventeen years we'd been outdoors for our annual March tasting of the new vintage.

Bugs were buzzing and green was greening and everything alive was squirming with energy and even proprietor Peter Geiben's news that snow was forecast for the following week couldn't dampen our spirits. After an hour or so we all heard a sound from the sky and looked up, but didn't see anything. A moment later Peter pointed skyward and said, "There it is." It was two large flocks of migrating cranes, several thousand feet aloft and very small, headed north to their summer home in Russia. The two flocks were trying to join, milling and billowing as if to form letters in the sky, crying to one another to establish a flying formation, their cries echoing through the air as if they were lonely or afraid. But they only told each other, *Follow me, follow me. I sense a wind. . . .*

Sigrid Selbach was with us, and I reminded her of the previous time we'd been here when it was warm enough to taste outside. We set a table in the quiet parking lot, and the sun was in my eyes, and when the first wine was poured I turned my head to the left and spat onto what I *thought* was the ground, but it was in fact the dog's *head*. Poor old Sam. Lying there enjoying the sun just like us when *splat*, some plug of viciously high-acid young Riesling lands on his innocent head. This year I spat into a little bucket. I ain't into traumatizing no dawgs.

The wine had just been poured when we heard the cranes. It

was a Kabinett from the Nies'chen vineyard, and when I looked down into the glass it reflected the earth green and the sky blue, and when I sniffed this fresh little infant, with the lonesome birds calling one another, a thing was tied together from what had been only threads before.

A wonderful chef named Elka Gilmore once said to me that she wanted flavors so alive that they would be like holding your hand just below a ripe peach on its branch and the peach swoons down without even a touch because it is *ready* to surrender. A great young Riesling gurgles to you with all the delight of a baby playing peekaboo. Yet a whole sky was reflected in the glass, and a chorus of migrating birds played their eerie blue music.

But German Riesling is more than the lyric Mosel face. There's also the giddy extravagant Pfalz face (or "Pface") and the reserved, stoic Rheingau face. I used to work with a tiny family estate called Riedel, in Hallgarten, where they made passionately old-fashioned wines from barely seven acres of vineyards. The longer I bought from them, the richer I discovered their story to be.

Christine Riedel was nearing eighty years old when we first met. I'd been dealing with her son, Wolfgang, and she stayed in the background where she assumed she belonged. But she was hardly a weak-willed being; these were simply Old World manners. Wolfgang lured her out one morning with the promise of a venerable vintage to taste.

The wine made her less shy. I learned she had been widowed quite young, and that not only her husband but three of her four brothers had been killed in the war. She ran not just the household (or what was left of it) but also the wine estate, on her own. The Rheingau of those times was a region dominated by a few royal wine estates with lordly names. The small estates had little chance, and this small estate, with a mere *woman* running the show, had even less hope of survival. No one had reckoned on the irascible will of Christine! Her wines, improbably, were superb, leading the administrator of the most exalted estate in the region to call her "the top cellarmaster in the Rheingau."

It seems there was once a tasting to honor the birthday of Count Matuschka-Greiffenclau, proprietor in those days of the famous Schloss Vollrads. Christine Riedel showed the then-young 1959 Beerenauslese, which attracted the notice of the birthday boy. Thinking, I am sure, that he was offering the most cordial remark from a blue blood to a commoner, he permitted himself to observe to Frau Riedel how remarkable it was that a wine of such quality could come from a small vintner. He probably expected an awed curtsy. But Christine's life had been building to this very moment. "You know, Count," she replied, "our vineyards are less than two kilometers from yours. Do you imagine we receive the same sunshine, or does God in His wisdom hang a curtain between your vines and ours?"

The old wine Wolfgang had brought from the cellar was in a very tall bottle of thick green glass. The cork was eased out deliberately, still intact. The wine was poured quietly. It was deep greeny-gold, astonishingly; whatever it was, all that chlorophyll was still there. Oh, a *great* bouquet, enthralling, complex, a cathedral of fragrance, like leaves or tapioca pudding or orchids. As I was trying to fathom what it could possibly be, Wolfgang could no longer hold it in. It was a *1937* Hallgartener Jungfer Spätlese (an unexceptional wine), fermented dry, as was the rule of the day.

"That was the year I was married," Christine said. I couldn't stop looking at her face and her youthful blue eyes, and her hands as they held the glass. What things those hands have known. What life has passed before those eyes—an entire human life. The wine was majestic, dignified, almost theologically mysterious, with a sagey high note on the back of the palate and a smoky fall-evening mood of burning leaves; it had power and verve, it was still vigorous! It was full of ivy and grain. It told of a time when people dressed for dinner in their own homes. The room fell silent as we all opened our hearts to this winged messenger of time.

The wine itself was lovely, about as profound as wine can be, but the *experience* of drinking it with the woman who helped make it more than sixty-one years ago, and her son, and my friends, was overwhelming. I felt as if I'd received the tablets on which were carved the answer to every human riddle, but it was written in a language I did not read. It is hard at such times to think of wine as an isolated, discrete *thing*. Wine flows like blood through these lives.

Eventually Wolfgang spent more time attending to his first loves, art history and medieval religious architecture. The wines slowly declined as he became less interested. He sold off some of his best vineyards. The little estate's clientele of private customers was aging and didn't buy much anymore. I was very fond of Wolfgang and wanted him to be happy, but I mourned another loss in a vanishing world, story upon story, flame upon flame snuffed out. My tribute is paltry against the passionate dignity of these lives.

At times the serving of old vintages is ceremonial, but not always. Sometimes it's almost casual, as among close friends with a shared interest. (It always surprises me when people are indifferent to old wines, or when they taste but don't "get" them.) One year while I was visiting my portfolio's Champagne growers, I had a young colleague along, and when we arrived at Gaston Chiquet in Dizy, Nicolas Chiquet wondered what his birth year was. A birth-year wine was still a rarity to my young chum, but Nicolas has lots of vintages in the cellar and so the boys went off to scrounge around underground.

I sat alone in the living room in a state of advanced bliss. I hadn't expected it. I'd been around people—congenial, even beloved people, but still—every day for the past two-plus weeks, and the sudden solitude was a balm I didn't know I needed. The blackbirds kept me such company as I required with their noisy melodies. It was just after sunset, and they sang as if they'd been caught unaware by the twilight. I had three of my favorite things at hand: solitude, songbirds, and Champagne.

Nicolas returned with a 1981 in tow, along with the '88 and '85 vintages of his top bottling (known as Special Club). We started with the '88, which had been the available vintage when I had first visited this estate twelve years earlier. Alas, like a fool I had drunk all my own bottles before they were really ready—I may be smart but I'm not patient—and I remembered again how the '88 took its sweet time maturing. This '88 Club was disgorged in 2007, and man, it was surreal, with haunting fruit and texture and a vein of chalky terroir to balance; fennelly and mentho-lated and long; not powerful but incisive and remarkable; one of those *Well, this comes from somewhere* wines. Not a wave crashing against the rocks, but a full moon rising over dark fields. So we drank it and continued to the '85 and '81, relaxed and thought-ful, schmoozing accompanied by splendid old Champagne.

At times, though, it starts out innocuously enough, tasting an old vintage to honor another year of friendship and good business. But it can morph unexpectedly, and then it is very hard to be me, because the fugue state that ensues is a solitary one, and I'm shy about being über-emotional in a crowd.

I work with a Champagne grower named Geoffroy, and old wine has been a leitmotif for us since the beginning, when I surprised Jean-Baptiste Geoffroy (and believe me, myself) by correctly guessing four of the five vintages he poured me blind. "Are you some sort of *savant?*" he asked. Not a chance. It was easy, as I tried to explain, because the aromatic signatures of these Champagne vintages were very close to the same vintages in Germany, which I knew extremely well. So now, when our business is done, we taste something venerable, and one year Jean-Baptiste announced, "This year I'd like us to taste something in honor of my grandfather."

He disappeared into the cellar, returning with a wormy old bottle from what he said was his grandfather's time. The cork sighed out. The wine was poured, a serene, deep straw color. Oh, it was a perfect old-wine fragrance; mocha, carob, could almost be red Burgundy. The word *spellbinding* came to mind. A deep, tender old friendliness, sweet with history. Almost impossible to assimilate; it was berserk with intricacy.

Jean-Baptiste's father came in and joined us; he'd been busy in the cellar. "Started without me, I see!" he remonstrated.

The wine was a 1966. So juicy still, so redolent of burning leaves and winter truffles. What a vintage! A slightly scorched note came on as the fruit faded. Next Jean-Baptiste's wife, Karin, came in, carrying the new baby, with another daughter at her side. The older girl seemed about six. She took the baby, who looked around and cooed. Old wine, new life, what can you do? *It all floods in.*

How many "points" is *this* worth? Lives lived in wine; three generations sitting with us and paying tribute to a fourth. "When I taste a wine like this, and think of my grandfather's methods," said Jean-Baptiste, "why change them?"

In old wine, life is restored to us with all the bad stuff removed: no fights, no illnesses, no misery. Only the stately passing of seasons, again and again. Only the love, the strange indifferent love without *affection*, the love you hear between the notes and the sentiment.

Twenty minutes went by, and now the wine smelled celestial: scallops drizzled with butter and nutmeg, macadamias, spices, star fruit. The six-year-old was offered a taste. She tasted like a pro: sniffed, swirled, drew air into her small mouth. Did she like it? She was very shy around us strangers, but she managed to peep out a tiny answer: "Il est bon."

There is the reason to care about wine. There is the taproot. Each of the many times I've shared an old vintage with this family, there have been three generations present (and most recently a two-week-old rabbit named Noisette whom the youngest child wasn't letting out of her sight), and we taste without ceremony at the old table, and I watch as this particular form of beauty gestates within a family and a culture, an understanding that this is worth doing, that people can live good lives doing this.

In case you are thinking it's easy to be seduced by the romance of it all when you're over there with the family drinking their Champagne with the smells of lunch cooking, you're wrong. I am sentimental about many things, but not about beauty. Beauty is too important to be sentimental about, and besides, beauty is often hard and indifferent. The spell can steal over you at any time and in the most prosaic circumstances, unless you have made great efforts to insulate yourself against it. This I think is the key; to be available for the spell is very easy. All you need to do is calm down and look around. To be impervious to the spell requires a far greater effort—plus it costs more in lost quality of life. I suspect most of you would agree, in theoretical terms, but you're wary whether a mere wine can deliver such moments of meaning. We're terribly proud of being down-to-earth where wine is concerned. I know a guy who spends about ten times more than I do on wine and who'd pooh-pooh every word of this book. "Goes down, stays down" is his highest praise. The part of this take that's right is completely right; the only problem is, there's a vast part of it that he has refused to consider.

Yet I sympathize. The sacred without the profane is merely precious (just as the profane without the sacred is merely dirty), and there are loads of times when all you need to say is, "This is fucking great wine." I had a 2004 Muscat the other night from Müller-Catoir, and the *F*-word was flying around the room with every sip. It'd be fun to read a tasting note like, "Oh, man, fuck; I mean, not just fuck, but *FUCK*." I'd buy it, wouldn't you? In any case, it says more to me than the "melted licorice, road tar, and weasel dandruff" school of tasting notes.

The wine itself steers your response. A quiet, pensive wine won't propel you up from the sofa spewing profanities, unless that's, you know, your basic default position in life. One day last spring it had been stormy since early morning, rumbly and gloomy. Outside, the trees in Maryland were just leafing, in that virginal unbelievable green that's like no other. The leaves were still curled and modest, and from my eighteenth-story balcony the trees looked like a lace curtain of emerald. It was getting on toward dusk and the storms were passing, and a sudden moment of sunlight threw crepuscular rays against the black of the retreating sky as the rain blew north. For a few seconds the whole sky was a drama, a tragedy, a miracle that the hero didn't see.

I didn't plan it, but the wine in my glass was an obdurately youthful 1990 Riesling from my friends at Nikolaihof in Austria's Wachau. It was the Weingebirge Smaragd, all of 12.5 percent alcohol, and so pale and limpid I almost couldn't accept the ripe balsamic sweetness of the fragrance. I really don't know how this experience assumed the form of a "tasting note." I just know that when I stood with the glass on my balcony and looked at the sun-on-black of the vanishing storm and the sun-on-green of those wet new leaves, dark, light, and gleaming all at once, I knew there was no other wine that could possibly make this moment liquid.

Wines like these don't seek to be included in the world, or even in your world, because they already are. They didn't ask your permission, any more than the rain does or the leaves do. When you drink them, they *include* you. This is so unusual, this feeling of being invited and included, when so much of our experience is confined to being indulged or entertained.

Is there really enough time to waste on the unreal? But who am I to know what is real and what is false? Nobody; I have no authority. I only report what I experience. You're free to ignore me. But I know what I know, and there's no doubt in it. And I know that every time we accept the flashy in place of the true, we starve a being who lives inside us. A modest being, who won't even say when he is hungry—but late in your life you will see he is there, and there's no time left to know him, and he had so much to say to you.

E ven if I'm unusual in the degree to which I welcome the spell, it's hard to deny the uncanny ways wine embodies connections. Here is a story.

When I was in my early forties, I decided to search for my birth parents, having been adopted as an infant at a time when adoption was a very hush-hush matter. Eventually, and with the help of a detective who specialized in such things, I found them both, both alive, though no longer with each other (they were high school sweethearts), both in good health, and willing to see me.

It was biomom (as I came to refer to her) who led me to bio-dad. Biomom had been looking for me, and her suspicions were aroused by a phone call she'd gotten from the detective, whose ruse she didn't believe. So ours was a mutually welcome reunion. Biodad, on the other hand, had to be contacted out of the blue.

This man and his wife demonstrated new depths of human decency and kindness in the welcome that greeted my approach to them. But that's a tale for another time. Our first talk was over the phone, and I made haste to assure him I was a successful adult and professionally well-off—some who search are in straits—but in that first dazed conversation I didn't tell him exactly what it was I did for a living. We talked in a rearranged reality, and about ten minutes after signing off, he called me again. "I guess I'm not through with you yet," he said.

"So, give me a sense of you—what are your hobbies?" he asked.

"Well, I enjoy the mountains and love to hike, and I play the guitar and love music and have never quite abandoned my dream to be a rock star," I said. "And you?"

"Oh, you know, I'm a Jewish doctor, so I love to play golf." He chuckled. "And other than that, I suppose you could say I consider myself something of a wine aficionado."

"Really?" I said, trying gamely to pick up my jaw off the floor. "And are there any wines you particularly like, any favorites?"

"Well, I know they're not the most popular wines around, but I must admit I have a soft spot for German wines. . . . Hello? Are you still there?"

"Let me tell you what it is I do for a living," I stammered, and once I'd told him he said, "Wait a second, stay on the phone, I'll be right back. . . ." I heard his footsteps retreating and, in a moment, returning. "I have your wine in my cellar! My son gave me a case for Christmas last year."

And that is my wine story. Remember it the next time someone says you shouldn't take wine too seriously.

If wine connects to life, as I believe it does, then it connects to birth and to death. Old wines, especially, have a grave tenderness that consoles the darkness. I have often seen these old wines linked to the memory of the people who made them; you've heard the story of the Geoffroy tasting, and I can't forget a bottle of 1953 offered to me at Willi Schaefer to mark the twenty-fifth anniversary of our meeting. It was all of ten in the morning, but Willi's wife, Esther, was with us, and when the wine was opened she poured a glass and said, "Let me take a glass to your mother, Willi; she'll enjoy drinking a wine her husband made." I didn't know what part of the house was the widow's, and I'd never met her before, but it was exquisitely touching to think of her drinking this wine. What, really, was the fluid in that glass?

One year, as my "entourage" and I arrived at Stefan Justen's estate (on the Mosel again, but these growers seem to have the deepest collections of old vintages), I learned the melancholy news that his father had finally succumbed to the emphysema with which he'd struggled for many years. He was two weeks dead, but his son's demeanor was opaque (Moselaners are unfailingly correct except with intimates). But when he brought out the old wine, he told us it was in tribute to his father. Pause with me just a second. The wine was poured, and the glass lifted in condolence and sympathy and gratitude, not only for the wine itself, but for our inclusion inside the circle. At this moment, how it tasted doesn't matter. Wine makes life liquid and tangible. Father had died and we raised a glass to him, we who had known one another for many years and were united in the love of these wines, which brought us together at the start and had brought us together again.

Usually I sniff the wine for clues, but this was like nothing I'd ever encountered. The color was deep but not at all golden; rather, a chlorophyll-saturated thick green. The fragrance was sappy, verdant, boxwoody, forest floor. The palate was gorgeously confusing, full of old-wine mystery but still *stiff* and crazily fresh. It was dry—Stefan thought perhaps 30 grams per liter (3 percent) of sweetness; in those days a wine fermented until it felt like stopping. It was one of his final three bottles, he said, and he himself was tasting it for the first time. Were we ready to know what it was?

A *1945*, one of only three wines made by the Justens in that great tragic vintage. The wines were made by widows, grandparents, and children in the settling dust of the cataclysm. This wine was hidden from the occupying French until they withdrew in 1948. It was my first '45, too, and I was muted, flattened. There were wet eyes among my companions, but it was too sudden, too unreal for me; I needed this wine at the end of an evening of intimate conversation with beloved friends. We were late for our next appointment, and here was this strange green sap dancing in the glass as if it were immortal.

Although I'm very chummy with many of the growers with whom I work, Justen isn't one of them. We don't yuck it up. But each year he brings some old wines out when we've finished the work of tasting the new vintage. Stefan is a reserved sort of man; wine is how he conveys the value he places on our relationship. It is almost unbearably touching, and I can never let it show.

Still, emotion lives by its own rules and when it wants to appear there's little one can do to curtail it. Sigrid Selbach, as I've mentioned, sometimes joins me on my rounds among Mosel growers. One of her oldest friends is Hans-Leo Christoffel of the estate Joh. Jos. Christoffel in Ürzig, to whom I was introduced in 1986. Sigrid and Hans-Leo were school chums, and though each married other people—very happily in both cases—theirs is a rare chemistry, which takes the form of them cracking each other up. I am sure that in some way my holistic experience of tasting Christoffel is informed by their constant laughter.

One year when our work was done, Hans-Leo drolly asked if we wouldn't "mind" tasting something back a few years, having worked up quite a thirst tasting the new vintage. We supposed we could be persuaded.

The wine had that wonderful color in transit from young green to grown-up gold, a kind of palimpsest of youth and matu-

rity. I figured it was between twenty-five and thirty years old—
with that color it couldn't possibly be older. It had an entirely
heavenly Mosel fragrance that grew smoky as it sat in the glass.
The palate was long and dry, with delicate smoke in the finish; just lovely in its calm, meditative way. Guessing the vintage
would be difficult, but I was pointing toward 1966. Wrong. The
wine was a 1959, an Auslese, not one of the huge ones for which
the vintage is famous, but a delicate one from the same parcel
the current "three-star" hails from. I had never tasted such a
youthful and pensive '59, and while I was wondering at its beauty
I glanced over at Sigrid; she was chuckling with Hans-Leo, just
as these two friends have done since the first time I'd seen them
together twelve years earlier.

Sigrid first brought me to this house, and now here we were
again, drinking this '59—the year Johannes, her eldest, was
born. I started to cry because I didn't deserve to be there. I'd had
too many hands in too many cookie jars in my life. Silly, isn't it?
In order to try to *be* worthy, and because I felt so sentimental, I
rather ceremoniously thanked Sigrid for bringing me here and
for all the things that had led to this moment, trying desperately
to keep my voice from breaking. "Oh, now; it's too early in the
day for such compliments!" she sang out. And, perfectly, the
moment dissolved.

It occurs to me that we all are acquainted with "spiritual"
experience in various everyday forms. Think of nostalgia, a sudden awareness that time has passed, when our old life assumes
a roseate glow and the life to come seems all too brief. I suspect that anyone who has ever signed divorce papers has had
a moment of transcendence, no matter the relief. It has ended,
the dream has ended, the hopes and the plans, and now that

you're no longer fighting with this appalling Other you remember that you loved this person, and for many years you made a life and managed not to maim each other. And now you're just another person who failed, that's what it feels like, and suddenly you realize how *hard* it all is, trying to be half-decent and fair and loving and to live with your own disastrous personality, and we're all milling and colliding in the dark, and there is a great sorrow in it, but it somehow isn't exactly *sad*. My point is not that we should live in such a state all the time; it would kill us, not to mention bore those around us to catatonia. My point is that such states are a part of life, that wine can deliver them, and that it simply *makes no sense* to exclude them forcibly, as we far too often do.

If I live in a world with other beings who are as real as I am, I can never be entirely lonely. I can't make you feel this, though I can ask you to trust me. It isn't weird. Its *absence* is weird, and its deliberate absence when we ourselves have shoved it away is perverse. We're all afraid to die, but that's not nearly as sad as the number of us who are afraid to *live*.

Do I stretch my point too far, linking mere wine to questions of life and death? I'll entertain the thought. We are not all made the same way. We have to live the lives that come naturally.

I had a friend in Austria who was about the sweetest man who ever trod the earth but cast an indulgent eye toward my more mystical wanderings. The fiend would present supernal old vintages of his wines and then tease me when I sank into the spell they cast. Yet each year he brought another one out, and there I went into my silly trance. He'd cock his head as if to say, *You know, it is just wine*, and I'd cock my head back as if to say,

Well, in that case, why've you spent your whole life making it? Thus our affectionate impasse.

His name was Erich Salomon, and he was one of the many new people I met when I was first researching Austrian wine and assembling my portfolio. There were many remarkable personalities (the ebullient Ludwig Hiedler, the genial sage Willi Bründlmayer, the elegant-earthy queen Heidi Schröck . . .), but perhaps none as striking as Erich. There was a cheerful affection about him, as if he possessed a rogue gene that made him quiveringly ready to be delighted by the world. Happy the man who is born that way. It is entirely apart from the cultivation of optimism as a point of view. That never works. It is, rather, a piece of absurd good fortune to find in life a source of such cheer. In Erich it took the forms of generosity, collegiality toward other vintners, an instinct to kibitz, and affection for nature. I'll never forget his healing a tree that had been stabbed by the tines of a forklift. He bandaged the bark and watched over the wounded tree as if it were human. And a year later he showed it to me proudly and joyfully—"See? It's all better. You can hardly see the wound."

His wines, of course, were lovely, and imbued with his caring spirit. He didn't fuss over his sales. Each year he greeted my friends and me in his sweet, teasing way. And then one year he said he'd been ill. Didn't go into detail, but it would be like Erich to downplay it anyway, such was his tact. I didn't press; he'd tell me what he wanted me to know.

The following year brought the news that Erich's younger brother Bert would leave a career in wine marketing to assume control of the estate, with Erich at his side. Neither of Erich's two children was interested in being a vintner, and Bert's arrival was a perfect solution.

As the years passed, I'd see them together at times, and at other times I'd be told Erich was ailing but sent his greetings. One year he was in India on an ayurvedic cure. Last year when I visited the estate, I asked after Erich and was told he was on the mend from a debilitating flu that had laid him up for weeks, but that he'd be out to say hi. It was a mild spring day, and my group sat under the linden tree that Erich had nursed back to health all those years ago. Some of those traveling with me had never met him. I wondered how he'd be. And as we were an hour or so into the tasting, I heard a familiar voice, and there was Erich, loping across the courtyard with a huge grin and an entirely bald head. "It's my Bruce Willis phase!" he said. He looked hale enough, and he sat with us for ten minutes or so, saying little. He seemed almost apologetic, as if he didn't want to obtrude on our work on such a fine spring day. I tried to draw him out about India. I would have sat there forever talking with him. But he took his leave and strode back into the house, holding close the extent to which he'd had to rally his strength to come sit with us.

That was May. In December arrived the news I dreaded, that the cancer had killed him. He was in his mid-sixties but seemed younger. Men like Erich always seem younger. The evening we heard the news, my wife and I opened a bottle of a 1982 Riesling Erich had made, and which we had recently received. Karen had barely met Erich, but I needed to drink this wine with her.

The bottle was good, with a clean cork, a good, healthy color. Old wine does a trick, or something that seems like a trick. It starts out almost stale and musty, smelling not of itself but of the cellar in which it lay dormant and beating. In the first instant all old wines smell alike; they smell like "old wines." This one did, too. So we sat and drank this taciturn herald of time and memory and thought about the man who made it. Seven years before, Erich had renewed the lease on the vineyard from which it came, a site owned by the monks of the Abbey of Passau, who still receive a tithe of its production. He had told me the story of the ceremony when the new lease was signed, wondering who would be present for the next renewal, thirty years later.

The following spring when I was back at the estate, we sat with Bert and his family while a bottle of his and Erich's grand-father's wine, from the 1943 vintage, was served. At my request, we joined hands around the table. The wine seemed so fresh as to suggest the eternal. I thought of the '82 I had drunk that evening with my beloved. I remembered how it sat in our glasses, mute at first. And then suddenly, miraculously, it transformed itself, it found the fruit and tenderness with which it was born, it seemed to exhale in pure relief, free at last from the confines of the bottle, and the dark cellar. It sat there in our glasses, and my wife and I watched in wonder as it rose from the dead.

ACKNOWLEDGMENTS

I wish I had thought of this book's title all by myself. In fact, the man who thought of it was New York restaurateur Peter Hoffman, who hosted a wine dinner featuring a poetry reading between courses, and wines. Of course, I'd have thought of it eventually. Of course.

Robert "Bobby" Kacher got me my first job in the wine business. He took a leap of faith. I had no experience and was quite a wine bore. Although he and I disagree at times, and our philosophies could be said to be at odds, he is a great hero. He knows himself and is faithful to his truth—he has integrity.

Howard G. Goldberg first "discovered" me, in 1987, when my fledgling portfolio showed well in a tasting he attended. He has been an unfailingly generous and not entirely uncritical angel ever since.

David Schildknecht was in retail when we first met. We quickly became brothers in arms, and have remained so even as our interests have diverged.

Among the many people who have offered encouragement

and support beyond the call, Howard Silverman, Bill Mayer, Tom Schmeisser, Paul Provost, and Hiram Simon all stand out.

The first sommeliers to put my wines in their programs were real pioneers. They included Scott Carney, Andrea (then) Immer, Daniel Johnnes, and Steve Olsen. All are still in the industry in various capacities, and none has suffered an apparent neck injury from having stuck it out as far as they did.

Alice Feiring was instrumental in helping me find an agent and publisher. When I asked her we were barely even acquaintances, but she assisted me with a touching and nearly incredible generosity.

Marnie Old took time and care with this project, for which I thank her.

Betsy Amster is a wonderful agent and critic and friend.

Blake Edgar has been kind beyond measure as I taxed his patience with this manuscript.

I work with outstanding people. Kevin Pike, Liz DiCesare, Jonathan Schwartz, and Leif Sundström are all much more than colleagues; they are kin. My association with Michael and Harmon Skurnik has been a joy from the first moment, and remains the best move I ever made—in a rare moment of wisdom and lucidity—since entering the wine business.

Without the sage council and abiding friendship of Peter Schleimer, I could never have launched my Austrian wine program, not to mention I'd be a much less happy guy.

I thank every single vintner whom I have ever represented for the privilege of being associated with their fine work, and for the trust and friendship they have shown me.

But one family stands out. And a story wants to be told.

After I made my first trip to German wine regions, in May 1978, I returned in a state of fanatic wonder. And I immediately set about locating all of Munich's fine-wine retailers to see what I could buy close to home. One of these shops was in a basement in a near-in suburb, and I was browsing during my first visit when I heard the proprietor's voice admonishing a customer in tones of nearly theatrical snootiness. I looked around and caught sight of a young man, apparently an employee, with whom I exchanged a mutual raising of the brows.

I approached him and asked, "Did he really just say that to the guy?" and received the reply, "Oh, he's just warming up; it gets worse as the day goes on." And we were off and running, the first words of a friendship that is in its thirty-second year. I learned the young man was the son of a winegrower named Strub, in Nierstein, a village I had just visited. "Next time you come, please stop in at my winery," he invited.

Walter Strub was in the middle of his *Wanderjahr* when he had to return to the estate. His father had suffered a heart attack and his mother had burned her hands; Walter was needed. I visited him many times over the next four years, and we sat up many a night saving the world over bottles of wine at the kitchen table, as young men do. When I was preparing to return to the United States, Walter drove the four hours to Munich to pack up my cellar and have it shipped for me. He was the first vintner to let me taste prebottled wine before *dosage* was blended in to adjust the final sweetness.

When I conceived the notion of creating a German wine portfolio a few years later, Walter was the first person I visited. By then there was Margit, whom he soon married. I have worked with Strub's wines since day one, and have spent more pleasurable hours with him and Margit than with anyone else I know.

 This might not have happened had I confessed an appalling transgression I perpetrated early on. It was July, and I was in Germany putting the first version of my portfolio together, and I started with a visit to Nierstein, where Walter and Margit put me up in their attic guest room. It was my first day, I was jet-lagged, and we had stayed up far too late and drunk an absurd quantity of wine. Sometime in the night I had to piss with great ferocity. The house was dark, and its narrow wooden stairways were steep and creaky. I could turn on the lights and wake everyone, or try to stumble down and risk a serious and noisy fall. To make things worse it had started to rain. Hard. But that gave me a hideous idea. I could piss out the window! The rain would wash it away, and no one would ever know. Ahhhh-h-h-h!

 When I rose the next morning I looked out my window and saw I had pissed on Walter's father's *car*, and when I confessed this sordid business many years later, to gales of laughter, Walter said, "My father could never understand where this green spot came from on his roof!"

 When Hans Selbach died, I arranged to fly over for the funeral. I'd be on the ground less than thirty-six hours. I phoned Walter and said I'd drop by—Nierstein is twenty-five minutes from Frankfurt airport—to drink a pot of tea before making the two-hour drive to the Mosel. "Don't do that," Walter said. "I'll pick you up, and we can drive to the Mosel together, and then I'll bring you back to Nierstein." Hearing the friendship in his words, I nearly wept. He'd save me the expense, the exhausted drive, and the solitude. This is what a friend does.

 Lifelong friendships will invariably fly through weather from time to time, as ours has, and might again. But there isn't a single day I am not grateful to the Strub family—Margit, Walter, Sebastian, Johannes, Juliane, even Emma the piddling beagle (like I'm one to talk . . .)—for the simple miracle of being such good people. This book is written with love for them all.

Designer: Nola Burger
Text: 10/15 Janson
Display: Bodoni Roman
Compositor: BookMatters, Berkeley
Printer and Binder: Maple-Vail Book Manufacturing Group

The
GIRL
Who Could Read
HEARTS

SHERRY MAYSONAVE

BALBOA
PRESS
A DIVISION OF HAY HOUSE

Balboa Press books may be ordered through booksellers or by contacting:

Balboa Press
A Division of Hay House
1663 Liberty Drive
Bloomington, IN 47403
www.balboapress.com
1 (877) 407-4847

Because of the dynamic nature of the Internet, any web addresses or links contained in this book may have changed since publication and may no longer be valid. The views expressed in this work are solely those of the author and do not necessarily reflect the views of the publisher, and the publisher hereby disclaims any responsibility for them.

This is a work of fiction. All of the characters, names, incidents, organizations, and dialogue in this novel are either the products of the author's imagination or are used fictitiously.

Any people depicted in stock imagery provided by Thinkstock are models, and such images are being used for illustrative purposes only. Certain stock imagery © Thinkstock.

Printed in the USA.

ISBN: 978-1-5043-5111-9 (sc)
ISBN: 978-1-5043-5113-3 (hc)
ISBN: 978-1-5043-5112-6 (e)

Library of Congress Control Number: 2016902067

Balboa Press rev. date: 05/11/2016

Dedicated to my late beloved sisters:
Donna Horn Huie Thetford and Carolyn Horn Gordon,
and to my dear brother-in-law, the remarkable Mark W. Gordon,
who took such extraordinary care of our precious Carolyn.

CHAPTER ONE

*H*igh in the hills of Berkeley, California, the omen hung in the stillness of the late afternoon air like a full moon yet to rise. Seeking refuge, Kate Kindrick huddled in the branches of the walnut tree flanking the driveway of the two-story brick home at 537 Spruce Street.

Kate, a six-year-old who was clueless about the rare seventh sense with which she was gifted—the ability to read human hearts coupled with keen intuition—felt squirmy in her skin. She sniffed at the air, her nose scrunching into a wrinkle. An odd scent seeped into her pores.

Pointing her index finger at the sky, she held it there as a lightning rod, fully expecting something telling to stick to it. Within seconds, as if a definitive substance had pinged her finger, she brought it down mere millimeters from her eyes. Sleuth-like, Kate examined every nuance, paying extra attention to the whorl pattern on her fingertip.

She touched the whorl to her tongue. A fearsome shiver snaked through her, one so potent she jolted, almost falling from the tree. Her fingers clutched frantically, grabbing at the limb and its leafy offshoots. Her body jerked upward forcing her weight to shift. After multiple unstable wobbles, she regained her balance. Even still, a feeling of dread had taken hold, had set up residence as surely as if a horde of poisonous snakes had moved in, their aliveness slithering deep within her.

Inside the house at 537 Spruce Street, an angel waited. She hovered respectfully atop the mound of white icing, atop a thing on Earth called a birthday cake. Her skin appeared to be a translucent plastic, and her eyes were radiant like blue topaz. Her wings, a golden-silvery hue, shimmered in a feathery quiver.

The clock on the kitchen oven clicked, displaying new digital numbers. The angel blinked her eyes. It was now less than one hour before the party, the celebration of Kate's entrance on Earth six years ago. Kate's mother said it was the day she was born to life, and she was. And she wasn't. Not from the angel's perspective, anyway, for the angel had known of the percipient soul who would be named Kate eons before she was born to the Kindrick family that lived on planet Earth.

While eyeing the birthday cake, the angel allowed images to float through her, compelling visions and ponderings of what was likely to transpire long before the clock announced a new day. *Humans always had choices, especially about whether they received or blocked Divine guidance. But their disregard for the universal law—for every action there is a reaction—was often perplexing. Today, though, it was most troubling. Would the subjects in question listen? Would they take heed of the subtle inner urgings, the Almighty's whisperings, that if acted upon could prevent disaster? Or would they make such a misstep that it could spin into motion an entire series of tragic events?* Soon, she would know.

Hoping to shed her angst, the angel focused on the details of the cake. Although she did not partake of earthly cuisine, she was captivated by food, all the textures, colors, and combinations that humans concocted. She found the cake's aroma utterly enticing. What's more, the meringue frosting with its perfect peaks looked heavenly, like fluffy cumulus clouds that invited happy imagination.

Even still, there was no denying it. An ominous aura sheathed the Kindrick kitchen, which gleamed a lemon-yellow hue, one of Kate's favorite colors.

The angel reflected upon little Kate and how she enjoyed color, all colors except orange, that is. Kate loved to eat orange slices, carrot sticks, pumpkin pie, and tangerine popsicles. Nonetheless, she refused to wear the color orange or have anything in her room orange, not pillows or walls. The funny thing, though, was that Kate's hair was somewhat orange, the light burnt-orange shade of a freshly peeled sweet potato, and strikingly similar to the new hair of an Irish-Setter puppy.

Hair color didn't seem to be an issue for dogs, the angel mused. No matter what the breed, hair color didn't evoke howling, yowling, or any concern. And regardless of the exact color of their hair, almost all dogs had brown eyes. Some type of chocolate. Irish Setters were no exception. Take Keebie, for example. She was the Kindrick's Irish Setter, who was expecting puppies soon. Her eyes were similar to S'mores—milk chocolate mixed with a graham-cracker tan—that looked just right, warmly artistic with her burnt-orange hair.

Human eyes were not as predictable. Kate's eyes were green, resembling two big olives.

Much to the angel's chagrin, Kate's cousin, Marilla Marzy, often taunted Kate that she looked like a pizza with her olive-green eyes and saucy red-orange hair. More often than not, Marilla Marzy referred to Kate as *Pizza Girl,* saying it in such a way that her tongue spat out the name as if the pizza tasted rancid.

On the other hand, much to the angel's delight, Kate's favorite uncle—Terrence Ted, otherwise known as TT— admired Kate's unique beauty. He often told Kate that her red hair and green eyes gave her a look of royalty, like a real-life princess. On Kate's fifth birthday, Uncle TT had overheard Marilla Marzy tell Kate that she not only looked like a pizza but that she was uglier than plain old ugly.

TT had then quickly escorted Kate into another room. Caressing her cheek, calming her trembling chin, he had said, "Kate, look at me. I want you to get this. In no way do you resemble a pizza, not any type. And you are not ugly. You are beautiful, Kate. Seriously beautiful."

He had then stared off into space, his eyes locking into a reality that rotated on a different axis. His fists had tightened, gripping time, handfuls of seconds as they passed silently through his fingers. Then he said, "Let's keep in mind that with Marilla Marzy's father forbidding her to wear colored contact lens, she faces the world every day with mismatched eyes. One brown and one green."

The angel sighed at the memory.

The clock flipped its numbers again. Only twenty minutes now. A nervous shudder fluttered the angel's shimmery feathers. Then a dreaded calm, like the still before a storm, settled over her.

Mrs. Kindrick peered out the kitchen window and called out in her soprano voice, "Kate, come down from that tree. Your cake is ready for candles. It's almost time for the party."

Six candles waited on the granite countertop, laying in crisscross fashion next to the arrangement of stargazer lilies—Kate's favorite flower. Fragrant and fully open, the flowers resembled six-pointed stars. Bursting forth from each star's center was a cluster of antenna tipped with flat round eyes, all gazing upward as if they were unable to contain their fascination for Heaven.

Clutching her cherished toy, a Power-Ranger action figure, Kate skidded around the corner like a veteran baseball player sliding into home plate. Beaming a smile in the direction of the cake, she jumped to her feet and reached for the candles.

"No, wash your hands first," Kate's mother shrieked.

Kate sprinted to the sink and turned on the hot water. With sudsy bubbles lathering her hands, she scrubbed at the leaf stains from when she had fought to hold onto the tree limb. Eyeing the cake, she said, "Wow, Mama, my rainbow cake looks awesome."

Technically, it was not a rainbow cake, but Kate called it that because it had six layers, with each layer being a different color, each representing one year of her life. When cut, the cake would be a six-color delight. That is, six colors when not counting the white ⸺ White didn't count because white contained all colors in ⸺, even the colors humans on Earth couldn't see yet—the

gs' birthday cakes were decorated to the hilt with layers underneath being plain vanilla or chocolate. ⸺e bottom layer of her cake was red like watermelon while ⸺ ⸺ond one was pineapple yellow, and the third was kiwi green. The fourth layer was berry purple. The fifth was pink like the inside of a fig, and the sixth was sky blue topped with cumulus clouds of fluffy white frosting. A fruity rainbow with a serving of sky.

Perched atop the clouds of icing was Etta Ebella, the angel. Etta Ebella was the name bestowed upon her by Kate's grandmother, Grammy Mer, who gave Kate the doll the very day Kate was born.

Kate loved to hear the story of when Grammy Mer had presented the angel doll to her—when she was only two hours old. Kate's tiny eyes had been closed, all tightly squinched. But at the sound of Grammy Mer's voice, her baby eyelids had fluttered, had struggled a few seconds, and then opened wide. Then when Grammy Mer held up the doll, Kate's little mouth had begun moving, and tiny purring noises had come forth as if she was trying to talk. Later when Grammy Mer laid her in the bassinet and nestled the winged doll aside her, baby Kate had wrestled her infant arm from the swaddle and placed her wee hand directly on the doll's chest. The pediatric nurse had commented that in all of her years she had never seen a newborn do such a thing.

Although Grammy Mer was now ill, recently struck by an unexplained disease that confined her to a wheelchair and inhibited her speech, she was an award-winning grandmother. When her Grammy Mer was around, Kate felt like she was a precious jewel radiating purpose and value, felt like she was the most important little girl in the entire universe. Although her grandmother could no longer communicate with words, Kate felt completely loved by her. Yes, loved, all the way through to her bones—and beyond.

While rinsing the soap from her hands, Kate's eyes darted about the sunny kitchen searching the lemony walls for why the eerie feeling was inside the house, too. *Had it followed her indoors?* The walls provided no answers, had nothing at all to say.

Locking eyes with the angel, Kate watched the doll's wings flutter ever so slightly and her heart light up like a brilliant diamond. Kate cast a glance at her mother to see if she had noticed, but her mother, busy with the party napkins, was oblivious to Etta Ebella's magic. What's more, she honestly believed that Etta Ebella was just a plastic doll with no life in her.

To Kate, it seemed that many living people in the world possessed less life than Etta Ebella did. They were the ones that were plastic, not real at all. Kate could always spot them—the breathing plastic people.

Some sported wide smiles while their eyes shot angry darts all about them and their hearts quaked with fearful tremors. Others wore frozen frowns and had eyes filled with nothingness while their hearts contained heaps of icebergs. Some had eyes filled with thorns, and their hearts were stacked with sharp spikes—dagger-like weapons ready to shoot at anyone who disagreed with them. And worse yet, some had eyes resembling muddy gravel that blocked *all* light. Their hearts oozed with puss and scabs from hundreds of deadbolts locked tightly.

The breathing plastic people's hearts and eyes could look a million different ways. The most telling sign, though, was in their hugs: plastic arms and plastic hearts giving out no love at all, not even a smattering.

"Alrighty, Birthday Girl, it's time to put the candles on your cake," Mrs. Kindrick said.

To Kate, her mother's tone was an order, not an invitation. The good part was that her mom would allow her to put the candles anywhere on the cake she wanted. Kate's mother believed in fostering creativity, letting her young daughter have some choices that were safe and within reason while also allowing her to experience consequences. Like last year.

Kate fingered the raised polka-dots on this year's candles, remembering her fifth birthday, how she had intentionally dug her fingertips and the candles into the white fluff so she could lick the icing from them. When her mother turned her back, she had even moved the candles around a bit for a double dip. And her tongue had basked in the glorious taste of the meringue frosting. Delicious had quickly turned to dismay, though, when she discovered that meringue icing could not be re-fluffed after it was set.

Her mother had frowned, the corners of her lips turning downward when she had tried to smooth the gouges. She had even heated the spreader in an attempt to warm the icing, hoping to fluff it better. Nonetheless, the icing had remained obstinate, sticky, wrinkled lumps refusing to look like fluffy clouds ever again.

Kate's daddy had suggested that they scrape off the icing and make another batch, or that he rush out to buy a bakery cake for the party and save that one for them to eat later. But Kate's mother had said no, absolutely not, that the homemade meringue frosting was a sacred birthday tradition in her family. It was important to appreciate the icing, the cost of its ingredients, and its maker's love and labor in preparing it.

And so it was, the ugly cake had prevailed, had taken center stage before it was served.

At the family party that year, Uncle TT had said, "Princess, what's up with ushering in your fifth year with a jacked-up cake?" Interestingly, it had been early in Kate's fifth year that Grammy Mer had suddenly and mysteriously become incapacitated.

She must usher in her sixth year with a pretty cake, Kate thought. She must because she liked pretty, and because she didn't want anything bad to happen to anyone she loved. Not this year, not ever again.

"Mama, will you roll up my sleeves for me? I want them rolled up high, up past my elbows. They might mess up the fluffs."

"Good idea, pumpkin. Here, hold still."

While her mother made a small cuff with the soft knit fabric, Kate watched Etta Ebella blink her right eye—a playful wink—and then flash one stream of light from her heart. She clearly agreed with this idea of rolling up the sleeves. Kate's mother didn't see the doll's antics. Her focus remained immersed in making repetitive fabric rolls up one arm and then the other.

Picking up one candle, Kate held it by its wick and gently pushed it in through the thick icing, all the way into the cake part. After the second one, her stomach gave a burble as if the candle had poked through it. Nevertheless, Kate kept her attention on the art of planting the next four candles.

One by one, she set all six candles in the frosting—all without a single smudge. Her heart swelled with pride as she admired the design. The candles looked so pretty—in fact, simply beautiful—in a half-circle around the front of Etta Ebella, edging her dress perfectly.

"Now, Kadie Girl, is it a good idea to have the candles so close to Etta Ebella?" Kate's mother asked. "Remember, the candles will burn for a bit while we all sing the *Happy Birthday* song to you."

Kate heard the disapproval. There was no mistaking the way her mother said her name. When her mother called her Katie Girl that was clue enough, but when she changed the "t" to "d," as in Kadie, that meant her mother clearly disagreed with her choice. But no, Kate would not move the candles, couldn't move them without messing up the icing. She remained adamant; she wanted the candles exactly where they were, and so did Etta Ebella.

The truth was Etta Ebella didn't think placing the candles that close to her was a good idea, either. No, she didn't, not at all. Blinking her blue topaz eyes repeatedly, Etta Ebella had tried to warn Kate by sending a prickly sensation to invade her stomach.

Kate had felt it, the odd bristly burble, but she had chosen to ignore it.

"Alrighty, Kadie girl, have it your way," Kate's mother said. "Now run upstairs and change into your new party dress. It's all laid out on the bed for you. Your new sparkly shoes, too."

The door bell chimed three times in quick succession, a code. Her face alight with glee, Kate ran down the stairs at breakneck speed, all the while yelling, "Uncle TT is here!"

She flung open the door and could barely see her uncle's face because of the tower of presents he carried. "Wow, are all those for me?"

"Special delivery for Miss Katelyn Kindrick. Happy Birthday, Princess. You betcha, they're for you, one for every year you are old. They're bulky though, so lead the way to the party table."

Kate took off skipping toward the kitchen. "Mama, look, Uncle TT has brought me six presents."

"That bottom one looks mighty big. Terrence, you spoil her terribly."

The doorbell rang again. "I'll get that," Kate's mother said.

TT eyed the cake. "Your cake is beautiful this year, Princess, just like you." He started to walk away when a shiver slithered through him. He looked back to the cake, then all around the kitchen. Everything seemed in order.

After feasting in the dining room, the party guests began gathering in the kitchen near the cake table. Kate's grandfather, Poppy Pop, rolled in Grammy Mer's wheelchair and locked it into position.

Eagerly, Grammy Mer inspected the cake. On Kate's other birthdays, even when the cake was not appealing, like last year, she had felt joyous upon seeing the doll presiding over the cake like a guardian angel. But this year, her stomach knotted at the sight.

As everyone found their places, Kate hopped from one foot to the next, while eyeballing the mound of brightly wrapped presents. Her daddy's sister, Sammy Sue, and her husband, Sandy, each picked up a present and shook it a bit. One made a sound; the other didn't. Sammy Sue pointed to the one that rattled, suggesting Kate open it first.

Her mother's sister, Abigail, and her family— Abigail's husband, Vaynem, and their teenage daughter, Marilla Marzy— straggled in from the dining room. When they joined the birthday circle, Marilla Marzy stood a bit aloof from her parents.

Uncle TT came dashing into the circle and stood next to Marilla Marzy just as Kate's mother brought out the lighter for the candles.

Grammy Mer opened her mouth with the intention of saying STOP, but only an eerie garbled scream came forth.

Kate's daddy said, "Mom, you're starting the song before the candles are lit." He laughed, trying to lighten the moment of sad truth—Grammy Mer could no longer speak or control the sounds that burst forth from her.

Kate looked to Grammy Mer, searching her face. That strange prickle returned to her tummy as she tried to read her grandmother's expression. *Surely, it was a smile since it was time for her big birthday moment,* Kate decided. But little did she know, her grandmother's face muscles no longer worked on command, her brain incapable of sending the signals.

With a shrug of her shoulders, Kate placed a hand on the lighter alongside her mother's hand. Together, they moved it from one candle to the next until all six were blazing.

Kate's mother started the song. Others joined in on cue, all singing *"Happy Birthday to you. Happy Birthday to you."*

Suddenly, TT sneezed. And then again. And again. Over and over in rapid succession, he sneezed, thunderous rib-racking sneezes as if a massive cloud of fusty polluted air had descended upon him.

Giggles welled up in Kate. Others joined in, some laughing heartily. Poppy Pop slapped his knee. Kate's daddy swiped at the tears that seeped from his eyes as he howled. Uncle Sandy was bent double with deep belly laughs. Aunt Sammy Sue's mouth was open with a huge grin.

Kate's mother tried starting the birthday song again. Ear-splitting sneezes interrupted her attempt. She tried once more, to no avail; she clutched at her stomach like it was laughing, too.

TT continued to sneeze, the most monstrous sneezing fit he had ever had or anyone there had ever witnessed.

The only person who didn't laugh was Vaynem, Marilla Marzy's father, whose eyes remained on the cake.

Everyone else remained riveted upon TT's face contorting with the sneezes. Cartoon-like, TT's nose continued to twitch, especially his nostrils, as if more sneezing was yet to come.

When the twitching finally ceased, and Kate turned to make her wish and blow out the candles, her heart almost stopped beating.

The hem of Etta Ebella's dress was melting, the bottom of her left wing was turning brown, and her cheek had a large moist blister on it as if her whole face might dissolve away. A bright flame spiked from the angel's shoulder, rising all the way up to the ceiling.

Screams and frantic commotion flooded the Kindrick kitchen.

Kate's mighty wish on her sixth birthday quickly converted to a fervent prayer: *Dear Jesus, please don't let Etta Ebella die. It's all my fault. Please, Dear Jesus, please HELP us! We need a miracle.*

CHAPTER TWO

In San Francisco—across the Bay from 537 Spruce Street— Dr. Angelique Donahorn was not having a happy day, the angel's birthday. With the angel gone, missing for well over six years now, there was not a song to be sung.

With a heavy heart, Angelique stared at the cupcake. Peaks of creamy lemon frosting surrounded a lavender birthday candle that stood tall, its ample wick exposed. The cupcake honoree was older than one year, yet one candle was tradition, as was one fresh orchid bloom, a white paphiopedilum bellatulum variety, placed to the side of the candle.

Extending the ebony lighter, Angelique's slender hand hovered briefly over the cupcake. The wick instantly flared, spiking high like a church steeple. The flame reflected brightly onto the blue topaz, a 12-carat solitaire stone worn on her right-hand ring finger.

The flame danced and swayed, making the facets of a nearby Waterford crystal vase sparkle like diamonds. Pink stargazer lilies— two-dozen stems, if counted—overflowed from the vase. The slight heat from the candle flame made the open blossoms even more fragrant. Their sweet essence wafted about the spacious kitchen.

Peering into the facets of the ring, Angelique watched its bouncing refractions echo the candle flame. She decided that her beloved angel, though no longer with her, would still want her to make a wish. The angel would even approve a grand wish, one made in honor of her birthday. After all, it was the day the angel's earthly body had been completed.

Angelique pondered the options. Wishes floated through her brain like brightly-colored tropical fish swimming in an aquarium. *If she were here, which grand wish would Angel Eve encourage me to make?*

Suddenly, Angelique's heart surged with a deep longing. The surprising realization exploded in her mind. Instantly, Angelique understood. Without her conscious consent, as if the angel had taken charge, the wish had been made and cast into the flame. The potent sensation consumed her. The tingle of the once-caged desire, now set free, strolled through her. Its footprints—goose bumps—rippled down her neck, her back, both arms, legs, and ankles, even her toes.

Leaning forward, Angelique took a deep breath and exhaled, outing the candle's blaze. Passionate, her exhale was, forceful as if the candle had multiplied itself and a million forked flames had to be blown out for the wish to have any hope of coming true.

Tears unexpectedly sprang forth. She plucked a linen napkin from the stack on the counter and dabbed at her eyes. Her other hand reached for the orchid. Popping the entire bloom into her mouth, Angelique chewed slowly and deliberately, the aromatic flavors wrapping her taste buds in their gift. *It was better than butter lettuce*, she concluded, determining that someday she would eat an entire orchid salad. Swallowing with her eyes closed, she luxuriated in the clean, aromatic aftertaste of the orchid. Then, she began to laugh.

Since when do I believe that Heaven on Earth is possible? I've envisioned a peaceful world, one with no wars, and no high bridges. And I've wished to meet the love of my life—a unique and powerful man. And he's a sweet-hearted man, one who inspires me to soar with purpose. He's a man who I can truly love and a man who will love me in return, love me truly and passionately. I must be dreaming. She lifted her hand to her face and raked her fingernails lightly across her cheek bone. *I'm not dreaming. I'm awake.*

A mango born in a world of apples that's what she was; at least that's what her father always said about her. Being different was an affliction and an asset, both aspects working overtime to keep her career life full and her love life empty.

As time ticked on, the more birthdays she had, her heart had secretly yearned for true love, for a life partner. Questioning the likelihood of such, she had suppressed the desire to find a special mango man, had buried it deep inside her in a grave of doubt. Oh, she knew there were unique men in the world. She had dated her share of them, always pure infatuation quick to burn out. None had captivated her heart.

In hindsight, she had mistakenly connected power and uniqueness to bad boys. What a joke that was. *Bad boy types are the weakest men on Earth;* she conjectured, remembering that jerk, the writer, she had dated. And then, there had been that misogynistic academic, the impeccably dressed university dean who had tried to force himself upon her. Unsuccessful date rape attempt. That was the diagnosis. He was not the first to underestimate her physical strength, all because she inhabited a petite body.

Touching the candle, Angelique vowed to the absent Angel Eve that she would never again knowingly go out with a bad boy type. She would never again date a man like the attorney she had been involved with a few months ago. Vaynem. Such an odd name, but fitting in retrospect. What a worm. He'd been so charming initially, and an intelligent conversationalist. He had peaked her interest seriously, though, when he had said he wanted to make a difference in the world, especially for children. A Board Director for a children's charity organization—that's where they had met—he had been convincing. She was close to falling for him, had almost been seduced by his facade. Then she had discovered three of his secrets: he was married; he had a teenage daughter. And, he was a pornography addict. What a sneaky. snaky complexity he proved to be: confident on the surface while insecure and dark underneath. A bottomless ego-pit of a man, he was minus a heart. Instead, a power complex was the pump that beat in the center of his chest. Angelique sighed.

14

Now she was clear, crystal clear about what kind of man she wanted for her life partner. She wanted sweetness and kindness all mixed up with uniqueness, intelligence, humor, and confident inner power. Yes, she wanted a man who was trustworthy and stable, though courageous and creative, and most importantly, a high-integrity man, as her father had been.

Her father's orator's voice rang in her ears as she remembered him saying, *"Angelique, only be with a man who treats you as well as, or better than, I do."* She feared she had let him down for he had set a high standard—always loving, kind, honest, and generous with her, even when she acted like a brat. And surely her father was disappointed how far she had strayed from his advice, seeing and knowing from his heavenly perch.

Another beloved voice whispered; this memory was of her mama's wise words: *"Angelique, not every mother deserves her children's love. But, beware of marrying a man who doesn't love and respect his mother. She's his first love in a way, and the nature of his relationship with her embeds deeply in his psyche. If he hates her or is indifferent to her, he could easily turn on you. It may not be obvious at first, but when things don't go well for him, he'll blame you. Hold out for true love, Angelique; don't settle for neediness or mere possessiveness."*

Was there even one emotionally healthy man alive in today's world? Angelique wondered. Had her father been an anomaly? Were her expectations too high? Maybe she should forget the unique mango part and look for a regular apple man. Maybe that was the type of man Angel Eve intended for her: an ordinary, virile, Adam's apple man. *Would that type better balance her mango oddities?* Perhaps she would rethink that dinner invitation from the stockbroker she'd met on the plane from Johannesburg yesterday.

The cell phone on the black granite counter vibrated, sounding like a dolphin flipping against a rubber cage. Angelique swiped at the arrow on the lighted screen. "Bon Jour, juh, Sis. Comment êtes-vous?"

"Well now, don't you sound chipper, far cheerier than this morning," replied Annateresa, Angelique's sister. "And just what spell did you cast to disperse all that gloominess?"

Looking affectionately at the cupcake and the candle, Angelique said, "Come now, you know I don't believe in spells. But yes, I am feeling well."

Annateresa rendered a soft whistle into the phone. "What happened?"

"The birthday ritual for Angel Eve… one in her memory, anyway, for wherever she is or isn't in this world. Have you celebrated yet?"

Annateresa said, "Not yet, I am setting up the cupcake now. The conference ended a bit late today, and I didn't have time to find a fresh orchid. So I'm substituting a whale of a strawberry. Do you think that will work?"

"Sure, if it's a tasty one."

"It looks ripe, but Sis, I forgot to ask what you decided about Jonah's party tonight. Ange, please go. He so wants you to come."

After a brief silence, Angelique said, "I phoned him this morning and gave my regrets. I was feeling jet-lagged from my Johannesburg trip. And frankly, Sis, it feels awkward to go without you. Jonah is more your friend than mine."

"So? You're a big girl."

"Yes, and in the last hour, I have reconsidered. I'm thinking now that I just may go … drop in for a little while."

"Wow. Some other spirit has surely invaded your body. Since when do you change your mind or defy etiquette?" teased Annateresa.

"Jonah was quite gracious. He left the door open, saying that he was not taking no for an answer this time. He said to come early or late, that I didn't need to let him know if my plans changed," Angelique replied.

"I'm beginning to think that man has a crush on you," Annateresa said.

"Oh, Sis, get real. He's far too tall for my taste. And besides, it's you and him who have simpatico."

"Maybe my grand wish today should involve asking the angel to teleport me there so I can go to his party with you," Annateresa teased wistfully.

"Teleport?"

"Visualizing the exact location you want to go then instantly traveling through space and time to that place."

"What science-fiction book are you reading now?"

"Never mind. Listen, Ange, I know this was a hard day for you, but someday we are going to find Angel Eve or at least discover what happened to her."

"If we do, it will be nothing short of a miracle," Angelique said.

"Hey, *miracle* is your middle name. You create them wherever you go. Try trusting that everything is as it should be for now."

"There are children starving in Africa and other parts of the world. Little girls, who never go to school, aren't allowed to simply because they are female. Children abused, and mistreated, kidnaped, and sold as sex slaves. Is that how God wants it? Is that how it *should* be?"

Annateresa sighed. "Oh, Ange, what's happened to you? Did that guy you dated, the neurologist who believes we are just animals floating on a rock, mess with your head?"

"No. I believe there is a God. A *Higher Power* of some form. But I'm not sure what extent IT is involved in earthly matters, as for personal miracles," Angelique replied.

"Well, that's a start. I'm relieved to hear you say you believe in some almighty good out there." Annateresa said. "But what do you mean? Not sure about personal miracles?"

"I see miracles every day with my work. Science and technology combined with intelligent action. Even still, with all the medical advances today, we didn't have a miracle with Mother's health." Angelique said. Some of the day's sadness was returning.

"Maybe we did. Dying is the not the worst that can happen to a human being. Life dishes up far worse fates than death."

"Life doesn't. People do by their choices and attitudes," Angelique said.

"Come now, Ange, are you saying you would want mother alive racked with pain, unable to swallow or to breathe on her own? Or that I chose to be born with a deformed leg? That starving and abused children are choosing that life?"

"No, no, no, certainly not. I was thinking of my choices, one, in particular, not seeing Mother before she died."

"Angelique, let it go, once and for all. You were simply obeying Mother's wishes," Annateresa said.

"I am keenly aware of Mother's wishes. It's easy for you to say let go of it because you were there. You shared in her last days, her last moments."

The silence hung heavily.

"Sis, tell me again what mother said about my Angel Eve, about not bringing her to the hospital," Angelique said.

"I asked Mother often if she wanted me to bring Angel Eve to her hospital room. I thought it would be like having you there. But she would always say, *"Angel Eve is exactly where she belongs; she will do more good right where she is."* Of course, I thought that meant that Eve was in her usual perch—at home in mother's bedroom, sitting on the cushion in the window seat where she could see the outdoor patio."

Encouraged by hearing her mother's words and Annateresa's rendition of their mother's cheery voice, Angelique decided not to allow her previous good mood to be dampened. Changing the subject, she said, "So, my sweet sister, what are you and your Angel Ava wishing for when you light her special birthday candle? Something tall, dark, and handsome?"

"I'm not telling. No energy leaks on this big wish. I've learned my lesson," Annateresa sighed. "So, what are you wearing to the party tonight?"

"My birthday suit," Angelique crooned into the phone.

Annateresa chuckled, "You, who always dresses to the nines? My, but you are in a good mood."

"Yes, I am. And please know that whatever your grand wish is today, I wish it for you, too. You deserve it and more."

"Thank you, Ange."

"And Sis, I appreciate you holding the vision of us finding Angel Eve someday, for expecting a miracle." Looking out through the French doors at the full moon rising over the patio, Angelique said, "Isn't it almost time for sunset in Anchorage? You need to get that candle burning and cast your grand wish into its flame."

Glancing at the clock in her hotel room, Annateresa screeched, "E-gads, I must go. Ciao!"

"Bon Soir. Je tam," Angelique said.

Hmmm, what am I going to wear to Jonah's party? Something black.

CHAPTER THREE

At 537 Spruce Street, the gnarled knots thrusting outward from the branch of the walnut tree poked at Kate's hip bones like angry fingers jabbing at her in accusation. Her beloved angel doll, Etta Ebella, was a fragment of herself, now reduced to a charred mess. At least, her earthly replica was. And it was all because Kate had not listened to the odd feeling that had surrounded her on her birthday. And then, she had not paid attention to the prickly warning in the pit of her stomach. In retrospect, that feeling must have been about the candles. The whole thing was her fault.

Was the walnut tree mad at her, too? Kate wondered. The tall tree with its lush branches usually offered comfort. Today, it tendered none.

Heavy sensations filled her chest as if a pile of boulders were sitting upon it. Her body felt achy. When she had appraised the details of Etta Ebella's damage, an awfulness had risen inside of her like a monstrous balloon soon to pop, a misery so dreadful it had threatened to rip her head right from her body.

If only she could stay mad at Uncle TT, blame him and his crazy sneezing fit, she might feel better. At first, she wanted to hate him. This morning she had pouted, wearing the feeling of detesting him like it was a pretty new dress that would cheer up her spirits. But the pretty dress had turned ugly. Waves of nausea had rolled over her, cresting in her stomach and roiling up into her throat. She had heaved and wretched, vomiting ragged threads onto the grass.

The truth was, she couldn't conjure up condemnation of him without hurting herself. The very thought of not being close to her uncle anymore triggered an icy shiver to slink down her spine.

Tree leaves brushed against her as a small breeze rippled through the branches. Her mind floated with the breeze. Soon she was caught up in fun memories of her uncle. She giggled aloud, remembering how he would put baby carrots in his nose to mimic vicious nose fangs, and then make monster faces and noises, all just to make her laugh. What's more, he ate Jell-O without a spoon, an entire cup without getting a drop on his shirt or hands. Figure that.

Try as she may, Kate couldn't be mad at her Uncle TT for sneezing at her prime birthday moment. Disfiguring Etta Ebella was clearly her responsibility. It wasn't a complicated formula. Pure and simple, fire can burn stuff—people and things, alive or dead, animate or inanimate.

Besides, Uncle TT had not put any carrots in his nose that day. People, dogs, or horses usually have no control over sneezing—when they sneeze or how many times. When a sneeze comes on, it must express itself.

By mere chance, TT had stood next to Marilla Marzy, who had worn oodles of perfume to the party. Most people called her M&M, like the candy. Her nickname was mainly due to the mixed colors of her eyeballs, the one green, and the one brown. Some claimed it was because her first and middle name both started with the letter M. Whatever reason was the truth, Kate found it surprising that M&M had been called a sugary candy name since she was a baby, and she still wasn't sweet.

Marilla Marzy was a nut variety M&M; Kate believed. She had a hard center. When she got mad, she pinched and kicked the nearest person or animal. Even when she didn't seem angry, M&M could be downright mean. Kate once saw her kick a newborn kitten away from its mother's breast—it was nursing hungrily—just to see what the kitten or the mother cat would do.

TT had not seen M&M for a whole year, not since Kate's fifth birthday. He didn't know that she now smoked cigarettes and thought she could hide it from the family, especially her father—the only person, place, or thing that M&M feared. In that way, she was smart. But since when did drenching a body with perfume cover up the smell of cigarette-smoke saturated hair and clothes?

TT was allergic to fragrances. He couldn't burn aromatic candles nor could he use scented soaps, shampoos or lotions. Ironically, he smelled better than most people who could.

One time at a family dinner, Kate overheard her aunt—her father's sister, Sammy Sue, who was a University biology professor—explaining why people could be close to death when they sneezed. Just the tiniest thought of her Uncle TT dying, of losing him, made Kate's heart clench with agony.

TT was also allergic to shellfish. But it didn't make him sneeze, it made him swell. If he even came near a pot of cooking shrimp or lobster, his left eyelid would puff up like an inflated skin balloon. It would hang over his eyeball, which then became invisible, making him temporarily blind in that eye. His throat would begin to swell and to close. He would gasp for air.

Aunt Sammy Sue had said that Terrence Ted (TT), her youngest brother, must be careful when eating in restaurants because some chefs didn't understand that people could die from shellfish allergies. Sometimes chefs put shellfish in soups and sauces and garnished plates with them when the menu didn't properly list their presence. This worried Kate, because TT ate in restaurants almost all the time.

A writer and famous author, TT traveled a lot. So far, he had written seven novels. Hollywood had made movies based on five of his books. That would make some people get a big head, but from what Kate could see, her Uncle TT's heart was the biggest part of him.

Kate felt protective of her uncle, yet, in truth, probably not as protective as he felt of her. TT was fully aware that Kate had the rare ability to see and read human hearts, because he did, too.

Grammy Mer's shoulder pressed against the side of the wheelchair; her eyes were seemingly focused on the television. Instead of watching the screen, though, her mind's eye beheld the horror of the angel on fire and the doll's charred remains.

Heaviness pressed upon her, the weight of keeping a secret—the story of the doll and its previous owner. It weighed a ton now, multiplied by concern for Kate, her young granddaughter. The oddity of such unique talents— reading hearts coupled with intense intuition—plus all the corresponding sensitivities, could easily derail the child's life.

Having lived through the misery of being such a child, Grammy Mer understood that Kate faced many challenges living on this Earth planet where spiritual hearts were not prized. Hearts today seemed more and more defiled, she thought. Rarely did she observe a person's heart that was a golden chalice bubbling with love and gratitude. Instead, it seemed most hearts had become storage sheds for hateful grudges, spiteful warfare, and old, painful memories.

And then, there was the gross misunderstanding of hearts being labeled as the home of raw emotion. Her mother had said that the heart was where the soul resided. It was intended to be the center of wisdom, which combined the sagacity of both emotion and intellect. That is if a person kept his or her heart pure with daily exercises of forgiveness and deep prayer or meditation. Otherwise, painful issues not dealt with or healed were stored in the heart, which contaminates emotional, mental, and physical health, limiting one's potential of living true to soul's purpose.

Both her mother and her grandmother had taught her well, Grammy Mer reflected. And she, in turn, had mentored her youngest son, Terrence Ted. All four of her children were intuitive, but Terrence Ted's gifts fit into an entirely different category. And Kate's did, too. Her family lineage continued.

She shivered. Now that she was ill and unable to speak, who would take on the momentous job of mentoring Kate? Who had the capacity to comprehend the child's complicated talents? Who had the time and the patience to teach her to use them for God, not for peril or mere carnival curiosity?

The angel doll had been the appointed one. Now, Terrence Ted seemed the next obvious one to take the reins, but he was ultra busy following his path of purpose.

Could the angel survive? Was it possible that she could continue to operate from a melted plastic body? *Doubtful. The vessel was in ruin.*

Children like Kate needed instruction. Tangible experiences strengthened listening muscles. She must learn to recognize the Almighty's voice in the faintest of whisperings and the subtlest of urges. Sadly, Kate's mother, or her father, for that matter, didn't begin to grasp Kate's gifts or have a clue about how to develop them, however, fine people that they were.

Wishing to bow her head in prayer, she strained and struggled, but nothing moved. Her brain could not communicate with her neck. Not anymore. Thankfully, she could still think prayerful words. For how much longer, though, she did not know.

CHAPTER FOUR

*T*wo weeks after Kate's sixth birthday, Uncle TT took Kate and Etta Ebella for a ride in his new silver spaghetti car. It was one of those lamb-fettuccini sports cars that cost a lot of money, a Lamborghini or a name that sounded like that.

For the life of her, though, Kate couldn't see one thing about that car that resembled a lamb or any pasta she had ever seen. But it had the coolest doors; they unlatched from the bottom and moved upward to open. At night, the lamb-pasta car's headlights became eerie-looking metallic almonds that shone like a pair of alien eyes. Etta Ebella said they looked similar to the eyes of Beings from Uranus.

Uncle TT said they weren't alien at all, that his car looked more like the vehicles used by the magenta turnip-like Beings who lived deep inside the Earth. He had a point; the car was low to the ground and could probably zip along between narrow crevices of rock. But Etta Ebella said the doors were a Gull-Wing design, so surely, the car was not meant to be landlocked. Surely, it was meant to fly, like a spaceship or an angel.

When the neon-green hand on the speedometer had moved far to the right, and the trees along the highway had become blurs, Uncle TT said, "Kate, I've been thinking. We can't leave Etta Ebella looking like she has leprosy. Do you have any ideas about how to fix her?"

Kate got very still. Her heart fluttered, and she saw Etta Ebella flash with hope. "No. But I have been praying to meet an angel doctor."

She studied the chiseled features of her Uncle TT's face, searching for his reaction. Speaking of praying was risky, her mother had once said. But Uncle TT's chocolate-toffee eyes suddenly looked like the toffee was melting as light flooded them. The corners of his mouth tugged into a lopsided smile.

Uncle TT had been born with a tumor on the right side of his upper lip. Though it was benign, the doctors said that it must be removed as it would only grow larger. After two plastic surgeries and growing into manhood, the remaining bit of scar tissue was a whitish ellipse, like a teeny flying saucer. It typically became more visible when he was smiling broadly. It was showing at this moment, and to Kate, he had never looked more handsome.

Unexpectedly, his deep, resonant voice raised one octave higher with excitement as he said, "Kate, what a brilliant idea. I think I know just the person, a real angel doctor."

With a new focus, TT's eyes checked the mirrors, both side ones and the rear one, searching for other cars. He slammed his foot on the brakes and made a U-turn. With tires screeching, he accelerated in the opposite direction. Kate's mother would have said he was driving recklessly, but Kate felt completely safe as if she and Etta Ebella were suspended in a cocoon of the Almighty's handiwork.

Besides, Uncle TT knew what he was doing. He had advanced–degree certifications from two driving universities, the kind of schools that specialized in going real fast and making hairpin turns. The only thing Kate felt unsure about was if those car-racer professors had taught him how to talk on a cell phone when driving at high speeds.

His tongue curling with odd syllables, TT's eyes sparkled. It sounded like he had carrots in his nose again and was using them as microphones. Kate didn't have a clue what he was saying because he was speaking French. But by the look of the sparks flying out of his heart, something was going on, something other than the joy of driving his lamb-pasta car super fast.

Kate felt curious and wanted to ask Etta Ebella about the possibilities. One of Etta Ebella's philosophies was to stay open and ask a lot of questions, rather than jumping to conclusions. So Kate couldn't help wondering about the sparks. After all, they had been zooming along, seeming like they were one with the car, all of them floating above the roadway. Was it possible that Uncle TT had inadvertently absorbed one of the lamb-car's spark plugs?

When Kate turned to ask her, Etta Ebella's eyes and heart were lit up like a Christmas tree shining with thousands of white lights. When Etta Ebella was bathing in light and delight, it was time to be silent. Physics lessons would have to wait. Mystery was in the making.

Using one hand to steer the car, Uncle TT adjusted his phone earpiece. He tapped Kate on the knee, patting her in drum-like taps. "Kate, we're going on an exploratory adventure. Let's call your mom and get permission."

Kate knew what an adventure was, but that word *exploratory* puzzled her. She broke it down to the root word, *explore*. And then she began imagining she and Uncle TT donning miners' gear or scuba-diving tanks and goggles. Etta Ebella hovered over them with her wings all aflutter.

Her daydream was interrupted as she heard Uncle TT say, "Qué pasó, Brother?" That meant her daddy had answered the phone because Uncle TT and her daddy were brothers— sons of Grammy Mer and Poppy Pop. They always spoke Spanish for their greetings. That was when they weren't playing tricks on each other by disguising their voices.

Grammy Mer's and Poppy Pop's other children, two daughters— Sammie Sue and Ruthie Renee—didn't initiate such phone antics.

At least, Sammie Sue did not. A biology professor, she was usually serious-minded. But Ruthie, who lived in London and was an actor and playwright, joined in on her brothers' playful theatrics.

Grammy Mer had named all of her four children with matching initial consonants for their first and middle names, a long-standing tradition in her family. Kate's daddy's name was Kalin Kaiser; everyone called him Kal. Sometimes Uncle TT called him "KK" in a teasing voice. Then her daddy's eyes that were dark blue, like blue-corn chips all speckled with yellow flecks, would narrow as if that was completely unacceptable. Kay-Kay sounded like a girl's name. Uncle TT would yowl loudly saying, "Hey, Bro, it's you who gave me a name like Tee-Tee." And then her daddy's wide mouth would turn up and out in the goofiest of grins. On the other hand, if someone dared to call her daddy KKK, short for Kalin Kaiser Kindrick, he went ballistic.

Snug in Uncle TT's car, Kate thought about her daddy's name and the only time she had ever heard anyone use all three of his initials to address him. She drifted off into memories of the family get together from just last week. In the middle of dinner, Vaynem—Aunt Abigail's husband and Marilla Marzy's father—had called her daddy that name. Vaynem often spoke like he had wrapped barbed wire around each letter of the alphabet because he enjoyed hurting people with words. That day, his lips had coiled into a twisted smirk when he said, "Hey, KKK, can you pass me the salt and pepper?"

Kate had never seen her daddy's face turn as red as it did that day. Suddenly, his heart looked like a Grand Canyon disaster, full of oozing painful craters and gorges. He slowly placed his fork on his plate and said, "Vaynem, those are the initials of ignorance—of raw evil. Do not ever call me that again or speak that name in my home. Do you understand?"

Vaynem's tongue had moved smooth as silk as he said in a somewhat apologetic tone, "Sure thing, Kal. No offense meant."

Kate didn't see apology; she saw a gleeful look creep into Vaynem's muddy eyes. His eggplant-colored heart recorded and stored her daddy's reaction to that name, just as surely as if he had pressed the

28

"SAVE" button on his computer. Kate watched as the incident stuck in Vaynem's heart like a torpedo. She had to look away. It made her stomach hitch with queasiness to see the many weapons he had stockpiled there.

No one else at the table seemed to notice Vaynem's reaction, except maybe Aunt Abigail. She had begun wringing her hands. Marilla Marzy had kept her eyes on her plate and continued to eat.

Later that same night, Kate had watched a Power Ranger video in the den-kitchen area, while her parents washed dishes—the ones too fine or too big to go in the dishwasher. Her daddy had washed while her mother had dried and put things away. Unbeknownst to them, Kate only pretended to watch the DVD. Mainly she had watched her daddy's heart, which was usually soft and rosy, continually checking to see if it had returned to normal yet. She had secretly listened as they talked.

Kate's mother, whose name was Charlotte but whom everyone called Carly, was worried, too. Kate could tell because her mom's heart was pulsing, and her feline eyes, normally bright green similar to freshly cooked asparagus, looked dark, all cloudy with shadows.

Kate strained to hear all of her parents' words. Her ears had almost flown from her head when her daddy said, "I despise my initials; they make me feel ashamed to be a white man."

Her mother had put down the drying towel and massaged his shoulders. "Sweetheart," she said, "I'm glad that you told Vaynem he could not utter that name in our home. And I understand what you're saying. But Kal Kindrick, you are an incredibly good man. You have done nothing of which to be ashamed."

"I know. But."

"Seriously. The world would be a better place if there were more men like you. Maybe we should try to clone you."

With a mischievous glint suddenly appearing in his eyes, Kate's daddy had laughed and said, "Clone *me*? Why, it's females that make the world go round. I think we should take a shot at cloning *you*."

With her eyes shining anew, Kate's mother said, "You know that a world full of women would self-destruct soon enough. Though not quite as fast as a world full of men would."

"You think so?"

"I know so." She poked him in the ribs and then started to tickle him. He grabbed the drying towel and began chasing her around the kitchen popping it at her bottom.

Kate didn't know what cloning meant, but she felt happy. Her daddy's heart looked decidedly better, and her mother's eyes shone brightly again. Kate had run into the kitchen and started chasing her mother with another drying towel, even though she didn't know how to pop it. Her daddy had grabbed her up in his arms, and they both had tickled her mother. Soon they were all in a heap on the floor.

After she had her bath and had gone through her nightly tuck-in ritual that usually put her right to sleep—Kate had felt questions poking at her forehead, holding her eyelids open. She twisted around, finally turning onto her side. It didn't help. She then flipped onto her back and asked her mother to tickle-scratch her arms. Facing upward, she could now contemplate the cumulus clouds painted on the ceiling.

As Kate mused over the clouds and reveled in the sensation of her mother's fingernails lightly tracing erratic patterns on her arms, she revisited the incident that afternoon with Vaynem and her daddy's name. Kate mulled over some K words she knew: kooky, kangaroo, ketchup, kick, king, kid and kiss. None made sense as for her daddy's angry reaction. "Mama, you know Daddy's initials, KKK. Why did that name make his face turn red?" Her mother's mouth opened and closed multiple times. No words came forth.

"Daddy sure was mad at Uncle Vaynem today. What does that name mean?"

"Well, Kate, it's complicated. It's about an organization, a hostile one, called the KKK. It was formed many years ago, long before your daddy and I were born."

"What's hostile? Is that a gun holder?"

"No, pumpkin, that's a *holster*. Hostile means unfriendly, opposed to, or even mean."

Kate pinched up a section of her leg, holding it between her thumb and forefinger. She examined her pale skin. "Why did Daddy say he was sad to be a white man? Actually, his skin is not white; it's kind of pink with some brown freckles."

Deciding she couldn't skirt the issue, Kate's mother said, "Our family is part of the Caucasian or Anglo race, so your daddy's skin is called white, like yours and mine is. Long ago here in America, there were some Anglo men who believed their white skin made them more important than those who had other skin colors. And that is utter nonsense. People have no control over the color of the skin they are born with or any of their physical characteristics. That's genetics."

Kate knew that word *genetics* because her Aunt Sammy Sue, a biologist, specialized in genetics. On Christmas last year when Aunt Ruthie was visiting from London and the family was all together, Sammy Sue had initiated a tongue-curling experiment. They discovered who could curl their tongues and who could not. Aunt Sammy Sue had said it was all genetics. Kate and her mother were the only ones there who could not curl their tongues.

"Kate, are you listening?"

Kate nodded, "Yes, Mama. I was just thinking about our tongues. Mine and yours. They can never curl."

"Yes, pumpkin, you and I were born with flat tongues, and that's that. The KKK men stupidly believed they were superior simply because they were born with whitish skin—skin they didn't choose, couldn't control, and had nothing to do with creating. Some thought their white skin gave them a license to do bad things to anyone different from them."

"All their names started with K's?"

"No, their personal names were varied, but they formed an organization, a secret club, called the Ku Klux Klan. They killed and hurt many innocent people. Mostly African American people."

"Were they like that Hit Littler man that did bad things to the Hanukah people?" asked Kate.

Carly's eyes instantly dilated with surprise. "Why yes, Kate, exactly right."

Feeling glad—for the moment—that she wasn't born a boy, Kate asked, "Were there any girls in the KKK?"

"I'm not sure, but that's a good question. The KKK people wore disguises so no one would know who they were. They didn't have the courage to show their faces."

"That's spooky." Kate tried to absorb the information. Shadows zigzagged across her furrowed brows and prominent cheekbones, her thoughts going to her best friend, Jillian, and her parents, Jophia and Dr. Joe. "Mama, why are Jillian and her family called African American? Jillian says they have never been to Africa, and they don't even know anyone there. She says that she's as American as I am."

"Jillian is, indeed, correct. She is truly an American with no need for other distinction. The Africa part has to do with her family's roots, her lineage, like Grammy Mer's family came from Ireland. There was a point in time where Grammy Mer's grandparents were labeled as Irish American."

"But we are not called Irish American."

"You are right, Kate; it's not fair. Yet it's complicated. Some people take pride in naming their heritage. They prefer that while others don't."

"Mama, is that organ thing called the KKK still going today?"

"No, not like it was in the past. But yes, there are people in the world who mistreat others based purely on their prejudices."

"I hate them!" spat out Kate, putting all the poisonous feeling she could muster on each word.

Instantly, Carly's eyebrows shot up making a severe arch. "Oh, no, you don't, Kadie Girl. That will make you no different from them; hating them will make you one of them."

"What do you mean, Mama? Why are you mad at me?"

"Oh, pumpkin, I'm sorry. I'm not mad at you, not at all. But it's very important that you understand that hating people is never the answer. Hate is what fuels the prejudice machine; it's destructive to everyone."

"Is that like a juicer machine?"

Biting her lower lip, Carly said, "Well, yes, in a way, it is. Prejudices and juicer machines both take the juice out of fruit, paying no attention to whether the fruit is good or bad. Do you know what the word prejudice means?"

Kate's shoulders inched up near her ears then released into a shrug. "Not really but I think that 'pre' part means before. Like I went to preschool before I went to the big school, you know, kindergarten."

"Yes, my pumpkin, that's part of it, prejudice is about PRE-judging. It's about not liking someone, being afraid of them, or even hating them for no reason other than they are different from you. Maybe they don't dress like you, walk like you, or think as you do. Maybe they go to a church that uses a different name for God."

Kate stared at the clouds. Thoughts raced through her head. *Some mothers would not let their daughters do a sleepover at Jillian's house. Some people eyed Grammy Mer, talking to her like she was dumb or was a baby just because she was in a wheelchair. Some kids made fun of Marilla Marzy because her eyes didn't match, and her stomach was far bigger than her head.*

"Kate, I do understand why you want to hate mean people. It seems like it would be a good thing to do. But that's a trick. Try thinking about it this way: Hate is like a monster machine that is destructive. It has an engine that needs gas to operate like cars and airplanes do. When we hate people or judge them unfairly, our thoughts and feelings put gas in the hate monster's fuel tank, which makes the monster hate machine get bigger, hurt more people, and enable it to disguise itself more cleverly."

Kate envisioned an enormous and grotesque looking SUV, a putrid chameleon-green that could change colors and easily camouflage itself. Gigantic body-builder arms, more like bat wings with bulging biceps, came out of each side and pulled screaming people inside. Its tinted windows and windshield prevented anyone from seeing who or what was driving. Poisonous smoke poured out of its giant tailpipes, like serpents squirting lethal venom, as it went speeding around the world destroying people and animals everywhere while it grew bigger and more powerful.

"Mama, was it the hate monster's machine that made those airplanes fly into those big buildings, killing nice people, that 911 thing?"

Carly winced. "Yes, my little pumpkin, it was the monster hate machine; indeed, it was."

Rising from the edge of the bed, Carly yawned and stretched. She pulled the covers up around Kate's neck and whispered, "My sweet pumpkin, my little cuddle bug, you just focus on loving as many people as you can. And fill your brain, every day, with as many happy thoughts as it can hold. Fill it so full that it has to bubble over with smiley faces."

Kate buried her nose into her mother's neck and breathed in the smell of her, honeysuckle mixed with whiffs of gardenia. She usually loved it when her mother hugged her up close. But tonight, Kate felt restless. She wanted to talk to Etta Ebella.

After her mother had left the room, Etta Ebella had simply nodded that Kate's heart observations that day were completely accurate, especially what she saw happening in her daddy's and Vaynem's hearts.

Then in her bell-toned voice, which always made Kate's ears ring, she told Kate that Earth people were so silly when it came to issues of race. She said the so-called white people were a mixture of all human skin colors because white contained all colors in it. Some day, Etta Ebella prophesized, people will learn that everybody is in each other, merely loving themselves when they love others. Those who hate others are simply hating and hurting themselves, like stabbing their own hearts with butcher knives. Kate just couldn't imagine anyone ever committing such a horrible act.

Just this past summer, Etta Ebella had reminded Kate that there were good and bad people in every race and every country. Her job was to stay focused on their hearts.

So when they watched the Olympics, Kate had tried to read the hearts of all the racers. And sure enough, some had kindness in them, and some had spitefulness in theirs. So far, Kate could say one thing for sure: this race thing was a big deal, for she could surely see mean-spirited competition at the center of many people's hearts.

Kate had forgotten to ask Etta Ebella about that little swimmy thing she saw in her mother's heart that night, but she was too sleepy. Although her eyelids were sealed shut for the night, she wrestled with two more forehead tugs before surrendering to the dreamy darkness: *Why did Grammy Mer and Poppy Pop give her daddy a name with bad initials? And the color orange—maybe she had prejuiced it.*

Drifting off into a deep sleep, she had dreamt of a heavenly nursery where angels took care of babies and little children. In the dream, Kate's mother and Etta Ebella helped the nursery angels tend the babies. Kate's daddy, Uncle TT, and a big blue angel had worked on building towering walls of clouds to protect them from the hate monster. Kate had run between the two, in and out of the nursery, sometimes helping with the babies, sometimes helping with the cloud tower.

At the end of the dream, she had run back into the nursery and walked through the maze of cribs. A baby boy reached out for her. Kate turned to him and put her index finger in his tiny palm. His wee fingers instantly latched onto her, gripping her with all his might. As she peered into his blueberry eyes, Kate's eyes registered recognition. His little heart then sprouted a red rosebud, its tiny petals bursting with desire to grow and open to full bloom.

Kate yawned and stretched, wriggling in the car seat, stirring from the memories of the day that Vaynem had made her daddy so mad. She glanced over at Uncle TT. He was driving with focus. But she could see his mind and heart also busy with memories: ones of Grammy Mer when she could walk and talk. Kate fingered Etta Ebella's wing, the one not burned. No longer was she bathing in light and delight.

CHAPTER FIVE

*T*he lamb-pasta car was weaving through traffic on the downtown freeway. Kate decided that other people must also be trying to figure out the lamb part of the car, looking for its head, because they surely did stare at them.

As they passed the baseball park, home of the Giants, Kate was surprised and annoyed to learn that its name had changed again. She liked the old name, Pac-Bell, better than any of the new ones. And Etta Ebella did, too, the bell in the name and all.

Uncle TT slowed the car and circled behind left field so that Kate could see the 80-foot Coca-Cola bottle that towered like a darkened lighthouse in the kids' miniature park. Although she had seen it numerous times, Kate always experienced a physical surge upon seeing that tall cola bottle, as if caffeine and sugar were suddenly gushing through her veins. Etta Ebella would shiver and surge, too, but hers had to do with the power of marketing, especially on kids.

Kate looked for Giants' players coming and going from their workouts. Uncle TT, who loved baseball and had club-level seats, sometimes took Kate to an afternoon game. When a player got a hit or made an out on the opposing team, they would cheer for him, jumping and yelling like fan fanatics. And when a player hit a home run, Uncle TT would swing Kate up in his arms and dance her around, yelling in euphoric delirium.

Since it wasn't a game day, only a few people were milling about the ballpark, mostly people on skateboards and rollerblades. Kate looked every which direction, straining her eyes, but she saw no baseball players today, except for Willie Mays, who was frozen in time, embalmed in a nine-foot-tall bronze statue.

When they reached Nob Hill, Uncle TT parked the car in front of a building that had seven columns. Kate knew because she counted things, and besides, that's how old she would be on her next birthday. He pushed a black button, and his car door rose upward.

Uncle TT told Kate to hold on tight. She thought they might be making a speedy departure with tires screeching again, but he jumped out of the car and ran around to her side and opened her door. He reached in and lightly tweaked her cheek. In addition to being affectionate, Uncle TT enjoyed making Kate's full round cheeks look even rosier. Some people called them chipmunk cheeks, but he would say, "No way, Kate. You have cherub cheeks; chipmunks store nuts in their cheeks. Yours have no craziness whatsoever in them. Your cheeks hold valuables, like heavenly rubies."

Captivated by gemstones, Kate thought rubies were made deep inside the Earth, not in Heaven, but she wouldn't embarrass Uncle TT with that information.

"Okay, Kate, we're about to go inside. I want you to meet a new friend of mine. I don't know her very well yet. I only met her two weeks ago. Interestingly, it was on your birthday. After your party, I went to another party at Jonah's house."

Kate knew TT's friend, Jonah. He could play the piano beautifully without using any pages of music. Uncle TT said that Jonah played by ear, that he had never had a single piano lesson. It looked to Kate like he played with his hands like all other piano players did, and she had inspected both of his ears closely and couldn't see anything unusual about them. Even still, she knew that there must be something extra special about Jonah Caleebe because Uncle TT liked to hang out with him.

Jonah's exotic looks fascinated Kate. She thought he was a model, and looked for him in ads on television and her mother's catalogs. His creamy cappuccino-toned skin perfectly complemented his warm, golden eyes, which reminded Kate of freshly baked pecan pie. What's more, he was tall. But it was Jonah's short corkscrew hair that Kate loved the most. Uncle TT said they were dreadlocks, but Kate didn't see anything about them to dread. Besides, Jonah always wore the coolest clothes and shoes.

Not surprisingly, looking cool was easy for Jonah; he owned a chain of men's clothing stores, located in San Francisco, NYC, London, Hong Kong, and Madrid. Uncle TT had shown Kate all those cities on the globe, pointing out what countries they were in and where they were in relationship to the United States. He said that Jonah's stores specialized in hip designer clothing.

Kate knew that hips were important because her mother surely did talk about hers when she was getting dressed.

The wind picked up and tossed Uncle TT's honey-colored hair up on its ends. He brushed at it, using his fingers for a comb, saying, "Kate, my new friend's name is Angelique Donahorn. She is a doctor."

Kate's spine tingled upon hearing the name. Barely able to eek out the words, her voice cracked as she said, "Is she an angel doctor?"

Uncle TT's deer-like eyelashes fluttered for half a second, "Well, Kate, I don't know yet for sure. If she's not, I have a hunch that she can help us find one. What I do know is that she is a *plastic surgeon*, specializing in pediatrics."

Kate knew that pediatricians were kid doctors. While she didn't know what plastic surgeons were, her heart surged with hope because Etta Ebella's earthly replica was made of plastic. Grammy Mer had said she had searched the world over for the right angel for Kate. She had been willing to spend a lot of money, but none except Etta Ebella had the right face—sweet, yet powerful, too.

"Is this her office?" asked Kate as she eyed the building with seven columns.

"No, Princess, she invited us to her home." Uncle TT used his left hand—he was a lefty—to stroke his black trousers, smoothing wrinkles. "I've only been there one time. She has sophisticated taste; it's quite the place. You will want to use your best manners." He smiled into Kate's eyes as he reached up and tweaked her cheek again.

Sophisticated taste? Looking perplexed, Kate envisioned someone eating their fists. Seeing her furrowed brow, he said, "She has a very nice home with fine furnishings much like Grammy Mer's house, although different, too. You'll like it; she has artifacts and geodes."

Seeing as how she was going to a fancy place in the city with Uncle TT, Kate wished she was wearing her new purple birthday dress. She brushed at her right knee. They had stopped for lunch at Lancaster's in Jack London Square, one of their favorite places. There, ketchup had dripped from her fries and landed smack on the front of her jeans. Looking up at him, she said, "Do I look okay?"

Uncle TT looked her over from head to toe, his roving eyes not missing one iota about her. He pronounced his verdict with a tone of authority, "You look better than okay, Kate. You're gorgeous, like a real princess."

Hand in hand, they walked up the wide stone steps leading to the entrance of the columned building. Halfway up, on the fourth step, Kate felt Etta Ebella quiver. Kate stopped and looked around.

"What is it, Kate?" asked Uncle TT.

Before she could answer him, something shiny caught her eye. On the next step—right where Kate was about to place her foot— was a feather. She picked it up, and it felt strangely warm in her hand. What's more, it looked familiar, similar to the feathers in Etta Ebella's wings before they were burned—a combination of silver and gold and slightly shimmery. Eyes wide and filled with wonder, Kate held it up for Uncle TT to inspect.

"Well now, what do we have here?" he said.

A uniformed security guard opened the door for them, nodded and said, "And how are you two on this fine day?"

Uncle TT smiled and said, "We are extremely well, how about yourself?"

"Splendid, just splendid." The guard motioned them toward a large mahogany desk where a man wearing a navy suit and red tie awaited them.

Kate studied the man. His eyes, the color of mushrooms, were not as friendly as the guard's eyes that resembled hot-cocoa. The mushroom-man looked at Kate suspiciously, eyeballing the spot of ketchup on her knee. She knew what his dubious look meant: he did not like kids, and not many kids came into this building. She shifted her Hello Kitty bag onto her shoulder, with a decidedly possessive grip. It was carrying precious cargo—Etta Ebella plus her favorite Power Ranger figure, and now secreted away in a side pocket was the newly-found feather. She gripped the strap with fresh determination; she didn't want this man to get any ideas about taking her bag and unzipping it to inspect its contents.

The somber gray-eyed man spoke to Uncle TT in a flat-toned voice saying, "How can I help you, sir?"

"I'm Terrence Kindrick, and this is my niece, Katelyn Kindrick. We are here to see Dr. Donahorn."

The man squinted through his glasses that were perched halfway down his nose and read from a leather notebook. "Ah yes, Dr. Donahorn is expecting you. May I see a picture ID, sir?"

With a sly smile on his face, Uncle TT reached for his wallet and produced his driver's license.

The man peered at the license. "Please sign in while I notify Dr. Donahorn that you have arrived." He picked up the black phone and pressed a button, then began speaking French.

Kate wondered if he ever put carrots in his nose. When he talked, he sounded like he had something in each nostril. But he did not strike Kate as the kind of man who tried to make anyone laugh. Layers of gray-green storm clouds, all dotted with icy pockets, covered his heart. The icky looking pockets contained spiky bits of hail.

Uncle TT wrote his and Kate's names in the registry at the corner of the desk. Kate watched, remembering how her mother had said that TT had beautiful handwriting, more like that of an artistic woman than the typical man's scribble. He looked at his watch and wrote the time 2:45 PM in the Time-Arrived slot.

The man behind the desk nodded and said, "Thank you, Mr. Kindrick. You may step to the elevators. Dr. Donahorn will receive you on the seventh floor, number 729.

Once they were inside the elevator, Uncle TT motioned toward the silver panel with all the buttons. He said, "Floor seven, please, Mademoiselle."

Kate pushed the button with the numeral seven embossed on it, and the elevator moved smoothly upward.

TT made silly faces at Kate, making her giggle. He said, "Don't worry, Princess, the worst part is over. Getting an angel, a Power Ranger, and a mysterious feather past that dude was not an easy task, was it?"

Angelique Donahorn opened the black double doors flanked by two large bronze lions. A strange tightening spread into Kate's chest. Her breath caught in her throat. *Dr. Donahorn was beautiful, like an angel.*

Her skin resembled a warm snickerdoodle cookie, creamy beige with just a light dusting of tiny cinnamon dots across her nose. Reddish blonde curls, the color of buttered cinnamon toast, cascaded down just below her shoulders.

The doctor's dark blue eyes baffled Kate; they completely stumped her. Kate scanned her brain for every blue food she could think of and not a single one matched the color of those eyes. When food didn't fit, Kate thought about gemstones. Yes, they were most like sapphires, a pair of sapphires that were encrusted with honey-colored diamonds, like sparkling stars floating atop dark-blue ocean waters.

Yet what shocked Kate the most was what seemed to be an astonishing coincidence. Except for her eyes being a bit darker blue, her black clothes, and a tiny scar on the left side of her upper lip, Dr. Donahorn looked almost exactly like Etta Ebella.

CHAPTER SIX

"**B**on Jour, Terrence," said the doctor. She extended her slender hand to Uncle TT, who then cupped her fingers in his. Lifting her hand in an upward motion, he pressed it to his lips.

Not accustomed to such greetings, not Uncle TT's friends greeting him in such a manner or him kissing a woman's hand, Kate gaped. She wasn't sure what to make of it or what to look at first—the pulsing rotation that popped up in both of their hearts, or the blue topaz ring on the doctor's right hand.

"And you must be Princess Kate. It's such a pleasure to meet you. I've heard so much about you from Jonah and your uncle. Please, come in," said the doctor.

Princess Kate. No one had ever called Kate that name. Uncle TT called her Princess, but not Princess Kate as in a royal title.

With thoughts of tiaras and palaces twirling in her head, she glanced around the foyer. The floor, black-and-white marble tiles set on the diagonal and polished to a high sheen, glinted as if gilded treasures lay just beneath its surface. Prisms of light bounced on the marble, like tiny fairies skipping and jumping, playing hopscotch on the tiles. Kate looked upward, seeking the light source, and saw a massive chandelier with dangling crystals, which sparkled so brightly that rainbow prisms were cast all about the room.

43

Directly under the chandelier, a table hosted an enormous crystal vase filled with stargazer lilies—more stargazers than Kate had ever seen in one vase. She gulped. Of all the flowers in the world, Dr. Donahorn had her favorite flowers, and she had lots of them.

Orchestral music filled the room. It sounded familiar to Kate and then she remembered that it sounded like music that Grammy Mer often played.

"Ah, the soothing melody of Pachelbel's Canon in D. It's one of my mother's favorites," said Uncle TT.

"For real? It was one of my mother's favorites, too," Dr. Donahorn said.

Another sound rivaled the music, a soft tinkling. Kate stepped to the side and beheld a tall metal sculpture with water running through it. To the right of the waterfall sat a mammoth quartz formation with three stalagmite towers shooting forth from its base. Kate ran over to it and said, "Wow, this crystal is awesome. The biggest one I have ever seen."

Terrence Ted informed the doctor that Kate was a rock hound, that she loved all kinds of rocks, especially crystals and gemstones.

Dr. Donahorn smiled and placed her hand on the crystal. "It's okay if you want to touch it."

Kate placed her hand on the quartz base. Immediately, her hand began to tingle and feel warm. She then placed her other hand on the tallest of the crystal towers. A mild shock rippled through it, flowing up into her wrist as if she had placed her finger in an electrical socket. She quickly jerked that hand back. Bending down, Kate looked underneath and to the sides of the crystal, checking for an electrical cord plugged into an outlet. She said, "Is this crystal electric?"

"Well, yes, it is, but not in the way you think." Dr. Donahorn laughed. "It has no wires, and it's not plugged into any outlet. It's naturally electric."

Kate looked disbelieving at the palm of her hand. "It sort of shocked me," she said.

Dr. Donahorn looked closely at Kate's hand, examining it for redness. "I'm sorry that it hurt you. Most people can't feel anything or begin to know that this crystal emits electrical sensations. You are quite perceptive, Princess Kate. How about having some lemonade?"

Her feet seemingly glued to the floor in front of the massive quartz, Kate said, "Can I touch the crystal tower again?"

Uncle TT scooped Kate up into his arms. "Maybe later, Princess. It must not have hurt too badly if you want to touch it again."

Tucking her chin down, Kate said, "No, but it did surprise me. I've never touched an electric crystal before."

Dr. Donahorn said, "Let's go into the kitchen and choose something to drink. Then we'll go out to the patio. I have some other crystals out there. Those are calmer; they do not bite."

TT set Kate down carefully and put her hand in his. They followed Dr. Donahorn through the spacious living room.

Kate was stunned to see orange silk pillows mixed with purple and gold ones on the white sofas. The orange was a soft coral shade, the same shade as in the rug; nonetheless, it was orange. *Ugh.* Otherwise, the grayish taupe-colored walls and the high ceilings reminded her of Grammy Mer's house. Something else did, too, but she couldn't identify what it was exactly.

Dr. Donahorn's kitchen was light and airy. French doors opened onto a patio where Kate could see an array of plants and blooming flowers in large decorative pots, all flanked by a tall angel statue.

Etta Ebella quivered once again. Kate felt the doll's tremor all the way through the Hello Kitty bag that hung from her shoulder. *Uh-oh, what now?* With a tight grip on her bag, Kate's eyes darted back to the view of the patio. She froze, startled to see the angel statue's wing flutter, just ever so slightly. She stared hard; the statue's concrete wing was now still. Kate swallowed. Her throat felt big like it was knotting up to remind her not to speak of such things. It ached, feeling as if her throat had created a dam where no words could pass.

Observing Kate's fixed stare, Dr. Donahorn said, "We will go out to the patio in a few minutes. For now, though, you can put your bag here on this desk."

Bewildered, Kate looked to her uncle.

TT nodded, "Great idea, looks like the perfect place."

Not completely convinced, Kate set the bag down ever so carefully, making sure that it was erect. Etta Ebella was standing up inside the bag. Kate wanted her to have a clear view of the angel statue that was on the patio.

After citing a litany of beverage choices, Dr. Donahorn said, "What would you two like to drink?"

Uncle TT said he would have sparkling water. Kate chose pink lemonade.

A tea kettle hummed on the stovetop. A blue-and-white porcelain teapot awaited the hot water, and a platter of cookies awaited Kate, at least she hoped.

Dr. Donahorn arranged cups and saucers on a tray as she and Uncle TT talked about Jonah opening a new store in Mexico City. Kate watched as Dr. Donahorn's already shiny eyes brightened even more when she spoke of Jonah.

Kate's eyes roamed around the kitchen, taking in all the details. She eyed the platter of cookies. Her hand begged to touch one, to have one. Saliva churned under her tongue. Then her ears rang with the memory of Uncle TT asking her to use her best manners. She would have to wait until Dr. Donahorn offered them.

Curly pink and red tulips peered over the cookies, some leaning sideways out from the vase. Kate contemplated the tulips. Were they leaning their faces into the cookies to smell them, like people do to sniff flowers?

She continued to scan the kitchen and spotted a fruit bowl filled with mangos and apples, some green, some red. Kate loved mangos, especially the salad her mother made with them.

Next to the mango bowl, Kate eyed a small frame resting on an easel. She squinted her eyes, hoping to see the letters better. Written in a fancy cursive style, they were harder for her to read.

"Hope is the thing with feathers that perches on the soul."

– Emily Dickinson

46

Etta Ebella had feathers, and she was forever hopeful, but feathers stuck on soles of feet? Hmm. Kate moved around the counter and eyeballed Dr. Donahorn's feet, which were dressed in black high-heel sandals. No feathers were sticking out from them.

Does that feather I found on the front steps belong to Dr. Donahorn? Kate wondered. She sensed Etta Ebella quivering in the bag on the desk; even still, she was not going to say anything about the lone feather unless forced to; she hoped to keep it.

Spotting some children's artwork displayed on the side surface of the refrigerator, she moved in close to examine the bright colors and lopsided shapes. Many of the drawings were of a woman with wings. Three of the pictures showed kids lying in bed with the winged woman bending over them or standing next to them. Several had the words *Doctor Angel* written on them.

Photographs of three children occupied another portion of the refrigerator's side panel. Kate thought all three were girls, but she wasn't sure; they looked different. Their clothes and hair certainly seemed odd compared to the girls she knew.

"Well, Kate, I see you have found my children," Dr. Donahorn said.

"Your children?" Kate asked. "You have kids, Dr. Donahorn?"

"Please call me Angelique. And no, I don't have any biological children. Not yet, anyway. Those are my adopted kids."

Almost stuttering with surprise, Kate said, "They live here? With you?"

"No, I don't mean adopted in that way. They don't live with me. They live with their families in Africa."

"Oh," Kate said, her face all squinched, her brow furrowed.

"By adopted, I mean I sponsor them. I send money every month to help with their food, clothes, and school fees. Sometimes they send me letters and artwork they did at school. However, not all of those drawings are from them. Some were done by my young patients here."

"Do they call you *Doctor Angel*?" asked Kate.

"Yes, they do. And some of my patients call me that, too. You see, the first part of my name, Angelique, spells angel. So Princess Kate, how long have you been reading?"

Uncle TT's face beamed. He said, "Kate has been reading since she was three, at least some words and signs, right, Kate? The last I heard, she was reading on a third-grade level." He walked over to the refrigerator and tweaked Kate's cheeks.

Poking her Uncle TT in the ribs, Kate turned back to Angelique. "How old are your adopted kids?"

Angelique joined them and stood behind Kate. She inched in close to Uncle TT, her shoulder nestled against his. Although Kate had her back turned to the pair, when she looked out of the corner of her eye, she could see those spark things flying out of her uncle's heart again. And much to her surprise, some were flying out of Dr. Donahorn's heart, too. They seemed slower moving out of her heart, so maybe she didn't like to drive fast the way Uncle TT did.

Kate watched the tiny sparks, like fireflies dashing headlong into one heart and flying out the other, making a circle between the two. The lamb-pasta car was all the way out on the street. It couldn't be the car's spark plugs. *What did it mean?* She felt Etta Ebella bathing in light and delight.

Angelique pointed to the pictures as she began telling them about each child. "This is Narkeasha, she is 10, her name means *pretty*. In Africa, great emphasis is placed upon the meaning of names, so I did a bit of research. This one is Abeni, her name means *girl prayed for,* she is seven. And this cutie is Baina, who just had her thirteenth birthday. Her name means *sparkling*.

"They're all girls?" asked Kate.

"Yes," Angelique replied. "You know, Kate, many girls in Africa don't get to go to school. Their parents or guardians cannot afford it. There are no free public schools like there are here in America. Some families make it a higher priority to send boys to school before girls."

"That's mean," mumbled Kate.

Angelique nodded. "All of these children live in total poverty, far worse conditions than the poorest American families. Education is their only chance of having a better life."

"Have you ever met them?" Kate asked.

Smiling broadly, Angelique said, "Yes, I have met all three of them."

"Amazing. I just assumed you picked them from a website," said Terrence.

Angelique shook her head up and down as if to say yes, her red curls bouncing against her cheeks. "Initially, I chose Narkeasha from a website. Then during my residency, I had the opportunity to go to Africa and work on a mission project, performing plastic surgeries on children who had disfiguring birth defects or problems. That's when I first met Abeni and Baina."

"What sort of problems did they have?" asked Terrence.

"Abeni was born with a cleft palate and cleft lip." Angelique placed her index finger on the picture of Abeni.

"Palette? Was Abeni born with artist colors?"

"No, Princess, an artist palette is spelled differently," Uncle TT explained. "This palate refers to the roof of her mouth. A cleft palate means something is wrong there, like an opening, a hole, or a split in the top part of her mouth. At least, I think that's what it means."

"That is correct. Good explanation, Terrence," Dr. Donahorn said.

"A hole in her mouth? Could she eat?" Kate asked.

"Yes, Kate, she could eat, but slowly because she had difficulty swallowing."

"How old was she then?" TT asked.

"Abeni was only four when I first examined her. I was concerned about the care she would have after the surgery. So, I went to the village where she lived. There, I visited her home and met her mother. It was shocking how poor they were. Abeni's home was a hovel. Dirt floors, no plumbing, and no electricity. She had zero chance of ever going to school, especially with her speech impairment. Plus, she was going to need more than one surgery. I decided to sponsor her."

"Fortune surely smiled on her with you coming into her life," said Terrence.

"What about this girl?" Kate asked.

"Baina had cancer on the right side of her face. When the tumor was removed, she was left with a hole in her cheek. A hideous one. I was able to rebuild her cheek, but it took two surgeries before she looked normal again."

Kate thought about Etta Ebella's cheek. She didn't quite know how to ask the question; her mind was still trying to figure out exactly what Dr. Donahorn's work entailed. When the realization clicked in her brain, Kate blurted out the words, "Plastic surgery is for skin, not plastic?"

Angelique's tongue poked the inside of her cheek, forcing her lips to thwart their amused expression, "Well, Princess Kate, you're quite the thinker, aren't you?"

"Yes, she is, and she has big ears for words." Uncle TT patted Kate on her shoulder.

Kate reached up her hand to fondle her left ear. It was not big; it was its normal size.

"Yes, Kate, plastic surgery typically involves skin tissue, but in Baina's case, we also used a form of plastic to rebuild her cheek. She has a synthetic implant."

Aware that Uncle TT had placed his hand on her shoulder and was now applying light pressure, Kate decided he was sending her a coded message. Most likely, he was saying this is not the time to talk about Etta Ebella's cheek problem. She must have interpreted correctly because her uncle kept the conversation on the adopted girls.

"What is Abeni's condition now?" Terrence asked.

"Her mouth looks weird," said Kate.

After pouring hot water into the teapot and replacing its lid, Angelique once again nestled against TT's shoulder, standing behind Kate at the refrigerator. She tapped her finger gently on Abeni's photograph as if she was giving her love pats. "She didn't receive treatment when she was a baby for the deformity, so her mouth will never look normal. Though after three surgeries, it is vastly improved."

"Does Abeni's house still have dirt floors?" Kate asked, questioning how it could qualify as a floor when it was made of dirt.

With a sad sigh, Angelique said, "Yes, all of these girls live in houses that have dirt floors. But, you know, Kate, they are happy to have a roof over their heads, happy that they are not living on the streets. They feel lucky, especially that they get to go to school."

Kate peered at the photo, staring intently into the girl's faces. *How can they feel lucky when they are poor, living on dirt floors?* Marilla Marzy's face floated through Kate's mind. She wondered why some of these girl's eyes looked more sparkly and hopeful than Marilla Marzy's did when her daddy was rich. *Later,* Kate thought, she would ask Etta Ebella.

"What a marvelous thing to be involved with, Angelique," said Terrence. "What generosity. Please tell me how I can get involved."

"Me, too!" said Kate, her mind abuzz with visions of piggy banks. *Which ones of her collection would she open?* With a happy spring in her step, she skipped over to her bag to tell Etta Ebella that she was going to help a girl in another country go to school.

Angelique placed the pitcher of pink lemonade, a bottle of San Pellegrino, five glasses, and a small ice bucket with silver tongs on a black lacquer tray. "Let's go out on the patio. I will give you the details out there," she said, handing Uncle TT that tray. She carried a second one that had the cookies along with the teapot, three cups with saucers, a small plate of lemons, and a tiny pitcher of milk.

TT opened the door for them and motioned to Kate, who was stroking her bag. *Should she take it on the patio or leave it on the desk?*

"Kate, you can bring Etta Ebella with you," Uncle TT said.

"Is there a guest that I have not been introduced to yet?" said Angelique as she went through the French doors.

"I was just about to ask you that," Terrence replied. "There are more glasses and cups here than the three of us will need."

CHAPTER SEVEN

For Kate, the only thing missing from Dr. Donahorn's patio oasis was a tree she could climb. It was paradise.

Exotic geodes and crystal formations edged a thicket of green leafy plants—potted palms, ficus, and lemon trees. To the right, a three-tiered copper fountain played liquid melodies as water cascaded in rhythmic tones. To the left, a tall amethyst geode stood guard, winking at the purple and white orchids that graced the nearby table.

An array of colorful blooms—hydrangeas, peonies, zinnias, cyclamens, and banks of impatiens—created a living floral mural that teemed with such artfulness that surely it was designed and hand-painted by Mother Earth herself.

Enchanted, Kate imagined hundreds of flower fairies pirouetting on the lush petals. She waved and curtsied to the teeny tutu-clad creatures.

Dr. Donahorn handed Kate a glass of lemonade along with a cocktail napkin, white linen. She then poured San Pellegrino for Uncle TT and hot tea for herself. Using the tiny fork, they each took a thin slice of lemon.

"Kate, would you like some cookies?" Angelique asked.

Finally, Kate thought, the long-awaited words. Her hand hovered briefly over the cookie tray, choosing a chocolate one first. Her teeth sliced through the chunky chocolate super fast; she hardly tasted it. Then while sipping her lemonade, Kate munched the second variety, a petite cookie with pink icing.

Her mouth watered for more of the sweet buttery flavor, but she wanted to check out the angel statue. Placing the crystal glass carefully on the table, Kate walked over and reached upward, placing her hand on one of the angel's wings, making certain that it was stone. Although Kate knew that when it came to angels, they could be made of any earthly material and still be very much alive. That is, if you believed. And if you had eyes that could see the truth—the moving molecules; even manmade substances were in motion at their core.

After touching the wing, Kate's stomach prickled with an odd sensation, as if a porcupine had scampered through it. *Was the angel statue trying to tell her something?* Kate walked around to touch the other wing. It felt the same. But now a high-pitched hum pierced her left ear, like a beehive choir all singing *beezzzzzz* with their wings flapping in unison, which made her eardrum vibrate like it was a fine percussion instrument.

Etta Ebella had instructed Kate to pay attention when honeybee songs buzzed in her ears, saying it meant that an angel or angels were speaking, and she should listen carefully.

Kate commanded herself to be still, motionless. After mere moments of letting the honeyed tones waft through her, she felt the urge to look downward at the patio floor. Two steps behind the angel, she spotted a Ziploc bag filled with something shiny. Bending down to pick it up, Kate saw that the bag was slightly open. A feather poked out the top, a silvery golden one. It resembled the feather she found on the building steps. It was just like Etta Ebella's wing feathers. The bag bulged from the large number of them stuffed inside.

Feeling excited and a bit awkward, Kate stepped from behind the angel statue. Holding up the baggie, she said, "Look what I found. Behind the angel."

"Oh, for heaven's sake, my sister and I have looked everywhere for these feathers. Thank you, Kate." Angelique took the feather-filled baggie. "Annateresa will be quite relieved."

A bevy of high heels clicked on the patio. A woman's voice called out, "Did I hear my name? Are you talking about me?"

Kate looked up and felt like she was dizzy from seeing double. Leading the group of three females, a woman smiled mischievously, a woman that looked almost exactly like Dr. Donahorn. She had the same square chin and jawline, same petite bone structure. Staring intently, Kate could only detect minor differences. Her hair was a bit blonder, not quite as red. And her sapphire eyes did not have golden stars floating in them; they had silvery-white ones. Her eyes made Kate think of dolphins—ones with diamond-studded noses—playfully poking their sparkling beaks up through dark-blue ocean water.

Angelique walked toward the door, smiling as she embraced all the women, saying, "Welcome, please join us." Giving one of the women an especially spirited hug, Angelique said, "Monet, you are here! I hope Annateresa drove sensibly from the airport." The other two women exchanged impish grins.

Standing up quickly when the women entered, Uncle TT drew Kate close beside him, lightly tickling her shoulder blade as he placed his warm hand on her back.

Angelique said, "Terrence and Kate, I'd like for you to meet my sister, Annateresa Donahorn, and these dear friends of ours, Laura Capelle and Monet Lisette. Ladies, this is Terrence Kindrick and his niece, Kate Kindrick."

Kate eyed the women as they said hello. Laura looked like a model, maybe not as tall as runway models, but as if her face belonged in magazines. Her aquiline nose gave her a look of aristocracy, and her light blue-green eyes created a surprising contrast with her porcelain-like skin, which was as flawless as the face of a high-quality China doll.

Kate then focused on Monet Lisette. Something about her looked vaguely familiar. She was striking—tall and thin, with toasted coconut colored eyes that danced, reflecting luminously onto her gingerbread skin. Her dark curly hair was closely cropped accenting her pretty oval face.

Monet rushed over to them, extending her hand to Uncle TT. "Terrence, it's such an honor to meet you. I've heard so much about you. From Jonah, my cousin. And I love your books. I have read all but your latest one."

Kate's eyes widened in surprise; Monet was Jonah's cousin. Kate studied Monet's hands and ears, wondering if she played the piano the way Jonah did.

Shaking her hand vigorously, Uncle TT said, "Thank you, Monet. The honor is, indeed, mine. Jonah will be jealous we had this serendipitous meeting. He told me you were moving here, but he failed to tell me that you knew Angelique."

After everyone had exchanged proper greetings, Angelique passed the cookies and served the newcomers drinks. She then dangled the bag of feathers in front of her sister and said, "Sis, look what Kate found."

Ebullient, as she all but squealed, Annateresa said, "Where did you find these? We have searched everywhere for them." Clutching the bag close to her chest, she said, "Kate, thank you. These are rare and expensive feathers. We save them for our premium angels. But, I'm curious. Where were they?"

Kate was dumbfounded. *What did Dr. Donahorn's sister mean when she said "our premium angels?"*

Ever so lightly, Uncle TT squeezed Kate's arm, prodding her to answer Annateresa's question.

Kate stood and faced Annateresa more directly and pointed with her index finger, "They were right back there. Behind the angel statue."

Annateresa's eyebrows furrowed as she mumbled, "That's strange."

"Well, if they are rare and expensive," Terrence said, "we have another one for you. Kate found a feather like those on the front steps this afternoon." Turning to Kate and giving her a knowing wink, he said, "Princess, get your bag."

Sad to give up the feather she had found on the steps, Kate's arms and legs tingled as she walked into the kitchen and retrieved her Hello Kitty bag. She heard Uncle TT ask, "So, Annateresa, what business are you in, that you use these feathers? You mentioned *premium* angels."

"That's quite a long story, Terrence. But basically, I'm involved with two different businesses," replied Annateresa.

"Two?" Terrence asked.

"Yep. I'm crazy, huh?" Annateresa chuckled. "One is in medical plastics. I design customized pediatric prosthetic limbs. That should be enough, right?"

"Sounds complicated to me."

"It is. But I'm a bring-it-on kind of girl. A few years ago, we—Angelique, Laura and I—founded Angel Kids, Inc., an angel doll manufacturing business. That's where we use the feathers."

"Wow. Interesting mix. Medical plastics and angel dolls." Terrence said. "What did you study in school for such careers?"

"I majored in Mechanical Engineering. Plastics and pliable composites are my specialties."

Terrence eyed her appraisingly. "Mechanical Engineering? That's impressive. And you work with two different applications for plastics. Intriguing."

"Yes, I enjoy the diversity," said Annateresa.

Leaning into the group of women, Terrence said, "All three of you work in the angel doll business?"

"I design their faces and bodies," Angelique explained. "Annateresa creates the molds based on my designs. And Laura, our renowned fashion designer, designs the dolls' clothing."

Upon hearing that, Kate's heart soared with hope, and she could feel Etta Ebella quivering.

Terrence's eyes drifted to Monet.

Angelique caught his glance. "Monet has recently decided to join the angel-kids team as our financial specialist."

Speaking for the first time, Laura said, "You see, Terrence, initially we began the angel enterprise as a fun diversion from our primary jobs. Originally, our plan was simple. We wanted to give dolls to Angelique's surgery patients, children who had overnight stays in the hospital."

"All three of us had surgeries as children," Annateresa said. "We wanted to soften the ordeal, the scary hospital experience, for Angelique's young patients. And for other seriously ill children in the hospital."

In her somewhat hoarse voice, Laura said, "Actually, the three of us are in a state of shock that our angel enterprise has grown like it has. There just aren't enough hours in the day to do it all now, especially the complex financials."

"I'll say," said Annateresa. "We decided to recruit Monet. We're stealing her away from a prestigious CFO position with a medical group."

Smiling demurely, Monet said, "No, no, not stealing. Health-care finance today is far from what it used to be. I am quite happy to let go of that stress."

"So that's how Angelique snared you. Did she sweet talk you into believing there was no stress at Angel Kids, Inc.?" Laura teased.

"She did spin a sugary web. But, I've wanted to work with the twins—Angelique and Annateresa—since we were suitemates in college."

"The three of you were in college together? Terrence said.

Monet continued. "Oh, yes, the tales I could tell you there." Monet winked at the twins. "Then last year I met Laura. Her fervor for *living her dream* was contagious. So I set new goals. Mainly to reconnect with my creativity, and to work for a cause that I believed in." The corners of Monet's lips jiggled, causing the centers to pucker like she was sucking sweet-sour juices from a citrus-flavored Lifesaver, not quite content to let it melt on her tongue.

"For different reasons from my friends here," Monet continued," angels are a subject close to my heart. I believe that every child, well, actually everyone—the young and the old, the ill and the healthy— would benefit from having a special angel in their life."

Kate was fascinated. *The Donahorn sisters were twins.* Once again she studied their faces and bodies checking for similarities and differences.

Uncle TT said, "Kate, it seems that Providence has moved on our behalf by allowing us to meet the Angel-Kids team. Would you like to introduce them to your special angel, Etta Ebella?"

Kate skipped to the far back table, the one by the amethyst, where she had intentionally placed her bag a few minutes earlier. She had hoped that she wouldn't have to surrender the feather she had found on the steps. But now that it was time to show Etta Ebella to these beautiful women, the burned Etta Ebella who looked like an abused angel, not a dearly loved one, Kate's head hung low.

Fighting back tears, Kate unzipped her bag. She felt her cheeks getting hot like the candle fire was blazing through her pores, breaking her out in welts.

Etta Ebella, who was a master at reading hearts, could see that Kate was deeply grieved about the candle incident. Kate had repeatedly kissed Etta Ebella's singes, had apologized to her and pleaded for forgiveness so many times that her ears felt sore. Etta Ebella was not going to allow any more of this shame nonsense. Not in Kate's pure heart, remorseful as it was. If Kate continued harboring shame there, over time, it would make her sick—even debilitated or seriously diseased.

Summoning all her powers, Etta Ebella blinked her eyes exactly two times in succession. Immediately, her silvery-golden wings quivered and puffed up huge around her. With forceful intention, she locked eyes with Kate. The flower fairies stopped their dance, all turning to watch.

From the center of Etta Ebella's chest emerged an orb of golden light, resembling a mini Frisbee spinning around like a high-speed merry-go-round. Using powerful lasers, Etta Ebella blasted Kate with gold and purple rays of light, beaming them directly into the center of Kate's heart. She then splayed them onto Kate's torso, moving the rays from side to side and up and down, covering every inch.

Instantly, Kate's left ear began to hum with a high-pitched sound, the bee choir again. A feathery veil spiraled down over her, shielding her in private and freezing time—stopping all clocks and watches.

In Kate's mind's eye, the movie screen behind her forehead became illuminated. A movie was beginning. The first scene was of an angel woman working in a magnificent kitchen. She, the Great Angel Mother, was making honey-sweetened lemonade, lemon curd, lemon tea, and all kinds of delicious treats from her children's lemon orchards.

Oddly enough, this Great Angel Mother could not take any lemons from her children. They had to want to give them to her and then willingly place them in her apron basket. That looked easy enough. But when Kate looked again, she saw that the apron basket was far out of human reach. Throngs of disheartened children surrounded the Great Angel Mother, all holding up their lemons.

Feeling confused, Kate looked around. Then she heard peals of joyful laughter, side-splitting guffaws that were so contagious that even her stomach smiled, and her toes wanted to giggle. Her eyes widened in utter awe as the movie screen, now in virtual reality mode, displayed the most amazing scene.

A man who looked like *Jesus*, like the pictures of him Kate had seen—was having the time of eternity, belly laughing and playing as he helped all the children. His enormous arms worked like elevators. And they held everything in all galaxies and universes: planets, moons, stars, all races and nationalities of people, alien-looking beings like ET, and all species of animals, plants, and minerals. His arms still had room and the freedom of movement to lift the children up and down. He raised them up so they could give their lemons to the Great Angel Mother. She would then use them in her magical transformative recipes.

Kate heard a knocking sound. Then she saw herself wearing a purple dress with a gold sash. She nodded, and the arched crystalline door deep inside the most secret chamber of her heart opened wide.

The *Jesus* man stepped inside and wrapped his giant arms lovingly around her. While gently lifting up Kate, he showed her a hologram of the interior of her lemon, how it had turned brown on the inside. Its flesh was contaminated with the incident when Etta Ebella was burned. He showed her that it had happened because she had ignored the sign, not listened to Etta Ebella's wing wisdom that had prickled her stomach that day—her sixth birthday.

With his warm, galactic eyes twinkling with merriment, the *Jesus* man suspended her carefully into the puffy clouds so that she could drop the lemon into the Great Angel Mother's apron basket. The Great Angel Mother smiled when she saw Kate. Then much to Kate's surprise, she grinned and patted Kate's belly-button. "Is it an innie or an outie?"

It felt like the *Jesus* man was playing the piano on her ribs as he tickled her. Kate tried to say, "It's an innie," as she dropped her lemon into the apron basket, but the laughter took all her breath.

The Great Angel Mother's lips brushed Kate's ear as she whispered that she would turn this lemon into something good.

As the *Jesus* man placed Kate back on her feet, he kissed her on one cheek and then the other. Kate felt her entire body flood with love, like her veins no longer flowed with blood, but with ruby-red love lava.

Still surrounded by the feathery veil, Kate could not take her eyes off the movie screen as she watched other children be lifted up. Then the scene shifted. Her eyeballs nearly popped out of her head, feeling like they were being dribbled on the floor like basketballs. The *Jesus* man's and the Great Angel Mother's skin color, facial features, and language changed according to the child that was lifted up. They had white skin and spoke English for Kate only because she was Anglo. For a little boy named Jerome, the *Jesus* man and the Great Angel Mother became black, just like him. Then Kate watched as a little girl, Esperanza, was lifted up, and they morphed into brown and spoke Spanish. And for Guang and Genji, they were Chinese and spoke Mandarin. For this *Jesus* man, changing skin color or nationality was simpler than changing clothes. Whereas baby Jesus in the Bible was born on Earth as Jewish, this adult *Jesus man* was everybody, all people, all races. Children from every continent on

Earth, those above the equator and those below, were all personally handled by this *Jesus* man and the Great Angel Mother.

The movie continued. It was almost like watching a Power Ranger DVD, except that it was now obvious to Kate that God and Jesus possessed even more fantastical powers than any of the Power Rangers did. Even when the children who did not know about Jesus asked for help in surrendering their regret-filled lemons, the Great God Almighty heard them and responded instantly. No matter what longitude or latitude on the Earth planet they lived, the Almighty came to them. It appeared that God's ears had built-in cell phones with a GPS system that worked 24/7, even in outer space. With just a single thought, the Almighty could teleport from one place to another in less than a nanosecond.

Awestruck, Kate touched her forehead. From what she could see, God was everywhere all at one time, was everything, was in every particle, molecule, atom, and cell of all and every creature and thing that existed on Earth—and beyond.

That was enough of a brain-stretcher, yet with what the screen was now showing her, Kate thought her eyes had been struck by lightening. Operating with far more intellect and compassion than humans could possibly imagine or contain—human brains and hearts would burst wide open and spew their smallness with that much positive power inside—God took on the characteristics of that child's religion or cultural belief system. It was like changing a digital image on a computer screen, but without any clicking. Kate watched the *Jesus* man become one with Buddha for Buddhist children, with Mohammed for Islamic children, with Yahweh for Jewish children, with Krishna for the Hindu, and on and on. No child, no culture, no religion was left out.

Everyone and anyone could be lifted up to put their lemons in the Great Angel Mother's apron basket and have something good made from them if they but asked. That is, asked sincerely from that secret place deep inside their hearts.

When the movie ended, the flower fairies applauded. Ecstatic, they clapped and stomped wildly. Flower petals reached out as if to give Kate a million hugs in one embrace. The crystals and geodes spouted strobes of light that showered Kate in rainbows.

When she returned to Earth time, Kate's throat was a desert. "I'm so thirsty," she exclaimed as she turned around to see if the others on the patio had seen the movie, too. But they looked as if no time had passed, looking as if nothing extraordinary had just happened on Dr. Donahorn's patio oasis.

Speaking as if only thirty seconds had elapsed since she had skipped to the rear patio table to retrieve Etta Ebella, Uncle TT called out to her, "Kate, bring her over here."

Hiding Etta Ebella behind her, Kate walked to the main table and picked up her glass. She drank all of her lemonade. Every drop. It was the most delicious lemonade she had ever tasted.

Holding Etta Ebella behind her back, her voice was strong as she said, "My Grammy Mer gave me this angel on the day that I was born. Two weeks ago, on my birthday, I put the cake candles too close to her. She got burned. She needs an angel doctor."

Presenting her special angel, positioning the doll in front of her so that all could see, Kate said, "This is Etta Ebella."

There was complete silence, an utter silence that floated and hovered like a dense fog. The four women stared at Etta Ebella. They gazed as if they were in a trance.

Kate turned and looked behind her to see if Spider-Woman had suddenly leaped over the ledge. She looked all around and couldn't identify any problem that would cause their faces to wear such stunned expressions. *Had she made a mistake by admitting that it was her fault that Etta Ebella got burned?* She quickly checked her body for any sensation of a sign, any prickling in her stomach and there was nothing—only peace and calm.

Terrence uncrossed his legs and then crossed them to the opposite side, wriggling in his chair, making it squeak a bit. His eyes shining brightly, he looked to Angelique to Kate to Etta Ebella.

Out of the corner of her eye, Kate saw the angel statue's wings flutter, which was usually a good sign. But the silence hung heavy, so Kate wondered. Yet she couldn't feel worried. She was happy, still reveling in the sensation of floating in the Jesus man's arms. Although she didn't understand the women's reaction, she sensed that something important was about to happen—again.

Slowly rising from her chair, Angelique stepped toward Kate and said, "Why Kate, Etta Ebella looks like...like...she is...is...is...is." She spoke a few broken words in French and then her shoulders began shaking as tears streamed from her eyes. She sat back down as if in a daze.

Uncle TT took Angelique's hand and stroked it. His eyes appeared strained and his mouth twisted in utter bewilderment.

Upon hearing the French words, Annateresa jumped up and said, "Kate, may I see Etta Ebella?" Kate handed Etta Ebella to Annateresa. Laura also clustered around her, eyeballing every detail of the angel doll.

With a shy smile adorning her face, Monet Lisette sat still, shoulders back, perfectly erect in the wicker chair.

Kate blinked her eyes and watched a beautiful golden-copper light form around Monet's head. It glowed for a few seconds. Kate blinked again and then could no longer see it.

After examining the doll, Annateresa, ever so tenderly, placed it on Angelique's knee. Leaning in close to her sister, she all but whispered, "Sis, we have found her!"

Still holding Angelique's hand, Uncle TT looked around for Kate. He spread his left arm back in a wide arc and said to Kate, who appeared to be frozen like a robot in front of the angel statue, "Oh, Princess, come here."

CHAPTER EIGHT

The studio on the thirteenth floor of the columned building was silent except for the music, a flute symphony, which quietly soothed like anesthesia released through the stereo system. Etta Ebella lay perfectly still on one of the workbenches. Her blistered cheek bulged out with the remainder of her face taped off as if prepped for surgery.

Three skylights filtered sunlight throughout the room. The scored concrete floor created an informal ambiance for the three workbenches, positioned at strategic angles to create private workstations. A dark cloud moved over the sun, altering the light in the room as if an invisible hand had turned a dimmer switch dial to low.

Annateresa adjusted her goggles and switched on the light in the visor that cantilevered out like a roof over her safety glasses.

Across the room, Angelique stood at her workbench. She was also wearing safety glasses as well as a surgical mask and polyurethane gloves. She picked up the drill and changed the bit to a gentle buffer type. The tears from the previous afternoon, uncontainable when she saw the angel doll, were no longer in her eyes. Like a cloudburst in a desert thunderstorm, they now spattered against her heart.

Memories of her mother, Henrietta Donahorn, and of the day she died—now over six years ago—dominated her thoughts, grieving every cell in her body. Shaking her head in disbelief, Angelique pondered those six-plus years. It seemed more like it was a day last week, the day she had not made it back from France in time to see her mother one last time.

Memories of the plane's wheels touching down on the runway, the screeching sound, haunted her thoughts. She had immediately turned on her cell phone. When the screen lit up, it had shown four messages. As a doctor, she customarily received messages of a serious nature, and she took them in stride. But the dread of what those four messages would convey overwhelmed her. Instead of listening, she had scrolled for Annateresa's cell number on her favorite's list—had repeatedly pushed the dial button frantically, only to get a recorded message—time after time.

As she deplaned, her phone had buzzed. She had answered it almost before it rang. Annateresa's voice had sounded hushed as if she were in a sacred temple receiving communion. Without her sister saying the words, Angelique knew. There was zero respiration, zero pulse, and zero blood pressure in the body she had known as Mother. Henrietta Donahorn—her mother—was gone, was dead.

Angelique had quickly switched her phone off, feeling like an 18-wheeler truck was sitting on her chest, its tires digging into her lower abdomen. The *what ifs* had run rampant, playing chase through her mind, tormenting her soul.

If only she had paid attention to her dreams. She had dreamt of her mother sitting in an ornately carved chair with two angels at its helm, dreamt the same scene night after night. If only she had listened to the compelling symbolism, then she would have disobeyed her mother's wishes. She would then have honored her own needs: honored the desire to look upon her mother's face, to share her pain, to hold her hand, to tell her what a wonderful mother she had been, to tell her how much she loved her, to feel her warmth—just one more time.

Forcing her legs to walk through the airport, she found a restroom, locked herself into one of the stalls and wept. She thought that was the most alone she had ever felt in her entire life. Then when she arrived at the 729 condominium her mother owned in the city, it was unbearably worse. The emptiness had filled her up, spilling over her edges.

What's more, the angel had been missing, not in her usual place. Angelique had walked through every room, opened every closet and every drawer, looked behind draperies, and ransacked the beds, checking under each one. Her frantic search for the angel doll produced nothing. It was nowhere, not to be found.

That was grief enough, but as Angelique looked back now, she had not an inkling of the lonely road of sorrow that lay ahead of her. Her mother's funeral had been easy compared to the weeks, months, and years that followed. She could no longer call her mama to talk—about nothing and everything. She could no longer hear her mother greet her with *"Hello, Sugar."* She could no longer be the receiver of one of her mother's warm, enthusiastic hugs.

At times, she thought her heart would explode, actually break apart. The very thought of her mother not being there when she graduated from medical school, not there when she got married—if she ever did—and not there when her first child was born, if she ever had children, her heart would ache like it was experiencing a massive malfunction. Then the day she realized that she did want to have children and that her mother would never know those children and they her, she almost fainted. One particular realization was the worst: her children would not have a maternal grandmother to watch them grow, to fawn over them. It felt as if her heart had shattered into shards, releasing jagged remnants of her mother's love through her veins.

Henrietta Donahorn had been the quintessential mother, enveloping those she loved in a far-reaching protective aura. Both strong and soft, she was often called a *velvet hammer*. She had been accomplished and beautiful, with a distinct bell-like voice that cheered all who met her. Angelique remembered how her mother had carried herself, perfect posture as if she walked with a book atop her head. Many had looked up to her; many had counted on her insight and wisdom. Friends and extended family had called her "Henny" as if she was the protective mother hen of their world, too.

After researching family names, Angelique had been struck by how her mother's maiden name, LaBelle, had suited her so perfectly. Yet she had carried that name only a short period of her life as her mother had married her father, Jacob Donahorn, at a young age.

Her parents had enjoyed a soulmate kind of love, never wanting to be apart for any length of time. For Angelique, it had been interesting growing up amidst all that love and devotion. Yet she never felt like an outsider. Her father had been as devoted a parent as he was a husband. From the time that Angelique could remember, her father would say that she and Annateresa and their brother, Lawry—Lawrence Wilson Donahorn, had unique talents, and they had a responsibility to apply them for the benefit of mankind. They were born different, born with the "Finger of God" upon them, he would say.

Angelique remembered the inner conflict this had created, especially in her teen years. One minute she was yearning for it to be true, her heart filled with grandiose dreams and ambitions, and in the very next breath, she was feeling mad, resisting the pressure of such expectations. Her parents probably never had any idea of the wrestling matches taking place inside her. Most days, she remembered, rebellion had been the champ. It wasn't until she went away to college that she had even the slightest understanding of her father's belief that she was a mango in a world of apples.

When she had returned home after spring semester finals of her junior year of college, a new light had been shed on why her father had been so adamant that his children were extraordinary.

He was ill, recently diagnosed with pancreatic cancer. She had felt an untold urgency to get home and be with him. Upon her arrival, the shock of seeing just how sick he was, already near death's door, had reverberated throughout her entire body.

Late Saturday afternoon of the second week that she was home, her father insisted on standing. Obeying his request, Angelique and her brother, Lawry, helped him get out of bed. His feet purple and swollen, her father teetered from weakness. Asking their mother to hold his hands, he stood with her in front of the fireplace, its etched glass screen reflecting the red-orange sunset streaming through the adjacent window. He looked into his wife's woeful eyes and told her that God had shown him that they would soon have to part. The normally strong Henrietta almost crumpled, her shoulders heaving.

Continuing in a frail voice—a mere fragment of his usual orator's resonance—Jacob Donahorn vowed that as a young man, the exact moment he laid eyes on Henny LaBelle and her red hair, he knew that he wanted to marry her.

Then he said an odd thing: When he first saw her, he immediately knew that with her, with Henny LaBelle, he would have special children with unique talents, children that he could not have with any other woman on Earth.

Sometime after midnight, he died peacefully. It was Mother's Day.

Today, once again, Angelique felt the agony of being parentless, missing her mother and her father. Like an abandoned seashell, she felt vacant.

Picking up the plastic angel, Angelique repositioned her on the workbench and then tightened the clamps to hold her in place. Applying the drill to the angel's cheek, she began to buff away the blister. She had dreaded doing this, handling this angel that so closely resembled her, the angel doll she had made in her likeness after her father died. She made it as a gift for her mother, hoping it would be like a part of her was there, hoping her mother would not be engulfed by loneliness.

Angelique's mother had been ecstatic, had cherished the angel doll, had become so attached the two were inseparable. Her mother had talked to the doll, had sewn clothes for her—an entire wardrobe of outfits, treating the doll as if she were truly alive.

They had called her Eve, the very first angel doll that Angelique and her sister created. The second one, Annateresa's angel doll who was made in her likeness, was named Ava. She sat perched on Annateresa's workbench across the room. Ava had always lived with Annateresa, never with Henrietta. Ava had never been lost, only Eve.

With her left hand stabilizing the head of Angel Eve, who was now named Etta Ebella, Angelique picked up the drill in her right hand and began carefully smoothing the angel's plastic cheek. She stopped for a moment; her left hand was tingling. She gave it a good shake and scratched her palm through the glove. She then turned the drill back to the *ON* position.

Memories of her mother's face, the look of utter joy when Angelique had presented this angel doll to her, made Angelique's lips tug into a smile. The stretching motion resulted in a slight rise of the tiny scar on her upper lip. As her mother's smiling face and merry laughter took up more space in her mind, the raining tears in her heart subsided. In their place, invisible raindrops seemed to spatter all around her as a scent of clean, fresh rain permeated the area around her workbench. She glanced up at the skylight and held up her gloved hand, palm up as if checking for falling moisture. *Was there a leak?* There was none, just the aroma of the freshest, cleanest rain Angelique had ever smelled. An electric-like current flowed up her left arm, all the way up to her shoulder. The roof of her mouth and her tongue were also tingling fiercely.

It was as if the angel was doing something to her, something she could feel. *Was she talking?* Angelique put down the drill, unclamped the angel, and removed the remaining tape. She picked up the doll and looked into her eyes.

Each of the doll's eyes was a full carat of blue topaz. Captivated, Angelique stared into the rare stones that displayed *rutilation—a* gemology term. This meant the stones housed unique mineral inclusions—streaks of gold—inside the otherwise clear blue gems.

Suddenly, two topaz eyes blinked twice.

Busy at her workbench across the room, Annateresa peeked through her goggles, checking on her twin working across the room. She was worried about Angelique. Finding Angel Eve—the very sight of her in Kate's arms—had triggered a tsunami of emotion, tumbling the mountain of grief her sister had held tightly inside.

Thinking back, their mother, who was wise about so many things, had been wrong about protecting Angelique's studies that year. Annateresa had felt it at the time, but had not dared stand up to her mother, not when she was sick.

Funny thing about the tentacles of protective love—Annateresa thought, wishing she knew then what she knew now—is that they can become a tangled knot in the very hearts you're trying to protect. As unselfish as it had seemed then, their mother had clearly made a mistake by not letting Angelique come to see her.

Denial, disguised as protecting your children, was the issue. Irrefutable denial was what Annateresa heard when her mother was on the phone with Angelique and her brother, not long after the oncologist had delivered the bad news: the lymphoma had returned, and it had spread. Strangely, though, her mother's report to Angelique and Lawry erased almost everything the doctor had said. Her words rewrote his words as if that would delete the cancer cells growing in her body.

For Annateresa, the details of the meeting with the doctor that day were frozen in her mind like audio photographs in a digital camera. She could look at each frame, examine it, and it remained there in perfect order for the next viewing. Initially, the doctor had discussed what the latest scans revealed: the lymphoma was inoperable this time; there were multiple spots in her mother's lungs and two outside the lung cavity, near her heart.

Interrupting the doctor's report, her mother said, "Now Dr. Quickland, you know that I am a bottom-line person. What is my prognosis?"

The doctor immediately looked down, shuffled the papers in front of him. When he looked back at her mother, his hands were brought together, fingertips to fingertips, steepled together as in prayer mode. But the steeple was horizontal. It pointed at her mother as if that hand position would work as a compass for his tongue, guiding him to tell her the truth—nothing but the guarded truth.

Speaking slowly, he said, "Well, Henrietta, with effective treatment, there's a twenty to eighty percent survival rate, usually up to a five-year period. You have some things working against you, though. Just two years ago, you had extensive treatment—multiple rounds of chemotherapy and radiation—which is hard on all bodily systems. Plus, you have the separate condition of fibrosis in your lungs. This combination is tougher to treat, and the lymphoma has now spread into your spleen. A metastasizing between the chest cavity and the abdominal cavity is significant. All this puts you at *Stage Four.* He hesitated, waiting for the impact of those two words.

Her mother simply nodded, and then asked about treatment, specifically, how many sequential rounds of chemotherapy she would have to endure. The high number he reported back was the information that brought tears to her mother's eyes. Stoic tears, they were, vanishing almost as quickly as they had appeared.

Before Annateresa could maneuver the car out of the medical plaza parking lot that day, she heard her mother on the phone. She had called her bridge partner, saying she had received a good report from the doctor, and she would be at the bridge game that night. She would be there at 6:30 sharp.

Annateresa could understand her mother not wanting to broadcast the news of her recurring lymphoma to her bridge group. But then, she was flat out flabbergasted when she heard her mother call Lawry. "The doctor said there was an *"80% cure rate!"* She would be fine after several rounds of chemo; she had proclaimed to her son.

Thirty minutes later when she was on the phone with Angelique, her mother reported the same hopeful news, using the words *cure rate.* Words the doctor had never uttered. And she said it with exuberance. She was quite convincing—she dreaded going through the chemo again, but she would be fine. Annateresa had recently moved, taken a job in the Bay Area, so she would be nearby to help her through the rough periods.

Their mother's orders had been clear: Angelique was not to leave school; the third year in medical school was too demanding. By the time she made the round trip to California, she could lose the entire semester. And that was unacceptable, would derail Angelique's career track. Besides, it was just too exciting that Angelique had been invited to read her research paper at a medical conference in Paris on May 12. She was not to even contemplate coming home until after that. And better yet, they would all meet in Paris for a joint birthday celebration. Then, they would travel south to the Provence area and see all the family. Throughout their lives, Annateresa and Angelique had spent weeks each summer with their French relatives.

Her mother had laughed about needing to go on a diet before the trip. In her usual enthusiastic style, her mother's voice had projected the lively energy of vibrant health. What Angelique could not see through the phone was that the diet dialogue was a hoax, a red herring. Their mother was bone thin. She had dropped thirty pounds in less than six weeks.

Even still, a joint birthday celebration in Paris sounded enchanting. As she remembered now, Annateresa admitted that even she had latched onto the idea like a hungry fish biting an artificial lure. The mere thought of celebrating their birthdays in Paris had soothed her soul. Their mother had always made their birthdays incredibly special, particularly since all three shared the same day.

The twins had been born on their mother's birthday, May 15, precisely at noon. Henrietta said it was a sign from the Blessed Mother, a passing of the power, the LaBelle women's special lineage would continue with double force.

Fate had other ideas about their birthday that year. Their mother almost died with the first round of chemo, her body not strong enough to withstand such poisons. Dr. Quickland postponed further treatment until she was stronger, saying when they resumed, he would alter the chemo formula so that she was not so adversely affected. Annateresa now knew what that meant; he was changing it to a weaker potion. There would be no *effective treatment*.

Her mother maintained her ebullient denial, and Annateresa did nothing and said nothing that would erode it. The battle within Annateresa had raged ferociously. Her inner dialogue had formed fists of questions that pummeled away at her like she was their punching bag.

- Hope was an essential ingredient, the essence of life, at life's very core, wasn't it? Who was she to take that away from her mother?
- And if she did, would she then be held responsible for accelerating her mother's fight against death? ...for revving death's engine so it could speed across the inevitable finish line in a hurry to attain lifelessness?
- And if she told Angelique and her brother the real prognosis, would that destroy or tamper with her mother's will to live?
- Or was her mother simply holding up a brave facade for everyone, aware of what she was doing, like sleeping in a bulletproof vest in hopes of psychologically fending off a gun-laden nightmare?
- And for that matter, what were the facts beyond the physical data? And what did the doctors really know? They extended hope, saying her mother had an incredibly strong spirit and faith, saying that combination was the best medicine in the world. They claimed that was what it took to defeat such ominous odds. Could they be right?
- And weren't children supposed to honor the wishes of a dying parent?

Annateresa recalled deciding that this was not about her, that it was about her mother, who had the right to live and to die as she wished. So, Annateresa had remained silent. She had understood too late that her silence had served only herself. It had fed her own disease, the one she easily recognized in others but suppressed in herself—the sly sickness called denial: thievery that stole precious moments of intimacy, moments of truth and courage.

Pneumonia had set in, so severe that antibiotics had not touched it. Rather rapidly, their mother took an unexpected turn for the worse. Ironically, she didn't become comatose until Angelique's flight departed Charles de Gaulle Airport in Paris. Seventeen hours later when Angelique's plane landed in San Francisco on that May 15— their birthday—their mother had already taken her last breath mere moments before the plane touched down.

Angelique still carried an enduring sorrow and guilt for not being there. Whereas her guilt, Annateresa decided, was like a finely chopped salad all mixed up with the peace she felt from being the primary caretaker and from experiencing the amazing ending. The guilty ingredients had to do with not calling Angelique and Lawry to come sooner, not defying her mother's wishes—to have consciously protected the dying, while not also tending to the living.

Even today, she still felt defensive, Annateresa thought, remembering how she had hoped her sister would intuit the truth from her, from her tone of voice in one of her sister's regular calls. She and Angelique had been extremely close as children; they could communicate without saying a word. Nevertheless, Annateresa could not break through the psychic veil to her adult sister when it came to her mother's illness. It seemed that the longer Angelique was in medical school, cutting on cadavers, the less intuitive she became. Nevertheless, she had tried to send Angelique telepathic messages that their mother was quickly deteriorating, was dying.

In the end, Annateresa thought, she had no choice but to let her mother go. To hope and pray for her to continue living in such a painful condition would have been nothing more than cruel selfishness. She could only pray for God's mercy.

After it was all over, Annateresa recalled, she had been physically and emotionally depleted, been acutely fatigued for weeks. Yet she had felt enriched, had felt at peace, especially from what she was privileged to experience at the end.

The ending scene of her mother's life was etched in her memory in indelible ink, penned in beautiful calligraphy on the scrolls of her heart. Annateresa would never forget.

She swiped at her safety glasses, lifting the corners up to wipe the tears as she relived the memory. The ending had begun with intense words. Her mother had not spoken one word in hours; she had been completely unresponsive, eyes closed, comatose. The only sound was her lungs gurgling with fluid. Then as if her vocal chords were suddenly resuscitated, her enunciation became perfectly clear. Annateresa heard her mother speak, almost sing, as she slowly placed great emphasis on each word: "Oh ...I ...love ...you." Every syllable was a declaration, dripping with love and praise.

The words were not spoken to Annateresa, not meant for her, not meant for anyone alive on the Earth plane. Yet when those words were uttered, death's doorway opened life inside Annateresa, unlocking the immortal shield around her mortal ears, eyes, and heart.

In the quietness between the long spaces of her mother's breaths, Annateresa heard trumpets. Wings surrounded her as if a host of angels had entered the room. Angelic melodies filled the air, announcing the arrival of the *Divine*. A huge angel, carrying glorious banners, preceded this God presence of light that Annateresa could not see clearly, unable to behold the powerful brightness. IT had stood just behind her mother's bed. A magnetic vortex flowed forth from ITS outstretched hands, which seemed to be extracting her mother's spirit from her earthly body, drawing it out directly through the top of her head.

Aware that the end was near, Annateresa was standing beside the bed, her left hand on her mother's head, stroking her hair. Her right hand was tucked into her mother's fingers. When the *Divine Presence* began its magnetic pull, Annateresa's left arm had begun to tingle, from her fingertips all the way up past her shoulder, including the entire left side of her neck and face. Her tongue and the roof of her mouth had tingled fiercely. Then suddenly, the smell of fresh rain had flooded the room. It was the cleanest, purest rain as if a trillion snowflakes had exploded in the presence of intense sunshine.

Her eyes became open windows with the screens removed. Annateresa saw her mother's spirit body rise from her deathbed, walk through a crystalline arched doorway and sit on a magnificent chair—a golden-silvery one, ornately carved. Two angels pulled a strap across her mother's lap as if fastening a seat belt; then, flanking each side behind her, they held the top corners of the chair and flew upward.

As the angel chair ascended, her mother smiled and waved to Annateresa. It was the cutest wave, her palm forward, fingers together, making a distinct, but slight, horizontal movement. It was her mother's signature wave. That is, when she was happy.

The earthly body, the one lying on the hospital bed, gave one final exhale. Then there was nothing, nothing but absolute stillness. There was no following inhale, only startling stillness in the flesh that Annateresa had known as Mother.

Annateresa had yet to tell Angelique what she had experienced that day, didn't know if she ever would tell her—or anyone, or if she ever could.

Movement across the room caught Annateresa's eye. Looking over to her sister's workstation, Annateresa stared in wonderment. Surely the thick lenses of the safety glasses and her recent tears were distorting the scene across the room. She removed her goggles and placed them on her workbench. Annateresa stepped ever so quietly across the room, all the while wishing her prosthetic leg had the ability to tiptoe.

Gracious sakes, what was Angelique doing? Was she waltzing with Etta Ebella? No, she was fox-trotting and doing so with unabashed merriment.

Angelique slowed her dance, embracing the angel doll to her chest. In a hushed whisper, she spoke to Annateresa. "She transported me there, to the sacred moments of Mother's last breaths on Earth and her first breaths in Heaven. I smelled the rain, the purity of the beautiful rain. Oh, Sis, we did have a miracle. Mother received the ultimate healing."

CHAPTER NINE

pproaching the Bay Bridge, the lamb–pasta car inched along, moving more slowly than normal even amidst heavy traffic. In route to Berkeley Hills, 537 Spruce Street, Terrence talked on his cell phone while keeping an eye on the rearview mirror, constantly checking to see if the Jaguar was still following closely behind him.

Etta Ebella, wrapped in a lavender satin baby blanket, lay on the seat next to him, listening to his conversation as he tried to unravel the mystery.

"Hey, Pop, what do you remember about where Mother got Kate's angel doll?" Etta Ebella didn't hear a response. Poppy Pop must have spoken quietly, unusual for him.

"Okay. Then did you or she ever know anyone with the last name of Donahorn?"

Terrence removed one earpiece as Poppy Pop's voice suddenly boomed, filling the car. "Donahorn, is it? It rings a bell, Son, a distant one, though. I don't think it was anyone I worked with at PG&E. Let me ask your mother."

Etta Ebella could hear Poppy Pop asking Grammy Mer the big question. In the long pause, the only sounds were Poppy Pop's breathing and his fumbling with the phone. Finally, his answer: "Well, Son. It seems like I saw some recognition in your mother's eyes. But you know she can't move her head or her hands anymore. Not on command, anyway."

Terrence's heart plummeted. Finger signs had been the only way to communicate with her for five months now. It was devastating news. The car interior seemed to fold in around him. Barely able to disguise his shock, he said, "No, I didn't know. Just last week when I saw her, she still could." His throat knotted with tears. "Hey, Pop, I'm in a crunch of traffic right now; I'll have to call you later. Give Mother a kiss for me. I love you, Pop."

Terrence had taken his mother to so many doctors and medical schools that he had lost count. He had taken her to every renowned neurology specialist from coast to coast, and not a single one could diagnose her problem. All were in consensus that it was not Parkinson's, not MS, not ALS—Lou Gehrig's disease. Some said it was Multiple Systems Atrophy, meaning they didn't know what it was.

The one thing they all said was that her MRIs showed black areas, dead brain cells in her cerebellum and the central nerve between the brain lobes. Her brain would become increasingly incapable of sending the necessary signals to keep her body functioning properly. Her thinking brain would not be affected. Even still, she would gradually lose all voluntary and involuntary bodily functions. There was absolutely nothing that could be done for her, except to try and keep her comfortable. All doctors agreed it was too late for her to benefit from using an electronic communication board.

And to think it all started with her slightly tripping, walking out of her shoes—high heels. She always wore high heels, pricey high-fashion shoes. *How could this horror have happened to my mother, my beautiful, elegant, and graceful mother? My young mother? Dear God, she's only sixty-two. How can that be your plan for her, for us?*

Terrence's hands tightened their grip on the steering wheel. His mother was a talented interior designer, quite renowned and such a good, honest person, so loving and kind. She had the mind and memory of a computer whiz. And now, in addition to everything else, they couldn't ask her where, who, and how she had obtained the angel doll she had given to Kate.

Etta Ebella sighed silently. Already knowing the answers to the questions TT contemplated, she decided to listen to the radio that Terrence had turned down to such a low volume that he had forgotten it was still playing.

Her plastic lips wanted to part in amusement, somewhat disgruntled amusement, as she listened to the advertisement for the tanning salon. Why was it that so many white people wanted to tan, to darken their skin color while so many of those born with dark skin yearned for a safe and effective way to lighten theirs?

She chuckled to herself as she remembered a day just a few weeks ago when Jillian was over playing with Kate. Carly and Jophia, Jillian's mother, were having tea at the kitchen table while the girls played. Jophia had asked Carly what she wanted for her upcoming birthday, and Carly said she wanted a membership to a tanning salon because her legs were paler than two sticks of chalk.

Jophia had screeched, "Why, Carly, I am a black woman. I can't walk into a tanning salon and buy you, my white friend, a tanning membership." Carly's face had turned even whiter, then instantly red. She and Jophia had giggled and laughed so hard that rivers of tears had streamed down their faces.

When Jophia could finally talk without laughing, she had admonished Carly for even contemplating using a tanning bed, saying that was like climbing into a microwave and nuking your liver and other internal organs.

Carly had promised that it was just a whim because of their upcoming trip to Hawaii for a business conference with Kal's company. It was especially exciting because Kal would be honored as this year's top salesperson for the entire company, worldwide.

Carly had said she was thrilled for Kal, for what this meant to his career advancement. Though, admittedly, she had confided to Jophia, that one of her first thoughts had been of her legs, fearing they would appear ghastly *white* when stepping into the azure waters of the Pacific.

The women had snickered as Carly told Jophia about the self-tanning products that she and her sister Abigail had used over the years. With the sun-in-the-bottle stuff, sometimes their fair skin ended up streaked like a toddler's finger painting or worse yet, an icky yellowish orange, looking jaundiced like they had indeed cooked their livers. Jophia got so tickled she snorted, which had made Carly laugh until her stomach muscles ached.

Etta Ebella smiled inwardly at the memory. With that, she began pondering the paradox of American ideas about skin color. On one hand, there was prejudice against dark skin, and on the other, tanned skin was held up as the epitome of beauty. One recent news report said that some young women spent more time in tanning beds than they did in their sleeping beds. *Do they know they will eventually get giraffe-size freckles on their arms and legs, even their faces, and worse yet, skin cancers that eat away at their flesh?* Etta Ebella shivered.

Considering her job as angel guide to Kate when she went through the adolescent and teen years on her way to womanhood, Etta Ebella was also alert to Hollywood's ideal of female beauty—bone thin. She didn't want Kate to behave like some girls and women who forced themselves to vomit after eating, or purged with laxatives, or ate dangerously little to be thin, all in all ruining their health. The odd thing was, though, most of them were already perfectly beautiful but just couldn't see themselves properly. If it within her powers, she would make all mirrors on Earth beautify their subjects, as the eyes of the Almighty do.

The lamb-pasta car rumbled roughly around a corner, shifting her somewhat on the seat. She listened as Terrence tuned the radio to a sports channel. Earth's sports industry was an enigma to Etta Ebella. She had eavesdropped on many of TT's and Kal's conversations and learned that it took athletic talent and rigorous training to excel in sports. She was on board with that and with healthy competition that could improve skills and foster team building. Nevertheless, she remained puzzled about the gargantuan salaries paid to sports figures. One day, she had overhead TT comment that athletics offered high salaries due to ongoing physical injuries that shortened careers. Even still, Etta Ebella fretted over the disparity of salaries between professional athletes and teachers. Many athletes netted millions of dollars a year to perform ball feats while teachers—who fed and shaped the minds of children, the Earth's future—were paid pittances in comparison.

A bigger worry for Etta Ebella was Earth people's negative attitudes about motherhood and fatherhood. She wondered why the hardest job on Earth—when done with loving vigilance—was ranked low, not given its proper respect. How had scores of smart people evolved, or not evolved, to support such values? *Earth, what an odd planet.*

Quite unexpectedly, Terrence pushed the off button on the radio.

Etta Ebella watched his eyes fill with tears. She looked into his heart and saw how dearly he loved his mother, and how it took enormous strength for him to look at her now. Physically, she was a mere sliver of the beautiful, powerful mother he had known. Her neck muscles could no longer support the weight of her head, so it lolled to the side as she leaned heavily against the right side of the wheelchair. She could only utter nonsensical noises. If Terrence did not have the capacity to see his mother's heart overflowing with love and beauty, like a magnificent rose garden, Etta Ebella understood that he would now have difficulty feeling connected to her.

Sighing yet again, Etta Ebella jostled on the passenger seat as the lamb-pasta car failed to make friends with a chain of potholes. With her lavender blanket still cozy around her, she let her angel mind wander. She thought about how most Earth people could never explain the *why and how* of things, especially disease, not during their Earth life, anyway. In most cases, the answers they concocted missed the mark by gazillions of miles. That is except for their notions about the effects of stress.

As for other mysteries, most humans couldn't conceive of the intricate network of mazes connecting all people like tree roots in a forest. Most earthlings didn't tap into the heavenly blessings and mysteries Earth life served up in giant portions every day. Most didn't pay attention to or honor the multitude of directional signals generated by the Almighty's map.

Ironically, Terrence was one of the rare earthlings who did listen deep inside himself and continually watched for signs of being on-track or being off-track as for his best life path. Even still, he could not formulate the why of his mother's illness. Nor could he solve the mystery of how the angel, once named Eve, the one Angelique had made and given to her mother, had come to belong to Kate and was now named Etta Ebella. Not yet, anyway.

CHAPTER TEN

*K*ate sat in the walnut tree, waiting. The tree branches hugged her close in its giant arms, attempting to massage away her worry. After six long and miserable days without Etta Ebella, anxiety riddled her very core.

Although she remembered that Dr. Donahorn's heart had a pretty lilac-and-green swirl of color that appeared kind, Kate worried that the doctor was going to stake a claim of ownership to Etta Ebella. She could keep her forever. After all, Dr. Donahorn had made Etta Ebella.

Well, the truth of it was, Kate thought, Dr. Donahorn had only made Etta Ebella's plastic earthly image. She was not the ONE, who had breathed life into her. But she had named her Eve. The same name of the first woman in the Bible—the woman in the Garden of Eden who ate the *apple*.

A frightening image suddenly lurched in Kate's mind. There had been a Prada purse sitting on the kitchen counter in Dr. Donahorn's house. *Maybe she was not nice, maybe she was a devil.*

While Kate's mother had not allowed her to see that movie, *The Devil Wears Prada*, Kate had read the title on the marquis. And then, she saw it on a wall poster inside the theater. Kate wondered: *Was having a Prada purse the same as wearing it?*

What troubled Kate more than anything was the images she saw in Dr. Donahorn's heart: a cameo of an older woman who had angel wings sprouting from her shoulders; she was holding up a bell in her left hand. The woman and the bell had been surrounded by a grayish color that made Kate feel sad when she observed it. *Was it a sign that Etta Ebella truly belonged to Dr. Donahorn, should live with her?*

Kate's heart ached like it was fragmented, like an essential part of her was missing. She had tried to connect to the feeling of wholeness engendered by the Jesus man and the Great Angel Mother. But at night, sleep had remained near impossible, her purple sheets wadding underneath her like knotty broken bones poking at her skin.

Bad dreams haunted what periods she did sleep. *Nightmares.* She shuddered, remembering her dream about a huge, striped snake. It had appeared to be giving a speech in church, a strange church, not the one that she and her parents attended. The snake had stood up erect behind the pulpit. As the snake talked, it had slipped poisonous fangs into Kate's left arm, which had throbbed horribly during the dream.

Despite the angel doll's absence, Kate had felt Etta Ebella's presence at times. That and little inklings of the angel's love. But the darkness had loomed over her more, seeming to slide right underneath her skin, pointing to monsters under her bed. For the first time, she had slept with a nightlight and had cried out in her sleep. Even the clouds on her ceiling had turned stormy, not offering their usual protective fluff.

What's more, her parents were going on a trip, all the way to Maui, Hawaii. It was usually fun when they went away, but this time, she had to stay at Marilla Marzy's house for a whole week. *Ugh.*

Her Aunt Abigail—her mother's sister and M&M's mother—was nice and sweet, but Uncle Vaynem was scary. One minute he could be pleasant, and the very next breath, he could be yelling curse words and pounding his fists, threatening to tear the world apart. Maybe he would have to go away on a business trip. But Marilla Marzy would not; she would be there. *Yes, she would.*

And Etta Ebella would probably not be there. Uncle TT had said that Dr. Donahorn had encountered some difficulty with the repairs. She had to order a particular material to restore Etta Ebella properly, and that her dress needed repair by Laura, who was traveling with her fashion-design job. It was going to take another week or two. Kate fretted that it was merely a delaying tactic while Dr. Donahorn simply enjoyed having Etta Ebella and was still deciding about keeping her.

Besides, Kate didn't know if she could use the bathroom at Marilla Marzy's house, with or without Etta Ebella there. The recent nightmares had set off explosives in her imagination. She now saw snakes everywhere, particularly in the toilet. Purposefully avoiding the bathroom next to her room, she had tried using her mother's bathroom and the guest bath. Nevertheless, every time she lifted a commode lid, she saw an ugly, striped snake coiled in the water ready to strike at her.

Etta Ebella had told her that humans didn't use all the power in their brains, that peoples' bodies would obey the brain if earthlings but knew how to do it. So Kate was trying to use her brain to put a red stop sign on her lower parts, her bathroom traffic.

Deciding to climb higher in the tree, Kate stood and grabbed the higher branch with her right arm as she stepped up with her left foot. With leaves tickling her face, she climbed three more branches, and then two more—higher in the tree than she had ever climbed.

Etta Ebella would say this one was not a full-fledged branch, more like a limb. Kate's stomach agreed. The limb did feel a bit wobbly, but she could see over the top of her house, could see Spruce Street. This limb could serve as her spy station as she watched for the silver spaghetti car.

Carly peeked out the kitchen window, straining her neck to see the walnut tree. She couldn't see Kate anywhere in the low branches.

She decided that Kate had probably climbed down and gone to feed and brush Keebie, her before-dinner chore.

Kal waltzed into the yellow kitchen smacking his lips and whiffing the air with his nose, "Mmm, it sure smells good in here. What's cooking?"

"A kiss for my handsome husband," Carly said as she wiped her hands on a towel. She wrapped her arms around Kal's neck. "Just think, in a few days we'll be in Maui."

Kal slid his arms around her waist, brought her slim body up close to his, and leaned in to rub noses with her, "Yeah, we can kiss without interruption, and..." His words were cut short by the oven timer and the phone ringing at the same time.

Carly pointed to the timer, saying that she had to tend to dinner. He had to get the phone.

"Qué pasó, Brother?" Kal answered, seeing on the caller ID that it was TT's cell phone number.

Carly, busy getting the roaster out of the oven, listened to Kal's end of the conversation as his words bounced around on the yellow kitchen walls.

"You are? Wow, already? No, Kate doesn't know, but she is expecting to see you at dinner. Alrighty, we'll see you all shortly." Kal hung up the phone and stepped around the corner into the dining room as he had heard a noise on the window. His eyes roved over the entire room, paying close attention to the locks on all the windows. The noise must have been a bird accidentally hitting the glass. Projecting his voice into the kitchen, he said, "Table looks gorgeous, my bride. Fine china and all, eh?" Stepping back into the kitchen, he asked, "And just what is in this roaster? I feel like I could eat a horse."

"Well, then, you are out of luck. It's lamb, Osso Bucco."

"Cool. TT's favorite, isn't it?"

"Yes, I want dinner to be special tonight. It's rare for Terrence to bring a female friend to meet us. Do you think they're romantically involved? Or is it just about the good doctor working on the repairs of Kate's doll?"

"According to the tone I heard in Terrence's voice when he told me about meeting her, I'd say there's romance. Just don't know if it's one-sided or mutual. I do know that it's a darn good thing she is repairing the doll." Kal said.

"No question there. Frankly, Kal, I am concerned. Kate has not been herself without that angel doll around. She's missed her like the doll is a live companion, not a plastic toy."

Kal twisted his mouth around a bit. "Don't be too hard on our Katie girl. She's only six. It's her nightmares that are driving me nuts."

"Oh, the joys of sleep deprivation. We haven't had to get up with her so much since she was two or under."

"Yeah, we've been lucky. But as for the doll, isn't it common for kids Kate's age to pretend? Even to have invisible playmates?"

"I suppose. Though, the last child-development book I read said that a child's ability to distinguish between pretend and reality should be well defined by five years."

He slid the oven mitt onto his right hand and lifted the lid from the roaster. He lowered his nose over the pot and breathed in the savory aroma of the braised lamb shanks. "Kate has been ahead of the game in so many things, so what if she's a little behind in this stage."

"Good point."

"I think that Kate may be projecting my mom's persona onto the doll, especially as Mother is deteriorating so rapidly." Kal conjectured.

"Perhaps. But Kate was mighty attached to the doll even before your mother became ill."

He placed the lid back on the roaster and walked over to where Carly was working on the salad. Leaning his back against the counter, he popped a slice of mango in his mouth. "Let's don't get overly concerned yet. Remember, Mother played a huge role in Kate's first five years. Her debilitation has surely left a painful void for Kate. As much as it has for the rest of us." His eyes filled with tears.

"Oh, sweetheart," Carly said. She wrapped her arms around him, one hand stroking his upper back. "I am so sorry for what's happening to your mother. It's just terrible. She's too young for this."

Kal picked up a stray paper towel from the counter and dabbed at his eyes. "Worse than terrible. But as for Kate missing her doll, you know Mother encouraged Kate to believe that it was a real angel. One especially for her."

"You're right. I hadn't thought about Kate grieving for your mother through the doll."

"Maybe I need an angel doll, too," Kal said in a kidding tone, a weak attempt at derailing his emotional track. His eyes brightened though as he reached for a tomato sprinkled with basil leaves. Even still, the tomato caught in his throat as he swallowed, his tonsils knotting with sadness.

Carly saw his Adams-apple bulge as he swallowed, but sensed that her husband wanted to move on, and for the moment he didn't want more empathy, which could trigger an avalanche of sorrow.

Swatting his hand playfully, she said, "Stay out of my salad."

He quickly grabbed a mango slice. "By the way, where did Mother come up with that name *Etta Ebella*?"

"It's an odd name for sure," Carly said. Her brow furrowed, she stepped around Kal to the cooktop and added three shakes of truffle oil to the pot of potatoes. She watched the oil float up in artful swirls atop the boiling liquid. "I have no idea what inspired your mother when naming the doll. But, now that I think about it, the name, Etta Ebella, seemed important and somehow meaningful to her."

"Yeah, it did. I wish we had asked her about it then."

Stirring the potatoes, she nodded, "We will never know now, will we?"

"Probably not." Kal's shoulders drooped—his body's registry of regret. He cleared his throat. "How was our Katie girl this morning after last night's bad dreams? I surely missed seeing her before I left."

"She was fixated on our Maui trip, carrying on something pitiful, asking why she couldn't stay with Grammy Mer and Poppy Pop while we are gone."

"What did you say?"

"Oh, just that Pops has his hands full and that it wouldn't be fun, with the nurse there and all. Then she went through a long list of people. Asking if she could stay with Aunt Sammy Sue and Uncle Sandy or why couldn't Aunt Ruthie fly in from London to stay with her."

"Sammy Sue has to be in Boston for a conference that week, and Sandy's swamped with opening his new veterinary clinic." Kal eyed the tomato salad, zeroing in on a plump slice of mango.

"I told her that. And I explained that Ruthie could not possibly travel all the way from London just to babysit. And that Terrence would be in LA."

"Hmmph. She does *not* want to stay at Abigail's, does she?"

"No, she doesn't."

"Should we reconsider and get one of our regular babysitters for Kate?"

"I'm not comfortable leaving her with a teenage sitter, not for an entire week."

"What about one of the nanny services?"

"No way, not a stranger nanny, not after what happened to Sammie Sue's friend last year. That little boy will forever be brain damaged, an invalid, all because the woman shook him."

"Oh, yeah, I forgot about that. Real tragedy, that one."

"I just don't see any other choice than Abigail."

"Abigail will take good care of her. It's Vaynem and M&M that worry me." Kal's jaw tightened, his back teeth slightly grinding against one another.

"Vaynem will be there for only one weekend. He has a trial. Abigail said it was possible that the trial could run into the following week. If so, he will stay over in Seattle and not come home at all for that weekend."

"Guess we can hope for that."

Carly glanced around the kitchen, a nervous feeling suddenly scouring her stomach. "What did Terrence say? Is someone else, besides Dr. Donahorn, coming for dinner? If so, I need to set another place at the table."

Just as Kal opened his mouth to speak, a bird flew into the kitchen window, slamming its beak against it, sounding as if the window might shatter from the force of it. Carly jumped straight up, her arms flying upward, hands flailing the air as she danced a jig, her feet stepping high, marching in place.

Kal laughed—loud and heartily. Carly automatically did this when she was startled. She couldn't help herself; her body just took over. A comical sight it was, to say the least.

If this was her spy station, why did Kate feel that someone was watching her, spying on her? She twisted on the limb, looking all around. She knew that feeling of being watched. There had to be someone or something looking at her.

Continuing to scan the area, Kate turned back to face the opposite direction. As she adjusted her legs on the limb, her eye caught movement in the flowers across the driveway. Dark beady eyes stared at her.

A small rabbit inched its way out from the flowers. Kate wondered if it was a girl rabbit or a boy one. Whichever, it seemed to be moving in a direct line toward her. It continued advancing, even with a blackbird flying crazily around the tree.

Kate looked down at the rabbit, its head looking up at her. Something about its eyes reminded her of Etta Ebella. It was dusk and getting hard to see, but those rabbit eyes seemed to grow bigger and bigger, seemed to be pleading with her. Then she felt that odd prickly feeling again, the porcupine running through her stomach. *Uh-oh.*

Etta Ebella had told her that animals could have messages if you but listened. Kate sat very still and opened her inner ear, the way Etta Ebella had taught her to do. In seconds, her forehead furrowed. The bird and the rabbit both seemed to be telling her that danger was lurking, to climb down from the tree. Kate looked all around; everything appeared normal. *What could the danger possibly be?*

A gust of wind swept through the tree leaves and branches, rattling her spy-station. Just as she decided to climb down, she heard a loud buzzing noise. Looking up, she spotted an airplane circling overhead. Excitement raced through her veins. *Oh boy, she could wave to the plane and see if it would dip its wings at her.*

Kate loved to pretend that small planes were spaceships with aliens on board. She would wave crazily to them, let them know that she was welcoming them, and hope that they would give her a friendly sign in return. Maybe these aliens were from Neptune. And just maybe they had some extra-terrestrial machine that could zap Grammy Mer into walking and talking again.

Putting the danger warning aside, she shifted her body around and planted her feet upon the limb; she stood fully erect and waved to her new cosmos friends. Immediately, she heard a crack. The limb she was standing upon was buckling.

Kate turned and saw her spy-station limb tearing away from the main tree trunk. Extending her arm, she tried to grab hold of a sturdier branch. It was too late. Her feet tossed upward.

Leaves and branches scraped her face and arms as she crashed downward, flailing from one branch to another. A broken limb poked her in the eye. Kate's heart pounded against her chest, a non-cadent thud clunk.

Again her fingers grasped for a hold onto one of the larger branches. There. She caught one with her right hand. Her little fingers clutched frantically, though impossible for them to reach around the branch's entire circumference. As challenging as it was in her semi-upside down position, she craned her neck side to side. Out of the corner of her eye, she caught sight of another sturdy branch, one within her reach. Her left hand clawed the air.

Finally, her fingers curled around a woody substance. A young, flimsy limb, it splintered, hurling her down again. Her right hand, bloody and scratched, began losing its hold on the larger branch. She kicked, trying to wedge her foot against the tree trunk while also trying to retain her hand grip. Her foot flailed in the air. Not what she expected, the kicking action threw her backward. Her elfin fingers had no choice but to let go of their feeble hold on the larger branch.

Her mouth open, she tried to scream, but no sound came out. *Or did it?* There was such a loud roaring sound, such a high-pitched ringing in her ears, that's all she could hear. That, and the silent plea that shouted from her heart: *"Dear Jesus, please help me. I don't want to die! But if I do, please don't let my mother be the one to find me, all dead and smashed to smithereens. She'd be so upset that she'd lose the baby, not have any kids then. Please, she's the bestest mother in the whole world."*

"Kal Kindrick, don't laugh at me. Wipe that smirk off your face right now," Carly scolded with a half-smile. She was well aware that her *startled jig* must look hysterical, but she could not control the response. It was completely unconscious with her until she felt herself doing it. And even then, her movements had to play out, go through a timed cycle until her nervous system calmed down.

Before she had time to recover, the haunting sound of Keebie barking like a dog gone mad invaded the yellow kitchen walls. "What now? Has Kate not fed Keebie on time?" Suddenly, the kitchen window pane vibrated with movement as the blackbird flew into it once more.

Kal was the one startled this time, thinking it was odd for a bird to fly into the windows three times this late in the day, first in the dining room and then two times on the kitchen windows that were on the opposite side of the house.

Both of them turned, running toward the kitchen door at the same time. Carly shrieked, "Kal, something's wrong. Oh, Dear Lord, where is Kate?"

The lamb-pasta car was turning the corner at Shattuck Avenue as Terrence Ted clicked off his cell after speaking with Kal. *Why couldn't he shake this sense of urgency?* It seemed to be taking forever to get to

537 Spruce Street from the city today. True, his speed was lower than normal so Angelique could follow him in her car. But she was driving so slowly that he had almost lost her in traffic when crossing the bridge. She had practically stopped. *What was up with that?*

He disliked being in separate cars, especially her first time to meet his family, but she was *on call* at the hospital, and if she got called out on an emergency, she would need to leave before the end of the evening.

Tonight, he wanted to stay; he felt compelled to speak with Kal and Carly, about a whole string of things. For one, he really should get their permission for Kate to be involved with sponsoring a girl in Africa. Then there was the matter of the trust fund he was setting up for Kate; however, that was now overshadowed by the discussion of getting some more help for Pop, who was sounding exhausted and frazzled. That one couldn't wait. He and Kal needed to join forces and intervene, force Pop to hire a second nurse, a night nurse for their mother. Pop was setting his alarm for every few hours, getting up to turn her to keep her from getting bedsores. It was incomprehensible why Pop refused a second nurse. Surely it wasn't about money. If it were, though, Terrence would pay, and gladly so, even for round-the-clock nurses.

And then, although he knew he was poking his nose where it didn't belong, he had concerns about Kate staying with Abigail and Vaynem while they were in Maui. Abigail was a loving person and a conscientious mother, but Vaynem was an entirely different sort. *That dude was messed up.*

The memory of when he had first met Vaynem still haunted him. Interestingly, his body, on its own accord, had stepped back from Vaynem. Instinctively, like an animal perceiving danger, he had taken three backward steps before realizing what he was doing. Vaynem had noticed his reaction to him and had appeared oddly happy about it.

Terrence's pulse raced at the thought of Kate in the care of such a *Machiavellian egotist*. From what he had observed, the man had a cruel streak that dominated his heart, one that rivaled his aorta.

Why were they allowing Kate to stay in Vaynem's home for a whole week? Kal didn't like him or trust him. And Carly knew full well that Vaynem was beyond obnoxious. Had she been fooled by his monetary success as a lawyer or his clout in the church? It appeared that the man did genuinely love his church, and that was good—his saving grace, perhaps. Yet, as for the way he lived his life, he practiced Churchianity. Not Christianity.

Terrence's hands tightened their grip on the steering wheel, remembering the grim childhood story he had read in Vaynem's heart. *But Vaynem was an adult now. It was time for him to stop the negative cycles of the past and take responsibility for the heartless way he treated others.*

Carly had witnessed, first hand, multiple examples of his bullying and antics of purposeful malice, so it must be that Vaynem would be away on business that week. Surely, that's the reason Kal and Carly had made such arrangements for Kate.

Terrence continued to fume wishing that he could change his travel schedule that week to stay with Kate. He knew that even if Vaynem were going to be away, Marilla Marzy would be there. She seemed to be cut from the same cloth as her dad. In truth, though, the jury was still out on her. Right now, she was just a challenging teenager, a depressed one, and who could blame her with Vaynem for a dad. It was a known fact that he was long on punishment and short on love.

A prickling on Terrence's right arm, as if someone in the passenger seat had brushed against it, turned his attention. He glanced over at Etta Ebella. *Whoa.* If he didn't know better, he would claim she was standing upright on the seat, her wings puffed up huge while yelling at him to go faster, to hurry. *Holy Harry! That's ridiculous. I've got to rein in my imagination. It's gone viral on me.*

His stomach felt like it was manufacturing enough acid for twenty people. When having eaten properly, the only times he felt this way was when something was wrong. That is, wrong with someone he loved.

He glanced in the rearview mirror and speed-dialed Angelique. Yes, she had set her GPS system for 537 Spruce Street. With minimum explanation, he shifted gears and was off, speeding down the street like he was racing on the autobahn.

With both hands on the steering wheel and his eyes focused like a professional racecar driver, TT gauged his corners carefully. Two more turns and up a steep hill and he would be there. His expert eye looked out over the sleek nose of his Lamborghini and swerved to miss a blackbird. That was odd, but not near as odd as what he saw now. *Whoa, I need to see an eye doctor.* He blinked his eyes, but no, it was the same scene: A replica of Etta Ebella was sitting on the hood of the car, big as life, with a lavender light extending out from her in a two-mile beacon. Then, as if the lamb part of the car had come to life and commanded, "Open Sesame," the doors—the ones with the Gull-Wing design—seemed to open and sprout wings, flying the car up the hill, over the streets and houses.

Landing at the edge of the driveway, the lamb-pasta car screeched to a halt. TT leaped from the car and began running. Midway along the driveway, he heard a thrashing noise. Looking up, he saw Kate plummeting down, head first from the top of the walnut tree.

Both yelling Kate's name, both in a frenzied state, Carly and Kal came running through the back door. In addition to each other's panicky voices and Keebie's maniacal barking, they heard a loud thwack. Carly stopped mid-step, the sound was paralyzing, her legs instantly frozen, refusing to move.

Kal ran past her. "Oh, Kate, Baby."

Terrence Ted winced. He hadn't expected that limb to whack him in the head, nor had he expected her to land with such force. The crushing weight buckled his knees, almost knocking him down to the ground. But he had her, his arms wrapped around her tangled little body. He kissed her bloody forehead and said a silent prayer.

CHAPTER ELEVEN

The blondish red hair appeared glued to the side of the wheelchair, the unrelenting weight of her head pushing against the dark navy fabric. Grammy Mer—Karalyn Kalee Kindrick— tried to move the little finger of her right hand, tried one more time, all futile tries.

Recently, she had given up attempting to move her pinky or any other body part, had made peace with the impossibility. But today, she had to try, had to mobilize her zombie dead-to-her body, had to try and communicate, had to get Gordon's attention.

He was sitting across the room from her, appearing cozy in his leather chair, reading the newspaper—an indulgence she could no longer enjoy. Not only could her hands not hold any reading material or turn the pages, now her eyes would not move across the page from left to right, not on command, not anymore.

The television droned on loudly because it was time for the news. Gordon always turned up the volume extra loud, making sure she could hear every word of the news.

Not even politics could capture her interest this afternoon. In the past when she had felt this pervasive anxiety, she would go into a private room, drop to her knees, and with spirited heart pangs beseech the Almighty to intervene, to protect her loved ones from any harm that was lurking in their shadows.

One specific memory of doing just that floated through her mind's eye, the memory of when Terrence Ted was nineteen and had a motorcycle accident. That afternoon, she had been working at a client's home, measuring the rooms and windows in preparation for creating a design plan. Out of nowhere, a bad feeling had suddenly come over her, penetrating her very bones. It was so compelling that she had to excuse herself from her client, go to the bathroom and get down on her knees in prayer. The memory of those cold hard tiles digging into her knees flickered through her mind as she remembered her prayer that day.

An hour later, she received the call that Terrence had been taken to the emergency room, a bad accident. In the bigger scheme of things, his injuries—a broken arm, a cracked collarbone, bruised ribs, and a minor concussion— were minimal compared to how badly he could have been hurt. The man who had witnessed the accident, the one who had called for an ambulance and the police, had said that the scene was sublime—both the scariest and the most amazing thing he had ever seen. An oversized Hummer moving at a fast clip, he reported, had abruptly changed lanes, broadsiding Terrence. He claimed that both the motorcycle and Terrence went airborne fifteen feet or more, sailing over the top of the Hummer, landing on the other side of the street in a heap. The man didn't understand why Terrence's left leg had not been mangled from the collision and why the flip and fall had not broken his spine or neck.

That day, she had gotten her miracle, had her prayers answered. But today, although she had already prayed fervently for the safety of her family, she couldn't get on her knees, couldn't humble herself fully before the Almighty.

Now, all she could do was bide her time, wait for bad news, wait for the phone to ring. And it would, of that she was certain. She had not lived these sixty-two years without learning that she didn't feel this way without reason. Someone in her family was in trouble, in physical danger, perhaps already physically injured and maybe more than one person.

Kate's face, framed with her straight reddish-orange hair, kept floating through her mind, along with visions of Terrence, of him running. *But he is not jogging as for exercise,* she thought. *Terrence is running toward something important. He is scared.* Kate at times seemed upright, and then suddenly, her body would appear upside down. *What were those green things all around her? Leaves of a tree?*

Intermittently, the angel doll, Etta Ebella, was appearing on the periphery of those visions. So, the problem must be with Kate, somehow. *But how was Terrence involved? Why did he have such a stricken look on his face?* He had called earlier asking where she had gotten Kate's angel doll, but Gordon had said he thought Terrence had phoned from New York. Now that she thought about it, the bad feeling had begun inundating her, like a deluge opening all flood gates, moments before he had called.

At first, she had thought the anxiety was related to her anticipation of his question about how she came to possess the angel doll. She had been expecting it, now that he was friends with Henny Donahorn's daughter. It was regretful that she had only encountered Henny such a few times, only on three or four occasions, for it seemed that they could have been best of friends had they lived nearer each other.

If she could speak, could answer Terrence's question, it would involve the telling of such astonishing events that even Terrence would think she had lost cognitive brain function, too. Why, she could hardly believe it herself and had never even told Gordon. He had been away on business the day, the week, she had brought the angel doll home. He wasn't there to see the radiant glow coming from her bag, and from the doll's face. Only she and the angel saw. Well, that is, except for Henny and the other witness.

To this day, she felt awed, but it was too crazy, too risky to talk about it with other people. A clear decision had been made by all three not to tell anyone. Pragmatic as he was, Gordon wouldn't believe it; few would. Nonetheless, after some reflecting, she knew that tale was not the source of the consuming anxiety that gripped her this afternoon.

If only she could bow her head in reverence, surely her prayers would be more potent. Mentally, she tried to compel her head down, to bow, at least in spirit, as her heart cried out, *"Great Almighty God, my cherished Lord, thank you for all the miracles I have had in my life. I am immensely grateful. And, yes, I am coming to you asking for yet another. I am calling upon Your Almighty Greatness to protect my precious granddaughter, Kate, and my dear son, Terrence Ted. Wrap them in your mighty love and light. Wherever they are and whatever they are doing, protect them from harm. I know that all things are possible with You and that your will for them is all goodness. Praise and glory be to You, Almighty God of Heaven and Earth."*

Still not at peace, she wanted to begin *The Lord's Prayer*, the meditative ritual that she practiced for hours every day, now that she couldn't read, couldn't talk, couldn't walk, couldn't do anything but think. Addicted to prayer, she was. Prayer and Lysol. How she yearned to feel a Lysol can in her hand, to inhale the pure smell, to spray it all around the house making it germ-free. If only she could, she would for sure.

A cleaning service came in every week, but the house was not up to her standards, but then most people's immaculate was not up to her standards. No one could satisfy her standard of cleanliness. She knew that only too well, remembering how she had made Gordon mop and rinse the floors seven times before she would bring any of their babies home from the hospital. Thankfully though now, Gordon knew how to do laundry correctly. *No bathroom things were washed with kitchen things, but was he disinfecting the washing machine and dryer after every load?*

And what about their groceries? Most likely, he didn't always clean all the canned or packaged containers before putting them in their pantry or refrigerator. She almost gagged thinking of the germs. She had told Gordon to consider just how many handlers touched their food items: the manufacturers, the packers, the unpackers, the shelf stockers, the checkout clerk, and the bagger person. *And that's not to mention other shoppers who picked them up to read ingredients or those who coughed and sneezed on them.* She had instructed him to wipe all grocery items down with a disposable disinfecting wipe. He had made such a fuss that she had relented. Then she had asked him to spray everything with Lysol. But she had serious doubts that he did, at least not every single item and not on all sides.

Obsessed with cleanliness, yes, she was, no argument there, but nowadays, her only cleaning product was prayer. All she could attempt to clean today was her own heart and soul.

Silently reciting *The Lord's Prayer*, like a mantra over and over, the words took on a life of their own as they spilled inside her, soaping and rinsing all membranes. Her body drank the words, sipping thirstily from the Holy Chalice that bubbled over with purifying syllables: *"Our Father, who art in Heaven, Hallowed be thy name. Thy kingdom come; Thy will be done on Earth as it is in Heaven...."*

The third time through, she noticed that she had slipped into saying *"Our Father and Mother who art in Heaven."* She acknowledged the recurring contemplation. Even still, her brain offered no objecting filter to the thought that there must be a Divine Mother component to God. Surely, there was. Gender was present on Earth in people, animals, and plants, why not in Heaven? All people have both a male and female part, their Anima and Animus, whether they know it or not, and whether or not they are man or woman in physical gender.

If God created this world, with life birthing from female bodies, mammal life, anyway, why wouldn't God have a female element? The Bible refers to the "She" that brings comfort and wisdom. Was that the invisible, powerful "She" presence she frequently felt hovering around her wheelchair? *Could it possibly be that the Holy Spirit had a female element, the mother component to the Holy Trinity?*

The sound of Gordon's voice jolted her reverie of heavenly deliberations. "Kara, honey, it's time to catheterize you," he said as sweetly as if he was offering her a delicious dessert, like lemon meringue pie with a flaky crust, her favorite.

Gordon was *remarkable*, true to his middle name—Mark. Being ten years older than she was, who would have thought he would take care of her as they grew older, not the reverse?

She knew the first time she met him that he was indeed a special man, but she never dreamed he would have the capacity to do all the things he did for her now. Things a husband should never have to do.

Respecting what a private person she was, he had protected her from strange nurses. He had willingly taken on the tasks of doing the necessities that she could no longer do for herself. He kept her clean from head to toe, washed all her parts, brushed her teeth, and shaved her legs and underarms. He even styled her hair every day and applied a bit of makeup. Then there was the chore of dressing her—pulling and tugging clothes onto her body that could lend no help, dead weight with no cooperative movement.

Having never held a blow dryer, curling iron, or handled hot rollers in his entire life, styling her hair had been the most challenging initially for Gordon. And he knew her perfectionist's eye was judging his efforts, though, she couldn't tell him that one side usually looked fuller than the other. He called her his "Miss America" and teased her that when he was an executive at PG&E, he had sat at his desk and daydreamed about becoming a hairdresser when he retired.

Fixing her hair was now a laughable trifle compared to the tasks of administering the catheterizations and enemas—all on a prescribed schedule as recommended by the doctors. Even still, the diapers were ever present.

Poor Gordon. She felt ashamed. And yet, incredibly grateful. If only she could tell him that she would now accept nurses, and in multiples. Sadly, her attempt at words, raw noises not even syllables, made no sense to him. He didn't have a clue what she was trying to say. The kids believed they already had one nurse, but they didn't.

She was trapped, held hostage, inside her unresponsive body. He was entrapped, emotionally fenced in, as her sole caretaker. Even with profound love, no man or woman should suffer this kind of burden in caring for their spouse, not alone, not as a sole caretaker. It was too much.

Involuntary tears seeped from her eyes as voluntarily she began another prayer: *"Dearest Lord, please be with Gordon, my beloved— Gordon Mark Kindrick—as he cares for me. Give him strength and respite from my care. Lord, I've been naïve, believing my condition to be temporary. I was wrong to be so prideful, wrong to refuse outside help. It was my denial and fear. I'm so sorry. Please forgive me that, and for my ever-toiling perfectionism.*

I have foolishly taken my health for granted, particularly the needs of my body for regular food and rest. And I wish I had properly appreciated my mobility and the ability to communicate. Oh, Great Lord Almighty, hear my prayer. Show me the way to serve You. Help me to glorify You in some way while I'm in this debilitated state. If my illness can come to some good, I am a willing servant. My blessed Savior, I surrender my all to Thee."

"Kara, honey, are you okay? You're not acting like yourself."

At 537 Spruce Street, Terrence's car was parked haphazardly askew, blocking the driveway.

Parking on the side street, Angelique switched off the engine and set the parking brake. She surveyed the two-story home, noticing the back door. It was open, wide open.

She had expected Terrence to be waiting for her, to accompany her inside and introduce her. Now she felt awkward, wondering whether to walk in the back door unannounced, knock and wait, or walk around to the front and ring the doorbell.

Her steps marked with conspicuous uncertainty, she walked toward the driveway. Nearing the Lamborghini, she became aware of a humming sound. Then she noticed that the driver's door had been left open. Peering inside, she saw the knot of keys dangling from the ignition. And lying crisscross on the passenger seat was Etta Ebella, still wrapped in the lavender blanket. *Terrence left the engine running, his door open, and the doll in the car. How strange.*

Angelique eyed the doll, wanting to retrieve it. She decided against it as Terrence had said he wanted to surprise Kate, had said he couldn't wait to see Kate's face when she saw Etta Ebella all refurbished.

A man's shouting startled her. "Dr. Donahorn, Dr. Donahorn, come quickly. Please. It's Kate." The man bolted out the door, running toward her.

"What's happened?"

"She fell from the tree. Terrence got here in time to catch her, but she's injured. He is carrying her upstairs now."

"Is she conscious?"

"Breathing but not conscious. Can you please take a look at her?

"Yes, of course," Angelique said. She glanced at the car.

"Whoa. Terrence left the engine on. Please, hurry on inside. I'll take care of it."

Angelique nodded as she rushed toward the door.

Kal yelled, "Up the stairs and to the left. The first room."

Robotically, Kal steered the lamb-pasta car to a safe spot aside the garage and switched off the engine. He jumped from the seat, shoved the car door, harder than Terrence would ever have done, and went racing into the house. He ascended the stairs with hasty steps.

Entering Kate's room, his eyes immediately went to his daughter, his little peanut, who lay motionless, sprawled on the bed. Blood, leaves, and perspiration matted her orange hair. The gash on her cheek was bleeding, but not spurting as badly as the cut over her left eye was.

Terrence sat in the chair on the opposite side of Kate's bed, looking somber and ashen, the color having drained from his face.

Angelique continued examining Kate, checking for broken bones, swelling, and bruises.

Carly raced into the room, holding two kitchen towels. Following Angelique's directions, she sat on Kate's bed and held the towels firmly on the facial lacerations.

"Terrence, can you help me out here?" asked Angelique.

"Sure, what do you need?"

"A fresh lemon, one cut in half, please."

Carly shook her head vigorously, silently saying, yes, there are fresh lemons in the refrigerator.

Kal—who had been standing behind Carly, his hands placed protectively on her shoulders—immediately started toward the door, saying, "I'll get it, Brother. You stay put; you're still looking mighty pale." He picked up the pace as he ran heavily down the stairs, going clomp, clomp, clomp.

The olive-colored eyes, now red and bloodshot, fluttered open and the little voice cracked, "A lemon, Dr. Donahorn? What for?"

"Hello, Princess Kate, I'm glad you've awakened. I need a lemon because you have two cuts that are bleeding. They are in areas on your face where we can only apply light pressure without hurting the wounds and bruising you. We need some lemon magic."

Still woozy, eyes barely open, Kate said, "Lemon magic? Are the Great Angel Mother and the Jesus man coming?"

Great Angel Mother? Angelique loved pediatrics. Kids like Kate could come up with some dandy concepts. She found it fascinating to explore their capacious imaginations. Nonetheless, she ignored the comment, kept to the facts at hand, saying, "Fresh lemon juice, when squeezed directly from the lemon, has properties that stop minor bleeding and disinfect wounds. Nature's magic at work. Now, it may sting a bit. Are you up for that?"

Terrence stood. Still shaken, he grasped the side of the dresser to steady himself. He turned slightly catching a glimpse of the back of his head in the side dresser mirror. Off-key from his normal resonant voice, he said, "Whoa. If Kate's not, I am." He swiped at the back of his head. His hand dripped with blood.

At the sound of Terrence's weakened raspy tone, Angelique's head snapped upward to a view of the back of his shirt. It was blood-soaked. Her eyes followed the bloody trail upward and saw the laceration on his head, gaping and hemorrhaging.

Carly screamed like a banshee as if she had bled to death from a head wound.

CHAPTER TWELVE

*T*he hospital chair felt hard; Kal Kindrick could not get comfortable. Like scissors, his legs crossed then uncrossed. How had his world crumbled so quickly, altered in the twinkling of an eye?

An emergency-room waiting area was the last place he expected to be this evening. He should be at home, savoring Carly's marvelous cooking and sipping fine wine ...should be taking pleasure in the company of his brother and getting to know Angelique ...should be tucking sweet Kate into bed ...should be anticipating the upcoming trip to Maui ...should be celebrating being named the company's top salesperson.

The sound of his cell phone ringing felt invasive, jangling his nerves. But the sound of his Pop's voice brought instant tears to his eyes. Why was it that when trouble clutched him in its shadowy aura, the sound of a voice he loved could knot his throat and drop his heart to his knees?

Poppy Pop was sorry for calling so late, interrupting Kal's evening, but Grammy Mer was acting troubled and agitated. He couldn't understand her attempts at words, but he could read some of her feelings. This evening, she wanted to be near the telephone. Every time he moved her wheelchair away, she got a wild look in her eyes, moaned in weird noises, which was so unlike her. He had checked her blood pressure; it was elevated but not in the range where the doctor said to be concerned. Being married to her for all these years, he was well aware of her intuitive abilities. Something must be wrong—somewhere, with one of their loved ones. *What was he to do? Start calling the kids, beginning with the oldest.*

"Kal, how are you, Carly, and Kate? Is everything, everyone, okay?" Poppy Pop asked.

"Pop, so good to hear your voice," Kal replied, working to conceal the knot of worry choking his throat. "I was planning on calling you and Mother just as soon as I had more information. I'm here at Alta Bates Summit Emergency. We've got quite a situation here, triple trouble—Kate, Terrence, and Carly are all being examined by doctors as we speak."

"What?"

"Kate needs stitches, and she has possible internal injuries as her abdomen is a bit distended. Terence has a head injury; he is conscious, but we don't know the extent of his situation yet. With all that, Carly fainted. That's all I know for now. The doctors asked me to wait out here."

"Hells bells, Son, what happened? A car accident?"

"No. Kate fell out of the walnut tree by the driveway. She had climbed to the top. Terrence was coming to dinner and arrived just in time to catch her fall, but he got whacked in the head with a falling tree limb. You know how head wounds bleed, and then Carly fainted."

"My lands."

"Terrence's new lady friend, Angelique Donahorn, arrived right behind him and helped me tend to all of them. She called for two ambulances. She is in with Kate now, stitching her face. Did Terrence tell you that she's a pediatric plastic surgeon?"

"No, I didn't know that. But, sounds like it is fortunate for us that she is."

"She's also arranged for the best doctors on staff here to treat Terrence and to look after Carly. If it weren't for Angelique, I would be a total nut case right now."

"What's the status of Terrence and Carly?"

"The doctors are still evaluating Terrence's head injury; they're doing an MRI and some other test. Angelique insisted on having Carly examined, too, since she fainted. Pop, that's all the info I have right now. How is Mother?"

"Hold on while I tell her what's happened." Kal could hear his father relaying the scenario, heard his mother make an eerie gasping sound, and then his dad was back on the line. "Son, call us the minute you have any news, regardless of what time it is. Okay?"

"Sure will, Pop. Give Mother a kiss for me. Ask her to render up some of her mighty prayers for us."

"Okay, Son, will do. Remember, we won't rest until we hear back from you." The phone clicked off.

From behind him, Kal heard a female voice.

"Kal? Are you Kal Kindrick, Terrence's brother?"

Kal spun around, expecting to see a doctor. To his surprise, a shiny-eyed woman—one who looked almost exactly like Angelique—stood there, extending her hand.

"I'm Annateresa Donahorn, Angelique's sister. I wish we were meeting under different circumstances."

"You're Angelique's sister?"

"Yes. She asked me to check on you. Is there anything I can get for you, do for you while you wait?"

Kal's mouth opened to speak at the same time that he noticed the bag that Annateresa was holding in her left hand. The bag emanated a peculiar glow as if a candle were lit inside it. He said, "Your bag. Is there a fire in there?"

Annateresa looked down, turning the bag away from him. "Fire? No, no, it's just one of those copper metallic-colored bags." Motioning up toward the ceiling, she said, "This fluorescent lighting casts a strange luminescence upon the copper color, doesn't it?" She laughed as she began folding up the bag and said, "Actually, it's empty now. I just handed off Kate's angel doll to Angelique so that Kate could hold her while she was getting stitches."

"Etta Ebella?"

"Yes. Angelique asked me to retrieve the doll from Terrence's car. I understand that Kate is quite attached to her angel doll."

"Oh, yes, indeed, she is," said Kal, silently wondering why the pit of his stomach suddenly felt strange. "Wait a minute. You drove all the way to our house, from San Francisco to Berkeley Hills, to get that doll?"

"My starting point was this hospital, so it was just a few miles. I had business here at Alta Bates this afternoon."

"Are you a doctor, too?"

"No. I am a pediatric prosthesis specialist, so I work with doctors and hospitals all around the Bay Area." Annateresa replied.

"My, that's interesting. How did you get into that line of work?"

Annateresa smiled into Kal's eyes, which looked a bit glazed from shock, and boldly pulled up the hem of her long skirt revealing her bare ankle and shin. She said, "I've had a prosthetic leg since I was ten; it so changed my life that I was captivated by the technology and wanted to help other children."

Kal's eyes blinked in repetition. The skin on her leg looked somewhat abnormal, thick like she was wearing a support hose, but he could see that she was not. "Whoa, I am sorry. I must be overwhelmed with all that's happened. Please forgive me for asking such a personal question."

"No worries. I am proud of my leg."

"You and Angelique look so much alike. Are you twins?"

"Mr. Kindrick?"

The deep voice startled him. Kal pivoted around to see a young man wearing a white lab coat and a stethoscope around his neck.

"Yes, I am Kal Kindrick, and you are?"

"Quinn Avery," the doctor said. He extended his hand for a brief handshake with Kal. "I've examined your wife, and I believe that she and the baby are fine."

"You mean Kate? She is six years old now. Thank God, they're both okay." Kal briefly bowed his head.

Dr. Avery cleared his throat. His eyes narrowed, and one bushy eyebrow went up, raised higher than the other. "You can see your wife now, Mr. Kindrick," he said. "Come with me and I'll show you to her room. We'll be releasing her shortly."

Kal turned, extending his hand. He said, "Annateresa, please excuse me. It was."

Interrupting him mid-sentence, Annateresa said, "Go with Dr. Avery. I'll catch up with you later."

As they walked away, Annateresa heard Kal say, "You said Kate was okay, too. Is she also being released?"

"Who is the best sonogram technician in this hospital?" Angelique asked, using her most authoritative doctor voice.

The three nurses at the curved station all stared at her. The dark-haired young one said, "All our sono techs are good."

Angelique said, "I want the very best available. Sonogram results are only as good as the technician."

The tall nurse who was standing to the side, the man with the RN (Registered Nurse) badge nodded in agreement and said, "Then you want Jophia Josephesus."

Angelique watched as one of the other nurses rolled her eyes while another's face twisted with a smirk. "Jophia Josephesus?" Angelique asked. "Is she any relation to the orthopedic surgeon, Joe Josephesus?"

The gray-haired nurse, the one who had smirked, tilted her head back and peered downward through her eyeglasses that had slipped down onto her nose. She said, "She claims to be his wife." She looked down at the desk and began shuffling papers. Under her breath, she muttered, "The wife of Dr. Jo-Bone."

The RN jerked his head around, shooting her a disapproving eyebrow hook.

The younger woman, the dark-haired one with a ponytail—the one who had rolled her eyes—put her hand to her mouth to muffle her snickering.

Glancing at her badge, Angelique saw that the young woman's name was Priscilia Pereira. The older woman was Virginia Veetlehurst. Both women were LVNs, not Registered Nurses.

"Dr. Josephesus is one of the top orthopedic surgeons in the Bay Area," said the RN, whose badge identified him as Chancellor Wilmington. "We are proud to have him on staff here at Alta Bates Medical." Turning to the two LVNs, who still wore their sneers— their more telling badges—he directed them to check on patients in two different rooms, sending them in opposite directions. Sighing, he said, "Dr. Donahorn, I apologize for their lack of professionalism. This is not my usual station. Shall I page Mrs. Josephesus for you? I believe she is on duty tonight."

"Yes, thank you, Mr. Wilmington. Please page her for me."

"Oh, please. Call me Chancellor, or better yet, Chance."

"Chance, it is, if you will call me Angelique."

"On duty, it's Dr. Donahorn, but Angelique, it's a pleasure to meet you."

Returning her gaze to Kate's chart, Angelique caught sight of her sister turning the corner, arm in arm with someone. Annateresa was leaning in close to the woman as if secrets were being whispered. The woman was very attractive, quite striking.

"Jophia, good to see you," Chance said. "I was just about to page you."

Kate was twisting and turning on the gurney. The ice packs on her face had begun to feel like thousand-pound polar bears. Surely she was floating on an iceberg in the Arctic Ocean and about to be eaten by the bears.

She hugged Etta Ebella, nestling the doll closer—a blanket for her heart. At least she had the hope of getting warm when she had the sonogram, the test Dr. Donahorn had ordered. If you left the gram part off, she knew that word sauna. One time on vacation, her mother had let her step into the spa's sauna, just for a few seconds so she could see what it felt like. In a nanosecond, she was sweltering and had run right out to her dad. They had stood at the glass doors watching her mother, who had gotten so overheated that she had almost fainted that day, too.

My mama, where is she now? Awhile ago Dr. Donahorn had said that it wouldn't be much longer until she could see both her mother and her daddy. That now seemed like years ago.

Kate remembered the surprised look on Dr. Donahorn's face when she had first told the doctor that her mother was expecting a baby, explaining that was why she had fainted. That and she had a weak stomach. Dr. Donahorn had then asked when Carly had told Kate that she was expecting a baby. Kate had replied that her mother didn't even know yet, that she and Etta Ebella were the only ones who knew.

Kate had watched Dr. Donahorn's face run through a gamut of expressions. She had then directed a question to the nurse, asking her if Dr. White, the obstetrician, was in the hospital or on call. The nurse had said no she was not in today, but that Dr. Avery from Dr. White's group was around. Dr. Donahorn had asked the nurse to page him. When Dr. Avery came by, Dr. Donahorn had stepped outside the curtain. Kate couldn't hear everything they were saying, but she did hear the words "pregnancy test and examination."

When Dr. Donahorn returned, a volunteer girl was with her, one wearing pink stripes and pink lip gloss. Her name was Sally. She was to stay with Kate while Dr. Donahorn went to check on the sonogram and seek news of Uncle TT.

Some companion Sally was, sitting in the corner with her head in a magazine. *Star* was the title on the cover, Kate noticed. She was all cheery when she first entered the room, peering down into Kate's face, appraising Kate's stitches. Her eyes, which were light brown like roasted almonds, looked dull and lifeless. Their only sparkle was on the eyelids, which were caked with frosty blue eyeshadow that arched in half moons. She had stroked Kate's hand and talked about how she loved to sit with kids. Then, when Dr. Donahorn stepped out, and the green curtain closed, the girl had scowled at Kate, had pulled the magazine from her pink-striped apron pocket and sat down to read. Not one other word had Sally uttered.

Kate wished that girl would leave; then, she could talk to Etta Ebella. There were so many questions to ask her. *Did fainting mean that her mother had lost the baby? That miscarry thing?* Recently, Kate had overheard her mother talking to Aunt Sammy Sue, saying she was so sorry about the loss of her baby, about the miscarry or a word that sounded like that. Kate comforted herself with the thought that her mother would carry her baby right if she had a choice. *But maybe when my mama fainted she was thrown off balance, losing her grip. Maybe the baby fell out. And how was Uncle TT doing?*

Kate's head ached, but not as badly as her heart, which was beating like a drum, pounding out its cadent truth: it was all Kate's fault that Uncle TT was injured, and it would also be her fault if her mother had lost the baby.

Big questions jabbed at her. *What if Uncle TT dies? Or what if he ends up in a wheelchair like Grammy Mer, not being able to walk or talk?*

She yearned to tell Etta Ebella that she had new lemons, gigantic ones, for the Great Angel Mother's apron basket, all because she hadn't listened to her stomach about not climbing higher and not sitting on that flimsy tree limb. Even the blackbird and the rabbit had tried to warn her. She hadn't listened to them either.

And now, she didn't know if this time the Jesus man would lift her up to drop in her new lemons. She had stilled her ears, trying to hear his laughter, but there had been nothing, only the sound of her heart beating, pounding out the truth. She decided that Jesus must be mad at her, too.

A hand moved the green curtain to the side. A familiar voice said, "My sweet Katie Girl, what has happened to you?"

Kate peeked out from underneath the ice pack and was surprised to see Jophia Josephesus, who had large round eyes that radiated sweetness like pools of maple syrup atop buttermilk pancakes. Signaling to Dr. Donahorn, who was entering behind Jophia, Kate explained, "She is my best friend's mother, Jillian's mother."

"Yes, I was informed of that a few minutes ago," said Angelique. "Perhaps what you don't know, Princess Kate, is that Mrs. Josephesus is the best sonogram specialist in this hospital."

"Thank you, Dr. Donahorn, and please call me Jophia." Her eyes still on Kate, Jophia smiled and said, "Princess Kate is it now? Yes, my Jillian and Princess Kate have been friends since they were babies. Here, sweetheart, let me take a look at your tummy."

Sally, the young girl wearing the pink stripes, had jumped to her feet the moment the first rung in the curtain had moved. Nonetheless, Dr. Donahorn dismissed her from the room with a disapproving tone.

A rattling noise took over the room as the curtains parted again and a gray-haired nurse rolled in a cart with a machine on it. Instantly, Kate didn't like the woman who was pushing the cart. Her skin was the color and texture of the toasted croutons her mother sometimes made from old bread. And the woman's blue-green eyes looked like mold, like the kind Kate had found once in Uncle TT's refrigerator, growing atop some cheese. Not only did her eyes look moldy, but they also looked cold and hard as ice cubes.

Kate glanced at the woman's heart. It had lots of bumps in it, like ski slope moguls or like warts on a toad frog. The color radiating from her heart resembled a storm cloud, a greenish-gray black. No, Kate did not like this woman, didn't trust her, and hoped that she was not going to touch her.

The woman rolled the machine next to Kate's bed and parked it at an angle, catty-cornered. She reached down and plugged the machine into the wall.

"Thank you, Mrs. Veetlehurst," Jophia said. In the very next breath, she began explaining the sonogram procedure to Kate.

The woman ambled to the front of the cubicle, by the curtain. She stood there a minute with her glasses down on her nose and her mouth held tightly, slightly pursed. Dr. Donahorn nodded to her, and she disappeared through the curtain.

"Okay, my sweetie, this machine is like a big camera that is going to show us pictures of what going's on inside your tummy." Holding up a plastic bottle with a nozzle on the top, Jophia said, "And this is an essential ingredient."

"It looks like lip gloss," said Kate.

Jophia said, "Yes, it does. Instead of your lips, though, we are going to rub this glossy gel all over your tummy and then we'll place these sensors at various points on the gel." Jophia held up the clear acrylic pads, saying that they didn't hurt, that the entire test was painless.

"When do I go in the hot room?" asked Kate. Jophia squirted the clear shiny gel onto Kate's tummy. "Hot room?"

"You know, the sauna room where people get hot and sweat." Dr. Donahorn's eyes sparkled. She laughed and said, "Oh, I get it. Well, Princess Kate, this sonogram is not like that kind of sauna. This here is an ultrasound machine that creates an image with sound waves."

Turning the knobs on the sonogram machine, Jophia said, "Now, sweetie, I need you to put Etta Ebella up higher on your pillow, so the gel doesn't get on her. She's looking quite spiffy. We don't want her to get messed up again, now do we?"

"No, we don't." Kate spoke with resolution as she shifted the doll higher upon her pillow.

"Lie still now," Jophia said. "This gel makes a smooth surface, like a newly paved street, for this little monitor to adhere to and glide over your tummy and make pictures for us." When Jophia turned the large white knob, static and lines came up on the screen.

"It looks like a TV with the cable unplugged," Kate said.

"It surely does," said Jophia, her forehead furrowed. She turned the large white knob, and once again the machine gave no response. She bent down eyeballing the plugs on the back of the machine. Again, she moved the monitor over Kate's abdomen but no image came up on the screen. "Dr. Donahorn," she said, "I apologize for the long start here. Something is wrong with this machine. I will call the lab to deliver another one."

"That lady did it," Kate said. "She broke it."

Jophia and Dr. Donahorn voice's chimed simultaneously, "What lady?"

"The lady with the gray hair. I saw something in her heart, I mean, in her pocket. She took it off the back of the machine," explained Kate.

Jophia scrutinized all the fittings and plugs on the back side of the sonogram machine. "Well now, look at this. There is a misfit plug on this wire. It looks normal at first glance, but the connector is too small, which doesn't allow proper electrical contact from the monitor to the screen. This connector has been replaced; it's not standard. I've never seen one like this."

"Kate, did you see the lady, or anyone else, remove a part or add one to the back of this machine?" Dr. Donahorn asked.

Kate winced. It was the very first time Dr. Donahorn had not called her *Princess Kate*. Tears stung her eyes. Her face hurt, and now she had done something else wrong. What a terrible day. It felt like beavers had built a dam in her throat. Somehow she managed to eke out one word. "N-o," she replied.

Jophia stood upright; exasperation wrinkled her pretty face. She began pushing the sonogram cart toward the green curtain. She said, "I'll leave this one in the hallway and call the lab for another."

"Please wait, Jophia. Did you leave the incorrect connector intact?" Dr. Donahorn asked.

Jophia nodded. "Yes, I did."

"Good. If you don't mind, rather than call the lab, please return this one and have the lab manager document its condition."

Jophia nodded, "Got it. And I will personally retrieve another machine, one that works."

"Excellent plan," Dr. Donahorn said, returning to Kate's bedside. She covered Kate's gelled tummy with the sheet and then placed Etta Ebella back in Kate's arms.

The two women exchanged a knowing look. Jophia nodded and pushed the altered machine through the curtain.

After Kate had heard Jophia's footsteps grow dim, Dr. Donahorn said, "I'm sorry, Princess Kate. It's unfair to ask you such questions with all that you have been through today. But it's important that I know if you saw the lady disable the machine."

Looking up, Kate watched Dr. Donahorn's long eye-lashes, reddish blonde tipped with black mascara, flutter as she leaned in close, examining Kate's stitches.

"No, Dr. Donahorn, I didn't see the lady do anything to the machine with these eyes," Kate said. Her index finger pointed to the two olive wide-set eyes in her head. "But, b–u–t I did see …" her words tapered off as quiet little sobs escaped from her mouth.

Dr. Donahorn began stroking Kate's hair. In a soft voice, almost a whisper, she said, "It seems that you are an extraordinary girl, Princess Kate, that you have an extra set of eyes. Can you tell me more about what you saw with your special eyes?"

CHAPTER THIRTEEN

In room 1230 on the sixth floor of Alta Bates Medical, Terrence Ted followed doctor's orders and lay perfectly still, though his mind was buzzing like a working beehive. His head throbbed. He couldn't decide which was worse, the nausea rolling in his stomach or the splitting headache. The doctors wouldn't give him pain medication, something about a possible concussion, a possible subdural hematoma. An hour ago, they had given him nausea medication but it was working only so-so. At least, he wasn't throwing up anymore. He could endure hard-driving pain far better than he could handle vomiting.

Whenever he closed his eyes, his mother's face floated in front of him. At first, he thought that meant he was dying. His physical umbilical cord had been severed at birth, but another one remained, to be severed upon death, his or hers, whichever came first.

Despite the pain and physical discomfort, the enforced stillness had fostered contemplation. He realized now that he saw his mother's face for many reasons, one of which was she was praying for him. She always said that you get to be close to the people you pray for, particularly when you can't be with them.

He sensed that his mother was feeling what was happening to him, internalizing it. He had to find a way to call her, have her hear his voice, assure her that he was coping and would be okay.

Something about the events of the day had made him realize how fragile her health was. She was hanging by a thread, her time short. The last thing she needed in her condition was the stress of worrying about him.

Excruciating pain bolted through his head as he turned it only slightly to the side. Sure enough, though, there was a phone on the bedside table. His hospital bed was as horizontal as one could get—no elevation, no pillows.

The doctors had said for him to remain flat and motionless; movement could trigger more hemorrhage. They were reviewing his MRI scans now, deciding if surgery was necessary. Brain surgery.

Poppy Pop was half-dozing, half-watching the 10:30 news when the phone rang. He glanced at Grammy Mer and grabbed the portable phone.

"Pop. It's. Ter-rence." He spoke slowly as if each word were a complete sentence. "Am. I. Calling. Too. Late?"

Poppy Pop's voice shook; his eyes brimmed with tears. "Oh, Son, it's so good to hear from you. But you sound mighty weak. How are you, really?"

"I'm. Hanging."

"Are you in pain?" Pop asked.

"A little. Can Mother hear, too? Speaker. Phone?"

"No, Son. I'm sorry I haven't gotten around to getting the new phones we discussed. I'll put this one to your mother's ear, though, and I'll stay nearby. Call out for me loudly when you're ready. Okay?"

"K."

Poppy Pop moved beside the wheelchair and positioned the phone gently against Grammy Mer's ear. He bent down and spoke into the mouthpiece, "She's here, Son."

"Mother. I will. Be. Okay. He paused, taking a deep breath. "I feel. Your prayers. You. Rest. Mother, I. Love. You."

Grammy Mer could only breathe into the phone.

"Pop. Pop. P-o-ps."

"Son, I'm sorry. Your voice sounds weak, and I'm near deaf anyway. I don't know what you said to your mother, but she looks a bit more relaxed."

"Good," Terrence replied with all the strength he could muster.

"Kal called us about an hour ago and told us that he was on his way home with Kate and Carly, that both were going to be fine." Poppy Pop paused for a deep breath then continued. "He didn't have the latest on you, said they wouldn't let him in to see you yet. They couldn't wait around; he had to get his girls home to bed, he said."

"Yes."

No longer shaking, Poppy Pop's voice came on strong, now peppered with a touch of humor as he said, "Did your doctor friend tell you about Kate, her stitches and her distended abdomen from impacted bowels?"

"Yes."

"She had some silly notion that snakes had invaded their toilets, and she wouldn't use the bathroom."

"I heard. Kate. Nightmares. Etta Ebella away. Being repaired."

"You mean that angel doll?"

"Pop. I've got. To go. Nurse here."

"Wait, Son. I didn't get the news on your condition. Ask your doctor friend or a nurse to call us."

Abruptly, the phone line went dead.

"Son, are you there?" Poppy Pop spoke louder and louder, "Son!" After examining the phone, he placed the portable back in its charging cradle, saying to Grammy Mer, "The nurse came in. I think she made him hang up."

Poppy Pop kissed Grammy Mer on her cheek. He walked to the back of her chair and began pushing it toward their bedroom. "Alrighty, my Miss America, it's long past our bedtime. We can roost for the night now, rest knowing our chickies will all be okay. Kate will heal, and Terrence will be okay after some bed rest. He sounded pretty good considering. He just needs time to heal. That tree limb must have come down mighty hard on him."

What Poppy Pop couldn't see was that at Alta Bates Medical, the nurse had stomped into Terrence's room and jerked the phone from his hand. At that very moment, she was unplugging the phone from the wall and removing it from the room. Terrence was to stay horizontal, totally flat with no movement, no talking, and no visitors.

And what Terrence couldn't see, was that his mother, breathing ever so shallowly, still wore a mantle of worry.

CHAPTER FOURTEEN

Carly poured coffee into her favorite cup, surfaced with an embossed photo of a smiling Kate and Kal. Her fingertip traced lightly over the photo face of Kate, lingering on her left cheek and above her right eyebrow. *Stitches in that precious face,* she thought. *Oh, Lord, please help her heal without scarring.* While stirring two dollops of milk in her coffee, she checked the monitor screen on the kitchen cabinet. The form lying under the purple blanket was not moving. Kate was still sleeping.

Carly inhaled the aroma and took a sip of coffee. *Just a half cup this morning. Limited caffeine when pregnant.* Her hand went to her abdomen. Life was growing inside there, a brand new life. Joy leaped in her heart, a joy she had yearned to feel, a joy she had feared she would never experience again. After four years of trying, she had almost given up.

Trying, the very word, an overbearing drumbeat that wouldn't cease its rhythm, had hammered in her head, in her heart, in her veins, every day over the past two years. And then there was her upcoming birthday—her fortieth—a looming indictment of failure.

Her hand briefly lit upon her brow, fingertips massaging her temple, and then flew back to rest on her abdomen like a homing bird finding comfort in its nest. The angst-riddled drumbeat was gone, now replaced with a new tempo. A baby heartbeat. This morning, her approaching birthday, benchmark and all, felt far less daunting, even bright.

Carly surveyed the mess in her kitchen. The veal shanks in the roaster would have to be tossed out as would everything she had prepared for last night's dinner. With the rush to the hospital, there had been no time to refrigerate any of it. She despised such waste; even still, her smile was radiant, her face a chandelier.

Heavy footstep noises—thud, clomp, thud—on the stairway somewhat dimmed her beam. Oh, how she loved Kal. A near perfect man, if only he could have a lighter step when descending the stairway. He planted his feet on the risers, right foot then left foot, putting his full weight on each impact.

"Good morning, my love. How's my bride this morning?" Kal said, entering the sunny yellow kitchen.

"A little tired. Any word on Terrence?"

"I'm about to call Angelique. She stayed in the doctor's quarter's last night. She said to call her this morning. Want the first soft kiss?" He turned his freshly-shaven cheek to Carly's face and rubbed it, skin to skin. A vied for morning prize, Kate and her mother often competed for that first kiss after Kal shaved.

"It's my lucky day," said Carly, nuzzling Kal's cheek. "Kate will be jealous."

"Yes, she will. Poor peanut. Guess she's all tuckered out from yesterday."

"Looks that way," Carly said, eyeing the monitor screen.

Kal chose an oversized mug from the cabinet and filled it with hot coffee. "I see the milk carton here. Already upping your calcium intake?"

"Yes, I am. Oh, Kal. Can you believe it? We're going to have a baby."

His hand went to her tummy; he pressed it there for a moment. His head tilted back on his neck; he let out a gleeful whoop. Lifting her up into his arms, he cradled her like she was the baby and then swung her around in a circle of bliss.

The monitor screen sizzled with static and then the sound of Kate thrashing in her bed, and then sobs, screams, and chilling words: "Mama, Daddy. Help. Grammy Mer is crying. Help. Something bad is happening to Uncle TT."

Carly wriggled down from Kal's arms. They both started toward the stairs. "We're coming, pumpkin," Carly called out from the bottom of the stairs. They ascended rapidly and rushed into Kate's room.

Kate was sitting up in bed, her mouth wide open, bawling. Tears gushed from her eyes, dripping down her face. She clutched Etta Ebella against her chest.

"Oh, pumpkin," Carly sat on the bed, pulling Kate into her arms.

"You're okay, peanut. It's just a bad dream," Kal said, stroking Kate's hair.

"Uh huh. It wasn't a dream."

"Kal, please get me a dry washcloth from the bathroom. I need to blot around these bandages. They're damp."

"Can we change those?"

"I'm not sure. Last night is a blur. I know she wasn't supposed to shower today. Please ask Angelique when you call her."

Kal stepped into the adjacent bathroom. When he returned with the washcloth, his cell phone rang. "I'll take this in the hallway. He closed the door behind him and answered the phone. "Angelique. No, you're not calling too early. I was just about to call you." Kal went down the stairs. Thud, clomp, thud, while he talked.

In Kate's room, Carly used one hand to blot dry the bandages that covered Kate's stitches, paying close attention to the edges, all while rocking Kate in her arms. "What happened, pumpkin? What did you dream?"

"I wasn't dreaming, Mama. I wasn't."

"What happened then?"

"Etta Ebella woke me up. We saw Grammy Mer crying and Uncle TT with big bandages on his head."

"Come, pumpkin. Let's go downstairs and get you some juice."

With Kate clinging to her mother's hand, they descended the stairs.

"Where's Daddy?" Kate asked.

Kal stepped from the dining room, his phone to his ear. "Okay, I'll be there as quickly as I can." Kal's previous joy erased, his expression was grim.

"What's wrong?" Carly asked.

"It's Terrence. They're taking him into surgery."

In the surgical waiting area of Alta Bates, Kal signed the register at the reception counter. An elderly volunteer manned the desk that had five black telephones—all direct lines to operating and recovery rooms—and one white phone that connected to the information desk on the first floor.

"Mr. Kindrick, please have a seat; we'll let you know as soon as we hear from your brother's doctor."

"This all happened so fast. Who is the surgeon?"

"Let's see." The attendant looked at the printout on the desk. His finger, a cursor for his aged eyes, moved all the way down the page on the far left side—the patient name side, and then it traced evenly across the page. "That would be Dr. Lacholher."

"What kind of doc is he?"

"She is a neurosurgeon."

"About how long before I hear something?"

The attendant lowered his eyes again to the day's surgical schedule. This time, his finger quickly pointed at the Kindrick name found at the bottom of the page where the emergency add-on surgeries were listed. He moved his finger across to the center of the page and stopped. "No expected time frame listed here. Sorry."

"Hmm." Kal's eyebrows furrowed.

"That's common for emergency surgeries. Don't get overly concerned about it."

Kal nodded. "Okay. I'll try not to."

"There's a hospitality center in the back. Fresh coffee. Help yourself."

Kal nodded. "Thank you, I will." Kal got some coffee and then found a chair. He flipped through a fly-fishing magazine, too distracted and too worried about his brother to tackle any of the articles. Laying the magazine aside, he began looking around the room. People were scattered about, some sat alone, others sat in clusters. His eyes lingered on the family groups.

The door opened and a flock of folks, around fifteen people, entered. After signing in, they found an empty corner where they could all sit together. They rearranged the chairs into a tight, exclusive circle. One of the men appeared distraught, his eyes rimmed in red, his chin quivering.

After they were all settled, one of the women, the one who wore a canary-yellow cape, stood and went to his side. She dropped to her knees. She bowed her head. Every head in their group instantly lowered. The woman began to pray—loudly. Her voice boomed at such a volume that people from the hallway stopped and peered inside the room to see what was happening.

Kal squirmed in his chair. A believer in the power of prayer, he was. A believer in ear-splitting public prayer, he wasn't. *God can hear even the quietest and most silent prayer,* he thought. *Who, besides God and the people in her group, did this woman want to hear the words of her plea?* Kal wondered as he noted her eloquence. Her voice seemed to have built-in amplifiers. Even still, she was projecting it like she was the lead singer at a standing-room-only concert.

Considering her bellowing, Kal was surprised to realize that his head had bowed. Reverent and respectful, yes, that would be him. Rather abruptly, the woman's pitch turned shrill and her tone insolent. Kal lifted his head, looking to see how other people were reacting.

Some stared at the woman with shocked expressions; some covered their mouths to hide their jester-esque smiles or to muffle their laughter. Some sat with their eyes closed. One young man, who had been sitting alone in the opposite corner, had turned his back on the group and curled up in his chair, his legs pulled up into his body. He was in a near fetal position, a Houdini move considering his size and the confines of the armchair.

The attendant behind the desk paced, his eyes cast upward. Kal imagined that he was praying too, but that his prayer had to do with how to quiet the woman. She was now going into graphic, blood-shed detail of a car accident as if she were the first to tell God of what had happened and only through her prayer would God know all the particulars. The silent tenseness that had hung in the air of the surgical waiting area when Kal first arrived was now an audible aura of misery.

Scripture floated through Kal's mind. *A Pharisee, that's what she was.* He enjoyed that thought until an inner discomfort began gnawing at him. More scripture: *As ye judge, so shall ye be judged.* The words glided across his mind's eye as clearly as a banner on a television screen.

Sighing, Kal seized on the notion that the distressed man was blessed to have someone to pray so passionately for his wife and young daughter. *Poor guy.* According to the prayer, the man's wife and five-year-old daughter had been in a car accident, their car hit head-on by a dump truck. Hit and run. The dump truck driver, who had run the red light, had sped away from the collision. Both the woman and the little girl had suffered severe injuries. The woman was in surgery. It was yet to be known if she or her young daughter would survive.

Kal checked his watch. Terrence had been in surgery for close to an hour now. Once again, he silently prayed for his brother, his doctors, and the entire surgical team. His fervent plea asked the Almighty to guide their minds, their hands, and their instruments as they attempted to relieve the pressure on Terrence's brain, pressure from the hematoma. Kal's scalp prickled as he empathized with his brother. Scratching his head, he picked up the magazine again and tried to concentrate on one of the feature articles. Images of fishing rods and river streams battled visions of skulls and scalpels. And then there was the intrusive prayer for the man who could lose his wife and daughter. After about two minutes, Kal cast the magazine aside. When he stood to replenish his empty coffee cup, relief filled him. His sister, Sammy Sue, and her husband Sandy were standing in the doorway.

Kal called out, "Sis. Sandy. Over here."

They all exchanged hugs, wrapping their arms a little tighter, squeezing more firmly than normal—the warm, clasping kind of embraces that families give when one of theirs is in a precarious pose with life, dancing with death.

"Any word on Terrence yet? And what is going on over there?" Sammie Sue whispered, nodding her head in the direction of the cape-clad woman.

As they settled into chairs, Kal said, "No word on Terrence yet. As for the group over there, they came in about ten minutes ago, and the woman has been praying ever since."

"Can you call that prayer?" asked Sandy.

"It started out that way; it's now a didactic diatribe," said Kal. "They have a sad situation, though. The man's wife and daughter were in a car accident, hit by a speeding dump truck. They're both in critical condition."

"How tragic." Sammy Sue, not prone to obvious emotion, almost choked. "I am sincerely sorry for them, but is there another waiting area? That woman is screaming. It's insane in here," said Sammy Sue.

"No, this is it: where the doctors will expect us to be. There's coffee in the back if you want some. I was heading that way when you came in."

"I'd like coffee," said Sandy. "Honey, you want some?"

"Yes, please," said Sammy Sue.

"Beige?" asked Kal.

"Yes, lots of cream."

"Oh, yeah, a whole lot," said Sandy.

"Alrighty," Kal replied.

Sammy Sue sat staring at the praying woman, who ranted on and on. Then she eyed the man at the desk, who was talking on the phone. *Why doesn't he do something?* She shot him a professorial scowl, her eyebrows raised and yet also knitted together. He nodded to her, acknowledging her accusatory and expectant grimace.

"Here you go, Sis. As beige as coffee can get," said Kal. He and Sandy took seats on either side of Sammy Sue.

The man at the desk placed the phone back in its cradle. He stepped from behind the counter, pulling up his pants as he walked as if he were pulling up courage with each step. When he reached the woman, he tilted his head back, which put his nose in the air. He placed a hand upon her shoulder. She continued with her ranting. He squeezed her shoulder. She continued. He coughed and cleared his throat loudly. She continued. Some members of the group fluttered their eyes, but all kept their heads bowed. Some moved their lips mouthing her words or saying amen repeatedly every few sentences.

"Excuse me," the reception attendant said, his voice raised. "Excuse me."

At last, the woman stopped. She lifted her head and looked utterly surprised. Then her eyes narrowed with suspicion. "Yes? Is one of the doctors here to speak with us?"

"No, ma'am, but I must ask you to quiet down or move elsewhere. We have other families here, waiting for news of their loved ones, too."

"That's preposterous. You cannot tell us we can't pray here," she railed.

"Ma'am, I did not say you cannot pray here. I am simply asking you to lower your voice out of respect for everyone else here in this space. Or to go somewhere else."

"We are not leaving. And I am not done. How dare you interrupt my prayer?" She shook her head feverishly in disbelief of his audacity.

"Ma'am, we are receiving disturbance complaints from multiple hallways, including patient rooms."

A uniformed security guard walked over to the group. "I'll take it from here, Jim. One of the doctors in OR is calling the desk. The Kindrick family."

CHAPTER FIFTEEN

*A*t 537 Spruce Street, Kate, who sat at her miniature desk in the kitchen, was engrossed in drawing and coloring while her mother cleaned last night's dishes. Etta Ebella sat on the top right corner of the desk, her blue-topaz eyes watchful as Kate's picture evolved.

The orange marker seemed to wink at Kate. She picked it up and uncapped it. Her nose wrinkled. Hard as she tried, she didn't think the color orange was pretty. But today, it was the perfect color to use for the little girl's dress. Before coloring the dress, though, she would give the girl some hair. Taking the marker, she made orange strands sprout out from the girl's head, orange hair that appeared wildly out of control. Then she colored in the dress, all of it, entirely orange. Capping the orange marker, she placed it aside to the far edge of the desk.

Kate then chose the brown marker and used it to put dots all over the girl's face as well as her arms and legs. *Freckles.* She checked the skin on her arms, examining it closely. She didn't have any freckles, at least, not yet. She thought about Dr. Donahorn, who had a few across her nose. They were faint, like teeny cinnamon dots, quite pretty, Kate thought. This girl, though, the one in the picture, had big, unsightly freckles all over her. Next, Kate selected the red marker; she colored in ragged gashes on the girls left cheek and over her right eye.

Kate stared at the picture, checking the details of what she had drawn. A large tree dominated the scene that included an airplane flying low in a sunset sky. Sitting at the base of the tree trunk was a small brown rabbit, its neck atilt, looking up at a winged figure that sat on the uppermost tree limb. A blackbird hovered near that limb.

On the far right side, a man and a woman stood in the doorway of a house. The woman, who wore clothing except on her tummy, had a blue baby in the middle of her naked abdomen. Another woman lay on the walkway nearby. A pink baby floated in the air to the side. A dog, which looked somewhat like Keebie and had a bulging belly, sniffed at the prone woman.

Near the tree, a man lay sprawled on the driveway, a huge tree limb covering his head. The freckled girl in the orange dress was attempting to lift and drag the tree limb from his body.

On the left side of the picture, Kate had drawn a car at the end of a driveway. Next to the car was a wheelchair with a woman sitting in it. Kate picked up the yellow marker and drew zigzagged lines, like lightening bolts, from the airplane to the woman in the chair.

Looking over Kate's shoulder, Carly said, "Why Kate, you are becoming quite the artist. Tell me about your picture."

"Can we go to the hospital, Mama? I want to see Uncle TT and Grammy Mer."

"We cannot see Uncle TT, pumpkin. He's still in surgery, and there are strict hospital rules about children visiting surgery patients. Plus, I don't believe that Pops and Grammy Mer are going to the hospital today. Your dad's keeping them informed by phone."

Kate looked to Etta Ebella, focusing on her eyes, and said, "Uh huh, they are going. They're already there."

"It's such a challenge for them to get out of the house these days. I doubt it." Pointing to Kate's picture, to the couple standing in the doorway, Carly said, "Well, look at this. Is that me you drew with no clothes on my tummy?"

"Yes, I wanted to show the baby in there."

"It looks cute. So who is the woman lying down near the dog?"

"That's Aunt Sammy Sue."

"What's this?" asked Carly pointing to the pink blob floating near the woman.

"That's her baby. She didn't it carry right. It fell out."

"What do you mean, didn't carry it right?"

"I heard you say she had a miscarry."

"Oh, pumpkin. The word is miscarriage, and it certainly doesn't mean that Aunt Sammy Sue did anything wrong, not at all."

"Oh."

"Why did you color it pink and the baby in my tummy, blue?"

"Cause it was a girl. Ours is a boy."

"Kate, we do not know what Aunt Sammy Sue's baby was; we will never know now. And it's too early to know what our baby is. It could be a baby sister for you."

"It's a baby brother."

Across the room, the phone began to ring. As she walked toward the phone, Kate's mother shook her head in consternation. What was she to do with her daughter's strong will and her *I-Know* attitude?

Kate picked up the blue crayon. Bearing down hard, she colored the baby in the woman's tummy even bluer. Next, she selected the pink crayon and pressed firmly, making the floating baby an obvious pink. She looked to Etta Ebella.

Two topaz eyes blinked twice.

For the second time, Poppy Pop circled the visitor's parking lot at Alta Bates Hospital, hoping to find a spot near the front rather than in the parking garage. Bingo, there was a car departing from a handicapped space at the end.

"We did it, my Miss America. You must have been using your visualizing tricks."

Grammy Mer inwardly smiled. Sure enough, she had been visualizing, and this spot was by a tree and near the hospital entrance, just like she had seen in her mind's eye. She sighed with relief. Earlier she had worried that her visualizing had been diluted by her incessant prayers for Terrence, for God to watch over his surgery, to bless his doctors with perfect knowledge and skill for his condition.

Her mind had also been preoccupied with concern for Gordon. Last night, when he had lifted her from the bath, he had strained his back. This morning when he had lifted her into the car, he was in obvious pain, though, he had tried to hide it.

If only we had one of those electronic chair devices in our car, she railed at herself. Her belief that the Almighty was going to heal her had prevented her from taking such action when she could still speak, that and hiring nurses. *How foolish I've been,* she thought. *And now, my life is such a burden, particularly for Gordon.*

She sighed from the weight of her thoughts. *Dear Lord, my sweet Lord, please protect Gordon. Spare him from further bodily injury because of me. And please send us some help this morning, someone strong to help lift me out of this car. Dearest Lord, I pray that You watch over our Terrence, that he will be okay, will come through surgery whole, and have no complications and no lasting side effects. After that, whenever you decide the time is right, I am ready to leave this Earth. Dearest Lord Almighty, hear my prayer: take me home.*

Having no physical capacity to help Gordon, she began harnessing her mental power to send him a telepathic message: *phone Kal, who is nearby—just inside the hospital. Ask him to come out and help us.* Getting her into the car was hard enough, but the most taxing task for an ailing back was lifting her from the car and lowering her weight into the wheelchair. She added an extra oomph to the mental bubble, and then released it, directing it to Gordon.

Standing at the rear of their SUV, Gordon fidgeted with the wheelchair, delaying unloading it as long as he could. Almost all movement made his back ache. The idea of calling Kal surfaced in his mind. *Hmmm. Kal was not far away, inside in one of the waiting rooms,* he thought. *Kal could come out to the parking lot and lift her from the car and into the wheelchair.* He fingered the cell phone in his pocket. Scratching his head, Gordon decided against it. He could do this.

He pushed the chair aside Grammy Mer's door and set its brake. It had seemed like a good idea to have the chair closer than normal. But when he reached for the door handle, he had to turn his torso. A twisting movement. Immediately, he froze. He arched with pain, only to discover that was another wrong move. Agony. He panted, gripping the back of the wheelchair. Ever so slightly, he turned toward the car door again. Excruciating pains shot across his back and down his leg. His head bent, his upper body fell across the wheelchair.

"Pops, is that you?" A man's voice called from across the parking lot. "Are you okay?"

"Sandy. Thank God," Gordon said, barely audible.

"Here, let me give you a hand," Sandy said as he jogged up to the SUV. Bracing Gordon's back as he lifted him up, he said, "Take some deep breaths and then let's get you into this chair."

Gordon shook his head, a resounding no.

"Just for a minute, Pops. Until you can stand."

"Alright," Gordon said, breathing heavy, his tone disgruntled.

Sandy, a veterinarian who had a gift for assessing bodies in pain, animal or human, guided him into the chair. Sandy unlocked the brake and wheeled the chair around to face the car's passenger side.

Gordon pointed to the car door.

Sandy opened the door of the SUV. "Hey, Grammy Mer," he said, leaning in to kiss her on the cheek. "How are you?" Expecting no reply, he unlatched her seat belt and straightened the curved bean-bag pillow bracing her neck. "There now, is that more comfortable?" Knowing she couldn't turn her head or her eyes, he said, "I've got Pops here in your chair. His back is bothering him. Some spasms."

For a moment, Grammy Mer looked bewildered to hear that Gordon was in the wheelchair.

"He just needs to sit for a few minutes," Sandy explained to her.

When he had kissed her cheek, Sandy had noted a metallic smell coming from her skin. He scanned Grammy Mer's face and looked deeper into her eyes. What he saw startled him.

Memories flashed in Sandy's mind, ones of a dying Golden Retriever named Rusty. The dog's skin had given off a similar smell. The same complex look had been present in the dog's eyes. They had burned with desire to die, yet had shined with love and an unwavering faith of having completed his life, his service on Earth, all mixed with a new eagerness to serve in the heavenly realms. The dog had died in his arms. Sandy had never been so touched by an animal's death, had never witnessed a death faced so consciously, not by an animal or a human.

"Sandy, are you coming or going? How'd you find us?" Gordon asked.

"I'm going, got an emergency call from the clinic. Our new equipment is malfunctioning." Sandy swatted at a bee, then at another one that seemed to swarm around them.

"Well, that's too bad."

"No, it's good," Sandy said, swatting the bees away from Grammy Mer. "Otherwise, I would not have been walking through this parking lot right now. I'd still be inside with Sammy Sue and Kal."

"Is there any news on Terrence?" Gordon asked, wincing from his throbbing back.

"Yes, right before I left, the surgical nurse called the waiting area to give us an update. She said they were at the half-way point, would be about another three hours."

"Is that encouraging or worrisome?" asked Gordon.

"The nurse didn't mention any problems, said his vitals were all strong."

"Then we'll assume it was encouraging," Gordon said. His hand reached around to his back, where his knotted fingers massaged at it. "Where are Kal and Sammy Sue? Which surgical waiting area?"

"When I left, they were heading down to the cafeteria. Kal was starving, and they wanted to grab an early lunch, so they would be available as soon as Terrence was out of recovery. They didn't know you two were coming."

"Yeah, Kal thought he had talked us out of it. But we wanted to be here, as close to Terrence as we could get. Kara demanded it, in her way," Gordon said, a sheepish smile creeping onto his face.

"Well, as soon as you're feeling better, I'll get you two inside to join them. In a minute when you regain your breath, I'll take you through a series of stretches that will speed the process."

"Thank you, Sandy. We sure do appreciate your help."

Looking back to Grammy Mer, Sandy expected to see relief. And there was, plus she seemed fascinated by the two bees that circled her face. Leaning inside the SUV, he swatted at the bees again. "Are you okay, Grammy Mer?" he asked.

Sandy felt as if her piercing blue-green eyes had mouths with the capacity to speak many languages. Her message was clear: *I know that you saw. Please keep it to yourself. I know not when, not what day nor what hour.*

From what he had observed, Sandy knew full well that her time was short, if not immediate.

CHAPTER SIXTEEN

*J*n the cafeteria of Alta Bates, Sammy Sue and Kal arranged their lunch trays atop a small table. Sammy Sue's tray looked sparse in comparison to Kal's who had his filled with multiple plates, a spaghetti-and-meatball entrée, a large green salad, garlic rolls, and a three-layer slice of carrot cake.

"Are you and Carly still going to Hawaii later this week?" asked Sammy Sue.

Swallowing a knot of spaghetti, Kal said, "Guess that depends on how Terrence is doing. I may cancel."

Sammy Sue's back stiffened, she squared her shoulders. "Kal Kindrick, you have to go for your award speech, at the least. You have been named the number one sales person for the entire company. If you don't go, your bosses will discount you, especially for that potential promotion to VP."

Kal cocked his head to the side. "Maybe."

"Terrence would want you to go for your speech, even if he is not doing well. Actually, Terrence would want you to attend the entire conference, to maximize this opportunity."

"Thanks, Sis. I've been pumped about going, until now. You're right about Terrence. He's such a cheerleader for me, for all of us." Kal's eyes watered.

Sammy Sue nodded, remembering how Terrence had encouraged her to get her Ph.D., how he had always urged her to climb higher on the academia ladder, and how he had been there last month when she had the miscarriage. He had visited several times, had brought food, flowers, and spa packages.

Swallowing hard, she felt as if the small bite of salad were chafing her throat like it was an entire lettuce plant, a scruffy one with roots attached. She said, "Yes, Terrence is a cheerleader for me, too. And Kal, assuming his recovery is on track, Terrence would want you and Carly to stay over and take the vacation you've been planning."

"Yep, he would. What about you, Sis? Aren't you supposed to go to a conference in Boston?"

"Yes, and I'm already listed as the keynote speaker in the program, it would be problematic to cancel. And I have multiple meetings scheduled with specialty geneticists. It's a challenge to get on their calendars for phone calls let alone face-to-face meetings. However, I am seriously concerned about Terrence."

"Yeah, me too. And yet, I have a feeling that he's going to be okay."

"Ever the optimist, aren't you? Where is Kate staying if you both go to Hawaii?"

"With Abigail."

Sammy Sue's eyes narrowed. She turned over a tomato wedge, pushed it aside and laid her fork down.

"I know. I know, " Kal said. "Vaynem. He's supposed to be out of town on all the weekday nights, only home for one weekend. We've agonized over it but just couldn't come up with any other options. Mom and Pops always kept Kate when we traveled, so we never developed other overnight sitters. And we certainly don't want a stranger."

"What about Kate's friend, Jillian? Could she stay with her family? Jophia and Joe seem like such nice people."

"Oh, they are, but they work long hours. Jophia's mother lives with them and watches Jillian while they're working. She's getting on in age and undergoing some health issues. Jillian and Kate are too much for her; when together, they get all wired up and rambunctious.

Having eaten little, Sammy Sue pushed the salad around on her plate.

"Sis, are you okay?"

She cleared her throat. "I heard your other good news. About the baby. Congratulations."

Kal reached across the table and covered his sister's hand with his. "I'm sorry that our news comes so soon after your loss. This must be hard for you."

Sammy Sue nodded. "It's a difficult time. And being here in the hospital brings back some of the memories of my being here last month."

"Did the doctor ever say what happened?"

"No real medical explanation except for my hormones levels suddenly dropping. He did say that the tissue showed that it was a girl." Sammy Sue brought her napkin to her mouth as if wiping crumbs or salad dressing away, a disguise for the wail heard only by her lips. Their natural shape distorted, her lips quavered.

Kal bowed his head. "Oh, Sis, I am deeply sorry." Taking his fork, he began turning it in his pasta, mindlessly. A huge glob of pasta accumulated around the tines. "Kate would have been so excited to have a new cousin, especially a girl one."

"That's a mighty big bite of spaghetti, Brother." Sammy Sue gestured toward his plate, her napkin back in her lap. "Both Kate and Ruthie would have been excited about a new baby girl in the family."

Kal nodded. "Sorry. I'm starving, meager breakfast and no real dinner last night. How is our little sis? I haven't talked to Ruthie Renee in several weeks."

"She's well. She's been calling almost every day to check on me. Did you know that she has a leading role in *Midsummer Night's Dream*? It's premiering this week."

"Pop told me about that. He also said that a New York Broadway company was looking at producing one of the stage plays she's written."

"Yes, she's excited but holding her breath until the deal is cinched, in writing and signed."

"I'm touched that you and Ruthie are so close, even with her in London. Glad she's supportive of you, especially during this time."

"Kal, I am truly happy for you and Carly. I know you've been trying to have another baby for several years now. Sandy and I were just beginning. We'll start trying again in a few months." Hearing a rustle behind her, Sammy Sue turned in her chair. Her eyes widened, shocked to see her husband approaching.

"Yes, we are going to have a house full of beautiful babies," Sandy said as he rolled Grammy Mer next to Sammy Sue.

Poppy Pop hobbled up behind Sandy.

Kal dropped his fork and stood up, his mouth full. "Mom. Dad. What a surprise."

As close proximity to the patient as she was physically allowed, Angelique occupied a balcony seat in one of the operating rooms in the surgical area of Alta Bates. She peered through the Plexiglas watching the procedure down below. Unlike the usual times when she observed surgeries and concentrated on surgeons' techniques, she focused on this patient's condition, his vital signs and how the surgical team was responding to his data. Today, her attention was entirely on the patient, Terrence Kindrick.

Her cell phone vibrated with a new text message at the same time that her pager pulsed silently. She surveyed the text message and the pager. She grimaced.

Gathering her things, she stepped close to the glass. She stood, transfixed, for a moment. Then, she departed the observation chamber and headed toward the elevators, in route to the Emergency-Care helicopter on the roof of Alta Bates.

Kate retrieved her cookies from the vending machine tray. "Daddy, why can't I sit in Grammy Mer's lap? Please, can I?"

Kal poured coffee into Styrofoam cups, three of them in a cardboard carry-tray. "Kate. I've told you Grammy Mer is too weak to hold you in her lap. Her muscles don't work right anymore."

Kate stood clutching Etta Ebella in one hand, her cookies in the other, her eyes fixated on her dad.

Kal picked up the tray and took steps toward the doorway. "Come on, let's join the others."

He suddenly stopped, taking in the heartbreaking sight. His daughter's eyes were pleading in a stricken way, begging with earnestness. Her furrowed brow and the intensity radiating from her eyes made the bandages and bruises on her face seem to grow larger. With her lower lip puckered, she was a miserable sight.

"Well, maybe I could help hold you, support your weight while you sit in Grammy Mer's lap for just a few minutes," Kal said. "She would probably love that, too. We'll ask Pops. Okay?"

Kate hugged Etta Ebella up closer to her. She skipped and danced her way into the main waiting room. Kal followed.

Carly exited the ladies restroom located near the surgical waiting area. Preoccupied with news of being pregnant and the crisis with Terrence, she stepped absentmindedly into the hallway and angled across the traffic flow to the other side. Within three steps, she was met by another moving body, one walking briskly, the woman's pace almost a jog.

The two female bodies collided. Carly was knocked sidewise, against the wall. She heard a familiar voice.

"Ma'am, are you okay? I am so very sorry."

"Dr. Donahorn! Angelique. I am the one who owes the apology. I was paying little attention to where I was going."

"Carly. Is your shoulder okay?" Angelique began looking at Carly with doctor eyes, examining her visually. "Let's see, are you alright?"

"I'm fine. Really. No worries. Do you have any news on Terrence?"

"I can't speak for his doctor, but he seems to be tolerating the surgery well. They were ready to close when I left a minute ago."

"The family is in the waiting area. Everyone would love to see you. Terrence's sister, and his parents, Kal, and Kate. Do you have a minute?"

"I would love to, but I've been summoned to assist in an emergency surgery—an accident victim, a five-year-old girl. She is being transported to the pediatric critical care unit at Children's USFH in the city. Please forgive my haste. I must get to the helicopter now."

"Of course, go. I'm sorry I detained you." Carly watched as Angelique sprinted to an elevator door marked "Hospital Personnel Only" and swiped her badge. The doors automatically slid open. Angelique entered quickly. The doors closed rapidly, far more quickly than regular elevator doors.

Carly stood there for a moment and watched the elevator ascend at a rapid rate without stopping. Her eyes brimmed with tears as she thought of a child, a little girl like Kate, being in critical condition.

We were so lucky last night. Kate's tree accident could have easily turned tragic, she thought. A shudder fell over her. *What am I thinking? I am grateful that Kate's injuries were minimal but Terrence, who we all love and adore, is undergoing brain surgery right now because of it. His brain, for God's sake. Wake up. That is tragic enough. And with the brain, so many things could go wrong. I'm ashamed of myself, floating on this happy-to-be-pregnant cloud all day. "Oh, Lord, all of Heaven, please help us. If we lose Terrence, or even if he is disabled, the guilt and grief would completely unravel Kate. She would never get over it. None of us would."*

Leaning her head against Grammy Mer's chest, Kate felt a surge of joy, felt a warm hug embrace her, felt it as surely as if Grammy Mer had put her arms around her and squeezed. Then she felt hands on her face, stroking her. Kate's face began to tingle from the warmth, especially her stitches. She looked down at Grammy Mer's hands. They were still on the arms of the wheelchair, exactly where Poppy Pop had placed them so Kate could sit in her lap. Even still, Kate could feel Grammy Mer's spirit hands on her face, lovingly stroking her, healing her wounds.

When her dad had asked Poppy Pop's permission for Kate to sit on her grandmother's lap, Kate had immediately looked at Grammy Mer's face, trying to read her feelings. To Kate's delight, Grammy Mer's heart had suddenly buzzed with a swirl of purple. A rainbow had popped up amidst the purple. Each layer of the rainbow glowed as if all were made of faceted gemstones with the sun shining behind them. It had seemed to Kate that the rainbow arc was singing the words *"yes, yes, please."*

To the side of the rainbow, Kate also noticed a circle aglow with white light. Inside the circle, there was an image of a woman down on her knees, a woman who looked exactly like Grammy Mer, the way she used to look before she got sick. The woman was praying. An image of Uncle TT was floating in the circle.

Above the woman kneeling in prayer, Kate saw a hill dotted heavily with green trees. Atop the hill, the Jesus man stood; he was beckoning to Grammy Mer. She didn't say anything aloud, though. Kate was too afraid she wouldn't get to sit in Grammy Mer's lap if she did. Besides, everyone might think she was silly.

Basking in the glow of Grammy Mer's love, she hugged Etta Ebella tightly against her, pondering the meaning of the images in Grammy

Mer's heart. Etta Ebella had once told Kate that some day when she was older and saw things in people's heart, she would understand them. Guess she needed a lot more birthdays, Kate thought, because she certainly didn't understand all that she saw today.

"Alrighty, peanut, your time is up. Give Grammy Mer a kiss," Kal said.

"Come here, Princess. I have an empty lap," said Poppy Pop.

"What about your back, Pops?" said Kal.

"Before he left, Sandy massaged it a bit and had me do some exercises, specific stretches to help sciatica. It feels much better. Compared with this morning, it's amazing."

Kate climbed into Poppy Pop's lap and snuggled against him. Earlier she had observed his heart and saw an image of him hugging Uncle TT, holding him in a bear hug. Oddly, though, in the center of Poppy Pop's heart, there had been an image of him clutching a pink rose to his chest with tears streaming down his cheeks. The pink rose had its head turned down and seemed limp and withered. Kate didn't understand, except that pink roses were some of Grammy Mer's favorite flowers.

Kate remembered the many times she had helped Grammy Mer arrange or refresh flowers. She had kept fresh flowers, mostly roses, in every room before she was sick. And if a rose were ailing, Grammy Mer would cut its head from the stem and put it in a small crystal dish along with some water. She would also peel off any dry petals to make it pretty again. Poppy Pop knew how she loved flowers and took care of them. It made no sense why he would have a limp rose in his heart.

Today is a seeing day, Kate thought. That's what Etta Ebella called it when everywhere Kate looked she saw colors or images in people's hearts. Kate didn't intentionally look into people's hearts; the colors or images just popped up. Etta Ebella had told her to pay attention, had said that the angels were trying to tell her something about that person, and perhaps preparing her for an upcoming event.

Kate nestled her head against Poppy Pop. He felt warm and cuddly. Kate smiled at her Aunt Sammy Sue sitting across from them.

She was drinking the coffee her dad had brought to her. It was a beige color that to Kate looked more like oatmeal than coffee.

Kate observed her aunt's eyes; they were shades of nutmeg that were laced with cloves. The unique color looked just right with her auburn hair. Etta Ebella had said that God was the best designer and artist ever, unparalleled.

As Kate looked at her aunt, though, something about her aunt's eyes today didn't look normal. They didn't look as shiny as they usually did. Kate switched her attention to her Aunt Sammy Sue's stomach, wondering how the baby had fallen out of her. The miscarry thing. *Could it have fallen out of her belly button?* Kate wondered. *Maybe her navel came unbuttoned.* She would check hers when she got home to see if there were any possible way it could open. Maybe there was a hidden button, like on some clothing.

Suddenly, her aunt's eyes watered. Kate watched an image pop up in her heart, one of an angel rocking a teensy baby swaddled in a pink blanket. Sammy Sue cleared her throat and shifted in her chair so that she could see Etta Ebella's face. "Kate, how's your angel doll doing? She looks good as new now."

"She is. Dr. Donahorn fixed her." Kate ducked her head against Poppy Pop's chest, a worried feeling engulfing her.

Carly scanned the surgical waiting area looking for the family.

"Mama!" Kate called to her mother across the waiting room.

"Over here, honey." Kal waved to his wife.

She rushed over to them. "Guess who I ran into in the hallway?"

"Who?"

"Dr. Donahorn. I mean, Angelique. She said that Terrence seemed to be doing well from what she could tell. She said the surgery was almost over."

"The inside scoop. That's great," said Kal.

"Here, Pops, let me take that double load you have there." Carly picked up Kate and Etta Ebella and sat in the chair next to Grammy Mer.

"I think that angel doll has gained some weight," Poppy Pop chuckled. His hand reached for his lower back, his fingers rubbing at it.

"Honey, did you ask Angelique to stop by? She could meet everyone."

"Yes, Kal, I did. She wanted to, but she was in a great hurry, all but running to the ER helicopter. She said she had been paged for an emergency surgery. A little girl was being transported to Children's in the city."

"A little girl?" asked Kate.

"Yes, pumpkin, a five-year-old girl who was in a car accident."

"There was a man here this morning," said Kal. "His wife and young daughter were in a bad accident, a head-on with a dump truck. I think his little girl was five."

"I forgot to tell you, Kal," said Sammy Sue. "I heard some women talking in the restroom after lunch. You know the woman who was praying so loudly. I heard her on the phone saying that the man's wife had died, and the little girl was in critical condition. According to her, the child was being moved to Children's USFH."

Instinctively, Kal stood and went and placed his hands on Carly's shoulders, patting her. He bent down and gave Kate a kiss on the neck.

"Life," said Kal. "We just never know, do we?"

"The Kindrick family?"

"Yes." Kal stood and offered his hand to the doctor dressed in surgical scrubs.

All conversation stopped. All eyes went to the slim blonde doctor. "Christine Lacholher," she said, shaking hands with Kal. "And you are?"

"Kal Kindrick, I'm Terrence's brother," Kal said. "And this is Terrence's mother, father, and sister and my wife and daughter."

The doctor nodded. "Terrence came through surgery well. We were able to relieve the pressure from the hematoma. If everything continues to go well, and there are no complications, he should be up and running again in several weeks."

"Praise God," said Poppy Pop.

"That's great news," said Kal. Relief filled the family circle.

"He's still in recovery. Then he'll be moved to surgical ICU. He'll be there for a couple of days before we move him to a regular room. For now, we must keep him still and quiet. Limit visitors."

Kate felt the doctor's eyes—a greenish tan color like oregano, the dried sort in a spice bottle—upon her, looking directly at her like she was specifying that no children were allowed. Her eyes seemed to harden as she surveyed Kate's bandages. *She knows*, thought Kate. *Knows that it's my fault that Uncle TT had to have brain surgery.* Kate imagined that there was a part of Uncle TT's brain that was like a robot that recorded all happenings, and that the doctor had touched that part when she was performing the surgery. And then, she had viewed his memory of the tree limb hitting his head. Undoubtedly, she knew and blamed Kate.

"When can we see him?" asked Poppy Pop.

"Once he is settled in ICU, one person can go in for five to ten minutes every two hours." The doctor's eyes scanned the group, pausing on Grammy Mer.

"How long will that be?" asked Kal.

"Another couple of hours," said Dr. Lacholher.

Poppy Pop looked at his watch.

"Is there any chance you could make an exception for two people to go in to see him?" Kal asked. "Someone would need to accompany my mother, handle her chair. And my dad needs to get her home before long."

Kate could feel Etta Ebella trying to move her wings. Kate held her tightly.

Dr. Lacholher seemed to study Grammy Mer, her grayish coloring, her shallow breathing, her glassy eyes, noting that she couldn't move or speak. Checking her watch, she said, "Perhaps we can make an exception."

"Thank you, thank you," said Poppy Pop.

"Mr. Kindrick, can you handle your wife's wheelchair?"

"Yes, Doctor, I can."

"Pops, how's your back? Are you sure you can handle the chair?"

"Yes, pushing it is fine."

Doctor Lacholher said, "Then come with me. I'll escort you back there now. I think this circumstance warrants a double exception."

"Right now?" Poppy Pop asked, his eyebrows tilting upward. "Oh my, thank you."

"Dad, we'll wait here for you. Then I'll help you get Mother in the car, and I'll follow you home and get her inside."

"Thank you, Son."

As they departed, Kal could hear the doctor saying they would have to speak quietly and not to expect Terrence to communicate, that while he may not be able to open his eyes, he could hear everything.

Carly tilted her head back, looking upward to Kal. "So, sweetheart, now that Terrence's surgery went well, are we leaving for Maui on Wednesday?"

"Yes, my darling, we are."

Kate burst into tears, her bandages crinkling against her skin with the movement of her facial muscles. "You are leaving me at Marilla Marzy's house for a whole week?"

CHAPTER SEVENTEEN

*M*arilla Marzy was cheating; her gingerbread man skipped a space, dancing onto the Rainbow Trail, the shortcut to winning, although the card she had drawn pointed her in the opposite direction.

The Candy Land game lay spread on the den floor. Kate drew the next card. *Ugh.* It was an orange one, placing her in the Molasses Swamp where she would lose a turn. She was stuck.

"See, you're not such a smarty pants after all. Like you can't even win a game for four-year-olds," Marilla Marzy taunted.

"M&M, be nice to your cousin; she's our guest, and she's younger than you," Abigail called out from the kitchen.

"Not a guest I invited," Marilla Marzy screeched back to her mother. She leaned across the game board, inching her face close to Kate's and yelled in a mocking cadence, "I totally don't know why I'm playing with you. You look like a pizza, and you're stupid. Like, you know, you can't even win a baby's game. Is it time for your bottle of sauce or cheesy pacifier, Little Baby Pizza Girl?"

Abigail marched into the den. Hands on her hips, she said, "Marilla Marzy, you are acting rudely. You apologize to Kate right now. Put away this game and go brush and feed the horses."

Her full mouth set in a scowl, M&M got up from the floor; she kicked the game board. The gingerbread men and color cards went scattering across the room as if they were running for their lives. "I'm not putting this baby game away, and I'm totally not apologizing for telling the truth to little Miss Pizza." She strode into the kitchen, grabbed a package of Oreo cookies from the pantry. She huffed out the back door, slamming it so hard that the glass panes rattled like they might fracture and fissure until they resembled a splintered mosaic.

Kneeling down on the den rug, Abigail pulled Kate into her arms. "Oh, Kate, I am sorry. She doesn't mean what she is saying. She's stressed about an algebra test she had today." Abigail stroked Kate's hair while reaching for the Candy Land box. "Help me find all the pieces to the game. Then you can assist me in the kitchen; you can be my sous chef. Okay?"

Kate nodded then began crawling toward the sofa but stopped when she realized she was crawling on all fours like a baby. Instead, she stood up and walked to the sofa. She got down on her knees to reach the game pieces and cards that she had watched slide under the sofa to safety, hiding from the candy monster—M&M.

In no way did Kate want to do anything babyish, though she now felt like a baby, an ugly one, a pizza-girl baby, who wanted her mommy and a snack. Looking at all those candies and cookies on the Candy Land board had made her hungry. Maybe that was why M&M had taken the entire package of Oreos, a new package, a large one with three rows across and twelve in each row. Kate knew; she had counted them when helping Aunt Abigail put the groceries away. Kate's mother didn't buy such large packages of cookies.

"Okay, so that's done. Let's wash our hands. Then you can snap the green beans," Aunt Abigail said as she placed the game back in the cabinet flanked by bookshelves, the cabinet where the game Monopoly was also stored. Kate had wanted to play Monopoly, but Marilla Marzy had said that it took too long, and her daddy would be home soon and they couldn't have any games or toys out when he arrived.

Kate's hungry stomach emptied its craving for sweets and filled with the brackish taste of dread. Vaynem would be there soon.

M&M had been nice until today, had even played Chutes and Ladders with her last night, and she hadn't cheated, yelled, or called her names. *Was it the algebra test that had M&M stressed out or was it because her daddy was coming home?*

While drying her hands, Kate eyed the mound of yeast dough sitting on the floured board. She wanted to pinch off a piece and stuff it into her mouth. Her mother would have offered her a tiny piece, but not too big of one because it would rise in her stomach. Stomach acids didn't stop yeast action; her mother would say. Nonetheless, if her mother were here, they would each have a nibble of the dough. And later they would check their tummies to see if they were swelling up big.

Aunt Abigail didn't offer her a bite. She handed her a colander filled with already-washed green beans and showed her how to snap off just one end, not the curly one, the stem one, telling her how they were Vaynem's favorite. Haricots Verts, they were called in French, she said.

Uncle TT had already taught her about French green beans, although she couldn't say it the way he did. One time in a fancy restaurant, he had shown Kate the word on the menu, telling her that even though it started with an h, the first sound was more like saying air.

Thinking of her Uncle TT, Kate's heart clenched and her eyes stung with tears. He was still in the hospital. Etta Ebella had been praying for him, almost nonstop and had told Kate that she should, too. Kate had wanted to see him, but Aunt Abigail said that they would not let him have visitors yet, especially children.

Humming the ad jingle "I Wish I Were an Oscar Mayer Wiener," Aunt Abigail floured the rolling pin and rolled out the dough into a near perfect circle. "I just can't get that silly tune out of my head. I guess it's because we had hot dogs last night. Kate, do you ever get a song stuck in your head?" she asked while taking a large water glass from the cabinet. She dipped its drinking rim in flour and then used it to cut the dough into circles.

"Yeah, sometimes, I do. Last week the *Colors of the Wind* song from *Pocahontas* got stuck in my head. My mother told me to watch another movie, like the *Lion King* and to sing along with the *Circle of Life* song. I watched it three times before the Pocahontas one got unstuck," replied Kate, piling more snapped beans onto the waxed paper, their ends all going the same direction, precisely as her aunt had instructed her to do. They were now a bean choir, Kate pretended. A funny looking choir because the curly end of each bean resembled a skinny dolphin's nose or the beak of an alien bird. Kate wanted to pick up a grouping and have them dance around the counter singing through their skinny noses, but she didn't.

"Well, the *Colors of the Wind* song sounds like a more worthwhile tune to have stuck in your head, better than wishing to be a wiener. That's a good idea, though, to listen to other songs. Perhaps that would do the trick."

She started toward the stereo cabinet but then abruptly turned away. "No, Vaynem should be home soon, and he doesn't like music or the television on when he comes through the door; he wants silence so he can unwind."

"My daddy likes music and noise when he gets home. After kissing my mother and me, he turns on the stereo or the TV, if we don't already have one of them going," Kate said. She glanced up at Aunt Abigail and thought she saw her aunt's eyes get moist. Kate checked the countertop for onions. There were none. "Aunt Abigail, we could sing without turning on any music. That might help get the wiener out of your head. And if we hear his car driving into the garage, we can stop singing and be really quiet."

"Okay, in a few minutes. You be thinking of some songs while I finish the rolls."

Butter melted and sizzled on cookie sheets heating on the gas stovetop. Abigail moved them onto trivets on the counter. One by one, she took each dough circle, dipped it in the melted butter, placed it on the warmed cookie sheet, and then folded the top over and sealed the yellow butter into its center, pressing the edges together so that each dough circle became a half-moon.

Kate's mother made homemade yeast rolls, too, but she left hers round, full moon style, and she didn't use as much butter. Kate watched her aunt as she worked the remaining dough. The sadness on her face waned as her fingers pressed the yeasty circles. When the warmth from her fingers left each one, the butter sitting on its top became chilled, separating into little beads like hundreds of tiny moonbeam clusters.

Aunt Abigail's face now looked relaxed, her heart now glowing. These were her moon babies; she had given birth to each one; she loved each one. Grateful to be born, they loved her back with their shiny moonbeam hearts. They must be girls, these moon babies, Kate decided, as she watched a pink color swirl outward from her aunt's heart. With one final adoring appraisal, her aunt covered each cookie sheet with a fresh kitchen towel, like she was spreading a blanket over her moon babies so they could grow big when resting. Little did they know their destiny was to be devoured by humans, consumed by some who didn't appreciate their flavor, eaten greedily by others who couldn't even taste their most extraordinary ingredient—their maker's love all kneaded into their crescent-moon bodies.

The humming started again. The ad jingle on replay: "I Wish I Were an Oscar Mayer Wiener."

"Aunt Abigail, the wiener is in your head again."

"Oh, Kate, please don't let Vaynem hear you say that. He already thinks I have a wiener brain."

"What's a wiener brain? Does it mean that you have a long brain instead of a round one?" asked Kate.

"I like the way you think, Kate," Abigail laughed. "Yes, I have longitude versus latitude. Why don't you sing me a song? Help me banish the wiener one."

"The wheels on the bus go round and round, round and round, all through the town," Kate sang hoping to turn Aunt Abigail's brain into a round one. Abigail joined in as they finished snapping the ends from the beans. They were to the part about the babies going "waa waa waa, all through the town" when the phone rang. Aunt Abigail looked at the caller ID, shushing Kate before answering.

"Hello, darling, are you on your way home from the airport?"

That meant it was Vaynem. Kate fingered the Power Ranger figure hidden in her pocket. She hoped that Vaynem's answer was no, he was not on his way home. But she knew that wasn't nice to hope such a thing, especially when she saw her aunt's face tense up again.

"What? You haven't even left Seattle yet?" Abigail twisted her neck around and moved it from side to side as if trying to pop it. Her free hand massaged it like it hurt.

Upon hearing that Vaynem was in Seattle, Kate took the Power Ranger out of her pocket and began playing with it on the kitchen counter.

Crooning into the phone, Abigail said, "My darling, I am so very sorry. You've had such a hard week with the trial. Get home as soon as you can. I'll do the best I can with delaying dinner. I'm making some of your favorites, including homemade rolls."

Abigail's brows furrowed. She turned her face and body away from Kate and spoke softly, but Kate could still hear her say, "Vaynem, who is that laughing? What is so funny?"

Covering the mouthpiece of the phone, Abigail turned to Kate and said, "Kate, sweetie, why don't you play outside? Go down to the stables and help M&M feed the horses."

As Kate opened the kitchen door to leave, she heard her aunt say, "And what is that music? Vaynem, where are you?"

In the hay bin, Marilla Marzy sat cross-legged, upright like an Indian yogi who was meditating. She appeared to be in a trance, eating one Oreo cookie after the other. Seemingly unconscious movements, one hand repeatedly stuffed a cookie into her mouth. Her other hand repeatedly twirled the same long strand of dark hair. Her eyes appeared transfixed. Both the green eye and the brown one stood perfectly still as if they were locked in place. She stared ahead into the distance as if she saw a far off land—her own Nirvana:

> … a land where she was thin.
>
> …a land where potato chips were an important food group.

...a land where she could eat mounds of chocolate, cartons of ice cream, warm donuts by the dozens, and stacks of pasta with buttered garlic bread and never gain a pound.

...a land where she was born with eyes the same color. And if, by chance, she happened to be born with unmatched eyes, in that land she had a father who would allow her to wear colored contacts so that her eyes appeared normal to everyone else.

... a land where she was brilliant like Einstein and wildly creative like Salvador Dali.

...a land where her breasts were larger than her stomach.

...a land where people thought she was an angel instead of a witch.

...a land where she laughed in her sleep instead of screamed.

...a land where she had a beautiful name—a Goddess sounding name that didn't rhyme with gorilla.

...a land where she was loved and wanted by both parents.

...a land where she was not a mistake.

Kate skipped down the tree-lined lane, heading toward the barn. She felt happy to be outside in the fresh air, breathing in the reds and pinks of the sunset sky, which looked to her like God had spilled a strawberry-peach smoothie.

Finding the double doors of the barn closed, Kate put her ear to one door and didn't hear a sound, not even from the horses that should be inside. She didn't hear anything, but she smelled something. It wasn't manure, and it wasn't cigarettes, at least not the ones Marilla Marzy usually sneaked away to smoke.

Snorts and neighs suddenly startled her. Turning to the side, Kate saw the horses were still in the corral, standing against the gate, whinnying now as if they were talking. The shiny black horse, Mindy Midnight, raised her head and bobbled it as if she were motioning to Kate. She pushed her dark body against the white wooden fence. Daisy Daylight, the cream-colored horse, hung back, but she appeared to be working her mouth, almost like a cow chewing its cud. Daisy Daylight was hungry, Kate decided. The yet-to-be-born baby horse pushing on the insides of her stomach was probably demanding food, too.

Mindy Midnight shook her head from side to side as she neighed, rubbing her mane against Daisy Daylight's neck as if comforting her. They were best friends, just like she and Jillian, Kate thought as she wondered what they might be saying to each other.

Horses had their own language; Etta Ebella had said they did. So surely they were discussing why M&M had not brought them into the barn and fed them. And Mindy Midnight must want her black hair brushed, that's why she was rubbing her body on the wooden fence, scratching like a cat would do.

Marilla Marzy should be feeding or brushing the horses this very minute. Had something happened to her? Maybe a poisonous snake had bitten her, and she lay dying in the barn.

Kate put her ear to the door again. No sounds. She eased the door open. Thankfully, the lights were on and were blazing brightly. She stepped carefully inside the barn, leaving one of the double doors ajar, in case she needed to run for help.

Moving on tiptoe down the barn's hallway, Kate peeked in each stall. As she went farther, her skin prickled, her heart thumped visibly against her chest.

When she approached the hay stall, that nasty smell became more pungent. And there was a strange noise, a crunching sound. Peering around the corner, she saw Marilla Marzy sitting Indian style, her head folded down, her eyes closed. Her mouth was moving, chewing something. She had one hand on her stomach, and that hand was wearing a plastic glove; her other hand was busy twirling her hair.

The Oreo package was in front of her, almost empty. Only two cookies remained. They sat alongside a small plastic container that was not empty; its lid sat crossways atop the container. Around the inside edges, Kate could see white things wiggling like boiling noodles. Bending down to see the label, Kate tried to read the words: "Flat Stomachs Forever: White Magic Tape Worms; www.slimflats. com." While Kate wasn't sure about what it all meant. She knew that websites on the Internet started with the letter w, three of them in sequence, and she certainly knew that other "w" word—worms.

Without opening her eyes, Marilla Marzy stopped twirling her hair. She picked up an Oreo. Twisting her wrist, she removed its black top and set the other part back on the wrapper. With her gloved hand, she reached into the plastic container and pulled out a long flat wriggly worm, gave it a shake and folded it onto the Oreo icing. Quickly, she slapped the other cookie half on top of it. She took a deep breath and shoved the entire cookie-worm sandwich inside her mouth.

Placing the gloved hand back on her stomach, she swished the thing from cheek to cheek, not chewing. Her face contorted. She swallowed, making a gagging sound as the wriggly slid down her throat. Then she chewed, crunching the cookie halves loudly.

Kate's brain froze. She felt headless. Without any thought or command, her toes flexed, and she was off down the hallway, tiptoeing backward.

The hot liquid rising in her esophagus thawed her brain, reattaching her head. Bending over at the waist, she ran backward with her head down and her left hand over her mouth, that hand a vessel in waiting. Blind to where she was going, her back crashed into the barn door, the one that was open. The impact made it flop against the barn wall with a double wallop.

"Who's there?" Marilla Marzy screamed.

157

CHAPTER EIGHTEEN

*A*bigail's tears had liquefied her mascara, staining her cheeks. The punitive inner voice that dominated her mind warned her to stop this morose crying, to repair her makeup, and to put on her pretend face, the one she regularly wore nowadays. Makeup and clothes, they seemed to be the only things holding her together. Otherwise, she would not exist, would have no reflection in the mirror.

M&M and Kate could be coming through the door any minute, ready for their dinner, her inner voice railed. M&M was accustomed to seeing her crying like this, but Kate was not. Most likely, such displays of unhappiness didn't occur in her home. The child would surely recount the scene to her parents if she witnessed her aunt crying uncontrollably. No, Abigail could not risk Carly, her sister, or any of her family knowing the truth about her diseased marriage and the depraved man who was her husband. Other people knowing, that did it; that threat silenced her tears.

Where are those girls? They could be having such fun with the horses that they have lost track of time. *Who am I kidding? Marilla Marzy has probably hogtied Kate and is about to kill her. A chip off the old block, M&M was, much like her father. Not quite all the time, though,* Abigail thought, consoling herself as she applied new foundation. She dusted her face with matching powder. While lining her eyes and applying fresh mascara, she remembered how M&M had been rather sweet with Kate this week. Until today, that is. In fact, Marilla Marzy usually behaved well during the regular weekdays when it was just the two of them at home. It was the mix of her father's presence or the anticipation of his coming home that set her off into acting like him.

If you can't beat them, join them. Abigail pondered the axiom. Perhaps she should think more along those lines and begin donning fighting armor where Vaynem was concerned. Applying fresh lipstick, she studied her face, but then suddenly turned from the mirror. Rubbing her arm, she checked the doorway. *Had someone come into the room?* It had felt as if someone had brushed against her. She felt a presence, a distinct presence.

"Marilla Marzy, is that you? Kate, are you there?" Silence was the only response. She looked all around the bathroom and master bedroom suite. Gripping her cell phone, holding it poised to call 911, she began going through the house, each room one by one, looking under the beds and in the closets. She also checked for dust and disorder. She was pleased to see that every inch so far was spotless.

Vaynem discounted housekeeping as unskilled chores, yet he demanded perfection. He believed she didn't do any work because long ago she had acquiesced to his demands: he never wanted to hear appliances, not a vacuum cleaner, washer, or dryer. And he never wanted to see brooms or mops when he was home. Considering the perfectly ordered state of things, how could he not know that she toiled every waking minute either scrubbing or shining some part of the house, cooking, doing laundry, ironing, sewing draperies, or upholstering furniture? "Privileged child's play," he would say, yet he had forbidden her to work outside the home after she had paid off their hefty college loans.

In Marilla Marzy's room, Abigail noted the candy wrappers under the bed and a pile of clothes on the floor by the closet—both had accumulated since four o'clock when M&M had arrived home from school. Trashcan contents also caught her eye. Abigail peered inside at two empty laxative boxes. She would deal with that later. The possibility of an intruder in the house was far more terrifying.

When tiptoeing through the hallway to the main guestroom, the bedroom where Kate was staying, Abigail slowed her steps. The hair on the nape of her neck bristled. The doorway ahead summoned her, commanding her to enter. At the threshold, she halted. Her spine stiffened; her eyes widened. She gasped. The scene unfolding before her—though clear and unmistakable—was utterly unfathomable, was totally incomprehensible.

Inside the room, two topaz eyes blinked twice.

Kate crashed out of the barn, still running backward, unable to stop. Her back slammed against the corral fence, bringing her to a halt. A warm tongue licked the nape of her neck, triggering her stomach's release button. The hot liquid flowed up and out; she bent over heaving and gagging. Mindy Midnight neighed as Daisy Daylight pushed her nose under the fence and lapped up the whitish pink puddle Kate had made on the grass.

"No. Daisy. Daylight. Don't. Eat. That. Stuff," Kate said, the words coming one at a time, sandwiched between her gagging coughs.

A hand grabbed Kate's hair from behind. The plastic-gloved hand wrapped around her orange hair using it as a lever to jerk her head, tilting it backward. Kate's stomach heaved again at the thought of the worm juice from the glove getting on her hair, but the gloved hand held her captive. There was no escaping its grip.

Marilla Marzy's mismatched eyes fixated on Kate and spewed their brand of vomit—fear putrefied into hatred—all over her face. "What do you think you're doing, Missy?" M&M asked.

"I'm, I'm, uh, I threw up; my tummy hurts."

"You were in the barn, weren't you?"

The hand tightened; Kate's scalp ached. "What do you mean?" she asked.

"You know what I mean," said M&M. "Answer me, or, like totally, I am going to pull every hair out of your head. When I'm finished, you will look like a peeled tangerine." Then she took a piece of Kate's arm flesh between her fingers and twisted it like a door knob.

"Ouch. You're hurting me," Kate screamed.

"For the last time, were you in the barn?" Marilla Marzy asked.

"Aunt Abigail told me to come and help you. The horses were hungry and…," Kate stopped without finishing the sentence.

Holding tightly to the orange-red strands, she jerked Kate's head back repeatedly. Now every hair on Kate's head hurt, even her eyebrows. "Yes, I was. Was in the barn looking for you."

With a firm hold on Kate's hair, tilting her head back and her face upward, Marilla Marzy bent her head down, inching her face close to Kate's. She summoned a well of saliva to gather in her mouth. She spat it directly into Kate's open mouth. "Swallow, you little pizza baby. Right now, swallow," M&M commanded in a low, tight voice, a wild animal snarl.

Suddenly, Mindy Midnight reared up. Her front hooves extended over the white corral fence.

Releasing Kate's hair, M&M turned and jumped back, falling away on her knees as the mighty hooves barely missed hitting her shoulders.

Kate took off. Running. The trees lining the lane seemed to cheer her on as she ran as fast as her short legs would allow. She passed the tennis courts. The house was just around the corner. Now past sunset, the light was dimming, the air was chilling. A rock caught her foot.

The gloved hand nabbed Kate's shoulder. She went tumbling on the gravel.

"You stupid little pizza girl. You can't outrun me."

The gloved hand pushed Kate's head down. Marilla Marzy straddled Kate. Her mouth set in a sneer, she growled, "That worm juice is in you, too, now. It's mingling with your saliva and sliding down into your stomach right this minute."

161

Kate writhed on the gravel, the rocks digging into her back, as she tried to get away from M&M's grip. She cried, "Let me go."

Marilla Marzy leaned directly over Kate, blowing her worm breath all over Kate's face. "If you tell anyone about what happened in the barn, I will make you eat an entire container of worms, a worm pizza. Do you hear me? Do you?"

"Y-e-s."

"If you tell anyone, I mean anyone—a single soul—I will turn your angel doll into ashes. Do you understand me, Pizza Girl? I'll tie up her wings, douse her with gasoline, and set fire to her. Etta Ebella will be no more."

The back door to the house slammed, the sound of it banging shut penetrated the air.

Immediately, Marilla Marzy tore off the plastic glove, picked up Kate, holding her cradle style and began walking toward the house.

Abigail came running around the corner yelling, "What's wrong?"

When they met in the lane, Abigail glared at M&M. "What has happened? What have you done to her?"

"Mom, I am bringing her to the house."

"Why, Emmy, why? What did you do to her?" Abigail pleaded, her eyes roving over Kate's body and face, checking for new injuries.

"Mom, listen to me. Kate jumped at Mindy Midnight and threw a rock at her. The horse got spooked and began rearing up and bucking. When her hooves came down, they barely missed Kate's head. Kate took off running, and then she took a spill on the gravel. You need to carry her back to the house."

"I can walk," Kate said, wriggling down from Marilla Marzy's arms.

"Come here, sweetheart," Abigail said to Kate. Let's get you some ointment for your hands."

"I need to finish feeding the horses," Marilla Marzy said. She reached over and pinched Kate's cheek. "I'll catch up with *you* and that angel doll later, Pizza Girl."

CHAPTER NINETEEN

"*H*urry up. We're going to be late." Vaynem's voice boomed through the house speaker system. It was Sunday morning.

"We're coming," said Abigail. She, Kate, and M&M rushed into the garage where Vaynem was waiting, the car engine running.

"Marilla Marzy, take that i-Pod and put it in the kitchen. You are not taking it in the car. Not today. You left the lights on in your room, and Kate, you left them on in the bathroom. Both of you will weed the garden this afternoon when we get back," Vaynem said, bellowing like a bull as he got into his car, a dark blue Mercedes.

He sped out of the driveway. With every turn of the wheel, Vaynem ranted at them, a constant stream of complaints.

"Abigail, I don't know why you waste so much time on your hair; it's like pushing spaghetti around on a plate," he said. "And that blush and lipstick you're wearing is too bright. Who are you trying to be, Marilyn Monroe? Well, you can forget that when your chest only has two egg yolks on it," Vaynem said, his lower lip contorting downward.

Eyeing Marilla Marzy in the rear view mirror, he raved on, his lips twisting around like they were pinching and biting her as he spoke, "M&M, you will also move the new cord of wood after you finish the garden. You know my rules about electricity. I bust my butt all week to pay for you and your mother to live in the lap of luxury and do nothing. You could at least help with the electric bill. Lazy, that's what you both are, disgustingly lazy. And what kind of junk food did you eat this week while I was away? It looks like you have gained more weight; you look like a stuffed turkey in your skirt, both you and your mother do. And I am a speaker today. A man in my position shouldn't have to feel ashamed of his family."

Strangely silent, Abigail and Marilla Marzy sat there like two compliant hostages. Peering sideways to see M&M's face, Kate saw an image pop up in Marilla Marzy's heart. A building emerged, a skyscraper of pain, its jagged architecture jutting up toward the sky. Arrows were flying from the building as if it were a fortress, psychic arrows assaulting the back of her father's head and neck.

Suddenly, a wave shot into the back seat, a streak of blue that carried words upon it like surfboards riding atop cresting waves. The soundless message from Abigail warned: *Don't fight with the driver of any car in which you are a passenger.* The arrows slowed and then stopped.

The church steeple came into view; the Mercedes veered into a parking space. Kate got out of the car, holding Etta Ebella tightly. Abigail took her other hand and began walking toward the church.

"Oh, no, you're not. You are not taking that toy into the church, not my church. Your parents may indulge such irreverence, but I will not have it." Vaynem grabbed hold of Kate's left arm, right in the bicep. He squeezed hard. His thumb, a brutal weapon, mashed its way through to her muscle all the way to the bone. Vigorously, he shook her arm and shoulder, moving the joint back and forth like it was a martini shaker. Sharp pains shot through Kate's arm and neck.

He seized Etta Ebella, grasping her by one wing. Vaynem popped open the trunk and threw Etta Ebella inside—face down. He slammed the trunk shut and pushed the remote to lock the car.

Kate stood motionless, her mouth open and gaping. Tears sprang from her eyes.

"Dry it up, Kate, or you'll be banished to darkness in that trunk, too," Vaynem yelled as he began walking away. Walking briskly, he planted each foot in stomp mode. Marilla Marzy walked with him, matching his stride.

Pulling tissues from her purse, Abigail dabbed at Kate's tears. She whispered, "I am so sorry, Kate. Please forgive us. He's usually not like this. He's just nervous and stressed about being a speaker this morning."

"Abigail, quit coddling her. I will not be late because of that orange-haired twerp. Get over here now," Vaynem barked. He and Marilla Marzy waited across the street, both of them standing with their hands on their hips. Abigail grabbed Kate's hand, looked both ways for oncoming traffic, and ran quickly over to them, her high heels clacking on the sidewalk.

As they approached the church, near where people were standing in varying clusters, like grapes on a vine, Vaynem slowed his brisk pace. He took Marilla Marzy's hand and put his other arm on Abigail's shoulder. As they moved forward, people turned to look at them, nodded and smiled at the family going into the church.

Entering the church lobby, Vaynem smiled broadly, shaking hands with men and kissing women on the cheek, the happiest Kate had ever seen him. In the sanctuary, he chose a pew toward the front of the left side. Flanked by his daughter and wife, he sat holding Marilla Marzy's hand, having pulled their fist knot onto his lap. His right arm lay across the pew, his hand resting on Abigail's shoulder. Kate nestled close to her aunt, who was still holding her hand. They sat like a chain family, all link-locked together down the pew.

Organ music soothed Kate's nerves until a woman in the pew in front of her turned and scowled. Kate squinted at her; she looked familiar. Recognition dawned. It was the lady from the hospital, the one with the gray hair and moldy eyes, the one who had purposefully messed with the sonogram machine. Virginia Veetlehurst. She was turning her head back toward their pew, eyeing Kate in her peripheral vision.

Kate wondered if Dr. Donahorn and Jophia did a sonogram on her tummy today, would they see baby worms growing there? She had tried to spit out M&M's wormy saliva when running down the lane, but she still feared she had swallowed some of it. At the thought of it, nausea awoke in her stomach, stretching and yawning its way into her throat. And her arm still ached terribly. Pain. This week had been the worst of her entire life. Kate fingered her stitches, still covered with the white bandage. She yearned to lay her head in her aunt's lap and to lie down in the pew. She didn't try or even ask if she could. She knew. Vaynem would not allow it.

Virginia Veetlehurst crooked her head again. Kate looked down and focused on her Aunt Abigail's skirt, a raisin color that matched her aunt's eyes and hair. Kate thought her aunt looked beautiful, and she was almost as slim as her mother was, not at all like a stuffed turkey.

Kate checked her aunt's blouse. There were no egg yolks on her chest; they hadn't even had eggs for breakfast. Aunt Abigail had made homemade cinnamon rolls, Canadian bacon, and fruit salad.

On Saturday afternoon, Kate had watched her aunt roll out the yeast dough into a big circle, spread it with butter, and sprinkle it with cinnamon and sugar. Then she had rolled it up into a log and sliced it. When she placed the slices on the buttered pan, each roll revealed its spiral face. Her aunt had wrapped the pans tightly with plastic and foil and then put them in the refrigerator. She had said that she would get up early Sunday morning since the rolls needed to rise for a couple of hours before she could bake them.

That morning, after mere minutes in the oven, the aroma of the rolls baking wafted through the house, making Kate's mouth water and her tummy feel ravenous. Her taste buds were not disappointed. Unlike coffee that smelled delicious but tasted bitter; the rolls were as scrumptious as their aroma, the most delicious cinnamon rolls Kate had ever tasted.

Vaynem had woofed them down, eating them fast like his mouth was a garbage disposal. He had not sounded like a garbage disposal, though. The noises he made while eating the rolls had echoed with pure enjoyment. Even still, with each one, he had griped like a grackle bird. One was too sweet, the other not sweet enough, and the third didn't have enough cinnamon.

Still puzzled about why he had said Aunt Abigail had two egg yolks on her chest, Kate checked her aunt's curly hair for signs of spaghetti. No visible signs.

Kate's arm and shoulder were throbbing now, and she was worried about Etta Ebella. Vaynem had jerked her hard while grasping her by her wing. *What if her wing was broken? And how was she going to get Etta Ebella out of the trunk with Vaynem holding the keys?* As if reading her thoughts, Aunt Abigail pulled Kate's chin up toward her face and silently mouthed the words, "Are you okay?"

Kate slowly nodded yes as she tucked her chin down on the pink collar of her dress. Her throat tightened as she suppressed a sob. *Dear Jesus, please can I go home to my mother and daddy, go to my church where I can hold Etta Ebella and sit with Jillian?* She sat thinking about her mother and how she let her take Etta Ebella into their church. And she also let her take her *Hello Kitty* bag filled with crayons and coloring books—Jesus ones—so that she had something quiet to do during the sermon. Last week, she had looked through the newest Jesus coloring book for a picture of the Great Angel Mother, but she had yet to find a single picture of her.

Kate looked around the sanctuary, noting the differences between her church and this one. She eyed the artwork behind the altar—a dead looking Jesus hanging on a cross. It was a 3-D sculpture with blood running down the body of a lifeless Jesus, running like a water fountain in repeat recycle mode. *Was it real blood or fake, like watered-down ketchup or red wine?* Kate wondered. At the thought of real blood, her toes curled inside her black patent shoes. She sat staring at the cross, remembering the joy and uproarious laughter that had poured forth from the lively Jesus man she had seen, the Jesus that was full of energy and was exuberantly happy to lift up the children all over the world.

The minister's voice suddenly became louder, catching Kate's attention. He was introducing Vaynem as the next speaker, part of their yearly fundraising campaign, he explained. Vaynem strode to the pulpit and shook the minister's hand, then semi-hugged him, the fake kind of hug that men often did, just motions in the air, barely touching each other's bodies, slapping each other on the shoulders.

Vaynem stood tall behind the pulpit, gripping it with both hands as he scanned the audience. He smiled in a wide radiant beam that enveloped each and every person there. Kate thought he looked rather handsome in his dark suit, vertical striped shirt, and diagonally striped tie. She remembered overhearing the discussion between him and Aunt Abigail that morning about his tie. Aunt Abigail had said no, don't wear a striped tie with a striped shirt, but he had worn it, anyway.

Vaynem spoke into the microphone, varying his voice tones from hushed and reverent to loud and authoritative. He quoted scripture about separating the goats from the sheep. As he talked, Kate's special eyes kicked into operational mode. She watched puffs of gray fog emanate from the top of Vaynem's head, intermittently, like his brain was smoking cigarettes and blowing smoke rings. Reddish light radiated from his body and from his eggplant-colored heart, which resembled bruises and squashed red grapes. At times, it seemed that black snake heads—with their fangs exposed and flailing about— were poking outward from Vaynem's heart and also from his mouth.

Kate averted her eyes and tried to think of Jesus and the Great Angel Mother, all the time chiding herself for seeing and thinking of snakes. Her mother had told her that when she saw snakes it was her imagination playing tricks on her, especially when she saw snakes in the toilets. Her mother had said that was impossible, that snakes could not get into toilets through drain pipes.

Etta Ebella had said that imagination was a wonderful talent, a gift that helped to see possibilities and what was invisible to most people on Earth. Kate was trying to believe what her mother said was true, but so far, she was not entirely convinced. And now this, seeing snakes in Vaynem.

To distract herself from him and the pain in her arm, she let her eyes rove over the audience. Several older women were wiping at their eyes with handkerchiefs or tissues and getting out their checkbooks as Vaynem talked.

Virginia Veetlehurst was not one of them; her eyes didn't water, and she didn't touch her purse. Ever since Vaynem had been speaking, she had turned in his direction; yet, every few minutes she turned her head back and frowned at Kate. Her neck swiveled on her head as she took turns glowing at Vaynem and glowering at Kate. *Maybe she had a snake in her, too.*

The blue Mercedes sped down the roadway making its way back to the ranch. Vaynem's tongue was on a rampage. With every turn of the wheels, he barked angrily at them, sounding like an enraged Doberman Pinscher.

Fuming, Vaynem said that Marilla Marzy needed to learn to sit up straight and to hold her shoulders back, especially in church. From his pulpit perspective, she had looked like a sloth all slumped down, and that position had made her stomach look even bigger. How had his gene pool produced such an unsightly offspring? Well, it must have been Abigail's genes as evidenced by her ugly niece.

Speaking of Kate, she needed to learn to show respect by keeping her eyes forward on the pulpit, listening to the speaker, and not eyeing the people in the audience. There was no excuse for not behaving properly in church, regardless how young one was, he had said. And why did her booster seat have to be in his car, he had inquired, saying if it abraded even one spot of leather he would bill her parents for the cost of reupholstering the entire back seat.

Cringing, Kate wondered if this was what it felt like to ride inside the Hate Monster Machine. She wanted to curl her body into a ball, or better yet, fold it into a tiny triangle so she could slide between the seat cushions and into the trunk where Etta Ebella was. Never before had the thought of riding in a car trunk seemed appealing.

She wanted to hate Vaynem but, according to her mother, if she did, then she would be just like him. *Ugh, that would be horrible;*

snakes lived in his mouth and heart, and he had weapons there too. Was he evil, like a devil?

Etta Ebella's face flashed before her mind. She remembered how Etta Ebella had told her not to think about the devil. She had said to keep her focus on God because whatever a person thinks about will just get bigger in their life, and she surely didn't want Kate to feed and grow the devil. Etta Ebella had said that thinking about the Almighty in the midst of evil thoughts was like turning on a light in a dark room. Just flip the switch and the darkness would vanish. The God switch always worked; Etta Ebella had said.

Kate looked up at the lens cover on the side panel light. If she could turn that light on, would that make Vaynem act nice? Maybe she should just start thinking about God.

Vaynem continued spewing his poison, dousing them all: Kate would not be getting her doll back until the lunch dishes were done and the garden was weeded and properly so, to his satisfaction. And lunch. Why had Abigail decided to make a prime-rib roast instead of their usual Sunday fried chicken? Lazy broad.

As the car rounded the bend on the road toward the ranch, it suddenly jerked to the side. Vaynem grabbed the steering wheel with both hands, saying, "What the hay?" He wrestled the steering wheel. The Mercedes careened to the side of the roadway. Exhaling a stream of expletives, he shut off the engine and jumped out of the car.

A flat, the right front tire sat collapsed against the roadway. Vaynem paced around the car. Marilla Marzy opened her door and hurriedly got out, joining her dad. With her mismatched eyes cast downward, M&M studied the defunct tire like it was a masterful piece of art.

Peering through the car window, Abigail surveyed the roadway situation on her side of the car, the same side of the flat tire. The semi-paved shoulder was a welcome sight but the concrete culvert with an ultra steep gradient was not.

"Kate, wait here while I get out, and then I will come around and help you," Abigail said. "There's not much traffic this far out of town, but there's a sharp incline near this side. You might fall if you open your door. Wait for me, okay?"

Abigail opened the car door and stepped carefully onto the gravelly concrete. With the second step, the spike of her heel got caught in a pebble hole, catapulting her forward. She threw her arms back to counterbalance the forward motion. One arm went back further than the other, turning her toward the culvert. Arms flailing and one leg moving back and forth to get her heel out of the tiny pit, she resembled a stuck windup toy. Almost toppling down the culvert, she thrust her left hand outward and grabbed hold of the car's side mirror—just in the nick of time.

"You stupid cow. Stop that! You'll break the mirror. Get back in the car," Vaynem yelled at her.

When Abigail regained her footing, she readjusted the mirror. With a determined set to her shoulders, she took off her heels and marched around the rear of the Mercedes to the other side. She opened the back passenger door where M&M had been sitting and instructed Kate to crawl across and exit on that side.

Kate wriggled from the car, holding fast to her aunt's hand, which gripped her with an iron-clad resolve.

"Dad, pop the trunk so we can get to the spare and the jack," Marilla Marzy said.

"No way. I am not touching that tire," he said, pacing at the front of the car. Holding up his hands like he was a surgeon who was freshly scrubbed for surgery, Vaynem said, "I'm not sullying these babies with tire grease and grime."

Nor a wedding ring, Abigail thought. His hands held up, his fingers splayed, the absent wedding ring was conspicuous for a married man with a family. He had not worn one for years, ever since M&M was four years old. It had been so clever of him to lose it in the river when he was swimming with her dad and brother. She had given him a new ring for Christmas. He had thrown it in the trash, right in front of her, claiming that it was nothing more than a germ catcher.

Vaynem kicked the tire. It was only last week that the law firm's driver had taken his car into the dealership for general service and for the tires to be rotated, balanced and their air pressure checked. He had looked over the receipts and had phoned the service expert after the driver returned. If all had checked out so well, why had the car's air-pressure alarm malfunctioned? Not a single warning light or message had been displayed before the car had jerked to the right. His pricey Mercedes must have an electrical problem. Being Sunday, the dealership would be closed. Kicking the tire again, he coughed deeply and spat specs of phlegm onto it.

After inspecting the side mirror for damage, he returned to pacing in front of the car. His eyes surveyed the hills ahead while he talked on his cell phone.

With Kate in tow, Abigail opened the driver's side door. Quickly, she reached in and pushed the release button. The trunk lid flew open. Waiting anxiously, Marilla Marzy leaned into the trunk and began uncovering the spare tire.

Abigail walked to the back of the car. With one glimpse inside the trunk, she gasped, her hand flying to her mouth—it, too, surprised at the sight. Gingerly, she picked up Etta Ebella.

Kate held out one arm, the one not hurting, eager to retain possession of her angel doll. The rest of her body yearned to run far away since she didn't know what bad thing Vaynem would do when he saw Aunt Abigail getting Etta Ebella out of the trunk.

Abigail appeared frozen, her arms and hands extended upward, clutching Etta Ebella inside the trunk lid, the only visual curtain between her and Vaynem. She stared at Etta Ebella as if she had seen a ghost.

Two topaz eyes blinked twice.

Uh oh, Kate thought, now that she could see Etta Ebella and see that her heart was aglow and that her wings had inflated, all puffed up big. Her doll body was surrounded by a swirling and glowing vortex, emanating light and heat that looked different from when she was bathing in light and delight. And this did not seem like a situation where feeling delight was appropriate, anyway, except for the fact that she was almost out of the trunk and about to be reunited with Kate.

Marilla Marzy, who was engrossed with inspecting the spare tire and fumbling underneath it like she was searching for buried treasure, didn't even raise her head. She didn't see Etta Ebella's light show.

Abigail's eyes held Etta Ebella's laser-like gaze for a few seconds more. Then she slowly turned and placed the glowing angel doll in Kate's arms. Like magic, upon Kate's touch, Etta Ebella returned to her normal angel-doll self, seemingly lifeless.

"Abigail, what do you think you're doing?" Stomping back to where they were standing, Vaynem thrust out his hand to take Etta Ebella away from Kate.

Abigail grabbed his lower arm and said, "Vaynem, you stop it right now. Kate is our guest. She is only six years old, and she has done nothing wrong. You are the adult, stop acting like a bratty kid."

Stunned by her mother's words and tone, Marilla Marzy dropped the car's instruction booklet and immediately stood up. Bumping her head on the trunk lock, she rubbed it as if dazed.

"Piss on you," Vaynem said, swinging his other hand forward, fisted and aimed to hit Abigail's face. A car horn sounded. He dropped his hands and turned around as a white Mazda pulled up beside them.

"Vaynem, are you all having a problem?" called out a woman's voice.

"Why, Mrs. Veetlehurst, thank you for stopping," Vaynem said, oozing with niceness, his church voice again. He walked over to the Mazda, which was caked with flecks of mud.

The girl on the passenger side—Tessa, Virginia Veetlehurst's 22-year-old daughter—had rolled down the car window so her mother could speak to them. Vaynem leaned in toward her pretty face and long blonde hair. She flashed a toothy smile and tossed her hair like it was a horse's mane.

Vaynem winked at the girl and said, "We've got a flat tire. Do you know the name of the automotive repair shop in that new retail complex about fifteen miles to the north? I want them to send a tow truck. Information was no help without the exact name."

Marilla Marzy bit her lip and returned to reading the car manual. Abigail viewed the hillside.

"No, sir, Vaynem, I don't," said Mrs. Veetlehurst. "I don't go over there. That new complex is in the opposite direction from my work."

The girl shrugged her shoulders in an exaggerated way, making the wide-necked fuchsia sweater she was wearing fall off her left shoulder. It draped down on her arm, exposing her lace bra—also fuchsia, which showcased robust cleavage. Without returning the sweater to her shoulder, she fluttered her mascara-laden eyelashes and peered up to Vaynem saying she didn't know the name of that automotive repair shop, either.

"Hey, if you don't mind a detour to drop me off at home first, Tessa could give you a ride up there. I have to get lunch and be at the hospital at three. Do you want to bring the tire?" asked Virginia Veetlehurst.

"No, I don't. But if Tessa will give me a lift, I'll come back with the tow truck driver."

"Sure thing, Vaynem. My pleasure," said Tessa. The word *pleasure* flourished on her tongue. She elongated the word into ten syllables, savoring each one on various taste buds with her pointy pink tongue licking her upper lip for the finale.

Vaynem winked at her again. Reaching into his suit jacket, he pulled out a white handkerchief. He placed it on the door handle and opened the car door, protecting his hands from touching the muck that was thick on the handle. The entire car was spackled with mud, much like the texture of a stucco wall.

Climbing into the back seat, which had newspapers strewn across it, Vaynem grimaced. The soles of his expensive alligator shoes had no choice but to rest atop trash that filled the floorboard —Styrofoam cups stained with coffee, Krispy Krème wrappers, and Taco Bell bags containing old burrito remnants. His aquiline nose instantly wrinkled restricting its air intake.

Resurrecting the white hanky, he used it to press the window button, rolling down the dusty glass. He cocked his index finger like a gun and said, "Abigail, you and the kids get back in the car, lock the doors, and turn on the emergency flashers. If anyone stops, ignore them. Don't talk to them."

Stoned-faced, Abigail stared at him.

Vaynem flashed his fist at her as the muddy Mazda sped away.

Abigail motioned them all in the car.

Marilla Marzy slammed the trunk lid and then jumped into the front seat. "I'm riding shotgun," she said.

Abigail scurried Kate into the back seat, and then obeying Vaynem's instructions, she locked the doors and turned on the emergency flashers. She also placed her hand on the automatic gear shift, trying to move it, making sure the gear was set in "Park."

Marilla Marzy said. "Mom, activate the emergency brake, too."

"Yes, I'm doing that now."

Seemingly willing prisoners, they lounged on the plush leather seats watching the muddy Mazda climb the hill. When it had made it halfway, Abigail began rolling up the sleeves on her silk blouse, giving her wrists some breathing room.

Marilla Marzy hugged the door, tapping the handle with her fingernails, drumming it rhythmically.

Squeezing Etta Ebella into her as if they were one, Kate prayed for miracles, for her arm to stop hurting, for stomach acids to dissolve worm juice, for Uncle TT to be released from the hospital, for him to appear suddenly in his lamb-pasta car and rescue her. And she prayed never to see Vaynem again unless her parents were with her.

When the muddy Mazda topped the hill, Abigail said, "Okay, let's do it."

Marilla Marzy opened her door and jumped out of the car as if the seat were a trampoline.

Abigail motioned to Kate to get out of the car. She grasped Kate's hand, took a blanket from the trunk and walked to where the sloping concrete culvert ended, several hundred feet away from the Mercedes. She folded the navy blanket onto the grass. "Kate, sit here and hold onto Etta Ebella. If a car goes by, don't move. You are safe here."

"What are we doing?" Kate asked her aunt.

"You'll see," Abigail replied as she jogged back to the flat tire.

Marilla Marzy already had the tire iron in her hand. She handed it to her mother. Abigail placed the L-shaped bar on a wheel lug and she and M&M both leaned their weight on the tire iron, turning the lug counterclockwise. The first one loosened. Repeating the process for the other lug nuts, they worked like a well-oiled machine.

Abigail remembered the first few times she had car problems after she married Vaynem; she had always called him. His classic response to any of her problems was one question: *Why are you calling me?* Even the day she had called telling him his toddler daughter had fallen on a rock in the yard and had a gaping head wound, which was bleeding profusely, his response had been the same—*why are you calling me?* She had thought he would want to know, had hoped he would meet them at the hospital emergency. The wound had required multiple stitches in little M&M's scalp, and in the protective layer underneath it, the dura mater membrane. The doctor had asked if the baby's father had been called. *Yes, he had, and no, he was not out of town.*

Marilla Marzy handed her mother the tire jack.

From the grassy area, Kate watched the front right side of the car rise high and higher.

Abigail screwed off the already-loosened wheel lugs and placed them carefully on the asphalt. Then she removed the air-deprived tire from the wheelbase. Marilla Marzy lifted the spare out of the trunk and rolled it over to her mother. They both hoisted the good tire onto the wheelbase.

Sitting on the blue blanket, Kate watched as her aunt and cousin worked on the tire. She pretended the blanket had hidden properties and was a powerful safety net. Here eyes, on alert, scanned for danger. Clusters of fluffy white clouds caught her attention. She searched them, looking for angel wings. *Maybe the Great Angel Mother's kitchen was located somewhere in those clouds. And just maybe, Jesus was there, too.* Unless he had morphed into a teddy-bear cloud, she couldn't identify any shapes that looked like him, nor could she spot anything even remotely akin to angel wings. Mostly, the clouds looked like peaks of meringue frosting.

Thinking of her birthday cake, she heard her stomach rumble with hunger. *Or was it that odd feeling—a message from Etta Ebella—or was it simply because she was scared?* Kate turned and looked behind her to make sure that a river of snakes was not crawling in the grass. Her olive-green eyes detected none; her special eyes didn't either. Then it must be baby worms or worm juice eating at her stomach, Kate decided.

Clutching Etta Ebella, she worried about what was going to happen when Vaynem returned. *Would he beat them, pummel them with his fists making ugly bruises, or was he mad enough and mean enough to go so far as to kill them?*

Yes, he would kill them dead. She could see it all now. Considering how furious Vaynem was, he would probably strangle Aunt Abigail, after first pounding her face with his hands fisted tightly, covered with the white handkerchief, and then he would use those unsoiled hands to tear Etta Ebella apart. He would make Kate watch the horrors. After that, he would kill her in some tortuous fashion, probably pulling out all her hair, since he had said it was ugly and said that he hated red hair, especially straight red hair.

He would throw their bodies into the field. Kate wasn't sure whether Vaynem would murder M&M or try to enlist her help. Sometimes he acted as if he loved her, if one could call his weird way love. Other times he acted like he hated M&M as if he were ashamed of her. *M&M had helped with the tire, and he was still mad at her for not sitting up straight in church and for having a big tummy, so today he would kill M&M, too.*

Kate's arm throbbed from Vaynem's big fingers squeezing and pushing on her bone. And now she could feel his manicured hands around her throat choking her neck. A honey bee buzzed in front of her, lighting upon a yellow daisy growing nearby. She watched the bee. The sound of its buzzing penetrated her ears.

Etta Ebella began pushing back from Kate's tight grip; her wings began inflating. The bee buzzed even louder than before. Two topaz eyes blinked twice.

The air whirred around her. "Kate, visualize miracles, not disaster," Etta Ebella hummed, her bell-like voice vibrating in Kate's ears. "Worrying and imagining bad things happening are poisonous to positive possibilities. Worrying activates and energizes the very thing you don't want to happen."

Etta Ebella's inflated wings shimmered in the midday sunlight. "Kate, focus. Use your imagination to visualize a miracle, a positive and safe outcome for everyone in this situation. Open up to the possibilities."

Gold and silver particles, like tiny metallic fairies, danced all around Etta Ebella, adding to her winged oration: "Kate, miraculous solutions can come in a myriad of ways, in as many ice-cream flavors as you could ever dream up. Sometimes the miracles even appear in a disguise, as in a flavor that tastes bad to you at first."

Etta Ebella's wings fluttered as a distant church bell tolled thirteen times. "Kate, ask God for a miracle. Tell God *Thank You*; feel the gratitude in your heart. Give thanks and praise for the miraculous solution—even before it happens."

A wonderful miracle, what could that be? Kate wondered. Maybe they could get the tire changed in time to drive away before Vaynem returned. But where would they go? They shouldn't go the ranch, *should they?*

Kate sat on the blanket, mulling over more miracle-versus-disaster possibilities. Perhaps the Great Angel Mother would ask Jesus to lift up her mother and daddy from Maui and set them down right here in this meadow. Then she would be safe, even if Vaynem came back.

Possibilities abounded, floating through Kate's brain like ocean waves at high tide. Maybe her mother and daddy could walk across God's grid that Etta Ebella said went all around Earth, connecting all people, all places. But that might take too long, so maybe they could get on God's rail, that Holy Grail thing. That word *Grail* was a disguise, a code, but the G meant that the Holy Rail belonged to and was operated by God, the one, and only Great Almighty. Kate decided that was a good choice.

In her imagination, she visualized her mother and daddy clinging to one of the poles inside God's rail. They had to hold on tight as they tried to maintain their balance. It moved at supersonic speed, and people didn't usually ride on it since it transported Holiness everywhere, including outer space. Maybe God wouldn't mind if her parents rode on it today so they could come and protect her.

Kate's head began to hurt. Her gaze returned to the bee, to its wings fluttering as it perched on the fuzzy brown center of the yellow daisy. She let her imagination flutter with the same rhythm of the bee's wings.

She began seeing the lamb-pasta car speeding over the hill. Uncle TT was healthy and smiling broadly. He pushed the button on the gull-wing doors, and she climbed inside. Aunt Abigail and M&M got in, too, and they all raced away to safety. Oh yes, that possibility felt better; yes, decidedly better than Vaynem murdering them.

But wait, Uncle TT's car didn't have a back seat. They wouldn't fit. There had to be another solution, but what?

Suddenly, the movie screen behind her forehead lit up. Uncle TT's face loomed in front of her eyes. He said, "Princess, call me. Use your cell phone. Or ask your aunt to bring you to the hospital to see me or to Lancaster's, our favorite burger joint at Jack London Square."

Thoughts of her cell phone almost jolted her out of the reverie. Her phone, which was to be used in emergencies only, was back at the ranch in her Hello Kitty bag. Vaynem had said she could not take the bag to church, had made her leave it in the kitchen.

The movie started again. In it, she and Etta Ebella were with Aunt Abigail and M&M at Lancaster's—the restaurant she and Uncle TT went to sometimes, the one located at Jack London Square not too far from her house.

Uncle TT, who usually liked fancy food, said that sometimes there was nothing better than a juicy burger and a milkshake. Lancaster's certainly had delicious ones. Kate's mouth watered and her stomach rumbled at the thought of munching on crispy French fries slathered in oodles of ketchup and sipping a yummy chocolate shake.

In the movie, Kate saw that she, Aunt Abigail, and M&M, who were wearing the church clothes they had on today, sat in one of the padded booths at Lancaster's, hungrily eating their lunch. Etta Ebella sat next to Kate.

Abruptly, the happy scene changed. Out of the blue, something hit their table, turning it on its side and sending their food flying into the air. People crowded around them, aghast expressions flooding their faces. An ambulance siren whirred as it pulled into the parking lot. Aunt Abigail gripped her hand as the two of them went running after the ambulance men carrying a body covered up on the stretcher. The men loaded it into the ambulance and slammed the doors shut.

Kate felt hot tears searing her cheeks. Suddenly, the lamb–pasta car careened into the parking lot. But Uncle TT was not driving it. All she could see were the two dark hands that gripped the steering wheel.

Why, Uncle TT would never let someone else drive his silver spaghetti car, Kate thought. Even still, in the movie, the driver's door raised and those same dark hands snatched up her and Etta Ebella, lifting them inside the car.

The movie stopped, the screen went blank. The bee buzzed in Kate's ear again; it circled her head and flew over to the Mercedes.

Kate blinked her eyes repetitively as she touched Etta Ebella's wings, now their normal size. Her fingertips grasped for the blanket underneath her. *Was it there?* She felt as if she had traveled to a distant world. Nonetheless, she was still sitting on the blanket near the edge of the grassy meadow that was adjacent to the roadway.

As Abigail began replacing the wheel lugs, Marilla Marzy semi-rolled, semi-carried the deflated tire to the trunk and threw it inside. She stepped back to her mother. Like a well-rehearsed dance, they leaned their body weight on the tire iron, turning the wheel lugs, this time clockwise to tighten them.

Abigail pumped the jack and lowered the car back into its normal position. One more time, she and Marilla Marzy performed their dance duo, leaning their weight on the tire iron, getting each wheel lug as tight as possible. They stood up, surveyed the tire and did a high five. Marilla Marzy began carrying the jack and tire iron back to the trunk.

Kate stood and attempted to clap, but her arm hurt too much when she tried to bring her hands together. Instead, she called out, "Wow, Aunt Abigail, my mother doesn't know how to change a tire!"

Abigail smiled slyly. She gazed at the hill, checking for signs of a tow truck or the muddy Mazda returning. No cars or trucks were coming down the hill; none drove on the roadway at all.

Opening the car door, she removed a package of hand wipes from the console. She scrubbed her dirty hands.

Abigail gazed back at the hill. She gasped, "Oh, Emmy, we don't have the car keys. Your dad has them."

CHAPTER TWENTY

Jn room 1230 on the sixth floor of Alta Bates Medical, Terrence Ted slept, his left foot twitching under the blanket. His eyelids wriggled, appearing as tightly wrapped tissue paper covering puffer fish writhing on a hook.

Abruptly, his eyes opened wide. Unwrapped, they were now, startled in their sockets. The dream. The images had been extremely vivid, and the emotions that came with them were intense, yet to be dispelled.

It was one of those special ones—an electrified, red-letter dream—the kind he had occasionally experienced since he was a young child, the kind that came true, at some point in time. Upon awakening from this one, he had instantly understood the symbolism, particularly the baroque chair flanked by angels. As for the other parts, he knew that many of the scenes would play out in minute detail in his waking life and precisely as depicted in the dream. This time, it was to be soon, of that he was certain.

Pain from recent surgery or not, he must find a way out of this hospital or a way to enlist some help. It would be disastrous if he didn't. And in the dream, he had promised her.

Cocking an ear, he listened for voices and noises in the hallway. Hearing nothing, he flexed his arm down aside the bed, his fingers searching for metal. He pulled his cell phone from under the mattress.

On the island of Maui, Carly paced the white sand beach at the Four Seasons Resort in Wailea. She watched the black snorkel bobbling on the blue ocean water several hundred feet from shore.

Kal has found a reef, she thought, as she watched him approaching darker waters, ones purplish in color. Hopefully, he was viewing a plethora of tropical fish, the colorful world of underwater art they both loved. Sea life, its unique shapes, designs, and colors—from vibrant spectacles to muted hues—rivaled displays of museum quality masterpieces. It was impossible to think of humankind taking credit for any color amalgamation or design when viewing the artistic genius that nature provided.

Clutching her cell phone, Carly squeezed it as if she could force it to ring. They had been trying to call Terrence since early morning, late morning California time. When he hadn't answered his cell, Kal had called the main hospital line. The operator said he was still listed as a patient and had dialed his room. There was no answer. They had sent him text messages, too, but there was yet to be any reply.

To make matters worse, she could not reach Abigail or Kate, either. Her stomach felt like the baby was kicking every inch. But it was too early in the pregnancy to feel baby movement. If Terrence was okay, then something had gone wrong for Kate. Surely that was the source of this terrible feeling. Her little daughter must need her now, this very minute, and was yanking on the invisible umbilical cord that connected their mother-daughter bodies, linking them together across the Pacific, from California to Hawaii.

Abigail was taking Kate to the Moxsin's family church this morning. But the church service should be long over by now, and still, there was no answer on the house phone at the ranch or on Abigail's or Kate's cells.

Carly fretted. *After all that had happened with Kate falling out of the tree and Terrence's surgery, I should have stayed home with Kate while Kal attended the conference. At the least, we should have returned home when the conference had ended yesterday. We should not have extended our stay. Shoulda Woulda Coulda. If only.* Too much money on the line, they had decided, with her airline ticket being non-refundable and the high costs to change their return flight to an earlier date. Paltry pennies, though, if something bad had happened to Kate or had gone seriously wrong for Terrence.

Terrence had been right; Carly decided, wishing she had not left Kate in Abigail's care. Vaynem's temper was completely unpredictable. And then there was Marilla Marzy, who acted far worse when her father was around, trying to win his approval by matching or outdoing his wickedness. The two together could easily spell disaster for Kate.

What was I thinking? Weeks ago when they had first planned to extend their trip after the conference, she had felt desperate to get away with Kal. She had hoped that by being near the sea, they could get pregnant again. That formula had worked the magic when trying to get pregnant the first time. Since Kate's third birthday, they had been trying to have another child, but they had not been able to get away to the ocean until now, not alone, anyway.

And why hadn't I realized that I was already pregnant? The bigger question: *Why did I not fully trust the hospital tests?* It wasn't until she was in Maui that the symptoms appeared and the reality had taken hold. *Furthermore, how had Kate known? How had a six-year-old child known, especially a mere few weeks into the pregnancy, when I, an adult woman, didn't know my own body?* Carly sighed with exasperation as she remembered Kate saying that Etta Ebella had told her. *Yes, right, a talking plastic doll that could perceive such things. Jeeze Louise.*

She looked out over the Pacific waters, her eyes watchful for Kal. They usually snorkeled together, but today, the motion of the waves had made her queasy.

Kal's bald head popped up above the cresting waves. He waved to her, adjusted his mask and began swimming vigorously toward the cove where she stood on the beach.

Understanding his intention, Carly sought relief from the swelling anxiety. Her toes burrowed deeper into the white sand, taking cover in God's grit.

In Boston, Sammy Sue was winding down her speech, *The Impact of Viruses on Molecular Genetics*. Leaning closer to the microphone and lowering her alto voice, she spoke the last sentence with a resounding tone of authority. Thundering applause followed. She nodded in appreciation and then forced herself to remain gracious during the standing ovation.

People crowded the podium, hoping to speak with her. Her eyes, though, searched the crowd for Nigel, her cohort. She had to find him and let him know that she was leaving the conference early, leaving two days early for no explainable, logical reason, at least none that would make sense to him.

Science. Logic. Those tenets ruled their world. Nevertheless, she would not ignore this peculiar wariness urging her to go home early. After all, she had to consider the prescience prevalent in her lineage.

Yes, she was ready to admit that she had inherited her mother's family's Merlin-Gene, her pet name for intuition, non-scientific as it was. Albeit, she didn't seem to have it in the off-the-chart quantity that her brother Terrence had it encoded in his DNA.

Hermetic that Terrence was, he disputed that fact. He argued that she had it in the same dose as he, that she had not allowed her intuition to function freely, had not honored it, thus giving her brain the command to squelch it, for it to atrophy like an unused muscle. An intriguing theory, she would consider the topic for her next area of research.

Only last week she had asked herself how many birthdays did she need to have before she listened to this Merlin-like knower that lived inside her like a computer chip in the middle of her gut. She knew, though, if that part of her body were dissected, nothing unusual would be found, not from a physical medical perspective, like love could not be found in any part of a physical heart, not medically speaking.

Even still, this instinct in her gut had proven itself correct again and again, right about big things, right about little things, and right about people; yet, she had battled it, using sanctified logic as the weapon of choice for murdering any unaccounted for urges, feelings, and perceptions.

Just last month, she had a sudden urge to see her doctor, her obstetrician, ten days earlier than the scheduled regular appointment. She had ignored the feeling; she was not having any symptoms that would raise a red flag, would warrant an unscheduled visit. She had rationalized the feeling as simply first-pregnancy jitters. Perhaps if she had gone in to be checked then, they would have discovered that her hormone levels were off, that she was in danger of a miscarriage. Perhaps with treatment, she would not have lost the baby. Maybe, maybe not, but if she had listened, she would not carry the burden of the looming question.

Then there was that frustrating Tuesday last week. She had felt an urge to take her umbrella, but there was not a cloud in the sky, and when she had checked the weather forecast on her cell phone, no rain was predicted. She had left the umbrella in the trunk of her car. Sure enough, she came out of the meeting and was caught in a horrendous deluge. With her hair and clothes dripping, she was drenched from head to toe. Of all days to get wet, the day she was to preside over a department meeting; consequently, she had to go home and change to look presentable. Beyond annoyed at herself— again, she had vowed to listen to this other sense that seemed to know things in advance, warning her, or better yet, giving her the opportunity to be prepared.

Science had yet to give credibility to this type of intelligence. But in her personal life, arguing with it and trying to prove it wrong had only facilitated erroneous choices with aggravating consequences, sometimes lasting and painful ones. Cause and effect.

This time, she would listen. And not only would she listen, but she would also take it one step further. She would *act* on it. For now, though, she had no clue what accounted for the feeling. When she had spoken to Sandy last evening, he had said all was well, that he had stopped by to see Terrence at the hospital, and his recovery was progressing, that he was out of ICU, now in a private room. Nonetheless, her body told her something was wrong, told her that she needed to go home. *Action, not questions,* she reminded herself. *Why choose regret and unnecessary suffering?*

Not seeing her cohort, Nigel, she gathered her notes from the podium, picked up her briefcase, and began making her way to the door. Halfway to the exit, her cell phone received a message marked urgent. Ensconced in the darkness of her briefcase, the phone was incapable of playing any message. Its battery had lost its charge, had gone dead.

At Gatwick airport in London, Ruthie Renee Kindrick boarded flight number 307. Her roasted-chestnut hair tumbled over her shoulders, happy to be free of the blonde wig that had made her feel as if she looked like a summer squash.

Stage makeup stained her face. People stared. When she had checked her bags, the ticket agent had examined her passport photograph suspiciously. In his flight uniform—all starched and ironed—he had resembled a bobble-head toy, with his body remaining perfectly still while only his head moved up and down as if the flesh on his neck was hiding a spring-loaded coil. Again and again, his eyes had peered down at her photo, and then moved back up to her face, and back down at the photo, and then up again searching her features for pattern matches to her passport photograph.

There had not been time to remove all the makeup properly. She didn't care; she could not repress this inimitable inner feeling any longer. Yes, she was well aware of her penchant for dramatics, but it truly seemed that there was a hoard of twenty-foot-tall wings flapping and swooshing manically all around her, a chorus of angels clamoring, "Fly home, fly home, fly home, now!"

CHAPTER TWENTY-ONE

Although her mother's eyes were radiating terror and Kate's were floating in an ocean of salty tears, Marilla Marzy could not stop smiling. This time, it was not due to her spitefulness. This time, she had good reasons. She and her mother had changed the tire, and all in record time—something her dad could not do. What's more, it was twice now her mother had called her that pretty name, *Emmy*.

More importantly, she had a secret. One that would banish the terror from her mother's eyes and stop Kate's tears just as surely as if she had a magic wand. Leaning far into the trunk of the car, her torso extended, Marilla Marzy unzipped a flap, one hidden under the space where the spare tire would normally be placed. Her fingers groped blindly inside the narrow dark pocket, then pulled out a set of keys.

Dangling them proudly in her hand as if she held the keys to the Emerald City, she said, "Mom, I'm starving. Let's go to McDonald's. Like, I'm so hungry, I could eat three Big Macs."

Abigail's eyes narrowed in disbelief at the sight of the car keys, then soon widened as the sound of a roaring truck motor snapped all her senses into hyper-alert mode. Instantly, all heads turned and looked at the hill, expecting to see the tow truck zooming toward them. Instead, from the opposite direction, a dump truck rounded the bend, gunning its engine full force as it gained momentum to begin its climb up the hill. Rocks and chunks of gravel fell from its sides, flying in all directions. Abigail and M&M jumped back from the roadway to miss being hit. Like hail from a storm cloud, the gravel pelted the Mercedes, denting the hood, the sunroof, and the driver's side door.

Within seconds of the dump truck passing by them, Marilla Marzy yelled, "K64R484, K64R484."

Abigail marched around the car surveying the damage. Safe on the blanket, Kate watched the dump truck continue to spill its load, chipping away at the innocent highway as it chugged its way up the hill.

Marilla Marzy leaped into the front passenger seat of the car and jerked opened the center console. Grabbing a notepad and pen, she scribbled K64R484.

Abigail waved her arm in Kate's direction, "Come, sweetie, hurry so we can go." Holding Etta Ebella securely in one arm, Kate stuffed the blanket under her other arm, the throbbing one. When she was running up the concrete incline, the blue blanket slipped from the back of her arm, falling into the culvert.

"Oh, sweetie, you dropped the blanket," called out Aunt Abigail.

Kate stopped to run back for it.

"No, no Kate, just leave it. Let's hurry." Rushing Kate into her safety seat, Abigail quickly fastened Kate's seatbelt. Moving like a race walker, Abigail jaunted around the car and leaped into the driver's seat. She turned the key waiting in the ignition. The Mercedes' engine purred despite its gravel-dented body.

Abigail glanced up the hill, then behind her. Accelerating—with no pause to fasten her seat belt—she spun the car in a U-turn and began driving away from the ranch. Incessantly, the driver's seatbelt sensor beeped, screeching its warning.

As the blue Mercedes rounded the bend, a yellow tow truck topped the hill and began its descent.

In San Francisco, Angelique loaded birthday balloons, streamers, and two handsomely wrapped presents in the trunk of her car. She checked her watch. They were on schedule for the surprise party; even still, an invasive sense of exigency had been her companion all morning.

The Bay Bridge. Her Gephyrophobia. Was that the source? She could fly in airplanes, large or small, and experience no fear, yet driving across large bridges induced panic.

And now, what was delaying Annateresa and Laura? Earlier, they both had been dressed and ready to go when she had headed for the elevator. She had left the 729 door ajar for them as they said they were coming right behind her.

She peered into the open trunk and checked the cake box. The German chocolate cake looked perfect, his favorite. *He will love it,* she thought.

An annoying beeping sound fractured her cake fantasy. The trunk timer was whining, alerting her that it had been open for more minutes than the car thought proper. It sounded like one of the heart monitor machines at the hospital, except those methodical little screams said a human being was in serious trouble.

Thoughts of the day her mother died floated through her mind. Had her mother's heart monitor screamed before it flat-lined? Or had some merciful nurse or doctor removed it from the room before the end, knowing its shrieks would make no difference? Considering her mother's advanced cancerous condition and with her Living Will on record, there would have been no code blue, no resuscitation attempts.

Odd that such a document is called a "Living Will" when in fact, it's a "Dying Will." Enough of the morbid thoughts, Angelique lamented to herself.

Placing her hand palm down on the trunk lid, she pushed downward. Upon hearing the click, she immediately reopened it, wanting it open for the quick placement of their gift bags. *Annateresa and Laura would surely be waltzing out of the garage elevator any minute now.*

The anxious feeling swept through her once again. She rubbed the face of her watch, checking the time. They should be driving out of the garage this very second, or better yet, already across the Bay Bridge by now. Deciding to call her sister, she opened the driver-side door and reached for her purse. The silver cell phone was easy to see, even inside the silver silk pocket of the pewter purse. It was flashing. The now familiar number splayed across the screen. It was Jonah.

Scotch tape clung to her lips. Using her elbow, Monet Lisette pinned the wrapping paper against the gift box. With her alternate hand, she stripped the tape from her plush mouth and deftly applied the tape to the paper fold.

Today was possibly a birthday he would never forget. Was he tuned into the Heaven and Earth birthday cycle? Born on Earth, die to Heaven. Die on Earth, born to Heaven.

The copper paper glinted in the sunlight. The rays pouring in through the open windows made the metallic balloons, embossed on the tone-on-tone gift paper, shine like new pennies. *Pennies were from heaven*; her grandmother used to say. Affection shining in her eyes, Monet reflected upon her Gram. Oh, how she missed her grandmother's happy and loving presence here on Earth.

Monet's demure smile broadened as she remembered her Gram saying never to walk by a penny, to always pick it up because it was a sign an angel was watching over you.

Her Gram had claimed that copper pennies were extra special for three primary reasons. Copper's excellent electrical conductivity was one, and then there was the fact that copper, in the right dosage, was an essential mineral nutrient for human and plant health. But it was the third reason that she loved the most. The alchemical symbol for copper—a circle sitting atop a cross—was the symbol of love and beauty, and it was also the symbol of the female.

Admiring the paper, Monet placed another piece of Scotch tape on a strategic corner. She had selected this paper ever so carefully. Its copper color reminded her of Angelique's hair and two other women's hair, one of whom she could not disclose that she had once met.

But maybe after today, the secret would release her.

CHAPTER TWENTY-TWO

The Mercedes cruised down the street, its seatbelt sensor still beeping loudly. Now secure in leaving the curvy ranch road behind her and enjoying an easy flow of traffic, Abigail tugged on her seatbelt strap and managed to secure it, all the while keeping one hand on the steering wheel. She flipped on the blinker and began moving into the left turn lane.

"Mom, like, what are you doing? McDonald's is the other way," Marilla Marzy said, twisting around in the passenger seat as if that could change the direction of the car.

"Emmy, I know you're hungry, but I want to go somewhere different today. Besides, Kate's parents prefer that she not eat at McDonalds."

"Like, why? Like, how whacko is that?"

From the back seat, Kate spoke up, "Aunt Abigail, what about the roast cooking in the oven at the ranch? Could it catch the house on fire?"

"No, sweetie. I had the oven set on a timer. It was set to shut off promptly at noon. I'm sure Vaynem will have Tessa or the tow-truck driver drop him by home. He will probably eat some of it."

M&M tossed her head like she was practicing one of Tessa's flirtatious mane moves. She said, "Dad will not eat that roast. He's too mad, and when he finds us gone with the car, he'll think we

195

drove on the flat, ruining the rim. He'll be ready to kill us, like, he will probably hunt us down."

Abigail pursed her lips and put one finger across her mouth. *Shush.*

"Mom, after lunch we need to report that dump truck driver and call our insurance agent about the damage."

"Yes, Emmy, we will. I'm proud of you for getting that license tag number. That was quick thinking."

"Hey, there's a Taco Bell up ahead on the right. Do Kate's persnickety parents let her eat there? Mom, I'm so hungry. Go there or to Wendy's," M&M demanded.

"No fast food today. Let's treat ourselves to a special lunch. We've earned it. If we want to be treated well by others, then we must treat ourselves well." Abigail glanced down at her skirt to see if any tire grease had stained it. "If we hurry, we can make Sunday brunch at one of the waterfront restaurants at Jack London Square."

Kate's ears perked up at the mention of Jack London Square.

"But, I'm, like, craving a burger. I had my mouth all set for a Big Mac."

"Lancaster's at Jack London Square has burgers. Uncle TT takes me there sometimes," Kate said, daring to make the suggestion.

"That's a marvelous idea, Kate. It's been years since I've been to Lancaster's. I remember its view of the water, which I am craving today. Lancaster's, it is." Abigail sang out the words happily.

Kate's stomach smiled, and Etta Ebella began bathing in light and delight.

Marilla Marzy slumped in her seat, but only for a half-second. She sat up and flipped down the visor. She opened the mirror and scrunched her mouth and nose, scrutinizing her face. "Mom, can I borrow your, like, you know, your lipstick?"

Abigail's neck snapped to the side in surprise. "Why yes, Emmy, you can."

Clicking her teeth together, M&M examined them in the visor mirror. One was slightly crooked. She applied the plum-colored lipstick and then practiced sucking in her cheeks, like a model.

"Okay, Mom, if we are going to start treating ourselves well, does that mean that I get to wear colored contacts lens?...and get to have my teeth fixed?"

The two horses, Mindy Midnight and Daisy Daylight, trotted over to the corral gate, their ears erect, listening to the raspy car engine that drove onto the private road.

The muddy Mazda chugged to a stop on the circular driveway in front of the towering stone home. In defiance of typical ranch-style architecture, the home's three stories reached for the clouds, standing tall in the midday sun.

Upon entering the house, Tessa said, "Mmm, something sure smells good." She followed Vaynem through the massive foyer and up the stairs. Her fingers, chipped pink nail polish and all, stroked the ebony stair rail as she ascended behind him. "Did your wife start lunch before you left for church?"

"Yes, a prime-rib roast. The *lazy cow* didn't plan my Sunday favorite, fried chicken," Vaynem replied, walking into the master suite bathroom. Reaching into his trouser pocket, he removed the white hanky, now spotted with mud flecks, and tossed it into the hamper. Immediately, he turned on the hot water, lathered his hands with soap, scrubbed them, and then rinsed them well, letting the warm water flow over his palms and fingers, the soap suds disappearing in the white marble sink. Repeating the soap and rinsing process two more times, he examined his hands and nails after drying them on the plush, white towel.

"Fired chicken? Are you from the South? You don't sound like it."

"That's because I have lived in California for over twenty years, probably longer than you are old. The South? Not quite. I grew up in Texas, so did Abigail. How old are you, anyway, Miss Tessa?" Vaynem asked.

"I've had exactly twenty-two birthdays," replied Tessa, who lounged on the bed, her fuchsia sweater falling off her shoulder again. She turned on her side so that the neck of the sweater lowered even more, its wool fuzz balls rubbing against the fine fabric of the duvet cover, aqua silk piped in chocolate brown satin. "I'm old enough to like what I see when I look at you, Mr. Big Shot. Come over here and join me."

Vaynem moved from the bathroom's double doors to the end of the bed, his striped tie already removed, his shirt collar open, his fingers moving with a practiced precision as he undid the remaining buttons.

"I could be your Sunday fried chicken today," Tessa teased.

Sliding off his lizard belt, Vaynem laid it carefully across the back of the wing chair. Flexing his bare arms and chest, he said, "Get off that silk coverlet."

Tessa lolled on the bed, enjoying the feeling of the cool sumptuous silk on her shoulders. Puckering her full lips into a pout, she said, "That's not how you talked to me two weeks ago in the backseat of your car," she cooed.

"You little tramp, I said for you to get off that coverlet. Right now," Vaynem yelled.

The intense furor emanating from his eyes convinced her to jump up from the bed. Tossing her hair, Tessa looked askance.

Grabbing her arm, he yanked her over to him. He shoved her against the wall and pushed his body against hers. "Be my fried chicken, you say? That requires biting." Like a ravenous vampire, Vaynem's teeth dug into her lower lip and then moved to the softness of her neck.

Her eyes fighting mad, Tessa tried to push him away. He bit her again. Blood trickled onto the fuchsia sweater. Her wail was quickly followed by a vitrified howl from Vaynem as her knee jabbed his groin. *No one called her a tramp and got away with it.*

His skin now as pale as a clean, white handkerchief, Vaynem's body slumped, writhing with pain. As he mustered his strength, his hands formed fists, one aiming toward her chin.

Her knee rose up for another well-aimed blow. Collapsing, he yelped like a wounded animal. She shoved him into the wing chair. He rolled toward the windows—the opposite direction from the bed and the floral rug—his pale, hairless chest juxtaposed against the dark hardwood floor, his arms thrashing, his legs coiling into a fetal position.

Darting to the bed, Tessa yanked off the duvet cover. Grasping it by one of its corners, she wadded it and rubbed the silk against her neck, streaking it with her blood. She stomped the other end with her boot, digging her spiky heel into its hem, ripping the aqua silk away from the chocolate satin edging. Pursing her lips and swishing her tongue, a well of saliva roiled in her mouth. She spat the sticky dribble onto the aqua silk and then dug her teeth into the moistness, their sharp edges tearing and fraying the silk fibers.

"How's that for biting? Enjoy your precious coverlet now," Tessa growled as she threw the tangled aqua mass directly onto his ashen face. Tucking her purse under her arm, she raced down the stairs. When flinging open the front door, she heard his cell phone ringing.

In the corral, Daisy Daylight's tongue lapped water from the corral trough, her stomach bulging heavily with her unborn colt. Mindy Midnight flipped her tail as if she were swatting flies. She leaned heavily on the corral gate, watching the Muddy Mazda speed down the tree-lined roadway.

With his left thumb hooked into his jean pocket and his boot heel scuffing against the roadway's rough pavement, the tow truck driver spoke into his cell phone. "No, sir, that's what I said. I'll say it again. There is no blue Mercedes on the side of the road. There is no car at all by that culvert or anywhere past that hill, or around the bend all the way up to the stop sign."

"That can't be true. Did you check the mile marker?" Vaynem asked.

The tow truck driver turned his head squinting at the mile-marker sign a few hundred yards away. "Course I did." *You white-collar greenhorn.* His gaze drifted from the fluffy white clouds to the grassy field. "Sir, the only blue things out here are the sky and a blanket down in that culvert."

CHAPTER TWENTY-THREE

"**L**adies, right this way, please," said the maitre d' at Lancaster's. "How about a booth today?"

"As long as it has a view of the water," said Abigail.

"But of course, Madame." He led them to one of the curved, upholstered booths in the waterfront section of the restaurant. Smiling, he watched Kate place Etta Ebella close by her side and smooth the skirt of Etta Ebella's dress.

Kate studied his eyes while he squared up the rectangular menus. She remembered him and his eyes that resembled shelled-pistachios, green with golden brown flecks.

"Ladies, we have our Sunday brunch buffet available today, or you may order from our menu. What is your preference?"

Marilla Marzy reached for the menu. "I want a burger."

"Menus it is." His wide smile crinkled when he placed one in front of Kate. With one pistachio eye a-wink, he said, "Would your special friend like a menu, too?"

"No, thank you," Kate said, tucking her chin down shyly onto her pink collar.

"Oh, I remember you now, you and your winged friend here come in with your uncle, don't you? How is he? We haven't seen him in awhile."

"He's sick, in the hospital," Kate replied. She reached for Etta Ebella and held her tightly, trying to visualize miracles, trying to erase the icky feeling that pointed its gnarled finger at her, saying it was all her fault that Uncle TT was in the hospital.

"I'm sorry to hear that. Please give him get-well wishes from all of us here at Lancaster's. He causes quite a stir when he comes in, people wanting their books signed. We enjoy that and hope to see him soon. Now, missy, we usually put your winged friend in a booster seat. Do you want one for her today?"

"No, not today," replied Kate, clutching Etta Ebella in her lap, remembering how fun it was to eat here with Uncle TT. He always treated Etta Ebella as if she were a real angel like Grammy Mer used to do.

At the thought of Grammy Mer, Kate's heart swelled with love. Suddenly, the room seemed to spin in a circle. Kate's special eyes kicked in, opening wide. In Kate's vision, Grammy Mer walked through the front door of the restaurant. She wore high heels, stood tall, and walked perfectly. Her gaze was directed at Kate and Etta Ebella. In Grammy Mer's heart, Kate saw an image of the Jesus man giving her grandmother an exquisite pink rose. A small honey bee perched on the edge of the rose's outer petal. And then, the spinning stopped as abruptly as it had begun.

Kate rubbed her eyes, remembering that she had dreamt about Grammy Mer last night. In the dream, Grammy Mer looked the way she had before she was sick, before the wheelchair. She wore a fancy lace dress and shiny high heels, pointy-toe style. She had stood by Kate's bed, patting her arm and stroking her hair, saying she was going away to a beautiful place. "Someday, we will be together again. Kate, I love you with all my heart," she had said, her voice clear and strong, and, oh, so sweet.

Kate's eyes squinted from the bright light. She looked up at the ceiling. It was not spinning, and the lights were normal now. She then looked to Aunt Abigail and Marilla Marzy. They were busy reading their menus. She touched Etta Ebella's wing; it was its normal size. Kate looked back to the front of the restaurant to see if Grammy Mer was still there. The vision of her was no more.

The muddy Mazda came to a halt on the tree-lined roadway. It sat there, its motor idling, betraying its driver's non-idle thoughts.

Moving the gear into reverse, Tessa backed up several feet and parked the car. Somewhat angled, its right rear tire dug heavily into the soil to the side of the pavement, and its right fender rubbed abrasively against the bark of one of the tall walnut trees. The tree responded by allowing its woody skin to knock off some of the mud from the car's fender, revealing the white paint underneath. The kinder act.

Tessa got out of the car and scurried amidst the tall trees lining the roadway. At the white wooden fence, she held onto the post and placed one foot on the lowest plank, then the other foot, and pulled herself upward, elevating her position. She leaned her torso over the top rail to better survey the lay of the land. Peering through the thicket of trees within the fenced meadow, she could see the horses in the corral. Farther up the interior lane, the tennis courts sat empty, the slight breeze stirring the nets was the only movement in that vicinity.

Returning to the rear of the car, she opened the trunk and found the tool box that her father had kept there. Touching the metal box, she felt her fingertips recoil at the steel of sadness, at the thought of her father's hands toiling, his endless labor, his fruitless labor, using the tools held there. She stroked the metal remembering how her father loved to hate life. Brushing aside the despair, she flipped open the lid. Finding the device she needed, she donned the work gloves he had stuffed into the section intended for the hammer.

She climbed over the wide-planked white fence that sat behind the line of trees flanking the roadway. That was easy enough; it was the second fence that was worrisome. Was it hot, its wires zapping any potential intruders or any attempting escapees, frying their nervous systems with its electrical currents? Knowing Vaynem, the answer was yes.

Taking a deep breath, Tessa touched one gloved finger to the top wire, while almost simultaneously jerking it back. No shocks or tingling sensations gripped her. She tapped another wire, this time leaving her finger a bit longer. Surprisingly, she felt nothing.

Unlocking the handles of the wire cutters, she placed their jaws on the barbed wire and squeezed, slicing through one strand. It fell to the ground. The next wire stubbornly opposed her repeated efforts to disconnect it. She squeezed the cutters, twisting and turning them vigorously; her hands ached. Finally, one more strand broke free. She labored on a third and a fourth to no avail.

Throwing the cutters down on the grass, she stepped on the lowest strand of uncut wire while lifting the upper two wires of the fence. Ever so carefully, she put one leg through and then ducked down, slowly moving her upper body through to the other side. Three of the upper sharp barbs lashed at her, snagging her sweater and scraping her shoulder. The pain was far less irritating than Vaynem's stinking teeth had been. *Besides, what's a little more bloodshed today? Her mission was worth it.* She moved her other leg through the fence and stood on the grass.

A rush of jubilance flowed through her. Ah, victory was sweet, even if she had donated part of her sweater to the fence, its wires looking as if a fuchsia-colored lamb had escaped through them.

Running like a jack rabbit, Tessa zigzagged through the green meadow, darting behind this tree and then that one, working her way up to the corral. "Oh, rotten potatoes," she said. "I should have taken off this sweater." Its bright color was easily visible, even from a distance. But then, she didn't think he felt like standing yet. Although, when he did stagger up, he would be standing directly in front of the windows that viewed this rolling greenbelt, all dotted with trees—walnuts and oaks.

After running a bit farther, she stopped behind a large oak, its burly trunk shielding her. Catching her breath, she rested her head on the layers of bark while listening to the horses. The sounds were eerie. Almost words, the horses' neighs seemed to be an odd syllable conversation, with one of the horses seriously complaining, and about something important. *Is one of them in pain?*

Peeking around the side of the oak tree, she saw the horses at the back of the corral. One was lying down by the water trough. After assessing all the pathways, Tessa changed her strategy, deciding to complete her mission by approaching from behind the barn, not from the side of it.

The two horses in the corral stared at the girl in the torn fuchsia sweater. They both watched:

> ...the girl who slipped silently into the barn.
> ...the girl who came out of the barn with a long leather strop in her hand.
> ...the girl who walked boldly to the corral gate, unlatching it.
> ...the girl who swung the gate to its most open position.
> ...the girl who looped the strop through the gate and the corral fence, tying the gate open, securing it with multiple knots.

Their ears erect, their eyes not blinking, their neighs on mute, they watched the girl:

> ...the girl who ran back into the barn and returned with a bucket of oats

…the girl who spilled and scattered the oats outside the corral gate—all down the tree-lined lane.

…the girl who threw the bucket against the barn door.

…the girl who once again ran among the trees.

…the girl who climbed through the two fences, leaving behind more of her fuchsia sweater.

…the girl who got into the muddy Mazda and sped away.

CHAPTER TWENTY-FOUR

*A*pproaching the Bay Bridge, the red Ferrari changed lanes, moving to the far right, the slow lane, which was not his usual preference, but today, he had been told to drive cautiously. "How you doing so far?" asked Jonah.

Looking through the windshield, Angelique remained focused on the horse emblem on the hood of the car, not on the bridge, not on the heavy traffic, and not on the water down below. Without moving her head or looking at him, she said, "I am okay."

Jonah noted that her voice was shakier than he had ever heard it. He'd best try to distract her. "So, I only heard part of what happened. What exactly transpired with Annateresa's dress?"

"Oh, Jonah, I couldn't believe my eyes when I returned from the garage after you called. The sight was beyond comical; it was hysterical. Annateresa had been wearing one of Laura's new designs, an experiment of sorts, an unusual cut, particularly for delicate fabric. She had assigned all the stitching to her new intern."

Suddenly, a blaring car horn interrupted. Angelique's words ceased, her jaw tightening, her lips closing abruptly.

Jonah eyed the rearview mirror. Behind him, lights flashed on and off. The driver of the yellow BMW obviously wanted him to go faster. *Sorry buddy, not today,* he thought to himself. *Why is that goofball flashing lights at me when he is in the slow lane?* Jonah made no adjustments to his speed.

The driver accelerated, narrowing the distance between the vehicles to mere inches.

Yo, dude, you're loco, Jonah thought. Aloud, he said, "Angelique, I'm sorry, but I need to speed up; this banana Beemer behind me is trying to peel my bumper. With all this traffic, he's dangerous."

A regretful trigger it was, that word *dangerous.* Angelique's eyes instantly glazed over; and then, as if her brain had robotically issued crisis alert signals, her eyelids locked down, covering the once-sparkling sapphires. Her arms folded, gripping her body in a hug, and her chest heaved with rapid, shallow breaths. With her jaws clenched tightly, she forced out the words. "Just. Go. Get across. As quickly as possible."

Jonah maneuvered the gear shift. Checking his side mirrors carefully, he changed lanes and accelerated, leaving the BMW in the slow lane. The crazy guy moved upon the bumper of a Prius, flashing his lights and honking at that car now. *What is wrong with that dude?*

Jonah focused his attention ahead, despite the urge to watch for the Beemer in the rearview mirror. As if Moses were there parting waters, the traffic on the bridge seemed to move automatically to the slow lane, leaving a clear path for Jonah to drive like a rocket, his favorite style.

"Are you breathing?"

"Yes," she said, her voice almost a whisper, her eyes closed, her head tilted back on the seat's headrest.

"Well, when you feel like it, you can open your eyes. The dirty deed is done. We have successfully crossed the bridge," Jonah announced with pride.

Vaynem got out of the steamy shower, wrapped a towel around his waist and padded down the hallway to his home office. Standing over his desk, he booted up his laptop. Clicking on one of the websites registered on his favorites list, he typed in his password and a specific command. Within seconds, a map appeared—a map showing a swath of city streets and a pulsing red dot. Bingo. That's where they were, Jack London Square.

His face wore a look of triumph as he formulated his plan. Yes, it had worked out splendidly to have the tracking device planted behind the dash of the Mercedes. Last week, it had revealed his law clerk's antics. When taking the car to the dealership for service, the kid had driven the Mercedes around town for an hour, had even driven the car over 100 mph. When the young clerk had returned the keys, Vaynem had said, "You're fired." The kid's look of astonishment was still a source of pleasure.

He had yet to deal with his daughter *if he could call her that, mutant that she was.* She had it coming because of her shenanigans, taking his Mercedes out at night two different times now. How she had obtained the keys was the mystery. When he had that piece of the puzzle, and when that orange-haired twerp was out of his house, he had plans for M&M, and no candy she enjoyed was involved.

The white towel fell away from his waist. He threw it over his shoulder as he strutted down the hallway. Halfway, he stopped in front of a decorative mirror and flexed his biceps and practiced shaping his face into various expressions. *It served him well to have the ability to transform in a nanosecond, going from dazzling smile to* menacing scowl.

Upon entering the master bathroom, he stood in front of the full-length mirror, moving in various stances, reveling in every micro-inch of himself. His right arm came above his head and extended outward as if he were popping an imaginary whip. *Yep, the strop in the hay barn would be perfect,* the heavy leather strop that he had used to break Mindy Midnight when she was a filly. His personal brand of candy—breaking fillies, human or animal—tasted delicious to him. *Yes, indeed, that strop would be just the ticket for Marilla Marzy, for Tramp Tessa, for Cow Abigail, and even once again for Miss Mindy Midnight.* The mare's recent egregious behavior—refusing that expensive stallion he had brought in for breeding—had enraged him. *Much revenge to plot,* he mused.

Checking his watch, he hurried to finish getting dressed. Eager to get going, he was also savoring yet another spiteful pleasure to indulge. It would take less than five minutes. He deserved it after all that had gone awry on this Sunday, the flat coupled with not having his fried chicken. He finished packing and walked down the hallway back into his study. He dropped his hanging bag—packed with a week's worth of suits, shirts, and toiletries—onto the leather sofa in front of the windows.

At his desk, he moved the cursor to his favorites list and selected the same website as before. He typed in his password and this time, a different numbered command. Was the meteorite Jaguar on the Bay Bridge yet? Yes, there it was, halfway across, stalled in the far right lane. *Perfect. I'll have to send that goon mechanic an extra tip, a large bottle of Jack Daniels, Blue Label.*

His heart pulsed with satisfaction, contemplating the degree of raw fear she must be experiencing. "Well, Doc Angel, how does that feel? You made a big mistake saying you wouldn't see me anymore, and getting that restraining order," he said aloud, only he and the walls hearing. "Let's see what kind of state you're in at your new boyfriend's party this afternoon, that is, if you ever arrive. And if you do, what kind of party will it be without a birthday boy?"

He sat there, inhaling the pleasure of visualizing her panic at being stuck in the middle of the bridge—her sweaty palms, her rapid breathing, her twirling a long strand of that blondish red hair, her heart pounding, her blood pressure rising, her throat closing, her bridge phobia in full bloom.

Vaynem smiled. *What a fine day it was after all.* Some things had gone as he had planned. He shut down his laptop and slipped it into a padded sleeve in his briefcase. Grabbing the hanging bag from the sofa, and with his briefcase gripped tightly in his other hand, he headed for the stairway.

The oversized trash bag sat waiting at the top of the stairs, precisely where he had positioned it. Drawing his leg back, he gave the bag—filled with the aqua silk comforter that Abigail had designed and sewn—one swift kick. The bag tumbled to the bottom of the stairs.

Marilla Marzy squirmed in the booth, eyeing the restaurant décor. "This is dope, Mom. I dig this place."

"I like it, too. Beginning today, Emmy, we are turning over a new leaf and treating ourselves supremely."

"Then, like, I am ordering dessert first," Marilla Marzy said, her eyes focused on the lower section of the menu. "Yum, they have lava cakes."

"No, Emmy, we are going to dine properly. You must have an entrée that includes protein first, and then you can have any dessert you desire," Abigail said, her shoulders set with unmistakable resoluteness.

Marilla Marzy looked appraisingly at her mother. Lowering her head into the menu again, she mumbled something indistinguishable. Under the table, her hand repeatedly squeezed the side of her abdomen. She sulked, questioning what had happened to her mother who had once been easily manipulated.

"Kate, what are you having for lunch today?" asked Abigail.

"I'm not very hungry now. Can I just have some lemonade and some French fries?" Kate asked. She rubbed her arm and looked nervously around the restaurant.

"Pizza Girl, if I have to eat protein, so do you," retorted M&M.

"I believe they have a kid's menu, Kate. What do you usually order when your Uncle Terrence brings you here?"

"I get the kid's burger, plain, or the grilled cheese with fries on the side."

"Mom, hello. Your cell phone is ringing," said Marilla Marzy.

Abigail fished the phone from her oversized purse. She looked at the number flashing on the screen and hit the side button. The ringing stopped. "Cell phones in restaurants are one of my pet peeves. I am not answering now."

"It's Dad, isn't it?"

Abigail didn't respond. After her phone had beeped to announce a new message, she swiped at the arrow. Gasping, she said, "Twenty missed calls? Why, this is the first time I've heard it ring. I'll deal with this later." She turned her phone completely off and placed it back inside her purse.

"Where is that waiter? I'm ready to order. I'm going to have the calamari, a bacon cheeseburger with fries, and two orders of the lava cakes," announced Marilla Marzy. "You said we were going to dine properly, and that means ordering a starter, an entrée, and a dessert."

Abigail never raised an eyebrow at M&M's robust order. She simply nodded as she contemplated what she could do or say without embarrassing her. Emmy had experienced enough battering today. She would let her daughter enjoy this time before they had to face the monstrous situation awaiting them—the dented Mercedes and a venomous Vaynem. Dread filled her stomach, stealing her appetite. "I will have the Crab Louie salad, the small one."

After the waiter had finished taking their orders, M&M said, "Mom, where are we going when we leave here? Like, I don't think we should go home."

"We'll see, Emmy. I'm working on a plan."

"We could go to my house. I know where there's a key," said Kate.

"No, like, totally, that's one of the first places Dad will look for us."

"Most likely, he will not be bothered with our whereabouts. He will pack for next week and then take my car and go to the airport for his evening flight," said Abigail.

"Are you kidding? He wouldn't pack for himself. You always do it for him. And you know, like, totally, he would not drive your car. He wouldn't be caught dead driving a Yaris. He will try to find us so he can get his glorious Mercedes back. And to punish us because we didn't do as he said, you know, wait for the tow truck, and because you gave Kate her doll back, and, like, because you..."

Interrupting, Abigail reached across the table and put her hand on M&M's. "Emmy, let's just enjoy the view and not discuss your father right now."

Abigail's eyes looked stormy as they took in the view of the eastern waters of the San Francisco Bay. A fog horn sounded. She shifted her gaze and stared into blue topaz.

CHAPTER TWENTY-FIVE

The highway patrol officer leaned into the open window of the Jaguar sedan, his State-of-California badge glinting in the sunlight. The pupils of his brown eyes instantly dilated to their largest setting; such beauty always had that effect on him. Today was, indeed, a lucky day for Officer Duarte Cruz for there was not just one beautiful woman in the car; there were two.

"Ladies, what has happened here?" Duarte inquired in a far kinder voice than he'd intended when he was approaching the stalled vehicle that was blocking traffic and creating a hazard on the busy bridge.

Annateresa said, "Officer, thank heaven you are here. We need some help to get the car out of the way. The engine just suddenly stalled. I cannot get it to start."

From the passenger seat, Laura held the cell phone to her ear. Her head tilted to the side, as she observed the young CHP officer staring at her. Breaking his gaze, she looked back to the small plastic card she had pulled from her wallet. "Yes, that's correct. I am mid way on the Bay Bridge and need a tow truck as soon as possible. No, I need a flatbed truck, not a regular tow truck; my friend's car is a Jaguar XJR."

"Triple A is sending a truck," Annateresa explained.

When Laura clicked off the cell phone, the state patrolman felt disappointed. What could he do to get her to talk some more? She had one sexy voice.

Rifling through the desk in the kitchen, Vaynem found the extra keys to his wife's car, a Toyota Yaris. Grimacing, he remembered their disagreement. Abigail had never appreciated that car; she had wanted a nicer one. *Where did she get off thinking that she deserved to have a luxury automobile? She was spoiled enough, living in the lap of finery, not lifting a finger.*

Ironing, cleaning, cooking, gardening, and sewing was doing nothing in today's world, simple *housework* that was child's play compared to his complex job as a lawyer. Though he had to admit, Abigail had a knack. Their home was beautiful, and she had made all the draperies, upholstered chairs, and refinished old furniture to make it so. And it had made him mad, surprisingly so, when Tessa had lolled on the comforter his wife had designed and made by hand.

His stomach rumbled. Using pot holders, he took the warm roasting pan out of the oven, placing it on the counter. He removed the roaster lid. Taking a large knife, he sliced into the meat, through one of the rib sections. Holding the cut portion over the stainless-steel sink, he hungrily sank his teeth into it. In seconds, he had devoured it, his teeth ripping at the shreds of meat attached to the bone. His jaw open and front teeth jutted forward, his incisors scraped the marrow from the bone. *Mmm, no question, the cow could cook.* But it was Sunday; he should be feasting on fried chicken.

After wiping his mouth with a paper towel and thoroughly washing his hands, he reached for a glass in the cabinet. Not bothering to close the cabinet door, he filled the glass with water and drank half. Using the remaining liquid, he swished it in his mouth and spat it into the sink. Little bits of meat mixed with his saliva clung to the sink's sides.

After checking the time on his watch, he picked up his bag and briefcase and went through the kitchen door that led to the garage. He placed the hanging bag into the trunk of the Yaris. Since, in a few moments, he would pack the trash bag there, too, he left the trunk open. According to his plan, he would dispose of the ruined comforter in the dumpster in the parking garage of his apartment in the city, after he returned from Las Vegas. Abigail knew nothing about the apartment, of course. She honestly believed that he traveled every week.

He placed his briefcase on the front passenger seat and returned to the doorway that led to the kitchen. Before entering, he poked at one of the numbered buttons mounted on the wall. The garage door behind the Yaris began opening. Adjacent on the same wall, an electronic panel caught his eye. A small red light was flashing. It signaled that the electricity to the fence had been turned off. He pushed the button, pressing it until the panel registered a green light, restoring electricity to the barbed wires.

His wife was dumb as a rock. Her priorities with electricity were all wrong. She would rather run the AC or heat, rather than have their property protected. Another lesson, he had to teach her. Perhaps he would have his goon break in one night. Terror, even in small doses, worked well on her.

Planting his feet angrily, Vaynem stomped back into the kitchen and picked up the plastic bag with the comforter. Halfway to the door, he stopped. The trunk to the Yaris had been smaller than he remembered. *Would it fit?* And there would be little time to transfer it to the Mercedes. His goon would already have the tire replaced, bent rim and all, but time would be limited to make it to the airport on time.

With quick jerky motions, he removed the aqua silk mass from the bag and tossed it onto the kitchen floor. With his foot, he moved it around, his crocodile shoes spreading it on the floor like a wrinkled picnic cloth.

Going to the refrigerator, he surveyed its contents. *Yes, the dishes Abigail had prepared ahead for their lunch today would work splendidly.* He removed the casserole of garlic-mashed potatoes and hurled the dish onto the comforter. Smashed bits of the black ceramic and globs of creamy potatoes created an abstract design on the aqua silk. Reaching back into the refrigerator, he found the crystal bowl with the fresh asparagus salad. It was next to go splat. He jumped back so as not to get any of the oil-based vinaigrette dressing on his pants or shoes.

The pans of yeast rolls she had left to rise caught his attention. He jerked the kitchen towels from the dough, now having risen over the sides of the pan. Using a large fork, he stabbed at them, squashing them flat before flinging them onto the mashed potatoes. He looked into the refrigerator for more items. The bowls of fresh strawberries and whipped cream, prepared to top the homemade shortbread cakes, were perfect. *Ah yes, they would add nicely to his artwork, the strawberry juices providing a splendid concealer for Tramp Tessa's blood stains.*

For the finale, he stood on the opposite side of the island. A set of long metal tongs extended his arm the precise length he needed to give the roasting pan a spirited shove. The roaster careened off the granite counter, spattering juicy remnants on walls and cabinets. Prime rib au jus flowed into the mashed potatoes, mixing with broken crystal and ceramic shards, melding into the marinade that now drenched the silk and satin fibers.

Standing back, he admired his artful creation. *Anger management,* he chuckled. Furthermore, the message was clear. *To have the privilege of sleeping in my bed, of living under my roof, Cow Abigail is never to disobey me, and she is never again to vary the menu on Sunday.*

Sporting a carnal grin, Vaynem set the security alarm, its panel tucked behind the winding staircase and quickly exited through the front door.

CHAPTER TWENTY-SIX

"Jonah, this plan doesn't make sense to me. If I understand correctly, you will drive Terrence's car while I drive your car. And I am to follow you. Why?" Angelique sat in the driver's seat of the red Ferrari, looking intently at the buttons and knobs, trying to remember the details of the tutorial he had given her moments ago.

Jonah sighed, shaking his head as if saying he didn't understand either. "Angelique, I wish I could explain. Maybe you haven't known Terrence long enough. Are you aware of his, you know, visions?"

"Does this have anything to do with Kate and her angel doll?" asked Angelique.

"Yes, we are supposed to pick them up from Lancaster's. The aunt's name is Abigail. My understanding of the situation is limited. I'm simply following his instructions."

"Okay, no more questions. Let's go. I'm on my A-game now."

Holding keys in his right hand, Jonah tossed them up in the air, catching them with his left hand behind his back. "Alrighty, but at some point, I want to hear the rest of the story about that dress unraveling. That must have been one beautiful sight." He whistled loudly, cat-call style, obviously thinking about seeing Annateresa unclothed, her dress a pile of threads on the floor.

Angelique rolled her eyes and started the Ferrari's engine.

A few moments later, the lamb-pasta car backed out of the garage at 537 Spruce Street, where it had been parked since Terrence had been in the hospital. When it drove out of the driveway, the Ferrari followed closely behind it, a lamb and horse caravan.

Kate tried not to look at the calamari. Her stomach flopped around with wormy memories. If only, M&M—or Emmy, as her mother now called her—would let the waiter remove the dish. They were already eating dessert, and yet, every once in a while, M&M forked a calamari and stuffed it into her mouth along with chocolate lava cake bits.

When she had a particularly large calamari dangling from the tines of her fork, Marilla Marzy paused and scowled. Her green eye and the brown one both bore into her little cousin, reminding Kate never to tell their wormy secret.

Kate squirmed in her seat, stroking Etta Ebella's wing.

Aunt Abigail sipped a cappuccino, her raisin eyes now resembling black licorice jelly beans as they bulged with bewilderment.

Marilla Marzy had gone to the bathroom three times, staying for ten minutes or more each time. Lunch was taking forever. Still, she ate, occasionally burping, more often grabbing at her stomach as if fire-breathing dragons were flogging her innards.

Bored, Kate stirred the melted ice cream floating in her dessert dish. While watching the tiny vanilla vortex her swirling spoon had created in the glass, she felt her napkin slide to the floor. Setting Etta Ebella aside, she slid down in the booth, reaching for the napkin with her foot. She couldn't reach it, so she tucked her head under the table. Her napkin was wet. What had spilled? Kate peered around and was then so shocked by what she saw that she bumped her head on the tabletop trying to get back up into her seat.

"Help, Aunt Abigail, Emmy's uh…sick. Yucky," Kate screeched.

"What, what's wrong?" Abigail stood and then saw the stream of liquid flowing down her daughter's legs.

Marilla Marzy, whose skin had lost all its natural pink color, sat unmoving, seemingly paralyzed. Suddenly, her chest heaved and food bits and liquid began spewing from her mouth, projectile mode. People in the booths next to them jumped, moving quickly away, out of range of the putrefied rain. The entire restaurant came to a halt, everyone staring.

"Someone, call 911," a woman screamed. Waiters ran every which way, dropping plates and glasses.

The charming restaurant, which had earlier felt like a safe sanctuary to Kate, was now utter chaos. The disgorgement from M&M's mouth didn't stop, except when the stream was temporarily paused by her choking screams.

CHAPTER TWENTY-SEVEN

Rounding the corner of the circular driveway, Vaynem stepped onto the stone pathway that led to the garage. What he saw caused the veins in his neck to bulge. "What the hay?"

Armani ties, Brioni shirts, and Zegna suits lay scattered on the main driveway in front of the garage, high-dollar designer clothes chewed and spread among piles of manure—horse manure. On Vaynem's right, Daisy Daylight was lying down in the shade of an oak tree. She was breathing heavily.

With her backside to Vaynem, Mindy Midnight's nose poked around in the trunk of the Yaris, sniffing the fragrant spilled toiletries. Her back hoof rested on the leather hanging bag, or what was left of its shredded parts and the broken toiletry remnants, which lay crushed in pieces under the car's bumper.

Vaynem stood there as if in a trance. Without a word, his hands went to his belt buckle. Quickly, he jerked the lizard belt free from his trouser loops. Yelling obscenities, he popped it at Mindy Midnight, slapping one side of her rump.

She jumped, sidling her rear around, her neck twisting to face him, snorting with her nostrils twitching. He popped the belt again, this time grazing the side of her face. Mindy Midnight's lips rolled backward, baring her large teeth. She bucked and reared up, her two front hooves suspended mid-air as they aimed to strike the man with the belt, the man who had mistreated her again and again.

Vaynem stepped back just enough to miss the blow. When Mindy Midnight's hooves came down on the driveway, her nostrils appeared to be having spasms. She snorted loudly; then she let out one horrendous horse sneeze, her nostril hairs riddled with after-shave lotion.

The sneeze blew Vaynem back, one of his crocodile shoes landing in a rounded pile of manure. The gooey slickness sent him skidding across the driveway. He lost his balance, falling onto the concrete. While scrambling to get up, his hand slipped into another manure pile, defeating his brief attempt at verticalness. Horizontal again, he lay on the driveway.

No, not his hands. They could not get dirty. He examined his manicured nails. Dung coated the cuticles, and gooey droppings clung to the underneath side of his nail tips. His palm was completely covered. Repulsed, he freaked, his heart raced; he felt as if he couldn't breathe.

A black hoof came down on his lower leg and foot. Mindy Midnight lifted her other front hoof and stepped to the side of him. For seconds, her full weight remained poised on the one hoof.

When his ankle bone shattered, Vaynem's scream could be heard for miles, his pain rankling every square foot of the ranch acreage. Only the horses heard.

A uniformed EMT rushed into Lancaster's. A second followed quickly rolling a gurney. The wait staff and patrons stood huddled together in the back corner, as far away from Marilla Marzy as they could get.

Abigail, who had remained amazingly calm, motioned the EMTs over to the booth where she had managed to get M&M into a lying-down position. She wiped her daughter's face—covered in perspiration—with cool, moist napkins, having dipped them into her water glass, still filled with ice. She cooed to her that everything would be okay, that help was on the way. Her voice oozed with reassurance, as any good mother's would, while disguising how scared she was for her baby girl; albeit, a teenage one.

Kate sat on the other side of the booth, holding onto Etta Ebella for dear life. The doll's wings quivered against Kate's heart. Tears streamed down Kate's face.

The EMTs worked like robots in fast motion. They turned the table on its side to better access her body. In minutes, they were wheeling M&M out of the restaurant.

Abigail grabbed her purse and threw a wad of money on the seat cushion. She took Kate's hand, pulling her along. "Hurry, sweetheart." Kate felt like her arm was being yanked from its socket as they ran.

Even outdoors, Marilla Marzy's moans and screams hung heavily in the air, interspersed with her gagging and coughing up an icky liquid. One of the EMTs turned to Abigail. "Ma'am, you and the little girl cannot go in the ambulance. You will have to meet us at Alta Bates Emergency."

"But my car's two blocks away."

"I'm sorry, Ma'am. There is nothing I can do. We don't have room, and we don't know yet what we're dealing with here. It's not the kind of situation where we can take a little one," he said, nodding in Kate's direction.

The ambulance doors closed, locking M&M inside.

Abigail burst into tears.

At that very moment, Kate spotted Uncle TT's silver spaghetti car turning into the valet parking lane. She squinted her eyes; was it Uncle TT's car or one like it? Clearly, it was his car, but it was not Uncle TT driving, and he did not let anyone drive his lamb-pasta car. The Lamborghini's gull wing door opened and a male voice called out, "Kate, over here."

Abigail's eyes narrowed, looking suspiciously at the driver as he got out of the car. "Who are you?" she asked.

Before Abigail could stop her, Kate jumped into the man's arms. "Aunt Abigail; it's Jonah; it's okay." Wrapping her arm around Jonah's neck, she said, "Jonah, you're driving Uncle TT's car. Why?"

"I have no idea who you are. Leave us alone. That's my daughter in the ambulance. I have to get to the hospital, to Alta Bates." With anger rising in her voice, Abigail said, "Kate, come here, right now. We cannot waste time."

The siren whirred as the ambulance pulled out of the driveway, almost colliding with a red Ferrari.

Jonah, holding Kate and Etta Ebella in his arms, stepped toward Abigail, extending his hand, "Hello, I am Terrence's friend, Jonah Caleebe. I'm sorry for the circumstances with your daughter, but Terrence asked us to pick up Kate. He somehow thought you would need to make other arrangements for her today, that there was a problem."

Her forehead wrinkled, Abigail stammered, "What, Terrence, what? And who is *us*? Oh, I cannot cope."

"Here's Angelique now," said Jonah, pointing toward the street. He raised his voice speaking loudly, almost yelling. "She is also a friend of Terrence and she is a doctor. She can take you to Alta Bates and help you with your daughter."

Angelique's high heels clicked on the pavement as she ran over to them. She nodded to Jonah; she had heard his cues. "Abigail, I am Angelique Donahorn. Come with me. I will drive you to Alta Bates and take you through the physician's entrance. It's much faster."

Exasperated, Abigail looked one to the other. "Kate, do you know these people?"

"Yes, they're Uncle TT's friends. Go with Dr. Donahorn. She'll help you and Emmy."

For a brief second, Abigail looked to Etta Ebella. The two topaz eyes blinked. "Okay, let's go," Abigail replied.

Angelique took Abigail's hand in hers, and they ran toward the sidewalk. The Ferrari raced away, all before Jonah had time to get Kate properly settled in the lamb-pasta car.

"Your uncle told me to loop this seat belt around you twice since we don't have your safety seat," Jonah said. "He's some dude, isn't he?"

Gently, especially considering his large hands, Jonah wrapped the seat belt around Kate. When he lifted her arm to put it through the loop, Kate winced. He tugged on her elbow a bit to pull her arm on through the loop. Kate burst into tears.

"Whoa, Princess, I am sorry. I guess I'm not any good at handling little tykes like you. I'm used to handling bulky fashion trunks."

"It's okay," Kate said, her flowing tears negating her assenting words.

"Has something happened to your arm?"

Kate could only nod. In her lap, Etta Ebella blinked her eyes three times in succession.

Jonah's sweet, pecan-pie eyes darted from Etta Ebella to Kate, as if the pecans were disturbed. He looked back to the angel doll sitting perfectly still, seemingly inanimate now in Kate's lap. Must have been his imagination, he thought. That doll didn't look like one of those with a computer chip that moved its eyes at random. *Or did it?* Focusing back on Kate, he said, "I'll have Angelique or a nurse check out your arm when we get to the hospital. Okay?"

"Can I see my Uncle TT?" Kate asked.

"Oh yeah, way better than just see him, you can help us celebrate his birthday. Do you like chocolate cake?"

Kate's fair skin blanched. Her hand flew to her mouth as she stifled a gag.

A yellow BMW rounded the bend on the ranch road, speeding past the culvert that now housed a blue blanket.

A few miles away, Vaynem lay on his driveway, his leg mangled, his pain escalating with every nanosecond. His cell phone held in his lone clean hand, Vaynem spoke, breathing deeply between words, giving the man directions, and then the code for the entrance gate.

Mindy Midnight stood under the oak tree, giving Daisy Daylight affectionate and comforting nudges, encouraging her to stand up and move. Daisy Daylight staggered up, lumbered along, following Mindy Midnight to a thicket of trees by the pond, the opposite direction from the barn. Once behind the grassy knoll, Mindy Midnight gave a short series of neighs to Daisy Daylight, who immediately lay down in the tall lush green grass that was completely out of sight from the house.

Fifteen minutes later, the BMW sped along the tree-lined roadway for the second time. Vaynem lay sprawled awkwardly on its back seat. He was barefoot and shirtless, his shirt having been drenched from the water hose when his goon had power-washed his hand. It registered with him, the pleasure he saw in the man's eyes when using a more forceful spray than needed. The smirk on the guy's face, when seeing Vaynem's predicament and his pain when being lifted into the car, had also not gone unnoticed.

"Boss, I'm telling you the tire had already been changed. The spare looked perfect."

"Impossible," yelled Vaynem. "You stupid idiot; you must have looked at the wrong tire."

The BMW suddenly halted. The car sat there, its motor idling, the driver staring out the window, staring at the smoke. He opened the car door to get out.

'What are you doing? You stupid baboon, I need to get to the hospital right now," Vaynem said, his speech faltering between breaths.

"I need a pit stop, Boss. Just a second." The driver walked over between the trees to the white wooden fence. *Hmph*, he thought, noticing that some of the wires of the second fence were down. Shiny metal caught his eyes. A pair of wire cutters lay strewn in the grass. Pink fuzz sizzled on the wires; some chunks of the fuzz had dropped into the grass. Wisps of smoke wafted upward.

The BMW once again sped down the roadway to the entrance gate. *Stupid idiot and a stupid baboon, was he, now? Well, okay.* If that's what he was, then there was no need to report the cut electric wires, the smoke, and the pink fuzz sizzling in the grass.

His eyes alight with glee, the driver said, "So, Boss, about your Mercedes, there is one thing you should know, aside from the tires, which are all fine. I walked around that car five times. By the way, it was plenty tough to locate it in that six-level parking garage. I finally found it parked on the top deck squeezed between two over-sized SUVs, which had blocked the signal. You need to upgrade your spy software."

"Get on with it, what about my car?"

"I don't think you'll be any too happy when you see it. The entire driver's side and the roof are completely covered with dents like it was in a hail storm or a drive-by shooting."

Vaynem clutched at his chest, feeling like he couldn't breathe. Pain shot down his left arm.

Watching Vaynem gasp and writhe in the back seat, he adjusted his rearview mirror, not even trying to conceal his contemptuous leer. The driver said, "Boss, is Alta Bates okay? It's the nearest hospital."

CHAPTER TWENTY-EIGHT

*T*he wheelchair sat empty, as did the cabernet-colored leather chair. The television screen was not droning loudly. It was blank.

Gordon's heart raced. Feeling frantic, he fumbled with the keys. Finally, the key fit properly into the dead bolt. He locked the house and ran to get into the ambulance.

The EMT was adjusting the oxygen mask, sliding the tubes above her ears, pinning down some of the reddish blonde strands. He motioned Gordon to squeeze into a small space aside the gurney. His adroit hands worked quickly as he sought a vein for the IV drip.

Ever so gently, Gordon took his wife's other hand in his and leaned over her ashen face. He so wanted to look into her eyes, the beautiful blue-green eyes of his Miss America, but they remained closed. He spoke softly. "Kara, honey, we're heading to the hospital now. Dr. Christianson is meeting us there. He'll make everything okay."

The EMT exchanged a glance with the driver, their eyes meeting in the rearview mirror. He nodded and the siren whirred.

The young LVN, Priscilia Pereira, wheeled the patient down the hallway of the neurology floor of Alta Bates.

"Where exactly are you taking me?" Terrence asked.

"I've already told you that your doctor ordered an MRI, " she said, glad that he could not read her face, glad for the fabric brace that kept his head from turning, glad for the chin strap that kept him from turning to look upward at her while she walked behind him.

"But I had a CT scan and an MRI yesterday, just a few hours ago. I was cleared to sit up for short periods."

"Yes, I know, but the technician misunderstood yesterday's orders and failed to get all the post-surgery views the doctor requested. This morning, your doctor asked for additional images."

Priscilia turned down a small hallway, making her way through the hospital maze. She had to avoid the head nurse's station. After all, she could lose her job for what she was doing. This patient, recovering from a craniocerebral injury and surgery, was still restricted regarding movement. An MRI had not been ordered.

She checked her watch. Ten more minutes. Then it would be time for the injection. A syringe filled with sedative waited, hidden in the confines of her pocket. Sedative was not its only contents; the potent liquid was laced with shellfish serum.

CHAPTER TWENTY-NINE

*A*ngelique flashed her physician's badge and waved to the security guard at the doctors' entrance at Alta Bates Medical. He nodded. She rushed Abigail down the hallway and through the wide double doors of ER. After speaking briefly to the charge nurse, Angelique stopped at one of the twelve sets of green curtains in the first hallway. A plastic plaque mounted on the wall identified the cubicle as ER-4. She told Abigail to wait in the hallway.

Adjusting her neck lanyard, rendering her physician's badge full-view status, Angelique slipped through the curtains, introduced herself to the two nurses though she recognized one. First, she asked if a doctor had examined the young patient yet and then explained that the girl's mother was waiting just outside. Both nurses bobbled their heads in consent. Moving the curtain a bit, she asked Abigail to come inside.

Abigail stepped into the cubicle. There, she saw one nurse checking Marilla Marzy's blood pressure while another nurse on the other side of her bed was attempting to insert an IV into her daughter's hand. That nurse, a robust blonde man who had an RN badge clipped to his blue scrubs, a tag that bore the name Chancellor Wilmington, focused on Marilla Marzy.

He said, "Honey, I know you are hurting, but I need you to be as still as possible." His hand gently placed on M&M's wrist as if calming her, he nodded hello to Abigail and then to Angelique. He said, "Dr. Donahorn, to answer your question, Dr. Sibler has performed a brief exam. She ordered an IV, lab work, and an abdominal sonogram."

Tears mixed with mascara blurred Abigail's vision. Her daughter's face was deathly pale, and her moans were haunting. Surprised that she was already wearing a hospital gown, Abigail suppressed the images and stench of M&M's soiled clothes. She hoped they had put them in the trash. If they had not, she would.

The nurse, a small Asian woman, who was affixing the blood pressure cuff, said, "Now that your mother's here, perhaps we can get your name."

M&M tried to speak, but her mouth was blocked by a small plastic container that was attached to her mouth. A receptacle to catch regurgitations, the contraption resembled an oxygen bag and was attached with tubing behind her ears.

After recording M&M's blood pressure and other vitals, the nurse put the chart in the slot attached to the foot of the bed. She placed a small plastic tub on the bed next to M&M and said, "I'm removing this bag. From now on, you can spit up into the tub. Okay?" Her hands clothed in white latex gloves, she removed the plastic bag and carefully zipped the top liner to its closed position. "I'm taking this to the lab," she said to the other nurse. She placed a white washcloth in M&M's free hand. Her sneaker-clad feet padded out through the curtains.

The remaining nurse tilted his head in M&M's direction. "Her name and age?"

"Marilla Marzy Moxsin. Fifteen years old," Abigail said, patting her daughter's leg.

M&M shook her head vigorously, a vehement no.

Guessing at her daughter's intended communication, Abigail said, "That is her formal name, but she prefers to be called Emmy."

While clutching her stomach, M&M slightly moved her head, indicating yes.

"Emmy, it is, then," said the nurse, in a matter-of-fact voice, his tone modulated like an NPR radio host. He double checked the IV needle and adjusted the drip rate on the IV bag hanging above the bed. His cleft chin pointing in the direction of Abigail, he said, "Have you checked in with the admitting office yet? They are expecting you to check in there first. Paperwork, you know."

"Not yet," said Abigail, her eyes filling with tears again.

"Don't worry; we will take care of your daughter."

"Abigail, it is best if you check in now; they will need your insurance information and, more importantly, your signature since she is a minor. It shouldn't take too long. I'll show you the way," Dr. Donahorn began opening the curtain.

Now that space was clear on one side of the bed, Abigail stepped close to her daughter. "Emmy, I'll be back as soon as I can."

Terrified eyes, one brown and one green, stared back at Abigail, both were pleading for help.

The young CHP trooper turned off the flashing lights of the patrol car as he neared Alta Bates. He drove into the visitors' parking lot and found a space near the front entrance.

Regretful that the drive from the bridge had not taken longer, he eyed Laura's porcelain skin—her arms and legs—from what he could see of them.

From the passenger seat next to him, she extended her creamy soft hand, reaching over to his on the steering wheel. "I don't know how we can begin to thank you, Officer Cruz," she said in her forever hoarse voice, the one he found ultra sexy.

"Yes, we are grateful," said Annateresa from the backseat. "Not only for the ride and for rescuing us on the bridge, but also for finding that tracking device illicitly placed on my sister's car."

"We would love for you stay and join us for the party. The German Chocolate cake we have in your trunk is beyond delicious. An extra large serving is yours if you'll stay," said Laura.

"My, that sure sounds good since I missed lunch, especially if I could have a big corner piece," he said. An unabashed boyish grin spread across his face, showcasing his dimples and sculpting his cheeks.

Laura chuckled, "Only if I get the other corner piece—my favorite, too."

Officer Duarte Cruz checked his watch. "Well, I guess I can at least help you ladies get all your party stuff inside."

Guiding Abigail down the ER hallway, Angelique noticed that some of her morning anxiety was returning. It couldn't be the dread of the bridge this time. Thoughts of her mother were floating through her mind again like they had done intermittently all morning. Her mother's face intermixed with concern for Terrence. *What a puzzling day.*

Marilla Marzy's situation appeared serious, but she was in good hands with Dr. Sibler. Her reputation was stellar, particularly as a diagnostician.

She would get Abigail squared away at the admitting office; then she would go to Terrence's room and check on him.

Angelique's pager beeped. Expecting it to be conveying the arrival of Annateresa and Laura, she was in for a surprise. The message was marked urgent, from Jonah.

A yellow BMW careened into the emergency entrance at Alta Bates Medical. It slowed and parked near the end of the driveway, away from the large sliding doors of the public entrance. "Boss, I'll go inside and get help. Get someone to bring a stretcher."

"Okay. Hurry it up, though. After this, I want you to drive back to the ranch and get rid of those horses. No mercy shots. I want ugly."

"Sure thing, Boss. Ugly is my pretty."

"Break the black one's legs, and then kill the white one in the sight of the black one. Then shoot the black one in the stomach and leave her to bleed to death."

"Beautiful. Consider it done."

As he walked away from the car, an ambulance with full sirens whirring pulled into the same curved driveway, quickly turning into the second driveway marked *Ambulances Only*. It backed up to the private doorway.

The BMW driver suddenly stopped walking toward the public entrance to the emergency room. Instead, he walked to the side of the building. His boss would just have to wait. Let him lie in agony a few more minutes. Grinning, he lit a cigarette.

Jophia Josephesus entered the images in the hospital database and rolled the sonogram machine through the curtains of ER-4. That was one sick girl. Eager to hear what Dr. Sibler would say about these pictures, she rushed down the hallway.

It was a trek to the main lab. After the incident last week, all equipment had to be returned immediately, signed in and signed out. Inefficient, but necessary, she thought, remembering the incident with Kate and that nurse's aid, Virginia Veetlehurst.

Halfway back to the lab, she found herself no longer thinking about the alleged antics of Virginia Veetlehurst or that odd mass she had observed when doing the sonogram on that teenage girl.

Instead, she was daydreaming about what the hospital would be like if it had inspiring artwork, original art instead of mundane posters on the gray walls. Grimacing, she caught a man's eye, a man heading in the opposite direction, a man she knew well—Alta Bates' premium orthopedic surgeon—her husband, Dr. Joe Josephesus.

"Hey, hey, what a nice surprise," he said.

The sight of his handsome face sparked pure joy in her heart. Twelve years now, they had been married, and his wide smile still made her feel like a schoolgirl. His square jaw spoke volumes about his inner strength and the brightness of his eyes still captivated her.

Familiar with the annoyed expression she had been wearing before she saw him, he said, "You know, my bride, this hospital doesn't need fine art on the walls with beauty like you gracing the space."

Suppressing a giggle, she kissed her fingers and pressed them onto his arm. "Want to grab some coffee? I'll have a few minutes after I drop the equipment in the lab."

"Oh, babe, I would love to but I have been paged to ER—a man with a crushed tibia."

"Alright, my love. We'll catch up later."

His eyes twinkled. His long legs strode down the hallway to ER.

"Mrs. Moxsin, have you been able to reach your husband yet?"

"No, Dr. Sibler, he must be on an airplane. He is not answering his cell phone."

"Your daughter is very ill. She has an intestinal obstruction. I've called in the leading gastroenterologist in this hospital, Dr. Morgan Ryan. He is reviewing the scans and tests results now. He has asked for a surgeon, Dr. Valeah, to review the case."

Abigail swallowed hard. "Obstruction? You mean, like a tumor?"

"The images are not consistent with a hard mass, but there is clearly a blockage."

"Surgery? She seems a bit better now. Aren't there medications to try before jumping to surgery?" Abigail asked.

"The NG tube we inserted earlier has drained off enough fluid from your daughter's stomach to relieve some of the pressure; that's why her symptoms are improved. But we are concerned that the obstruction is cutting off the blood supply to the colon. In this case, we cannot tarry. We need your permission to perform surgery, your signature on this form."

Dr. Sibler handed Abigail a clipboard. A pen dangled from a chain attached to the top of the board. "Please review this form. We'll do our best to answer any questions that you have. I must remind you, though, that time is of the essence."

CHAPTER THIRTY

*A*bigail gripped her cell phone. Feeling alone and scared, she looked at her daughter, who was ashen and writhing with pain. "Okay, Dr. Sibler, I will sign, but I would like to scan, quickly read over, the release form first. I'll just take a... ."

A sudden outburst of loud obscenities fanned the green curtains, interrupting Abigail mid-sentence. Her face froze. Marilla Marzy's mismatched eyes flew open.

A man's caterwaul of unholy screaming penetrated their cubicle. It sounded as if it were magnified, piped over a loudspeaker, although the *a capella* cacophony originated four rooms down in ER-8. The baritone voice was yelling, cursing the nurses, castigating the hospital, demanding another doctor, screeching that no African-American doctor was touching his leg, certainly not doing surgery on it, and no Indian, Muslim, Jewish, Asian, Hispanic or woman doctor was touching his leg, either.

Abigail knew that baritone voice. It was Vaynem.

"Oh, for Christ's sake," said the fair-skinned nurse working in ER-10, "this is California." She sighed as she continued hooking up the heart and respiration monitors.

Her colleague's head swayed from side to side, a blonde lock of hair falling onto his forehead. "What makes you think that California is devoid of prejudice?" he asked.

The intern, a Middle-Eastern doctor sporting a perfectly cut auburn bob, who stood at the foot of the bed, rolled her eyes and tilted her head in agreement, but made no comment as she checked the patient's ankles and feet for edema.

The patient didn't comment either, but not because she lacked the desire. Her eyelids fluttered, yet she could not speak. Wordless, the only sounds that came from her were heavy breathing and gurgling in her lungs.

"I apologize for the nature of our conversation, Mrs. Kindrick, and for the commotion down the hall. It's a rare event for Alta Bates ER," said the nurse, Chancellor Wilmington. "Your husband will return shortly from submitting your insurance information. And Dr. Christianson should arrive soon." He spoke surprisingly softly for his oversized burliness, which was not a common trait among male nurses. If he weren't wearing scrubs and the RN badge, he could easily look like a professional football player or a bodyguard. His hands, though, were those of a dancer. With artful gentleness, he lifted the patient's head and adjusted the pillow under her shoulders, trying to make it easier for her to breathe.

A hand, ensconced in a white latex glove, parted the green curtains, making a small slit-like opening. From behind the curtain, a female cleared her throat in that commanding attention sort of way. She said, "Chance, are you where you can step out for a minute? Your presence is needed in ER-8."

Jophia smiled at the text message, "How about that coffee? I'm free after all." *Perfect,* she was already heading to the cafeteria. She slowed her pace to key in her reply.

At the coffee kiosk, she ordered two large lattés, one with cinnamon and one with extra vanilla. While waiting, she eyed the cafeteria tables, clusters of people here and there, some tables occupied by visitors, some by hospital personnel. Two nurses stood to leave from a small table for two in the corner. *Yes, that table would be perfect for her and her sweet husband to enjoy a few relaxing moments together.* Although there were plenty of other tables, she wanted that one. It looked cozy.

In her mind's eye, she surrounded that table with white light and visualized Joe and her sitting there, all while sending the table a message: *Wait for me.* Her mental exercise complete, she watched as a man carrying a food tray started toward her chosen table, but as he neared it, he turned away, opting for a different table.

It amazed her how few people could stand in the presence of white light. Smiling to herself, she was confident that no one else would sit there now. Energetically, the table belonged to her for at least a few more minutes. She loved employing this bit of quantum physics in her daily life. It worked for parking spaces, and for creating space away from smokers, and for designer clothing that she wanted to buy, but only when it was marked down to an affordable price.

Balancing the over-filled cups on the tray, Jophia headed for the back corner. Just as she leveled the tray on the table, an unfamiliar voice called to her. A long arm reached from the next table. A hand was extended to her before she could speak.

"Mrs. Josephesus? I'm Jonah Caleebe, and my little friend here would like to talk to you. Excuse me for not getting up, but my lap is quite occupied."

"What?" Jophia said, jerking her head to the side in surprise. "Why, my sweet Katie girl, Princess Kate, what are you doing here?" Jophia's smile quickly turned into a frown. "My goodness, what has happened to you now?"

Kate's head rested against Jonah's chest, her body appearing tiny curled in the lap bowl his long, lanky torso provided. One arm held Etta Ebella, and the other was in a sling, propped on a small pillow. Still wearing the bandages on her facial stitches, she was a sight, looking like a disaster survivor.

Nearing the table, Dr. Joe said, "Well, look who's here. Is this our Kate?" Gently, he patted Kate's head, and then he extended his hand to Jonah. "Joe Josephesus," he said, introducing himself.

"Pleased to meet you, sir. I'm Jonah Caleebe, a friend of Terrence."

"Hey, Princess, what's happened to your arm?" Joe said, furrowing his brow.

Kate, who been about to drift off to sleep, looked bewildered and tired. She yearned to close her eyes. They fluttered as she tried to think of how to explain what had happened to her arm. Then she saw Dr. Donahorn approaching their table. She relaxed into Jonah's lap.

Holding a folder of X-rays, Angelique joined the coffee cluster. "Hello, Jophia. It's good to see you again. Is this your husband?" Extending her hand, she said, "Hello, Dr. Josephesus. Angelique Donahorn. It's such an honor to meet you. I've heard about you and your great work for years."

"Dr. Donahorn. The pleasure is indeed mine. I can say the same for you."

"Please call me Angelique."

He pointed to his chest. "Joe." Bending down to look at Kate's arm, he said, "Now, what has happened to our Katie girl?"

Exchanging an exasperated look with Jonah, Angelique said, "We aren't sure. It appears that at a minimum, she has a bruised bone. Her arm was hurting whenever she moved it, so Jonah paged me. I took her to X-ray and put a sling on the arm to minimize movement and pain until we could arrive at a diagnosis and proper treatment. If you have time, Joe, I'd like for you to review her X-rays."

"Absolutely." Dr. Joe pulled up an adjoining chair. "Kate, do you mind if I examine your arm?"

"Jonah, Dr. Josephesus is an orthopedic surgeon," explained Angelique. "A Stanford scholar, he's known as the one of the very best in the Bay Area. Have you two met?"

"Yes, we did, but I didn't know that I was meeting a celebrity."

"Now, don't give him a big head," laughed Jophia, her eyes shining with pride.

Dr. Joe gently removed the sling and pulled up her sleeve. Kate winced. His lips stretched across his teeth, an expression of disgust. The bruise, a blurred thumbprint, loomed on Kate's upper arm. Recognizable to him, he had seen more outlines of thumbs than he ever wanted to see on children's and women's upper arms. An imprint like that usually meant the humerus was also bruised and was possibly fractured which could cause future orthopedic problems—both arm and shoulder difficulties.

"Kate, I know that your parents are away on vacation. Someone with some muscle has squeezed your arm super hard. Who was it?"

"My uncle."

Incredulous, Dr. Joe asked, "Terrence?"

"No, no, no, not Uncle TT," cried out Kate." It was Uncle Vaynem, Aunt Abigail's husband."

"Honey, Abigail is Carly's sister. Kate is staying with her this week while she and Kal are away," said Jophia.

"Did your aunt bring you to the hospital?" Dr. Joe inquired.

"No, Jonah did," Kate said quietly, her chin tucked down, resting on her pink collar.

Trying to explain, Jonah said, "Terrence contacted me around noon today requesting that Angelique and I pick up Kate. Long story short, Kate's teenage cousin became ill. Kate's aunt, the girl's mother, is with her in the ER downstairs."

"Her cousin? Would that be Marilla Moxsin?" asked Jophia.

"Yes, that's my cousin," said Kate.

"Moxsin?" Angelique asked, swallowing hard.

"Kate, you said your uncle's name is Vaynem? Is his last name Moxsin, too?" asked Dr. Joe.

Jophia noticed her husband's clenched jaw and how that tiny little muscle near his earlobe was flinching, betraying his otherwise calm face.

Kate nodded yes, leaning her head back onto Jonah's chest. She felt Etta Ebella's wing astir.

"Vaynem Moxsin is your uncle? You have been staying at his home this week?" Angelique blurted out the questions. Her sapphire eyes were ablaze, visibly disturbed.

Slowly, Kate nodded. She watched as a red flare shot out from Angelique's heart. *Uh-oh, Dr. Donahorn is mad,* Kate thought. The red flare was not unlike the red swirl she now saw in Dr. Joe's heart. Kate felt Etta Ebella's wing shudder as if it had been hurt when thrown into the trunk of the car, as if it, too, was angry at Vaynem.

"Jonah, can you stay with Kate for a few more minutes? I need to speak to Joe and Jophia in private."

"Sure, Angelique, I'm down with that." Jonah winked at Kate. "The princess and I have a date with the fountain in the courtyard. We're going wishing." He jangled the coins in his pocket.

Dr. Joe replaced the sling on Kate's arm. Standing, he said, "You two have fun wishing. Angelique, let's step down the hall. I want to review these X-rays."

Although Jophia didn't know Angelique Donahorn well, she was adept at reading her husband's countenance. Judging by his face and hers, trouble was brewing, and it had to do with the man named Vaynem Moxsin.

CHAPTER THIRTY-ONE

In room 1230 of Alta Bates, the new festive appointments contrasted sharply with the otherwise stark room.

Balloons, a dazzling bouquet, adorned the rolling tray table, which also served as the resting place for a square-shaped cake. The cake's icing showcased marine-blue calligraphy style lettering: **Happy Birthday Terrence.** Thirty-five candles, dark chocolate in color, were placed in a latticework design around the lettering. Sophisticated and handsome, the cake reflected bespoke detail.

On the bedside table, a square crystal vase held lush tropical flowers. Blackish brown pebbles filled the vase. The dark pebbles in contrast with the flowers—red Ginger mixed with orange-and-blue Bird of Paradise—perfectly complemented the German chocolate cake and the balloons, which almost looked edible themselves— chocolate brown orbs that shimmered with milk-chocolate and pewter-colored glitter.

An exquisite bow, multiple strands of textured ribbon—red, orange, and marine blue—all edged in dark brown satin, graced the balloon cluster. The bow's strands flowed downward like painted rain, all the way to the tabletop. Pewter serving plates, square in style, and brown linen napkins waited next to the cake.

As for people, the hospital room was empty. No doctors. No nurses. No visitors. No patient.

"Mr. Moxsin, you must quiet down, or we will call security to escort you off the premises. We have patients here that are fighting for their lives," said Chancellor, the tall, burly nurse.

His eyes like a rabid watchdog, Vaynem studied the blonde man. "Are you a doctor?"

"No, RN. Here, let me take a look at your leg," Chancellor gently lifted the sheet.

"Get out, don't touch me, you faggot nurse." Vaynem spat the words, his spittle coating each syllable with irascible bile. His neck veins protruded outward like inflamed exclamation points.

"Sir, you will need to make other arrangements for treatment."

"This hospital cannot refuse me treatment. I'll sue," he yelled, his left arm flexed, his hand fisted, repeatedly clenching and unclenching.

"This hospital is not refusing you treatment, Mr. Moxsin. You are refusing to let this hospital's staff, a highly qualified staff, treat you," Chancellor replied, grateful for his brief stint in law school.

Seething inside, Chancellor walked through the curtains and collided with a woman, the mother of the girl in ER-4, a woman who looked scared and was wringing her hands. A combination he detested. But somehow, being so close to her upward turned face, the icicle forming in his heart melted away for she had the saddest, yet most luminous, dark eyes he had ever seen. Something inside him lurched. Chancellor stood stock still.

Abigail held his gaze for mere seconds; she then stepped to the side, demure in mien, and disappeared through the green curtains to her husband's bedside.

"What are *you* doing here?" Vaynem screeched even louder, his voice a barbed baritone boomerang gone wild in the ER. "You stupid cow, all of this is your fault." Escalating hypertension spiked along with his rage. Vaynem clutched at his chest, gasping for air. His breath, it wouldn't come.

"Help!" screamed Abigail. "Someone, please!"

CHAPTER THIRTY-TWO

*M*onet Lisette sat by the fountain in the courtyard at Alta Bates Medical. She sat staring at the coins in the water, pondering the thousands of wishes they represented. Some were wrapped in prayer for ill or dying loved ones while others seemed cast into the fountain with the joy and celebration of new births.

She sat quietly, eyeing the abundance of copper pennies in the fountain's water, while thinking of her grandmother, of angels, and of the birthday present in the bag at her feet—the present wrapped in copper balloon paper. The party was a mystery now. She had been there at four o'clock as planned, and no one was in room 1230. Something had gone awry, just as she had thought it might, but it seemed early yet, according to her premonition.

She relaxed into the soothing sounds of the fountain. While basking in the coin reflections, Monet's heart stirred. Unexpectedly, a hoard of unspoken wishes surfaced. Wishes and desires that she had previously secreted away, had held captive by her strong will and fierce independence—her not wanting to be obligated to anyone. Pride and shame, tangled knots inside her, stunted her life as surely as if she was taking human growth suppressants.

Only today did she recognize how her ardent pride labored to keep her shame repressed, simple shame for being human—an imperfect mortal—and how she alone had cut herself off from receiving many of life's blessings. Today, they felt tangible, those blessings awaiting her if she could but receive them.

The realization shook her soul, awakened her unconscious slumber. Her gaze turned upward with childlike awe, remembering how as a little girl she often searched the sky for answers. Studying the varying shades of blue in today's sky, she eyed the storm cloud in the distance but preferred the small fluffy white clouds that floated freely in the vastness. She squinted her eyes, purposefully defocusing in an attempt to see with the eyes of her inner child like her Gram had taught her to do. The ensuing wind whispered sweetly into her ear, saying it was the perfect day to set wishes free.

She rummaged through her tote bag, a *Louis Vuitton*, bought for its quality and because it was the same color as she—spice brown, just like her hair, her eyes, and her skin. Not a walking example of contrast, she was born monochromatic, and that pleased her greatly.

Retrieving her wallet from the bag, she unzipped the coin section and focused intently on the array of coins as she contemplated which one would be best for her first wish. *A copper penny, of course.* Not a matter of cent value, it was simply that copper was on her mind today—copper pennies, copper wrapping paper, and memories of copper-colored hair and a copper glow emanating from a plastic angel doll.

Possibilities that defied common sense, yes, infinite possibilities were on her mind. On a whim, she took five pennies and cast them into the water, all in one fling, her heart bubbling with its own fountain of hope.

The young CHP officer couldn't wipe the smile off his face as he walked down the hall of Alta Bates Medical. *Taller, surely, he was taller.* He laughed at himself while keeping an eye out for a vending machine. With the birthday boy missing, he hadn't gotten to eat a chunk of that cake, and now his stomach rumbled. Funny, he hadn't noticed any physical discomfort when in the presence of Laura, but no longer under the spell of her beauty, he was hungry with a capital H. *That woman is way out of my league, but it sure was fun to entertain the thought that she was flirting with me.*

Rounding the corner, he almost collided with a wheelchair that held a man with a bandage around his head. After apologizing profusely to the man, his eyes went to the nurse. The sight of her face evoked such surprise that he almost stuttered when he spoke her name, "Priscilia!"

"Hey Duarte, I have to get this patient to the lab," she said hurriedly, almost out of breath.

"Oh-kay," he said as she pushed past him. *"It's good to see you, too,"* he mumbled under his breath. *Hmm, maybe she was just surprised to see me, to see anyone from our Portuguese neighborhood here in the hallways of Alta Bates.* Turning back, he called out to her, "Hey, Priscilia, where's the nearest vending machine?"

He waited; he watched her begin to move away even faster, her ponytail jiggling and her back rigid as she pushed the wheelchair. Without turning around, her back to him, Priscilia flung out her right arm and waved it downward multiple times.

To Officer Duarte Cruz, her nonverbal cue was clear: Go away, don't bother me. Scratching his head, he walked onward. *This hospital is a maze. Surely, I passed that same nurse's station a minute ago.* Taking the left hallway this time, he spotted a sign, Surgical Waiting Room / Vending.

The candy bar thumped as it hit the metal. He put in more coins and, this time, selected the peanut butter cheese crackers. This token snack would have to suffice; he had to get back to work. Leaving the waiting room, he noticed a pretty woman sitting alone in the corner. She was quietly sobbing, dabbing her eyes with already soaked and wadded tissues—that is, when she wasn't wringing her hands. Seeing her despair, he wanted out of the hospital and fast. Traffic on highways and bridges—not crying, distraught women— was his domain.

Following signs to the nearest exit, he thought of Priscilia. *What was up with her?* At church and in their neighborhood, she was friendly, actually flirtatious, and with her, the flirting was not a fantasy. He had heard through the grapevine that she wanted to go out with him. He had been interested, until seeing her today. Her hurried rebuff and greediness with her smile had not put him off as much as the unattractive face of guilt she had worn like a billboard. *What was she hiding?*

At last, he could see sunlight. A door to the outside waited in front of him, though, this was not the doorway he had originally entered. *How did I end up by ER?* He fretted that he had become too dependent upon his GPS device and was losing his fine sense of direction.

He walked through the automatic door, grateful for the fresh air, and surveyed the signage with renewed determination. His car must be in the lot to the left. Rattling the wrapper on the candy bar, he peeled back the paper. Today, it was chocolate first.

Chomping the candy in an even rhythm to his walking, he watched a man get into a yellow BMW and speed out of the emergency driveway, tires screeching as he accelerated at a rapid rate. An approaching ambulance, with siren and horn both screaming, had to swerve to miss the BMW. The Beamer didn't slow or grant the ambulance right of way; it accelerated, although already moving at a speed that exceeded the limit in a hospital zone.

City streets were not his territory, but something about that car and its driver's blatant disrespect for the emergency vehicle made his blood boil. As the car roared down the street passing him on the sidewalk, he noted the numbers on the license plate.

Navigating the hospital parking lot, he found his patrol car more quickly than anticipated. He jumped in and within moments was speaking to the dispatcher. "Hey, Doug, I need you to run a number for me, 5BBK299." With his lights flashing, siren silent, he drove in the direction that the BMW had gone.

His radio emitted static, then came the voice of the dispatcher. Two sentences into the report, his hunger vanished, his adrenaline raced. His response to the dispatcher was marked with urgency: "Call Berkeley and Oakland PD and notify them that we have a link to a nation-wide WLM (Wanted List Male) who may be in the area. The way this dude is driving, he must be our guy. Send backup; he's probably armed."

CHAPTER THIRTY-THREE

Well, so much for going wishing, Jonah thought, giving up on his plan to get outdoors and breathe some fresh air. Kate slept curled in his lap. He was stuck. Oddly enough, he didn't mind, though, he'd never experienced a little one sleeping in his lap before, never thought he wanted kids. Clothes and fashion made up his world. With the long hours of managing employees, inventories, and accounting for multiple stores, he didn't even own a pet. Not that he would let a kitten or a puppy sleep in his lap. *Ugh, pet hair on his fine clothing, no way.* The funny thing was, Kate had spilled some lemonade on his high-dollar designer pants, and he hadn't reacted negatively. *Agh, I'm going soft, hanging around with Terrence.*

Jonah looked down at the little face pressed against his chest and studied her features. Amused, he watched her eyes dart back and forth, although her lids were tightly shut. She must be dreaming, he decided.

A commotion erupted near the coffee kiosk. A modish young woman juggling a large designer purse, which secretly housed a tiny dog, had dropped her latté when the Chihuahua—dressed to the nines in doggie fashions—had suddenly jumped from the bag. Beige liquid spilled everywhere as the dog, yapping loudly, danced in the frothy latté puddle amassing on the floor. The young woman screamed, "Elvis!"

Jonah tried to squelch his chuckle, but couldn't contain it as he watched the commotion. Then he spotted Annateresa stepping from the line; she was grinning back at him, and slashing one index finger against the other, signaling naughty, naughty on him for laughing.

Jonah was further entertained as he watched three other women—Angelique, Monet, and Laura—jump back to avoid the splattering spill. Their faces marked with bemusement, they carefully side-stepped the chichi Chihuahua, and all headed toward his and Kate's table at the back of the cafeteria.

Jonah pressed his index finger to his lips, pointing to the sleeping princess.

Completely tuckered out by the trauma of the tumultuous day, Kate slept. Within minutes of closing her eyes, she had sunk into a deep sleep, had been immersed in a dream where Grammy Mer sat in a beautiful chair, waving happily, blowing kisses to Kate. Two large angels stood on either side of the golden-silvery chair and guided it as it flew upward. Kate heard angels singing, harps playing, trumpets blaring, but most importantly, she heard the joyous laughter, the contagious resonant laughter she had so yearned to hear again.

The Jesus man stepped from the clouds and lifted Grammy Mer from the chair into his giant arms. The moment he touched her, she cried out, "I am healed! Completely healed!" Her voice an exuberant echo, she exclaimed, "Oh, my Blessed Savior, praises to you, my Precious Lord."

Tenderly, Jesus set Grammy Mer down in a lush garden— every blade of grass, every plant was perfectly manicured. Dew droplets clung to magnificent pink roses. Bees buzzed proudly around, flapping their wings in applause to their master creator and their loving caretakers, their queens—Mother Heaven and Mother Earth.

Jesus held Grammy Mer's hand while they ambled through the garden. He stopped by a stalwart tree. They—Jesus, Grammy Mer, and the tree—conversed in a language Kate did not understand. Radiating happiness, Grammy Mer reached out and lovingly stroked the tree's bark.

Walking onward, the Jesus man guided her around a flower bed edged with exotic grass, grass so green that the blades resembled faceted emeralds. They stepped onto a golden-silvery walkway that led to a wide arch that had no door. The arch marked the entrance to the Great Angel Mother's kitchen.

When she saw Grammy Mer, the Great Angel Mother stopped working and tossed the kitchen towel in her hand onto the counter. While in the air, the sky-blue towel folded itself and then landed neatly on the marble countertop.

Upon seeing Grammy Mer, the Great Angel Mother clapped joyfully. She wrapped her arms around Grammy Mer, hugging her like they were old friends. Taking Grammy Mer's face in her hands, she repeatedly kissed her on both cheeks, turning Grammy Mer's face from side to side. Then she rubbed Grammy Mer's navel, her hand moving in circles. She whispered, "It will feel better soon. Don't worry; you will forever be connected to them, your babies."

Donning a mischievous expression, The Great Angel Mother raised her eyebrows. Grammy Mer laughed and said hers was an outie, especially after giving birth four times.

An expression of gleeful pride dominating her radiant face, the Great Angel Mother pointed to a giant lemon meringue pie, Grammy Mer's favorite dessert, which sat on the marble counter. One unlit candle, white beeswax glistening with diamonds and pearls adorned the pie. A birthday pie.

The Jesus man motioned for them to sit at the table with him. The Great Angel Mother poured lemon tea into fine china cups that sat on matching hand-painted saucers. The cups had thin rims. Grammy Mer smiled, delighted, for they were her favorite type of cups. Mugs were too thick for her patrician taste.

A honeybee flew into the kitchen, buzzing around the table. The Jesus man nodded to the bee, and it promptly landed on Grammy Mer, on the left side of her upper chest like it was a brooch. The bee spread its wings wide and extended the length of its body, and instantly transformed into a golden cross. Within seconds, the bee cross became bejeweled, pavé style, set with hundreds of dazzling lemon-yellow diamonds.

Two new bees flew into the kitchen and buzzed around the table. The Jesus man gave a slight nod to them, and they orbited his head three times. After their third circuit, they aligned their bodies side by side, hovering several inches out from his aquiline nose. Perfectly synchronized, the two bees lifted their wings and blasted off, zooming directly into the Jesus man's eyeballs.

With his eyes glowing like two mid-day suns shining blindingly bright, the Jesus man reached over and gently touched Grammy Mer's bee-cross brooch. Instantly, scenes began to flash, his honeycomb eyes the viewing screen, the golden bee-cross brooch the projector. The pictures changed rapidly like a computerized slide show set on ultra high speed. Grammy Mer watched intently.

Kate couldn't see the slide show. But she felt as if she was physically there in the Great Angel Mother's kitchen, felt like she was sitting in the Jesus man's lap completely engulfed in a cloud of pure love. She could smell the sweet aroma of good things baking and taste the lemon tea sweetened with honey.

The slide show stopped. The pair of bees winged their way out of the Jesus man's eyes, flying over and around the table, whirling and gliding in a graceful dance, a bee ballet. After enjoying a few moments of their concert, the Jesus man lifted his hand to his brow, saluting the pair. They bent their bodies forward and dipped their wings, bowing to him. They then flew in single file through the arched doorway into the garden.

Grammy Mer took a sip of tea and lovingly fingered her golden bee-cross brooch, her fingertips fondling it like lost treasure newly found.

"Now, you are ready to plan your party," said the Great Angel Mother.

Suddenly a tiny Irish Setter puppy came running into the room. It stumbled, dazed like, then trotted over to the table and lay down, curling up by the Jesus man's feet. Its tail, the color of a freshly peeled sweet potato, wagged happily when Grammy Mer reached down and patted its head. In seconds, it was asleep. Moments later, a second puppy staggered into the Great Angel Mother's kitchen. It, too, was an Irish-Setter breed.

Cacophonous noise disturbed the scene, but it didn't come from the Great Angel's Mother kitchen, it came from Earth in the hospital cafeteria.

Reluctantly, Kate sat up, rubbing her eyes, surprised to see that she had slept in Jonah's lap. Yawning, she wanted to return to the dream, wanted to be in the Great Angel Mother's kitchen playing with the puppies and planning the birthday party.

Astonishment erased Kate's drowsiness when Dr. Donahorn said, "Well, Princess Kate, you've awakened just in time for the party."

Abigail sat alone in the back corner of the surgical waiting area.

The desk attendant, an older woman, eyed her carefully. It was unusual for this waiting area to host a family that had two of its members in surgery at the same time. This poor woman had her daughter and her husband in emergency OR, and there she sat all alone, no one to comfort her.

The attendant reviewed her notes of the coming and goings of the past two hours. A young doctor, that pediatric plastic surgeon, Dr. Donahorn, had come in to check on Mrs. Moxsin, had sat with her a while, had held her hand. Dr. Donahorn had come to the desk and asked for fresh tissues. While delivering them to Mrs. Moxsin, her pager had buzzed, and she had then left.

A bit later, Virginia Veetlehurst—an LVN that worked at the hospital—had entered the room and strutted directly across to where Mrs. Moxsin sat. She carried an index card in her hand. From what the volunteer could observe, it had a list of names written on it. The Veetlehurst woman had pointed to the list and talked intently in hushed tones to Mrs. Moxsin. She had repeatedly looked over her shoulder, looking back at the volunteers manning the desk, as if her words were top secret.

Mrs. Moxsin had pressed her fingers to her brow, at times slightly shaking her head in disagreement. Then she had shaken her head vigorously, giving a resounding final no to whatever case Mrs. Veetlehurst was pleading. The nurse had stomped out in a huff.

The phone ringing snapped the desk attendant back to present time. She picked up the receiver, listening intently. "Yes, I will tell her." Normally, she would call out the patient's last name and then someone from the patient's family would come to the desk for news. Instead, she got up from her chair and walked back to where Abigail was sitting. "Mrs. Moxsin, the OR nurse just called. Your daughter's surgery is almost completed. Dr. Valeah will be in to see you shortly."

CHAPTER THIRTY-FOUR

*T*he dump truck rounded the bend on the ranch road for its fifth time that day, its last load as sunset neared. The driver accelerated, commanding his old truck to make it up the hill one more time. Paid by the load, speed was imperative.

He spotted a blue blob in the culvert to the side of the road. *A blanket*, he surmised, and one that appeared to be in good condition. He could use an extra blanket, but there was no time to stop, not even a second.

With the weather prediction of high winds for later this evening, his speed was even more critical. High winds would blow away most of the dirt load since he didn't have a tarp. And if a hard rain came with the winds, he would lose it all. *Blast it.* He wished he had saved one of the heavier gravel loads for the last. Without delivering this load of dirt before sunset, he wouldn't get the bonus.

Blast that wreck I had last week. Hit-and-run was his motto, but now because of his latest incident, he couldn't use his good tar. It was bright orange. He bit his lip, chewing on its side. *Oh man, I hope no one reported my license number before I got that blasted orange thing off and hidden away.* After the wreck, he had changed roadways and driven slowly and cautiously for a couple of miles before pulling over to remove it. The new tarp he had bought the same day of the collision had ripped to shreds within days. *Blast the frigging cheap thing.*

Black smoke loomed in the sky, a larger and denser mass than the approaching storm cloud. He eyed the smoke. Must be a big fire, he gauged. *Hot damn.* His hands itched to steer the truck in that direction. But, he also had a hankering for that bonus.

Dollars and flames waged battle inside him. Gunning the engine, he kicked the accelerator repeatedly like he was slapping a horse's flank imploring it to "giddy up."

As the truck chugged up the hill, the driver stuck his head out the window, his nose in the air with the aplomb of a banny rooster. He breathed deeply, inhaling the smoke, so delicious to him. Raindrops splattered. He spit on his fingertip and held it out the window. Just as he had thought, the wind was changing direction.

If he could place a bet, he would wager that he would make it back in time to watch the fireworks. The way that blaze was already roaring, its flames were spreading quickly, faster than the raindrops were. And the strong winds had yet to arrive.

"The Moxsin family." The waiting area attendant stood up looking around the room for who would respond.

Abigail went to the desk. "Yes, I am Mrs. Moxsin," she said to the man. *Shift change,* she thought, noting that she much preferred the older woman who had been there earlier.

"Mrs. Moxsin, Dr. Valeah will see you in consulting Room A. Go on in, and have a seat. She will join you in a few minutes."

Confused, Abigail looked around the room. The man pointed to the doors along the back wall. A new wave of fear settled over her. *Why did the doctor want to speak to her in private?* Earlier, several doctors, still wearing their surgical garb, had come into the waiting room and spoken to families. Those patients were all doing well—good news for their families.

Once inside the consulting room, Abigail paced. Now she understood the setup as there was a door on both sides of the room. The doctor would be entering from the opposite door, not from the waiting area. Looking around, she noticed there was a box of tissues in the middle of the small, round table. Clearly, this was where they delivered bad news.

Aloneness engulfed her. Over the years, Vaynem's mandates had isolated her from her family and friends. She wished for her sister, Carly, who was the only family she had in the Bay Area and the only family member who had continually reached out to her.

Abigail was fully aware that she had shunned a ridiculous number of her sister's invitations. Vaynem had demanded it. But she couldn't blame him entirely for she had gone along with him, and at times, because she had been afraid. Yes, scared, and not only of Vaynem but also of the likelihood that if she and Carly shared intimate time together, her sister would see her pain. And worse yet, she might spill the truth about her broken marriage, the reprehensible truth about her husband.

Thinking of Vaynem and what he had done to little Kate's arm, Abigail worried over what Dr. Donahorn had told her: Kate's glenohumeral joint was fractured, and the humerus bone was badly bruised. Abigail had felt like an idiot, not knowing what that meant. Vaynem would say she was dumb as dirt, but she had asked questions, anyway.

Dr. Donahorn had been so kind and apologized for her use of medical terms. She had explained that the joint where Kate's fracture was located was commonly known as the ball-and-socket joint, the one that connects the upper arm bone to the shoulder blade. Abigail consoled herself that at least she had known that the humerus was the name of the upper arm bone.

Wringing her hands again, Abigail worried that Carly would never forgive her for allowing this atrocity to happen to Kate while in her care. Even still, she yearned for her sister.

Plucking three tissues from the box, she sat down at the table. *Dear God, please help me. What a complicated mess! Please God, I beg you, please take care of Kate's arm. Let it heal perfectly. And Lord, please, please, please let my Emmy be okay.*

CHAPTER THIRTY-FIVE

The elevator doors closed behind her. Priscilia began walking briskly, her brown ponytail bouncing as she went down the hallway. Her arms were aching, tired from pushing the wheelchair. The patient had tried to talk to her several times, but she had pretended not to hear him. Now he seemed to be napping. *How much longer could she keep up this ruse, and where was Mrs. Veetlehurst?* It was now long past time for her to take the patient as per their plan.

Priscilia was sick to death of Virginia Veetlehurst and her sneaky shenanigans, tired of feeling ashamed, tired of risking this job she needed so direly, tired of saying hundreds of Hail Mary's, and tired of going to confession every day. She had recently confessed so often, asking forgiveness for the same type of sins that Father Frank had called her into a counseling session. He assured her she was forgiven, but he had said that she must grow some backbone and start saying no to the woman who used her as an agent for wickedness.

Father Frank had said that since Mrs. Veetlehurst was the kind of person that purposefully acted wrongly against people of different race and religion from her, she would mistreat anyone who differed from her ideology, and anyone who dared to cross her. Priscilia knew that as true, knew it only too well for she had witnessed it all. Non-Anglo people were Mrs. Veetlehurst's primary targets, but sometimes there were even Anglos on her to-do list, like Priscilia's assignment today, the patient in the wheelchair she had pushed around for hours.

Then there were gays; Anglo or not, Virginia Veetlehurst despised them. Hospital gossip claimed that the RN Chancellor Wilmington was gay. Mrs. Veetlehurst often needled him and had performed sly tricks trying to trip Chance up on the job, just as she had done with Jophia Josephesus and countless others.

Then there was Mrs. Veetlehurst obsessive aversion to Catholics. She had told Priscilia that she was going to burn in hell if she didn't quit her church. She had proclaimed that the only way Priscilia could wash her robe white and have any hope of getting through the pearly gates of heaven when she died was to join Mrs. Veetlehurst's Protestant church and be baptized their way, completely immersed in their sanctified tank of holy water.

Father Frank's priestly collar would fly right off his shirt if he knew that Priscilia had questioned her faith, had almost believed Virginia Veetlehurst about Catholicism and about it being a sin to honor Mary. *Absolute lunacy,* Father Frank would say. *Mary of Nazareth, the woman who bore Jesus Christ in her womb and gave birth to him, deserved honor.*

In the counseling session, Father Frank had questioned Priscilia at length about Mrs. Veetlehurst and her prejudices. With his brows knitted together, he had remained perplexed as to why the woman had not acted biased against Priscilia since she was a second-generation immigrant from Portugal.

Priscilia had explained her family history, her Sephardic heritage, and how that had seemed scarier information for Mrs. Veetlehurst to discover. She had rattled on about how her Jewish ancestors had been expelled from Spain in the late 1400's, and how they were then forced by the governing powers of Portugal to convert to Catholicism. Doing what many Jewish families at that time had done to escape harassment, Priscilia's family had not only converted but they had also changed their surname. That's when Priscilia's family took the name of Pieria, meaning "pear tree." Centuries later, she had explained, Priscilia's grandparents had decided to retain the

Pieria name and to remain Catholic when they immigrated to the United States.

Priscilla told Father Frank that since she was scared of being one of Mrs. Veetlehurst's targets, she had decided that the best protection from the woman was to befriend her.

Faulty thinking due to Priscilia's paranoia and low self-esteem, Father Frank had chided, and he had added, "Priscilla, the 1400's were a very long time ago. Please!" She had tried to tell him that her mother was fixated on it and that her entire family still discussed their Sephardic heritage frequently. He had just stared at her, a blank look in his eyes. She had shivered, like a ghost from the 15th century was trying to live through her, trying to drive her out and inhabit her body.

Clearly, it was one counseling session Priscilia would never forget. Father Frank had even held up a mirror to her face and told her to look deeply into her own eyes and name some qualities and ways that she was similar to Virginia Veetlehurst. The shock of that nauseating thought had rippled through her like a virus.

At first, Priscilia had tried to derail that train by naming the ways she was not like Virginia Veetlehurst. She did not intentionally tailgate cars when driving nor did she tailgate with her grocery basket the way Mrs. Veetlehurst did when she was grocery shopping, trying to bump people on the backs of their legs, hurting them. And more importantly, Mrs. Veetlehurst was a squatter in public bathrooms. She voided her bladder, letting her bodily fluid spray all over the toilet seat, all with no regard for the next user or who had to clean up her mess. Mrs. Veetlehurst refused to use the paper toilet-seat covers while Priscilia layered them three thick.

Father Frank had blushed, had held the mirror up again, and had made Priscilia do the exercise. He pointed out that Mrs. Veetlehurst suffered from paranoia and low self-esteem, too, and that was why her acts against others gave her a feeling of power, that and a sense of superiority.

Priscilia had to admit to having the very same demons.

Father Frank had said she could have compassion for Virginia Veetlehurst, but that she must disentangle herself from the woman.

Priscilia had vowed she would.

Father Frank would be chagrined to see her today, to see her lack of courage, and to see her promise to him already broken with this inane antic against this innocent patient. *At least, she had not given him the shot, injected the shellfish serum,* even though Mrs. Veetlehurst had said the proteins would be good for healing his head wound and would make him drowsy, easier to manage.

Priscilia had been reluctant to give the injection. Something didn't feel right about it. But, mainly, she didn't want to touch it. The shrimp serum might get on her hands, and she could inadvertently touch her mouth, nose, or eyes. Then she would be in real trouble; she was allergic to shellfish. She hadn't dared tell Mrs. Veetlehurst about her allergy. Besides, the injection didn't matter now. Mrs. Veetlehurst would not have to know that she didn't give it. The patient had slept without it.

What could she do to disentangle herself from the revengeful Mrs. Veetlehurst and not be sliced to bits by her and her lawyer friend, that man named Vaynem who issued the orders? To her credit, Priscilia had not gone to any of their secret meetings; she was still short of the number of wayward deeds to qualify for an official invitation stating the location. Of course, Mrs. Veetlehurst didn't call these acts wrongdoing; she called them God's work or being God's instrument to bring justice to the world, to help purify it.

Trash-bin thinking, evil's thumbprint, Father Frank would say. His words rang in her ears: *Priscilia, it is absolute blasphemy to use God's name to do something harmful to other people.*

Reciting a rosary, silently in her mind, Priscilia caressed imaginary beads. She crossed herself then launched into the Lord's Prayer. Seconds later, she spun the wheelchair to face the opposite direction; she pushed the chair back toward room 1230.

"So, we're not in a parade, after all," he said, his voice strong and resonant again. His hands came down on the wheels, halting the wheelchair. "Come and stand in front of me. Let me see my kidnapper."

Priscilia checked the hallway. It was empty. She dropped her hands and stepped around in front of him. "I'm not a kidnapper."

"Maybe not, but you are an adult-nabber, a patient-nabber, right?" Terrence focused his eyes on her heart area, surveying the churning colors. To Terrence, her heart looked like a rainbow lollipop doused with muddy slime.

Priscilia tugged at her scrubs as a sense of nakedness ensconced her while standing there in front of him and his penetrating, but kind, eyes. She bowed her head, her neck bending from shame's weight. "I am really sorry."

"You say that quite convincingly. Alright, I accept your apology, and I won't report you. But you owe me one, and I am going to cash in on half the debt right now."

Her brown eyes bulged. "What?"

"First, you are taking me back to my room. Then, you are going to ER and find out if there is a patient named Karalyn Kindrick, who has been admitted. And if so, you are going to find out her condition, the name of the attending doctor, and her room number. And then you will come back to my room and give me a full report. Understand?"

Priscilia checked her watch. "Okay, but I need to hurry." Savoring her reprieve as she pushed him down the hallway, she wondered what the second half of the favor entailed.

They rounded the corner to room 1230. She pushed him through the doorway.

A chorus of voices chimed, "Surprise! Happy birthday!"

CHAPTER THIRTY-SIX

*A*t San Francisco International Airport, Sammy Sue waited at the baggage-claim carousel. She fingered the dead cell phone, lamenting the charger that had been packed in her checked bags, a fact she had not discovered until past security at Logan in Boston. No shops or kiosk selling such items had been near her gate, and the flight was already boarding. Typically, she packed the phone charger in her computer bag, but today she had been so preoccupied with her speech and the nagging feeling to leave early that she had hurriedly packed it in her primary suitcase.

With frustration mounting, she tossed the dead phone back into her briefcase that hung over the top of the raised handle of her rolling computer bag. One less challenge, she consoled herself, as it was hard enough to keep one hand near her computer while retrieving her luggage from the carousel without attempting it when holding a phone.

People pushed inward crowding around her, grabbing at their bags as they went along the conveyor belt. Disgruntled, she moved slightly to the left. *Drat it,* she had staked out her place. Why did people stand back and wait and then, the moment they spotted their bags, run up and shove other people out of the way, the very people who waited politely in one spot? If she weren't a scientist, she would write a book on baggage claim etiquette. *Then I'd be known as "The Bag Lady." Now that would be a different life.*

A young woman wearing ripped jeans and stilettos knocked into Sammy Sue as she struggled to lift a gigantic bag from the belt, a leopard-print bag that sported a red sticker—HEAVY. More fodder for her book, Sammie Sue fantasized. She would indulge this etiquette book-writing game to keep from becoming furious, and yes, righteous.

The same young woman bumped hard against her again, warring with another over-sized leopard bag. Sammie Sue grimaced, gritting her teeth though she decided that the spectacle was a juggling act worth observing. She turned to watch how the girl managed her two leopards to the door.

Feeling impatient, Sammie Sue sighed and turned her attention back to the conveyor belt jammed full of black bags. Swatting at the back of her neck—it felt as if a bee had lightly stung her—she jerked her head, whiplash style. It was not a sting on the back of her neck; it was a kiss.

"Hey, Sis, what are you daydreaming about, a genetic experiment?"

"Kal Kindrick, you almost gave me a heart attack. What are you doing here? Is Carly with you?"

"Well, there is nothing like a warm greeting from your sister." He grinned and gave her a kiss on the cheek. "Carly's in the ladies room. What are you doing here? I thought you were in Boston."

"I asked you first," she bantered, sibling style.

"Is that your bag?"

"Yes, finally. I was beginning to think it was lost."

Kal reached and single-handedly lifted the brown tweed Hartman. "There you go, Sis. What do you have in there, an entire lab?"

"Enough already. So, you've returned from vacation early. Why? I'm assuming it's not for little brother's birthday."

"No, but we did consider that reason. It probably won't make sense to you, the queen of logic," Kal paused, "but neither Carly nor I were having much fun because of this darndest feeling that we should come home. It wouldn't let go of either of us." Looking out over the crowd, Kal raised his arm and waved.

267

Carly weaved her way through the throng, her cell phone in hand. "Sammy Sue! What are you doing here?" She embraced her sister-in-law and instantly burst into tears.

"Honey, what's wrong?" Kal stroked her arm.

"Everything. We have to get to the hospital immediately."

Her dark ponytail bounced as Priscilia almost ran down the hallway. The nearer she got to room 1230, the more anxious and shyer she felt. *What if the party people were still there?* Standing outside the door, she decided to knock though the door was partially open.

"Come in," boomed the resonant voice.

Priscilia stood inside the door. The party folks, standing scattered about the small room, were chatting, their cake plates mostly empty.

"Okay, I need everyone to step out for a minute. My nurse is here," announced Terrence.

"I've got to get going, anyway," Jonah said.

"Me, too. We've kept you up too long as it is," said Annateresa.

"Okay guys," Laura said, "Annateresa and I don't have wheels. Can someone give us a ride or do we need to take BART or a cab back to the city?"

"My car has room for one of you lovely ladies," Jonah said, eyeing Annateresa. "But Angelique, how are you getting home now that your car was towed?"

"I can take you home later, Angelique," Monet said. "I'm not leaving just yet. There's another patient I want to visit." Monet gathered her purse, sliding its shoulder strap over her arm, her dark eyes casting a longing look at Etta Ebella.

Angelique's brows wrinkled in consternation; she said, "Thank you, Monet, but I am considering staying here tonight in the doctors' quarters. Call me when your visit is complete; I should have an answer for you by then."

"Let's solve our wheel problem downstairs," Annateresa said. "Ange, I'll text you our plan." She squeezed her twin's hand, worrying that her sister was simply avoiding the bridge with her plan to stay overnight at the hospital.

"Hey guys, thank you for coming, thank you for everything. It would have been a dismal birthday in the hospital. Thanks for lifting my spirits," said Terrence.

Jonah stepped to the bed, fisted his hand and knocked knuckles with Terrence.

"I owe you one, buddy. Thanks for all your help today," Terrence said.

"Anytime, my friend, gizzard wizard that you are," Jonah said, his fingers fishing in his pocket. "Here are your car keys," he said, laying them on the bedside table.

"We didn't go wishing," Kate said.

"One of us was sleepy, remember?" Jonah winked at Kate. "How about we have a wishing date on another day? I know where there's an even bigger fountain." Jiggling the coins in his pocket, he stepped toward the door.

Annateresa, Monet, and Laura all sent air kisses in Terrence's direction. "Happy birthday," they said, waving as they followed Jonah through the doorway.

The yellow taxi turned into the driveway at 537 Spruce Street. The driver got out and unloaded the bags from the trunk. Carly and Sammy Sue waited inside the cab.

"Can you give me a hand with these?" asked Kal.

"Sure, I'll help you get them inside if you'd like," said Charles, a tall man from Nigeria.

"That would be awesome. Thank you, Charles," replied Kal.

The Kindrick family called Charles whenever they needed taxi service. He kept his cab in immaculate condition, and he was always on time or early. Kal usually enjoyed talking politics or sports with Charles, who was exceptionally well-read. But today, on the way from the airport, a serious tone had hung heavy in the cab. Kal had been consumed with listening to the many phone messages, many of which delivered urgent behests and bad news.

They wrestled the luggage inside the door, including Sammy Sue's bags. Kal motioned for Charles to leave them at the bottom of the stairway.

"I'll just be a minute more," Kal said.

His head full of woeful visions—his mother hospitalized, Kate's broken arm, Keebie's puppy-birth complications, and Terrence who they could not locate or contact by phone—Kal marched back to his study and opened the file drawer in his desk. He searched through the files and found the one he wanted. He had dreaded this day, the day a hospital requested a copy of his mother's Living Will. Pop had made sure all the kids had a copy, a notarized copy. Kal tucked the folder under his arm and ran out the door.

The yellow taxi backed out of the driveway of 537 Spruce Street and turned in the direction of Alta Bates Medical. Time was of the essence. Kal had decided not to drive his car. Parking at Alta Bates could be as grueling as finding parking at a national league football game. Being dropped off at the main entrance would be faster and was far simpler.

Aware of the urgency, Charles drove as fast as was safe. They were only a few blocks away, so near they could see the hospital tower when traffic suddenly stopped. Multiple lights were flashing ahead; two police officers directed traffic. The lanes of cars, bumper to bumper, inched along.

"Can you see what the problem is, Charles?" asked Kal, craning his neck from the back seat.

"Not yet, I should be able to see in a minute," Charles replied. A shrill whistle penetrated the car, and they began to inch along. The police officer directed the cars, his whistle constantly blaring as he commanded them to go faster versus slowing down to watch the action.

"Wow," said Charles as the taxi moved into sight of what was causing the delay. There was a three-car pileup that involved a yellow

BMW, a police car, and a white Mazda, or at least a semi-white Mazda, as it was dirty, all caked with mud. "I've never seen so many law-enforcement officers for a simple car accident," said Charles. "There are Berkeley and Oakland officers and three state troopers."

"It must involve more than a traffic accident; they've got a handcuffed man on the ground by the BMW," said Sammie Sue. She sat by the window with a good view of the situation.

"Hey, look over here on this side," said Kal. "Three guys and a woman are pouring out of a black SUV, and they're all wearing FBI vests."

"That guy's in some major trouble," said Charles, peering into his rearview mirror.

Completely disinterested in the scene on the street, Carly interrupted. "Charles, are you available around 7:30 this evening? Ruthie's flight gets in around then. I'm afraid we may not be able to leave the hospital to get her."

"Good idea," said Kal and Sammie Sue, simultaneously.

"Do you have her flight number?" asked Charles.

"Yes, I scribbled it on a tissue in the ladies room." Carly dug the ragged tissue from her purse. "She's on American, Flight 922, scheduled to arrive at 7:21. She entered Customs in Dallas; this flight is from DFW, should you need to check on the actual arrival time. I'll leave her a message to meet you out front."

Sammie Sue shook her head in amazement that her baby sister, Ruthie Renee, was also on her way home. Yes, her family did, indeed, have the Merlin-gene. What's more, they were all listening to it.

My mother is dying. The thought seemed unbelievable. Panic filled her, an awareness of emptiness close on its heels. No longer the scientist, she felt three years old. Clasping hands with Carly, Sammie Sue pleaded, "Charles, can you drive any faster?"

The yellow taxi accelerated.

CHAPTER THIRTY-SEVEN

In room 1230, Angelique eyed the nurse suspiciously. *What was she doing in his room again?* She was not Terrence's nurse, Angelique knew full well, recognizing her from the incident the week before. She was not even assigned to this floor. *And what was that about her taking him for an MRI today?* Angelique had checked his chart; none had been ordered. Ever polite, though, she said, "Priscilia, would you like some cake?"

Jolted that Angelique had called her by name, Priscilia suppressed the desire to flee. Quite readily, though, she gave in to her saliva glands that were already moist with cake desire. "Sure, I'd love a piece," she said.

On the other side of the room, Kate curled on the hospital bed, sitting snugly against her Uncle TT's side. She had refused to eat any of the chocolate birthday cake. No amount of coaxing would convince her to taste it.

Kate studied the nurse with the root-beer cola eyes. She decided that the young nurse's heart seemed somewhat nice, although she didn't understand the image that appeared—a mini rainbow with a dark, storm cloud over it. Kate looked out the window to see if it was storming or raining. It was not.

Angelique, the precise way she cut the cake, captured Kate's attention. After the horrors of lunch, the mere sight of chocolate cake had nauseated her. Even still, Kate thought Uncle TT's cake was beautiful, and that made her happy. With such a pretty birthday cake, surely nothing bad could happen to Uncle TT or their family this year.

Kate nestled closer to her uncle, glad that the nurse was taking the time to eat some cake and not making her get down from his bed just yet. She looked down at her chest, wondering if her own heart had an image in it as it felt warm, purring happily with getting to snuggle close aside her Uncle TT.

Kate's bubble of happiness burst rather quickly, though, when Angelique said, "Okay, Princess Kate, it's time for us to go and see Dr. Joe. Time to get your arm set. He's done with surgery and ready for you."

Terrence looked perplexed. He had wanted Angelique to stay, but he didn't think that Kate should hear the news that Priscilia most likely had for him, not just yet.

"Alrighty then," Terrence said. "Angelique, can you check back with me when you're done? And hey, Princess, I want to be the first to autograph your cast."

Angelique lifted Kate and Etta Ebella down from the bed. "Sure thing, Terrence. We will see you later, sometime before Princess Kate goes home with Jophia. Besides, I want to clean up the party things."

Kate stepped back up to the bed and using her good arm, touched fists with her uncle, the way Jonah had done. His hand reached out and tweaked her cheeks, and then he rubbed Etta Ebella's head.

"Don't mess up her hair," Kate whined, her eyebrows drooping downward in a frown. She was sad to leave her Uncle TT, her arm ached, and her tummy rumbled, chocolate-cake repulsion mixing with dread that pain was ahead when Dr. Joe put the cast on her arm.

"Princess, I'm sorry. Your arm hurts, and you've had a lousy day, huh?"

"Yes," Kate said, tucking her chin down on her pink collar.

The nurse's cake plate was now empty; she had gobbled it without even really chewing. Keeping her back to the others, Priscilia had begun gathering the wrapping paper remnants, putting them in the trash.

Kate skipped over to her side. "Did you see the copper penny paper? Monet says it's good luck."

"Then maybe we should keep it." With a quick glance, Priscilia surveyed the mood across the room and said to Angelique, "I'll take this to the trash chute for you. It's just around the corner."

"A trash shoot? Are there guns?"

Angelique's cheek bulged, her tongue poking it in amusement. Priscilia laughed aloud.

"I want to see the trash get shot. Can I go?" Kate said almost dancing a jig.

Angelique looked to Terrence, deferring the decision to him.

"Sure, Princess," he said. "Remember to use your quiet manners, though. Patients on this floor need quiet; noise makes their heads hurt. Okay?"

Rustling the trash bag, Priscilia together with Kate exited the room. Kate danced along the hallway, thinking that if she was supposed to be quiet, then the guns must have silencers on them, like the ones she saw on that television show at Marilla Marzy's house. Her mother would turn orange when she found out that Kate had watched such a show. With the thought of her mother being away, Kate's eyebrows drooped again.

Back in room 1230, Angelique stood by Terrence's side. They exchanged an intense look, her eyes searching his, his eyes twinkling stars.

He lifted her hand, kissed it, and then pulled her close to him. "I love you," he whispered.

She jerked back, her free hand going to her brow. Her blue topaz ring glistened brightly aside her red tresses.

He pulled her back to him, "Thank you. My birthday: the cake, the balloons, the flowers, the presents, each and every one was magnificent. And Angelique, I am immensely grateful to you for taking such supreme care of Kate. Thank you."

Brushing her lips against his, Angelique squeezed his hand and hurried away to catch up with Kate.

Down the hallway, Etta Ebella was bathing in light and delight.

Angelique thanked Priscilia for disposing of the trash. Taking Kate's hand, she started toward the elevators.

Priscilia turned, going back to room 1230.

Perturbed, Angelique had wanted to ask Priscilia what she was doing in Terrence's room again. The memory—of how he had looked anxiously at the nurse when she had returned as if he wanted to be alone with her even when the party was still in progress— had stopped all questions. *It's none of my business*; Angelique chided herself. Even still, uncomfortable feelings continued to rise. A well of suspicion roiled. Ever her own interrogator, one particular question surfaced. *Egad, am I jealous?*

"It wasn't a trash shoot; it was just a hole where the trash slides down a metal tube to the dumpster," Kate said.

"Yes, Princess Kate, that kind of chute is spelled c–h–u–t–e."

Not interested in spelling today, Kate said, "Look, Dr. Donahorn, Etta Ebella liked that trash chute."

Angelique could see that Etta Ebella was, in fact, wearing her Christmas lights, bathing in light and delight, although one wing hung lower than the other. "Is her wing broken?" asked Angelique.

"Yes, a little bit, it is. Uncle Vaynem hurt it this morning before church. He grabbed her by this wing and threw her into the trunk of the car, hard and fast like she was a baseball." Kate explained.

Her rage barely concealed, Angelique said, "I'm so sorry Kate that you and Etta Ebella had to endure such mistreatment. I will do my best to repair her wing."

Back in room 1230, Priscilia halted at the door and tiptoed into the room. Silence was all that greeted her.

Terrence reclined with marked stillness, his head propped up on pillows, eyes closed, his lips pressed together, which made the tiny scar on his upper lip flat, barely visible.

"Mr. Terry, are you okay?" asked Priscilia, using the patient name Mrs. Veetlehurst had given her.

"Mr. Terry?" Terrence asked. "Oh, never mind. What information do you have for me?"

The way he had repeated his name, indignant like it wasn't his, rattled her, shaking the cage that imprisoned her brain. *So many dumb mistakes*, Priscilia thought. She had not even checked the patient's hospital ID bracelet; she had blindly obeyed Mrs. Veetlehurst as for room number. What if she had taken the wrong patient? Virginia Veetlehurst would be furious, would torture her, and would inject her with the shrimp serum.

Stunned, Priscilia stood like a wooden mummy; yet, nothing inside her was quaking in fear. The cage door ajar, thoughts and feelings swarmed, swabbing away layers of the wicked web she had allowed when she had stopped thinking for herself and began being a programmed robot, one owned and operated by Virginia Veetlehurst.

She could correct one of those dumb mistakes, she thought. She must retrieve the patient's cell phone, and quickly, remembering how she had taken it and stashed it in the linen closet on floor two, as Mrs. Veetlehurst had ordered. It made no sense to Priscilia why Mrs. Veetlehurst or her lawyer friend wanted the patient's phone.

Terrence watched the nurse stand in silence. Bits of mud flew out of her heart and brain, like bats cast out of their nests. Normally, he would have been intrigued. Today he felt impatient. "Miss Pereira?"

"Sir? Oh, yes. A woman named Karalyn Kindrick was admitted to ER this afternoon. Dr. Christianson is the attending physician. He has moved her to room 317."

"And?" Terrence said lifting his hand, rippling it like a flag, urging her to say more.

"She has pneumonia, among other things. She is in critical condition."

"Room 317? Not ICU?"

"No, from what I could overhear, there is not a lot they can do for her. The doctor was recommending hospice. But legal requires her Living Will to be on site before they allow hospice to work with her here. I heard Chancellor, an ER nurse, telling Dr. Christianson that a family member is bringing a copy."

His eyebrows narrowed. "Okay, it's now time for the second half of the favor. "Take me to room 317."

Priscilia shook her head, indicating her answer was no. "That patient is not allowed any visitors, only immediate family."

"Okay, I need a minute to leave a note for Dr. Donahorn. Please get my chair ready. I believe I qualify to visit room 317. Karalyn Kindrick is my mother."

CHAPTER THIRTY-EIGHT

The dump truck driver unloaded the dirt in the marked area and quickly made a call to lock in the time of delivery. His cell phone was still in his hand when he climbed into the driver's seat. "Hot damn, I did it," he said as he hit the steering wheel, slapping it in celebration of getting the bonus.

He tossed his phone in the open ashtray and gunned the engine, priming the pump for his next bonus—fire watching. As he turned left, leaving the construction compound, his phone rang. He eyed the caller ID, sighed, and answered, "Blast it, Tessa, what do you want now?"

Raindrops splattered onto the windshield. He noted their size, extra large, like splats of colorless egg yolks. He hadn't seen such large raindrops in California, not that he had been there that long. These looked more like the ones he was accustomed to seeing in Oklahoma, where a mega storm was guaranteed with that size raindrop.

He grimaced, looking at the cloud and listening to his niece rant about not having her own car, about her discontent to be at home alone, about her upset to watch the column of smoke from her front yard. The Moxsin ranch was on fire, and she wanted a close-up view of the blaze.

Annoyed, he began chewing on the inner skin of his right cheek; his jaw shifted as if he was giving a sideways whistle. He didn't care whose ranch was burning. He just wanted to enjoy the fire. Time was ticking; he couldn't take any detours.

A few months ago, when he had decided to move his house trailer onto his sister Virginia's property after her husband had died, it had not occurred to him that his twenty-two-year-old niece would be such a pesky pain in the neck.

"Horses?" he asked. Now that got his attention for if there was one thing he loved more than a big fire, it was horses. "Blast it, Tessa. Alright, I'll pick you up, but you be waiting for me at the highway entrance. I am not driving that half mile up to the house for you. If what you say is true, we've got to hurry."

He tossed his phone back into the ashtray and accelerated, his old truck straining to go faster.

Monet paced, walking one direction then the other inside the hospital waiting area on floor three. She wanted to pay a visit to the patient in room 317 but didn't know what to say to Mr. Kindrick, who she had never met.

She had walked past the room five times or more. The door had been closed. She couldn't just waltz in, introduce herself and ask for a private moment with his wife, his dying wife. Other family members would surely be arriving soon. She took a deep breath, deciding that she must try something, must offer some excuse, lame or not. This moment was her only window of opportunity. It was now or never.

Stepping into the hallway again, Monet eyed the numerals on the doors. She walked toward room 317. When she was three doors away, the door to room 317 opened. She watched Mr. Kindrick stand in the doorway a moment, then walk down the hallway. A nurse turned the corner, walking toward him.

Monet paused and pretended to search for something in her handbag. She heard Mr. Kindrick ask the nurse for directions to room 1230. The nurse turned the opposite direction and walked with him, escorting him to the elevators.

With her heart pounding, Monet slipped into room 317. She tiptoed over to the bed and spoke softly, "Mrs. Kindrick, my name is Monet Lisette. You may not remember me. We met at Henny Donahorn's home, over six and half years ago now. You and Henny were there discussing a design plan, one that you had made for the previous owner of her condominium." Monet took a breath as there was no response from Mrs. Kindrick. She continued, "I had stopped by to pick up some items that Mrs. Donahorn wanted me to take to Annateresa, one of her twin daughters who roomed with me in Chicago at the time." Monet paused, berating herself for giving too many details with such precious little time.

Lying perfectly still, Karalyn Kindrick appeared to be sleeping.

Monet stared at her. "It's about the angel doll, the promise I made to you and to Mrs. Donahorn that day, the promise to never tell."

Karalyn strained to open her eyes, to get them to flutter ever so slightly. No part of her moved.

Monet placed her fingertips lightly on Mrs. Kindrick's hand. "I've never told anyone what transpired that day. I've kept my word. But now, it's all become so complicated with Mrs. Donahorn now deceased and you ill, and Angelique, who made the doll for her mother, now friends with Terrence. I can handle all that, but Mrs. Kindrick, I am worried about little Kate, and the scared, guilty look in her eyes. While she seems to be getting over her fear that Angelique will claim ownership and take the doll from her, I see a bigger fear. One that indicates Kate thinks she is duty-bound to return the doll to Angelique because of its connection to Angelique's mother. I apologize, Mrs. Kindrick, for bothering you at such a time as this. But can you possibly grant me permission? ...give me your blessing to at least to tell a portion of the story to Angelique, Terrence, and Kate? I will only tell part of the story: how Mrs. Donahorn wanted you to take the angel doll home with you, how she wanted you to give it to your granddaughter and for it to be completely hers. I won't discuss the other details, amazing that they were, nor will I tell them that it was the doll's idea, or that she claimed that your yet-to-be-born granddaughter was her new assignment, direct orders from Heaven."

Karalyn Kindrick didn't stir, silence her only response.

Holding her breath, Monet waited, contemplating removing her fingertips from Mrs. Kindrick's hand. *She is paralyzed and maybe in a coma. Why, Mrs. Kindrick cannot give me a sign even if she wants to.* Monet's heart sank. Now it felt positively silly to have hoped for release from even part of the secret, even if her motive was to help Kate and, of course, the angel—Etta Ebella.

Just as Monet began lifting her hand, she felt a tiny flicker, a minuscule movement of Mrs. Kindrick's little finger, her pinky.

Suddenly, Karalyn opened her eyes and looked directly at Monet. She tried to speak, but no sounds came forth.

Monet gripped Mrs. Kindrick's hand. There, she felt it again, a teensy flutter of the little finger. Tears sprang from Monet's eyes. Permission was granted.

"Thank you, Mrs. Kindrick, thank you. You are such an inspiring woman. Seeing you that day at Mrs. Donahorn's house, seeing your keen faith and ready belief in the angel doll, the intense glow, all of it changed me forever, allowed me to receive healing. You see, I had an angel appear by my bedside when I was a young woman. She told me to stop dwelling on the past, a painful past." Monet's chin trembled from memories of enduring brutal abuse and rape.

"That angel had glowed, too. She implored me to put the past behind me, to move fearlessly into the future. I had decided the episode was a figment of my imagination, a hallucination of despair. I gave it no power, until I met you, met Eve—now Etta Ebella. After that day with you, there are times when that other angel comes to me. She even rides in the car with me sometimes, sits in the front passenger seat, wings and all. I feel safe now, protected, and incredibly blessed. Thank you, Mrs. Kindrick. I'm eternally grateful to you."

Karalyn Kindrick caught a glimpse of Monet's heart, a lavish fountain bubbling with gratitude, mere seconds before her eyelids closed. Without any warning, her lids came down involuntarily, shutting off her sight against her will. They would open only one more time later that day—one more time ever again, on Earth, that is.

CHAPTER THIRTY-NINE

"I'm sorry, Mrs. Moxsin. I know this must come as a shock." Dr. Valeah said. Her expression remained benign, though she shifted in the chair in the small consulting room, the only clue of her discomfort with delivering the distressing news.

"Tapeworms? You think she ingested tapeworms?" Abigail asked, dry-eyed.

"There's evidence to support that conclusion. We are still running tests, but we can verify the presence of adult tapeworms, and as of yet no larvae have been detected. Typically, when we find adult worms, they have hatched from larvae in contaminated food or fecal matter bacteria that the person ingested. In your daughter's case, there were numerous large worms, whole, all adult stage, and it doesn't appear that they originated from eggs."

"Are you saying that the worms caused the blockage in her colon?"

"Yes. The blockage consisted of adult worms and some partially digested ones that had become entangled together in a knot and lodged in the intestinal wall. The knot was about the size of a large lemon that allowed no fluids to pass through, making for a dangerous obstruction."

"How many were there?" asked Abigail.

"The knot has been sent to the lab; we will know the number in a few hours. But, Mrs. Moxsin, to help you understand, I can tell you that there were twenty or more whole ones."

Abigail reached for the tissues, repeatedly pulling the white softness from the oval opening in the square box.

"The good news, Mrs. Moxsin, is that we did not have to remove any of your daughter's intestines. She should heal quickly from the surgery."

"Well, that's a relief," sighed Abigail.

"My additional concern, however, is that your daughter's esophagus shows signs of frequent vomiting or extreme reflux, and over an extended period of time. Do you know if she was forcing herself to vomit after eating?"

"No. Not that I know. I had recently noticed some laxative wrappers in her bathroom, but I was waiting to confront her until my young niece was not staying with us."

"I have recommended that your daughter be evaluated by one of our staff psychiatrists, after she is feeling better from the surgery but before she's released from the hospital. I have requested Dr. James Johns. He specializes in eating disorders."

Abigail looked aghast.

Dr. Valeah reached out and touched her hand. "Mrs. Moxsin, unfortunately, eating disorders are not uncommon for teenage girls today. Nonetheless, bulimia and anorexia nervosa are serious health problems, both mentally and physically. Left untreated, organs can become damaged; the result can be life-threatening."

"But my Emmy is not thin."

"People of all sizes and weights can suffer from eating disorders."

"So then, you think my Emmy is bulimic?"

"Dr. Johns will help us determine that, but based on what I've seen today, yes. For the record, I have never seen a case like this, where tapeworms were intentionally ingested, but I have read about it. If it's any comfort to you, there is an article in this month's *Journal* that cites a growing number of cases, with the majority involving teenage girls."

"How would she get them? I mean, where do you buy such a thing?"

"The article suggested that there are sources, such as websites that perpetuate the myth of tapeworms—being able to eat large portions, especially of sweet or fatty foods, and still lose weight. Such sites encourage the ingestion of these nasty things for weight control."

Abigail dabbed at her mouth with the tissues.

Dr. Valeah stood, preparing to go. "I will continue to treat her for the next few days as will Dr. Ryan and Dr. Sibler. They will be following up with you regarding our discussion."

"When can I see her?"

After checking her watch, Dr. Valeah said, "She will be in recovery for another hour or so. As soon as she has fully awakened from the anesthesia, you can see her, probably in another half hour. Wait in the main area as before. We will page you."

Dr. Valeah had her hand on the doorknob, the door ajar when she turned back to Abigail. "Mrs. Moxsin, I know this is a difficult time for you and I also understand that your husband is undergoing cardio bypass surgery as we speak. Right?"

Only slightly nodding, Abigail sat looking dazed.

"This is a lot to cope with at one time. Can we call someone, a family member or a friend to be with you?"

Shaking her head no, Abigail raised the tissues to her eyes, dabbing at fresh tears. "Thank you, Dr. Valeah, but no, there is no one. My sister is out of town."

"Okay. Take a minute, if you want, though it appears that someone else has been assigned to this room for doctor consult," said Dr. Valeah, her eyes focused on the glass pane in the door behind Abigail. "Take care," she said and then went through the door to the doctor's hallway.

Abigail sat, paralyzed, her body as lifeless as the wooden chair, her eyes glazed as if dipped in waxy paraffin. When Dr. Valeah's comment, about someone else waiting for the consulting room, swam to the surface of her comatose brain, her head swiveled. She peered disbelieving.

The glass pane in the door revealed a profile that she knew well, was as familiar as the back of her hand. Standing against the wall just outside the door was her sister, Carly Kindrick.

The elevator doors opened. Angelique and Kate stepped inside. Two men stood in the back corner. One wore blue surgical scrubs, and the other was an elderly gentleman who wore a tuxedo and a bow tie, black-and-white polka-dotted silk. Leaning on a handsome cane, he was an eye-catching character, debonair with his white hair combed straight back from his forehead, a style that showcased his prominent widow's peak.

All conversation stopped when Angelique and Kate entered. Their inhibitor—a child's presence, Angelique presumed. Typically, only doctors and nurses rode this elevator located on the back side of the surgical wing.

As the elevator moved downward, Angelique sensed that one of the men, the older one, was studying her and not even bothering to be discreet. Annoyed, she was in no mood to be ogled. Her shoulders stiffened; she kept her eyes forward. Even still, out of her peripheral vision, she could see that he was tilting his head and leaning in close to her, his eyes angled toward her as if he was examining the contours of her lips under a magnifying glass.

Furious, she turned her head, aiming to give him a glare. Instead, she felt hugged by the warmth of his brown eyes. It was Dr. Maison Albert, a renowned plastic surgeon, an icon in the field. She had been but a child when she last saw him. According to hospital grapevine, he was mostly retired, no longer performing surgeries, but active as a spokesperson for multiple hospitals in the Bay Area. He enjoyed going to charity events, was quite the talker, and it was said that Dr. Albert never forgot a face.

Dr. Albert smiled broadly, "You're one of the Donahorn twins, aren't you? Are you the one that's now a plastic surgeon? Pediatrics, I believe I heard."

The elevator slowed to a halt on the second floor where the doctors' lounge and sleeping quarters were located. Angelique stepped from the elevator. "Yes, Dr. Albert, I am Angelique Donahorn." Extending her hand, she said, "It's good to see you; it's been years."

"The pleasure is all mine," Dr. Albert replied, his eyes wide.

The other doctor quickly exited past them. "See you later, Mace."

Gripping his cane, Dr. Albert leaned in close to Angelique, nodding toward the tiny scar on the left side of her upper lip. "That looks great if I say so myself. Have you had any problems with it?"

"No, you did an excellent job."

"Well now, is this lovely young lady your daughter?"

Angelique's red tresses bobbled back and forth, saying no. "Dr. Albert, please meet Kate Kindrick, a special friend of mine. Kate, this is Dr. Albert."

"Hi," Kate said, her fingers slipping inside the sling on her arm and feeling the texture of the new cast. She had been staring at Dr. Albert's brown eyes, deciding whether they looked like the vanilla beans her mother used when making ice cream or more like the liquid vanilla that her mother put in cookie dough and cake batters.

"Kindrick? You wouldn't be related to that author, that Terrence Kindrick, would you?"

"That's my Uncle TT," Kate said, beaming, hopping from one foot to the other.

Dr. Albert put his hand on his chin, in thinker mode. "Well, I'll be. You know, I did his surgery, too, same lip tumor as yours, except his was the right upper lip, the exact opposite of yours. If my memory serves me correctly, your initial surgeries were on the same day. It's odd, but I still remember that day, it was so unusual to have two babies with the same problem scheduled for surgery back to back. The nurses had called these unique hematomas marks of God, symbols of special souls.

I remember doing the surgeries and then talking to your respective mothers in the waiting room. They had sat together chatting up a storm; both red-haired beauties." His eyebrows jiggled, acknowledging his penchant for pretty women.

Shock rippled through Angelique, locking her eyes wide open.

"Dr. Donahorn, are you okay?"

CHAPTER FORTY

*A*mid hugs and tears, the Kindrick family gathered in room 317. Poppy Pop sat by the window with his chair pulled as close to the hospital bed as its bulk would allow. He picked up his wife's hand, "Kara, honey, all our chickies are here. We're all together. You can rest knowing everyone is well."

Clearing his throat, Gordon continued, "Terrence, our birthday boy, is here. His doctors say that he's recovering well from surgery. Today, he's sitting up in a wheelchair, but he will be up and walking by tomorrow. And can you believe our baby girl, Ruthie Renee, is here all the way from London. You should see her makeup. Stage makeup applied in London. Surely, it itches by now."

"Hey, Mom. Please make dad stop teasing me," said Ruthie, rubbing her mother's leg. Everyone laughed or gave their best attempt.

"Sammie Sue is here, too," Gordon said. "She came in early from Boston. Sandy is home with Keebie, who's in labor. Puppies well on their way, he says. And listen to this, Kal and Carly surprised us by coming home early from vacation, looking a bit tan from the Hawaiian sun. Kate's not in the room with us yet, something about getting her arm set upstairs, but she will be here later and they say, fine and dandy in no time."

Poppy Pop rose from his chair and stood by the bed. He leaned over and kissed his wife, "My Miss America, I'm going to step out and let each of our chickies have some time alone with you. I'll be just outside the door if you need me."

The old truck rumbled along the bumpy back road. "Blast it, I wish we had gotten here before the firefighters arrived and placed those dang barricades at the front and side entrances."

"There," Tessa pointed. "The turn is just ahead. At the fork, go right."

"Is this where we went jackrabbit hunting the other night?" he asked.

"No, that area is about five miles to the east," Tessa replied. "That sure was fun, though, running the Mazda up and down the rows, watching their long rabbit legs jumping, watching them trying to scramble out of the headlights and run from the bullets. Where did you learn to shoot like that?"

"Back in Oklahoma, a group of us went jackrabbit hunting regularly. We would take turns being drivers and shooters. Best target practice there is, shooting at jumping rabbits while riding on a car's hood, a car that's bouncing and sliding between muddy field rows."

"Do the farmers ever catch you? I would think they would turn their headlights and aim on you, tearing up their crops and fields like that."

"Not getting caught is part of the fun. That's why we try to go when it's the dark of the moon, never on a full moon. Course, sometimes we did it then, anyway, if there had been a big rain. The car wheels spinning in the mire and kicking up mud makes for twice the dare, twice the fun."

"Here's the road; turn here. Holy mackerel, feel the heat from that fire. This whole place is getting charred."

"Hot damn, this fire's awesome, but blast it, how are we going to find those horses? You know, Miss Tessa, they may already be burned or trapped."

"No, don't say that or even think that for one second," Tessa said, her fuchsia sweater falling away from her shoulder when she jumped down from the truck's cab. "We've got to find them."

CHAPTER FORTY-ONE

"*T*errence, you go first. Have your private time with Mother now. You're looking mighty pale again, Brother. You've been up too many hours," Kal said.

Arising from their chairs in preparation to leave, the other family members nodded in agreement, although they each cast longing eyes at their mother.

"Mother, we'll be in the waiting area," Sammy Sue said. Her eyes were moist as she patted her mother's leg. "I love you, Mother, so very much."

Ruthie Renee stood at the foot of the bed, feeling like she couldn't breathe. *Oh God, her mother was dying.* She had to lighten this mood, change states, had to assume a different persona. Her specialty, she was an actress, after all. "Mother, I'm going to wash my face, now that I can access my remover cream." She squeezed her mother's foot. "But do I really want to stop resembling a rhubarb tart?" Ruthie said, walking out of room 317 along with Sammy Sue and Carly.

Kal hesitated by his mother's bed. He leaned in and kissed her on the cheek. He briefly bowed his head, and then quickly caught up to Ruthie Renee. "Believe me, you do. But how about some good old soap and water, Baby Sis?" teased Kal.

"Not on theater makeup. Soap doesn't touch it. See, you don't know everything, Mr. Big Brother." Ruthie elbowed Kal in the ribs. "Anyway, I thought you liked rhubarbs."

Poppy Pop tried to laugh. His adult children easily reverted to their adolescent banter when they first saw each other. Normally, he enjoyed their repartee. But today, sorrow knotted his throat; laughter found no life in him, only sobs.

"Oh, Pops," Kal said, his arms going around his father's shoulders. He held him in a soft hug. Soon, they were all huddled together, weeping in the hallway.

Inside room 317, Terrence rolled his wheelchair near his mother's bed. He pushed back from the chair, using the chair arms to push himself into a standing position. Still weak from his surgery, he held onto the bed's railing.

Leaning over her, he stroked her hair and beheld her ashen face. "Oh, Mother," he said. No words beyond mother would come forth. His tongue felt paralyzed, like hers.

Terrence stood captivated, in awe of the sheer beauty of his mother's heart, her soul. His head bowed in reverence as he watched the colors swirl, like magnificent gemstones, the highest quality brilliant cuts shooting forth rays of light.

"Mother, I want to talk to you about many things—about God, about angels, about you, about me—but I cannot seem to formulate the sentences. Ironical for me, as a writer, yet words seem useless now, like void, scrambled letters."

Karalyn Kindrick's eyes fluttered, yet remained closed. The only thing that opened was yet another door deep inside her heart.

Terrence squinted from the brightness. Intense colors gyrated. A white light radiated from an amethyst swirl, her heart's center. He felt the diamond strobe of white light engulf him. He wanted to go with it, wanted to surrender all and go with her into the light—a nirvana-esque journey compared to staying without her.

Although no words were spoken, both she and the light gave a resounding no. He heard it clearly. A powerful magnet repelled his spirit backward.

"Mother, it's excruciating to imagine my world without you—to imagine my life without seeing you, without talking to you, without your love, without your prayers. Thank you, Mother, thank you for everything." *Oh God, those words sound minuscule compared to what I want to say.* "Mother, I'm immensely grateful to you for always being so incredibly wonderful to me, the greatest mother any child anywhere in the entire world could ever dream of having. Standing here today in your glory and seeing all the ways you nurtured me and how your strong will saved me more times than I knew, I fear that in return, I've fallen short of being the best son—you know when I was younger, my wild and crazy days."

Karalyn Kindrick's eyes flew open.

She didn't speak, but he heard her say, "Noooo, you have been everything I wanted in a son."

The colorful lights birthed a set of extraneous ears inside him. The subsequent sound was the most exotic, ethereal polyphonic he had ever heard. The colors were singing.

A cantata of love trilling through every cell of him, he clasped his mother's hand. "Oh, Mother, you don't need to be trying to take care of me, to exert yourself to make me feel better, not today, not anymore. I will be okay although a ragged hole will exist in my life every single day that I live on Earth without you here."

The colors' song was quieter now, a soothing psalm. Terrence's eyebrows suddenly rose into an arc, questioning if he dared. "Mother, I have a special request for you, for when you arrive on the other side. I guess it cancels what I just said about not taking care of me anymore, yet it seems different somehow, so here goes: After you cross over, if you can, if it's allowed, please give me a sign that you are okay. Heck, give all of us Kindricks a sign. Now make it a highly noticeable sign—electricity, a flickering of the lights, or something else spectacular—and maybe I can write it into one of my stories." Terrence Ted laughed at himself, the soft tinkling of an affectionate chortle.

He stood there, gazing upon her. He watched her mouth twitching, it trying to smile, too, but it was her heart that gave life to the smile. He saw it, that and the swirling vortex ensconcing a magnificent blue angel.

Enraptured with the angel, Terrence stared. Feeling as if the angel were prompting him, he said, "In addition to a sign, please visit me in my dreams, like you did today. Speaking of which, Mother, my answer to your question today is yes. I'm not saying it's easy, but, yes, I can let you go. I don't want you to suffer anymore."

The angel began revolving, turning in circles. A few seconds elapsed and it suddenly became Etta Ebella, who was holding Kate, cradling her, as if Kate were the doll. A lavender strobe shot forth from Etta Ebella's heart connecting to his, like a dart expertly hurled at its target on a dart board. A name was riding on the lavender wave, transmitting it as clearly as if his mother had said it aloud, slurred and all, "K-a-a-a-t-e."

"Do you want me to bring Kate to see you?" he asked. He waited.

Karalyn's eyes were now closed, her breathing labored.

"Yes, Mother, I hear you. I promise to continue being involved in Kate's life, to do my best to protect her, to help develop her unique abilities of reading hearts. And her intuition, just as you have done for me. And who knows what other gifts may emerge. She's something, Mother. She's like you. And just so you know, I recently established a sizeable trust fund in Kate's name; she will have the means to go to the best schools. With Kal, Carly, Pop, Etta Ebella, and me on her team, Kate will be well cared for and dearly loved."

The lavender light swirled all around him, hovering.

Terrence's lip quivered. "Mother, my time is up; the others are anxiously awaiting their turn with you, but there's one more thing.

You always said I was a different sort of soul, a mango born in a world of Adam's apple men, that it would take a unique woman for me, and that I should choose my bride extra carefully. It's still early to be sure, but Mother, I think I have found her, my perfect match, my mango woman."

The yellow light almost blinded him. Terrence held onto the bed's railing. Even still, he collapsed onto the floor.

CHAPTER FORTY-TWO

*M*arilla Marzy slept, an anesthesia and morphine induced sleep. The pallid pallor of her skin was beginning to dissipate.

Watching her daughter's even breathing, Abigail sat quietly in the vinyl recliner recently pushed into the corner of room 604 at Alta Bates. The door creaked open. Abigail stood, "Pastor Paul, it's so good of you to come."

"Abigail, I'm sorry to hear of all that's happened to your family today." Nodding toward the bed, the minister said, "How's our girl, Marilla Marzy, doing?"

"According to her doctors, she's doing well. They said my Emmy will be back to normal in a few weeks. They will have her up walking by late tomorrow."

"Emmy?"

"Yes, that's the name she prefers now."

Pastor Paul nodded, but his eyebrows denoted a question.

"The two M's together make Emmy," Abigail explained. "She's outgrown M&M, and bless her heart; she has never liked her real name."

"That was a family name, was it?"

"Yes, Vaynem insisted upon naming her after his mother. Strange, because he did not like his mother or get along with her. He often complained that she was a mean-spirited harridan."

"Well, you know, Abigail," Pastor Paul said, "scripture tells us that our earthly names will pass away with our earthly bodies. The Lord has a special name, a glorious and eternal name, for each of us when our souls enter the pearly gates."

"Yes, I've read that scripture to Emmy many times, but Pastor Paul, the afterlife is not a concept that most kids or teenagers appreciate. I've decided to give her a prettier name right now, today."

Suddenly, Emmy screamed out, "No, Daddy, no. Please stop, please don't."

Abigail stepped over to the bed and stroked her daughter's hair. "You are okay, Emmy, you are safe," she whispered.

"That's medication talking, giving her bad dreams," said Pastor Paul.

"Perhaps," Abigail said, stroking Emmy's thick dark hair, wavy tresses that did not lie flat against her scalp, beautiful hair that had body and volume.

"Is there any word on Vaynem yet?" he asked.

"Yes, he's come through surgery and is now in Cardiac ICU, standard procedure after bypass surgery."

"What about his leg? How did that happen?"

"He said something about the horses. I was already at the hospital with Emmy, so I don't know exactly what transpired. The surgery on his leg was done at the same time they performed the bypass surgery."

"Well, he will certainly be in our prayers. Quite a few church members, a hundred or more, have gathered in the waiting area downstairs, praying for him. Vaynem is much loved. We couldn't do without him. His devotion to the church does wonders for it, for all of us."

"He loves you and the church, too, Pastor Paul. How did you find out we were here?"

"Virginia called me. Virginia Veetlehurst."

The automatic blood pressure cuff made a swooshing sound as it began compressing against Emmy's arm. She screamed, "No, Daddy, no. Please stop, it hurts."

A nurse bustled into the room.

Pastor Paul placed his hand on Abigail's arm, and said, "I'm not going to keep you. I had hoped to have a word of prayer with you before I left." He eyed the nurse, taking her time checking the monitors, in no hurry to leave. "I'm going to see if I can see Vaynem for a few minutes, have prayer with him. Then I'll come back to check on you two in a bit. Is there anything I can get for you, some dinner?"

"My sister has already brought me a tray. But, thank you." At the door, she gripped his hand. "Pastor Paul, I, uh, I." Before she could finish her sentence, a wary feeling arose in the pit of her stomach. In an odd flash of thought, Etta Ebella appeared, shaking her head as if saying, *no, don't tell him, not yet.*

"Abigail, you can tell me anything." He peered into her tear-stained face, his ever-patient expression of concern concealing his appetite for secrets.

She dismissed his hand. "I'm sorry, Pastor Paul. I'm weary beyond words. I just wanted to say how much I appreciate your visit. Thank you for coming and for your prayers."

Pastor Paul leaned against the counter of the nurses' station at Cardiac ICU, studying the configuration. Eight ICU rooms, all with glass fronts, were arranged in a half-circle surrounding the nurses' station. Some had curtains pulled; others did not.

"I'll only be a minute. Say a quick prayer with him," Pastor Paul said.

"Yes, sir, but I need to check with his wife first. She has not seen him yet, and she has priority. Only one 10-minute visit per hour is allowed. If you go in now, and she arrives in a few minutes, her visit will be denied."

"I just spoke with Mrs. Moxsin in their daughter's room, 604. She knows I was coming directly to see him."

"Okay, a brief prayer, but are you aware that he is on a ventilator, that he cannot speak? Sir, have you ever seen a person immediately after quadruple bypass surgery?"

Sighing wearily, Pastor Paul said, "Yes, many times."

The nurse looked down, checking the patients' monitor displays on the screens below. In one glance, she could see Vaynem's blood pressure, heart rate, oxygen rate—all the vitals. "Okay, he's in Unit 8, there on the left. Do not stay more than five minutes." She looked at her watch, noting it on a chart. "Check back in with me as you are leaving."

When Pastor Paul turned away from the nurse, a man who was wearing a dark suit stepped up to the counter. "FBI. I need to speak to the head nurse for Intensive Care." He laid his badge encased in black leather atop the counter.

At the sight of the FBI badge, the nurse's eyes bulged. It was the first authentic one she had seen in real life. "That would be me," she said, her heart pounding.

"Please come with me, ma'am, to Mr. Vaynem Moxsin's room."

Overhearing the man's words, Pastor Paul paused briefly. His plump eyebrows knitted together into a unibrow as he veered left toward Unit 8.

"Sir, Mr. Moxsin has undergone bypass surgery, just this afternoon. He is still heavily sedated, incapable of speaking with the ventilator, a breathing tube down his throat."

"Yes, ma'am, I am fully aware of his condition. We are verifying his identity and location. Procedure, ma'am. Police guards are being posted at his door twenty-four seven. Every doctor, nurse, and visitor who enters his room will have to provide a photo ID and a credentials badge."

"Sir, this is ICU. We cannot be bothered with delays every time we go in and out of a patient's room. What if he requires emergency care, Code Blue?"

The man stared at her.

The computer in front of her flashed, alerting her to a message from the chief hospital administrator. Her eyes narrowed as she read the official command. She stepped from behind the counter and walked with the agent to Unit 8.

In room 604, Abigail flipped the side lever on the recliner, extending the footrest. After adjusting her shoulders, her eyes closed readily; yet, her thoughts raced. It was not medication making Emmy ask for her dad to stop. The poor child had been having night terrors and screaming those exact words while sleeping since she was five. How could she, the mother, have been so naïve?

It was as if Vaynem had cast a vile veil over her from the day they married. Her bridal veil had blinded her. But she had allowed it. She had stopped being true to herself, had stopped being herself, surrendering all her power to him. He had been sweet and alluring and then changed radically immediately after their wedding ceremony. Now, it all felt like a nightmare, like she had been in a deep slumber for centuries. No longer could she wrap herself in a net of denial. Changes were mandatory. Her daughter was eating worms.

It was bizarre to think that it was a simple visit from her six-year-old niece that had been the catalyst that awakened her, that had brought irreversible change. When Kate had toted in her doll upon arriving, she had believed it to be just that, a plastic doll with wings. The events that had then transpired were unspeakable. She couldn't discuss them with anyone lest she risked being restrained in a straitjacket and taken to the psych ward.

As mystified as she was, Abigail felt more clear-headed and less crazy than she had in years. Her newfound strength and resolve were indisputable. For the first time in decades, and even in the midst of the day's traumatic events, she had hope of a better life—one that did not include Vaynem.

He would be vicious with her. *Oh, yes, he would indeed.* She had lived with the man for over twenty years. He had not been kind or generous with her in marriage; he certainly would not be bighearted in divorce. She knew him better than he knew she knew. The apartment in the city, off-shore bank accounts, oil stock certificates and gold coins secreted away in his office safe, other women galore, stacks of pornographic magazines and X-rated sadistic movies in the attic—none of those were news to her. And they were tiny drops in a big bucket.

Considering his facility for hiding assets, Vaynem would surely connive and manipulate the divorce settlement, ensuring that she ended up with zero in her column. He would totally discount her contributions. He did not value her work in their home. He would give no credence to her working to put him through law school and then for years after every penny of her teacher's salary going toward paying off their college loans. His law firm would be untouchable, of course; it was already set up that way. Even still, he would tell people that she got everything.

According to the gospel of Etta Ebella, Abigail should not be engaging in these negative thoughts. But according to the gospel of Abigail, that was easier said than done when one was gripped in a vise of foreboding.

Etta Ebella's winged wisdom had asserted that Abigail's and Emmy's hearts would heal, and their lives would change for the better when Abigail expected miracles instead of doom. Her situation, Etta Ebella had claimed, would improve when she visualized what she wanted, not what she didn't want by engaging in excessive worry. And most importantly, Etta Ebella had said that when Abigail's heart overflowed with gratitude—a high-powered balm that magnetized all kinds of good and abundance to humans—she would be far better than merely okay.

Gratitude, Etta Ebella had said, was sorely neglected on Earth. Even still, there were mountains of miracles, of material blessings, and of spiritual gifts awaiting everyone, but most Earthlings were too guilty to receive them.

Guilt, Etta Ebella had said, was a thief, particularly of success, because guilt pushed goodness away. Some humans who carried guilt, she had said, found ways to sabotage their personal success and to punish their bodies with accidents or illnesses. Unconscious doings. The thing that Etta Ebella found the most puzzling about all this guilt business was this: most Earthlings who should feel guilty didn't, and those who shouldn't, did.

Regarding the divorce from Vaynem, Etta Ebella had instructed Abigail to think like an angel and to fight like a tiger—to be undaunted in standing up for herself. Abigail knew there was much ugliness yet to walk through, but she could do it. She would don her mud boots and slosh through the slime, all the while thinking of angel wings and blue topaz eyes…and, of course, the amazing power of her real creator.

The door creaked, the sound of hinges begging for lubricant. Abigail's eyelids fluttered. Exhaustion and shock wrestled them closed again.

Angelique and Kate stood outside the door numbered 604. Angelique had slightly pushed on the already ajar door and peered inside. Emmy was sleeping in bed; Abigail was sleeping in the recliner. Inching the door closed, Angelique whispered, "Kate, we will have to come back tomorrow."

Sobs welled up in Kate. A wail escaped her lips before she could even take a breath.

"Kate? Dr. Donahorn, is that you?" Abigail rose from the recliner and opened the door.

"Abigail, I am sorry to have disturbed your rest," Angelique said.

"I was not sleeping, I assure you."

"Princess Kate has an urgent question for you."

Abigail knelt down, pulled Kate to her, and rubbed Kate's cast. "Sweetheart, I am sincerely sorry about your arm. Please forgive me."

"You didn't do it, Aunt Abigail. It's not your fault." Kate said, clutching Etta Ebella in her free arm. "Aunt Abigail, do you remember where I left my *Hello Kitty* bag?"

"Yes, sweetie, it's in the kitchen at the ranch."

"We have to get it now," Kate said.

"Why? What's wrong?"

"My Grammy Mer gave me that bag. Something awful is happening to it. The Power Ranger inside the bag is melting."

CHAPTER FORTY-THREE

O n floor three in the visitors' waiting area at Alta Bates, Ruthie sat in Poppy Pop's lap, her long legs dangling to the floor, her legs longer than her dad's were. The Kindrick family sat huddled together. Two empty chairs waited in their circle. One was for Ruthie when she decided to depart her father's lap and the second was for Carly, who was roaming the hospital, on a mission to find Kate and Dr. Donahorn.

"So, have you guys thought about names for the baby?" asked Ruthie.

"Kate's favorites are Nate and Luke. She talks to her mother's tummy, trying out the names." Kal said.

"I didn't realize it was a boy," said Ruthie, turning her wrist to view her watch.

"Kate insists it's a boy, Kal said. "But we won't know the gender for sure until Carly has the amniocentesis."

Sammie Sue nodded, her hands clenched tightly in her lap.

"And what's on the list if it's a girl, names that start with an R?" Ruthie teased. She once again eyeballed her watch, checking the time.

"Too early for the name game. We're still getting used to the idea of having a baby, period." Kal sighed.

His eyes occupying a different space, Poppy Pop said, "I'd give Kate's prediction some credence. She takes after your mother, you know."

Ruthie slid from Poppy Pop's lap. "I'm blowing the whistle on Terrence, the time hog. He has far exceeded his allotted minutes with mother," she complained, departing the Kindrick circle in the waiting room.

"Pop, that reminds me," Kal said, "I've meant to ask you about my name. I know it was in honor of my grandfathers—Kalin and Kaiser. When did you and mother realize that you had given me a name with initials of three consecutive K's?"

"Well, if I remember right, it wasn't until we had signed your birth certificate that we noticed the three K's. You know, those were your mother's initials, too, after she married me. She said that with the two of you in the world being kind and humanitarian people, the bad frequency for such initials could maybe begin to change.

Ruthie jogged down the hallway. Bursting into the waiting room, she panted, "Kal, come help. Terrence has collapsed by Mother's bed."

CHAPTER FORTY-FOUR

The dump truck rumbled along the back road, now heading the opposite direction. The driver and Tessa jostled around in their seats, the rough road spanking them.

"For crying out loud, would you drive on the shoulder? These potholes are killing me. I can barely keep hold of her." In Tessa's lap, the newly born colt slid around atop her legs.

"Hang on. It's not long now." The driver eyed his side mirror, checking on his load in the back—Mindy Midnight and Daisy Daylight. "Hey, Tessa, does his wife know about our step-cousin connection?"

"No. Mr. Big Shot Moxsin keeps that top secret. We're white trash to him. Don't worry; the cops will never connect us. Everyone will think the horses burned. The barn and corral are gone, nothing but smoldering ashes now."

"Does he ever come to your house, to see your mother for those meetings, you know, the-who-gets-blackballed-next conferences?"

"Not really. Sometimes he brings a list for Mother telling her who to harass this week, but he never comes inside the house. He honks, and she runs out to his car. She's his android slave."

"Then, won't she tell him?"

"She is not going to know. This is our secret. The horses are going to stay in the barn at the back of the property, the one by your trailer, at least until we get ready to sell them. Mother never goes back there anymore. That old barn is where Daddy shot himself."

Carly carried Kate in her arms, toted her and Etta Ebella from room 604. "Sweetheart, you're tired, and rightly so, with the traumatic day you have had. I know you're worried about your Power Ranger, but I believe that you're just so tired that your imagination is malfunctioning. It's stuck in overload mode."

"No, Mama. It's not. My Power Ranger is melting."

"We have one more stop, and then I am taking you home, my pumpkin. It's late, long past your bedtime."

"But I wanted to go home with Jophia and spend the night with Jillian."

"I know, pumpkin, but there's been a change of plans, and for good reason. You'll understand soon. Daddy has something important to tell you."

"What?"

"My goodness but you and Etta Ebella are a heavy load." Setting Kate down by the elevator door, Carly said, "How about you walk by yourself? I'll carry Etta Ebella since you are tired."

"Is that what Daddy has to tell me? That my Grammy Mer can walk by herself and talk again?"

"No, pumpkin; it's not."

"She can, Mama, I saw her. She and the Jesus man walked in a rose garden, and they talked to a tree."

The man wearing the dark suit knocked lightly on door 604, opening it before there was a response.

Abigail, who had been talking quietly with Angelique, jumped up from the recliner. "Yes?"

"Mrs. Moxsin?" He looked from Abigail to Angelique.

"I am Abigail Moxsin."

He reached into his suit pocket and pulled out his badge. "FBI, ma'am. May I have a word with you?"

Angelique stood to leave, "I'll come back later, Abigail." She took two steps toward the door. Abruptly, she turned back and extended her hand to the man, "Angelique Donahorn, sir. May I speak with you when you're finished here?"

"K64R484, K64R484," screamed Emmy.

Abigail stepped to Emmy's bedside. "It's okay, Emmy. You're okay." Her fingers stroked her daughter's mahogany-colored hair, strong wavy strands that looked quite beautiful splayed across the white pillows.

After scribbling something on his notepad, the agent said, "Would that be Doctor Angelique Donahorn?"

"Yes."

"Dr. Donahorn, would you mind staying with the young patient here while I speak with Mrs. Moxsin in private? We won't be more than ten minutes. Then yes, I would like to speak with you next."

"Just look at this poster; it's ridiculously mundane. Similar ones are ensconced in cheap frames, hanging everywhere in this hospital," Jophia said as she and her husband walked toward the elevator.

"Yes, my love, they are," Dr. Joe said. "So tell me, are you suppressing an artist in you? You certainly are obsessed with having fine art."

"Me, an artist? No way, I can't even draw a stick figure, but I surely do admire those who are creative, those who can capture the essence of life on canvas."

"But why the bee in your bonnet about fine art here in the hospital?"

"Do you remember when our beloved Nannette was dying, and we went down to Monterey to see her?"

"Yes, indeed."

"The hospital there impressed me with its collection of original artwork, huge canvasses, at that. Colorful ones. It was uplifting, soothing and healing to view such beauty, such creativity, especially at a sad time. I'm determined to bring that quality to Alta Bates."

Dr. Joe pushed the elevator button. "Well, one thing is for sure. You've got a lot of energy around this. I will not be surprised to see these posters coming down soon."

"Enough about these second-rate posters. You look distressed. What's wrong, sweetheart?" said Jophia. The elevator doors closed. With just the two of them inside, she nestled against him and stroked his cheek.

"The Moxsin incident today has me riled up, his limiting which doctors and nurses treated him based on his prejudice against their race, religion, nationality, gender, or sexual preference. And I'm furious, and worried, about what he did to Kate. I did the best I could with her arm. We'll see how it heals."

"Poor little Kate. But that Moxsin man, what kind of person acts that way in today's world? Though, issues of prejudice do seem to be escalating in many arenas, especially religion and politics. Just look at the hateful warfare that exists now between the liberal and the conservative political parties. It's unprecedented. I am seriously concerned."

"Politics. I'm disgruntled with both sides. But did I tell you about what happened with an African-American man in OR last Thursday?"

"No. What?"

"He was prepped and ready for anesthesia when suddenly he freaked and demanded an African American surgeon or for a black doctor or nurse to be present during the entirety of his surgery."

"That's bold and rather outrageous. How old was he?"

"Mid-fifties. I happened to be in the adjacent OR scrubbing for a different surgery when they paged me."

"Did you try to talk some sense into him?"

"My words made no difference to him. He's lived a narrow life, has major trust issues. He wasn't as overtly obnoxious and belligerent as Moxsin, but at the end of the day, he was about as small-minded and extremist as Moxsin and that LVN. What's her name, Veetlehurst?"

Chancellor Wilmington pushed the elevator button and waited. He usually took the stairs for exercise, but tonight he was bone tired. At last, the elevator doors opened.

"Hi, Chance, how are you?"

"I'm bushed, Jophia, how are you, and you, Dr. Joe?" Chancellor eyed the wall panel and pushed the button to level two of the employee parking garage.

"I'm with you," said Dr. Joe, "but now Jophia here, she has plenty of energy. She's in the mood to discuss art. What do you think about the idea of having fine art hanging in hallways of Alta Bates?"

Chance laughed, his first time to laugh all day. "Sounds refreshing to me, albeit, highly unlikely."

"Oh, come now, Chance, you wouldn't sabotage my positive possibilities with doubt and disbelief, would you? I've set my intention. I will succeed not only at convincing, but also galvanizing, the design committee to acquire some original artwork, giving these hallowed walls a well-deserved makeover."

"That would be a boost for us all," said Chancellor. "Jophia, do you give tutorials? Sign me up for convincing and galvanizing."

"I would be delighted, Chance," Jophia said, "if you're interested in how to set an intention and achieve your best possibility."

"I'm game. Count me in. We sure could have used some of your magic in the ER today. What a ruckus." Chance said.

"I'll say." Dr. Joe's smile disappeared, a deep grimace instantly replacing it.

"How did that surgery go, Joe, you know, on the crushed tibia?" Chancellor inquired.

"I didn't perform that one, Chance. You heard the man's words. He didn't want me to touch his leg. The Chief and I talked. We decided that the patient had expressed his wishes clearly. Dr. Phillips, a new resident, performed the surgery; he was the only male, Anglo orthopedic surgeon available with Wong, Rodriguez, and me out of the picture."

"It's Moxsin's loss, and he doesn't even know it, his own craziness," Chancellor said.

His square chin cast downward, Dr. Joe nodded, "Yes, it's disturbing, particularly in today's global society, to come across blatant prejudices, and in an educated man, no less."

With disdainful disbelief, Chancellor's head swayed from side to side. A lock of blonde hair fell onto his forehead. "And worse yet, that man may never walk normally again, all because of his narrow thinking."

The elevator slowed to a stop. Jophia shifted her hefty purse to her other shoulder, "Who performed his bypass?" asked Jophia.

"Dr. Iqqash."

The wattage of Chancellor Wilmington's broad smile could have illuminated the entire hospital, even during a blackout.

The elevator doors slid smoothly open. Joe Josephesus pushed the doors-open button and held his finger there. "Mr. Moxsin failed to specify who could or couldn't touch his heart; he was unconscious. By the luck of the draw, he got the best cardiac surgical team in the entire Bay Area—Gooptka Iqqash and Lilah Lieberman."

"They are, by far, the best," Chance said.

"A knot of folks from Moxsin's church—headed by an LVN, who works here—tried to stop it," said Dr. Joe. "But Moxsin's wife approved the surgical team, signed the release form. More than likely, Mr. Moxsin will live to a ripe old age."

In room 1230, Terrence slept.

Angelique tiptoed into the room. She lifted a straight-backed chair and placed it carefully next to his bed. She sat in the darkness staring at him, studying the angles of his face, watching his chest rise and fall with regular breaths, peaceful breaths.

Her chest rose and fell, too, but hers with anger, regular rhythms pounding like a ferocious drummer. The young nurse, Priscilia Pieria, had confessed to obeying orders from Virginia Veetlehurst to nab Terrence and keep him from his room this afternoon, forcing him to sit up for hours. That time, combined with his birthday party and then his visit with his mother, proved to be too much for him.

Within her, another wave of anger crested with full fury—*Virginia Veetlehurst, such a narrow-minded, petty person.* Angelique grimaced. Kate had been right about her breaking the sonogram machine intentionally. When Priscilia was told that Virginia Veetlehurst was being held for questioning by the FBI, she had cried like a hungry baby. She readily confessed to a multitude of ill-intentioned antics orchestrated by Virginia Veetlehurst and Vaynem Moxsin.

It was an outrage for Terrence to suffer because of their hateful schemes. What happened today wasn't right on any day, but today of all days, when his mother only had hours, if that, to live. Terrence was now robbed of rare and precious moments with his family, cheated of the comfort that would bring him when his mother was dying.

Moving into a yoga position, Angelique stretched, hoping to calm herself. It was somewhat comforting, she consoled herself, to have told the FBI agent about Vaynem Moxsin being responsible for the injury to Kate's arm. She had also confided her suspicion that it was Vaynem who had placed the tracking device on her car and tampered with the engine so it would stall on the bridge. Interestingly, the agent already knew about the latter. One of Vaynem's employees, a man on the FBI wanted list, had been apprehended. Apparently, he was telling all.

Enough of this, Angelique thought, her shoulders relaxing. She checked her watch, 11:00 PM. She rose from the chair next to his bedside. She kissed her fingertips and placed them just above Terrence's lips, yet not touching them. He stirred as surely as if he had been kissed deeply.

She returned to the chair, changed her mind, and moved over to the recliner in the corner. She pulled the recline lever. In moments, she was asleep.

A short twenty-three minutes later, Angelique bolted upright, her back rigid, feeling that someone, something, had entered the room. She watched as a light, a lavender-colored glow, formed around Terrence. She checked the window. The draperies remained closed; no lights from the outside were reflecting into the room.

The light grew bigger, swaying around him, moving from head to toe. It even seemed to reach out to her. Angelique wrapped her arms around herself and rocked. Odd, she felt as if the light had hugged her. Subsequently, she experienced a heat encompassing her, a definite sensation of warmth, particularly notable in her heart area.

The light became brighter than before, and the lavender color changed to a deeper hue, more intense. It focused now solely on Terrence. It lingered for a moment, full force, and then it vanished.

The ensuing sound shook her soul, disturbed it at its very core. An agonizingly mournful cry it was, the sound coming from Terrence's lips. Every hair on Angelique's arms rose from her flesh, standing up straight in alarm, or awe. Quickly, she moved to his bedside.

Tears slid down his cheeks; his hand moved to his navel as if he experienced pain there, and yet, he was still asleep, sound asleep.

She stood there, transfixed, watching his tears. The minutes ticked by, ten or more. Her eyes, glazed from fatigue, suddenly brightened as a profound realization struck a deep chord within her. *Only a mango man would perceive the tearing of his heart the moment his mother died, feel the ripping of the invisible umbilical chord when she left the planet. Only a mango man could weep and remain so soundly asleep.*

Footsteps shuffled behind her.

"I'm so glad you are here with him," Kal said quietly. He placed his hand in the small of her back. His fingers tingled amidst her warmth. Although the room was dark, Kal saw her eyes sparkling brightly. The sapphire facets, all brimming with tears, filled the room with light, like two blue moons encrusted with diamonds shining in a starless night sky, both watching over his beloved brother.

"Your mother, his mother, she's gone, isn't she?"

His head bowed, "Yes, she passed peacefully about fifteen minutes ago, at 11:23."

CHAPTER FORTY-FIVE

*A*t 537 Spruce Street, two weeks to the day after Grammy Mer's funeral service, Kate slept. Nestled snugly in her favorite purple blanket, Kate dreamt.

The lavender-organza princess dress shimmered. Layers of ruffles cascaded from Kate's waist, which was wrapped with a coral-colored sash that tied in a bow at the back of the dress. A laurel of roses sat upon her head like a crown. Coral and lavender ribbons rained down from the laurel, flowing all the way to her waist. A basket filled with rose petals draped on her left arm, which looked normal, not in a cast.

Angelic music, a stringed aria —Pachabel's Canon in D—wafted in the air. In a domed gazebo, three musicians stood aside Monet, who was playing a harp, her long fingers stroking its golden strings. Etta Ebella, wearing a dress that matched Kate's, sat on the bench aside Monet.

Stepping onto the walkway, Kate began tossing rose petals onto the white satin runner. Rose petals—pink, coral, champagne, mango, and mauve—filled the basket. She tossed them as instructed, two handfuls with every step.

The walkway curved. When Kate turned with the arc, she glimpsed a bride behind her but she couldn't see the face through the veil. Focusing ahead, Kate saw that Uncle TT and Jonah stood at the end of the walkway, both wearing tuxedos and white orchid boutonnieres.

The dream became jumbled, suddenly switching to a scene of a wedding cake, a multi-tier tower sitting atop a table covered with a floor-length silk chiffon cloth. Hundreds of orchids, white paphiopedilum bellatulums, and greenery filled the space between each cake tier. Three tall urns on pedestals adorned the wall behind the cake. Each urn overflowed with lilies—stargazers and white Casa Blancas. The lilies' eyes, cinnamon-colored antenna centered in each flower, were all gazing upward, seeking Heaven.

Kate's gaze followed the lily eyes heavenward. There, far above the cake, was Grammy Mer, floating there, looking happy. Poppy Pop, who was standing on the opposite side of the cake table from Kate, was looking up at her, too.

Speaking in hushed tones, Poppy Pop told Grammy Mer that he was lonely and was already tired of waiting. And boom, just like that, he was up there with her. They embraced, and then began waltzing. Another couple joined them, dancing, too. The woman of the other couple had red hair, much like Grammy Mer's, but more coppery.

Trumpets blared. The Great Angel Mother made a grand entrance, joining the heavenly dance. Her arms cradling a baby, she swayed this way, then that. She waltzed over and presented the baby to Poppy Pop. The baby reached his hand out for Poppy Pop, who placed his finger into the little palm and gazed into the baby's eyes, which resembled the color of vine-ripened blueberries. Then the baby reached for Grammy Mer. She took him into her arms, swaddled him in his blanket, and walked inside a tree, its bark door closing behind her. And boom, in an instant, Poppy Pop returned to standing by Kate at the cake table.

The Great Angel Mother looked closely at the wedding cake and gave a whiff, smelling it. She clapped her hands with glee and patted her navel.

Abruptly, the dream switched to a birthday cake. It was a rainbow cake with seven layers, not counting the white frosting, that is. The bottom layer was raspberry red; the second one was pale orange like an apricot creamsicle while the third was lemon-pie yellow. The fourth layer was apple green; the fifth one was pink like a peppermint snowball. The sixth was lavender, resembling blackberry yogurt, and the seventh layer was sky blue topped with cumulus clouds of fluffy white frosting—seven-minute meringue icing that displayed tall peaks of perfection.

Etta Ebella stood atop the birthday cake, her silvery golden wings aflutter. She looked brand new, her cheek perfect, and her wings flawless.

Kate stood by the rainbow cake, her fingers clasping seven birthday candles. Carefully, she placed each candle on the cake, placing each one far away from Etta Ebella. She stepped back to admire her work. All seven candles glowed, but not from the cake's top; all seven candles were sticking out from the cake's sides, stuck into the icing between the first and second layer. They were spaced perfectly around the front half of the cake circumference.

The music started. "Happy birthday to you, happy birthday to you, happy birthday, dear Kate, happy birthday to you." The mighty wish floated into Kate's mind as the candles blazed and her family sang to her. *Hmmm*, that was the mightiest wish she had ever made on her birthday. Not to worry, she believed in miracles.

Honeybees circled the rainbow cake, flying in a counterclockwise direction. Kate's ears buzzed from the honeybee songs.

Speaking in angel-bell language, Etta Ebella pealed, "Kate, listening to, and then acting upon, the whispers of God are the keys to your happiness, to experiencing the serendipitous flow of Divine synchronicity. You have eyes in your heart and ears in your tummy. Let them guide you. Make choices based on what you hear and see with your special ears and eyes. Then, God's wondrous goodness can come into being for you. The Great Almighty will always take of you if you listen."

The honeybees whizzed into a U-turn, now orbiting the cake in a clockwise direction.

"Kate, wake up. It's time to rise and shine, my pumpkin. Today's a special day," sang Carly.

Slightly stirring, Kate rubbed her ears. They were there, still attached to her head. She felt her left arm; it still had the cast. "Is it my birthday?"

"No, sweetie, that's many moons away," Carly said, sitting on the side of Kate's bed.

"Why is it a special day?" asked Kate.

"For starters, this morning we are sending Zahra, your new friend in Africa, a care package. How about you make a pretty picture for her with your new markers?"

"I'm going to draw flowers for her since her name means flowering," Kate said. "Mama, tell me again what my name means?"

"Pure, my pumpkin, your name means pure."

"Pure pumpkin? Ugh."

"You silly girl," Carly said, tickling Kate on her sweet spot just under her neck. "So, Miss Pure Pumpkin, I have a busy day planned. After we mail Zahra's package, we are going to Aunt Abigail's. She and Emmy are excited for us to see how they've decorated their new apartment, and Aunt Abigail said she is cooking one of your favorites for lunch. We will be their first guests."

"What is she making?"

"Angel-hair pasta with olives and artichoke hearts."

"Yum, she makes the best."

"Emmy has something to show off, too. She got her new contact lens yesterday."

"Are they brown or green?" asked Kate.

"I'm not sure which color she chose."

"Brown. I think she chose chocolate-chip eyes."

"Either color, it's a celebration day for Emmy. So Kate, guess where we're going after lunch?"

"To see the puppies."

"Yes, but this afternoon, we get to bring them home with us, Keebie and all five puppies. Have you decided on their names?"

"Bagel, Biscuit, Pancake, Waffle, and Toast are their names. Muffin and Donut are the ones that died."

"Hmph. Maybe you should decide on their names after breakfast."

But Mama, I wanted to wear a princess dress and go to a wedding today."

"A wedding? Whose wedding?"

"Do we have to go to Aunt Abigail's?"

"Yes, sweetie, we do. It's important that we give her our support right now. Hey, my little pumpkin, Aunt Abigail has an extra special treat for you when we go to Uncle Sandy's clinic to get the puppies."

"What?" Kate yawned, wriggling on her peach-colored sheets.

"There's a new boarder at the vet clinic," Carly said. "Aunt Abigail has arranged for you not only to see it but also to feed it."

"A kitten," exclaimed Kate, now sitting up in her bed.

"Far bigger than a kitten. It's Daisy Daylight's new baby, her colt, Molly Moonlight."

"Cool! Can I see Mindy Midnight and Daisy Daylight, too?"

"Yes, they are all at Uncle Sandy's vet clinic, thanks to Emmy for getting the license number of that dump truck.

"Mama, after we get back home with the puppies, can we go and visit Poppy Pop?" Kate asked.

"We'll see. That will be about time for me to start dinner."

"Maybe we could invite Poppy Pop over here for dinner. He could eat with us, and I could show him the puppies."

"That, my pumpkin, is a mighty fine idea. I'll call him this morning. You know, Kate, Poppy Pop's birthday is next week. Remind me to ask him tonight what kind of cake he wants for his party this year."

"Blueberry. He'll want blueberry."

"A blueberry birthday cake?" Carly's eyes rolled upward trying to envision a blueberry cake.

"Mama, isn't it cool that the puppies and Molly Moonlight have the same birthday as Uncle TT and Grammy Mer?"

"Well, yes, the colt and the puppies were, indeed, born on Uncle TT's birthday, but Kate, that was the day Grammy Mer passed away. It was not her birthday."

"It is now. Her new birthday in Heaven. Etta Ebella says so."

"Come, my pumpkin. It's time for breakfast." Carly planted her dainty feet on the floor. "A puffy pancake is already baking in the oven."

"Mmm, yummy! Mama, I'm going to draw giant pink roses for Zahra, like the ones in the Jesus man's garden. And I'm going to draw a picture of the Great Angel Mother and the lemon birthday pie she baked for Grammy Mer's party. Mama, the pie was huge, and it had a tall birthday candle with real diamonds and pearls."

Kate slid off the bed, her purple nightgown falling around her ankles. Clasping Etta Ebella in her arm that wore the cast and her new Power Ranger held in the other hand, she padded down the stairs, following her mother into their sunny yellow kitchen.

Her thoughts not on breakfast, Carly walked into the kitchen as if on automatic pilot. She poured Kate some juice and then washed the fresh blueberries waiting in the colander although she had already washed them before waking Kate.

Fretting over her daughter's belief that her plastic doll could talk plus her seeming inability to distinguish reality from her imagination and dreams, Carly wondered if Kate should be evaluated by a child psychiatrist. While what seemed to be Kate's imagination did prove correct quite often—her Power Ranger had melted in the fire at the ranch—the child had a major reality problem about the doll.

Fearing that Kate suffered from delusional psychosis, Carly had discussed the doll issue with Angelique last week. Surprisingly, she had seemed amused, completely unconcerned. Even still, Carly felt disturbed. She decided that immediately after breakfast, she would call the office of Dr. King, a highly touted child psychiatrist, to schedule an appointment for Kate.

After drinking her juice, Kate ran to her desk, her very own workstation in the den-kitchen area. She placed Etta Ebella and her new Power Ranger next to each other and unzipped the packet that held her colored markers. "Mama, did you get to see the birthday party for Grammy Mer, the one that Jesus and the Great Angel Mother had in Heaven? It was the day Grammy Mer died here and was then born into Heaven, on Uncle TT's birthday, now her birthday, too."

The kitchen lights flickered on and off, two times in succession.

Etta Ebella's heart lit up like a diamond. If her plastic lips could smile, she would have been wearing a brilliant one. Instead, her face and heart were aglow.

Standing with the refrigerator door ajar, Carly looked at the ceiling fixtures, then to the wall switch. Neither she nor Kate had touched the controls. She stood trancelike, staring as if the refrigerator's contents had abruptly disappeared, as if every shelf and drawer were empty. Phantasmal images of a smiling Grammy Mer warmed the coldness. In other-worldly scenes, Grammy Mer walked arm-in-arm with Jesus in a rose garden. Their arms were linked through intimacy rather than physical support as Grammy Mer walked easily and fully erect.

Suddenly, Grammy Mer turned and spoke directly to Carly. "Get out of your head, Carly. Open your heart and unlock your spirit eyes. Dare to see the world as a little child does. Everything—and I do mean every single thing—is alive in The Light of God." She paused to cup a pink rose bloom, its lush petals fully open. Her smile radiant, she continued, "Carly, I am completely well here. There is an afterlife, and it's utterly blissful. Have faith and breathe in God's amazing love for you."

Possibilities, ones unlikely to Carly, pressed upon her brain. She shook her head in disbelief. *Get a grip. This is nonsense.* Her eyes blinked repetitively, banishing all improbable thoughts. The food items returned to Carly's view. She reached inside the refrigerator and removed one lemon.

Kate sat at her desk working on her picture for Zahra. Colored markers splayed across the desk; she opened caps, peering at the colors. "Mama, do we have any silver and gold markers? I need them to draw the Great Angel Mother."

"No, Kate, we don't. While we're eating, you can tell me what this Great Angel Mother looks like, describe her to me. By the way, who told you about her?"

"Etta Ebella did, and then the Jesus man lifted me high up into the clouds to put my lemon into her apron pocket. I saw her kitchen; it's humongous."

"Your lemon?" Carly said, eyeing the freshly cut lemon on the counter.

"Uh huh. My mistake lemon. It was all brown and yucky on the inside, from when I didn't listen to my stomach and put the candles too close to Etta Ebella, and she got burned. The Jesus man showed it to me."

"Kate, use the word yes instead of the slang words like 'uh huh.' It's important to speak correctly."

"Yes, Mama."

"And what do you mean, the Jesus MAN?" asked Carly, her voice tones fraught with suspicion.

"Well, the man I saw, the one who helped me with my lemon, looked like Jesus, like the pictures I have seen of Him, but ...um, er ...I don't know why. Are you mad at me, Mama?"

"No, Kate, I am not mad at you. Thank you for telling me."

"Oh, yeah, I remember now. Etta Ebella said that Jesus was born on Earth as a human baby, and He grew into a man, but He was also God's son. She said that when He lived on Earth, he was part man, part God. Can we buy some new markers today? Some silver and gold ones?"

"Maybe, if we have time." Carly removed the skillet from the oven, setting it on a pad on the counter aside the lemon. With her hand in motion, she squeezed both lemon halves onto the pancake. Lemon juice, clear liquid mixed with a bit of pulp, flowed freely over the egg-laden pastry, all across its top and sides, some sliding underneath it. Next she sifted powdered sugar atop the lemon glaze. The sweet powder rained from the sifter like manna from Heaven.

Carly cut across the round pancake making triangular slices. She lifted two juicy servings onto a plate and then dotted each slice with blueberries. "Kate, here's your breakfast. You can finish your drawing after you eat."

The kitchen lights flickered again, two times in succession, just as before.

"It's Grammy Mer," squealed Kate. "She is saying hello to us."

When Carly lifted her eyes to survey the gone-haywire chandelier, an unusual coppery colored light caught her attention. Searching out the source, she blinked. The astonishing sight baffled her. The plastic doll's face was aglow, emitting a clear and copper-colored luminescent. What's more, the doll's chest—resembling a ten-carat brilliant-cut diamond with a mid-day sun shining upon it—was flashing a rainbow of colored prisms about the room.

Carly gawped, her heart rate rising rapidly. The tiny heart growing in her womb began to beat faster, too. It was bathing in light and delight.

Two topaz eyes blinked twice.

AFTERWORD FROM THE AUTHOR:

The inspiration for this story, *The Girl Who Could Read Hearts*, came to me in a vivid dream. One night in August of 2006, I dreamt of visiting a cemetery. There, I stood stock-still, facing a tall angel statue. Mesmerized by the statue, I was staring intently at the angel's face when I became aware of something—an unknown force—from behind that tugged energetically at my back, as if "it" wanted me to turn around and look. I turned. And, lo and behold, there was my beautiful, red-haired sister, Donna, who had died in May of 2003. She was smiling broadly, and she was dancing happily atop a mountain, a cliff of sorts with red-rock layers evident.

Looking healthy and radiant, Donna wore a formal gown, the same dress she had worn for the official ceremony and banquet when she was installed as president of the Lubbock Board of Realtors in November of 2000. In her right hand, she held a megaphone, which she would occasionally put to her mouth, and then she would yell at me in a cheering kind of way. Otherwise, she danced; she smiled; she laughed. This scene continued for quite some time. The bounteous love, joy, and enthusiasm she radiated pierced the very core of my heart. Clearly, she was showing me that her spirit was alive and happy in the afterlife—what some call the "other side." She was also sending me another message via the megaphone, and exactly what that was eluded me in the dream. For the rest of the night, though, words tumbled endlessly through my mind as I tossed and turned with restless visions.

Early the next morning, I sat down at my computer with coffee cup in hand. I began writing on my current book project, my second non-fiction book, which was then two-thirds complete and under contract with a high-powered literary agent in Dallas. In the weeks before the dream, I had been finding the work tedious and lackluster.

Unexpectedly, I suddenly placed my cursor on "New File" and this story began pouring out. The words flew effortlessly onto the pages as if I were not the one writing them. Thus, my first novel, *The Girl Who Could Read Hearts,* was born.

The story segments that deal with death are based on my true experiences when present with many of my family members as they passed away. These sections, in addition to others, also reflect my wondrous encounters with loved ones' spirits after their physical deaths.

When I was a little girl, I had multiple mystical experiences that opened my mind and warmed my heart, changing my perception of life on Earth. I learned at the mere age of five that the real me—my soul—existed separately from my physical body. I don't just believe there is an afterlife; I KNOW there is.

If there is one message I wish this story to convey, it is this: Almighty God will take care of us in our Earthly lives, too. That is, if we listen to and act upon the Divine guidance that can come as subtly as a mere whisper of a feeling, a slight bodily sensation, a fleeting thought, or a dream. As humans, we tend to box in and limit the power of God's amazing love and care for us. I challenge you to open up and expand your God box. Gifts await you.

May this story enrich your heart, your mind, and your soul.

Peace and Blessings,
Sherry Maysonave